CW01183155

FORGOTTEN VIKINGS

To Leanne!

A Harvey

To Lane!

Alonzo

FORGOTTEN VIKINGS

NEW APPROACHES TO THE VIKING AGE

ALEX HARVEY

AMBERLEY

*Boandi goðr Alex
let ræisa bók fyrir
Dettori, kunu sina*

First published 2024

Amberley Publishing
The Hill, Stroud
Gloucestershire, GL5 4EP

www.amberley-books.com

Copyright © Alex Harvey, 2024

The right of Alex Harvey to be identified as the Author
of this work has been asserted in accordance with the
Copyright, Designs and Patents Act 1988.

All rights reserved. No part of this book may be reprinted
or reproduced or utilised in any form or by any electronic,
mechanical or other means, now known or hereafter invented,
including photocopying and recording, or in any information
storage or retrieval system, without the permission in writing
from the Publishers.

British Library Cataloguing in Publication Data.
A catalogue record for this book is available from the British Library.

ISBN 978 1 3981 2209 3 (hardback)
ISBN 978 1 3981 2210 9 (ebook)

1 2 3 4 5 6 7 8 9 10

Typeset in 10.5pt on 13.5pt Sabon.
Typesetting by SJmagic DESIGN SERVICES, India.
Printed in the UK.

Contents

Maps 6

byrja; To begin 12

Dawn 15

Rise 37

Storm 63

Shadow 92

Journeys 122

Power 172

Nemeses 197

Flux 222

Faith 244

Fate 274

endir; Conclusion 299

Further Reading 300

Index 347

Maps

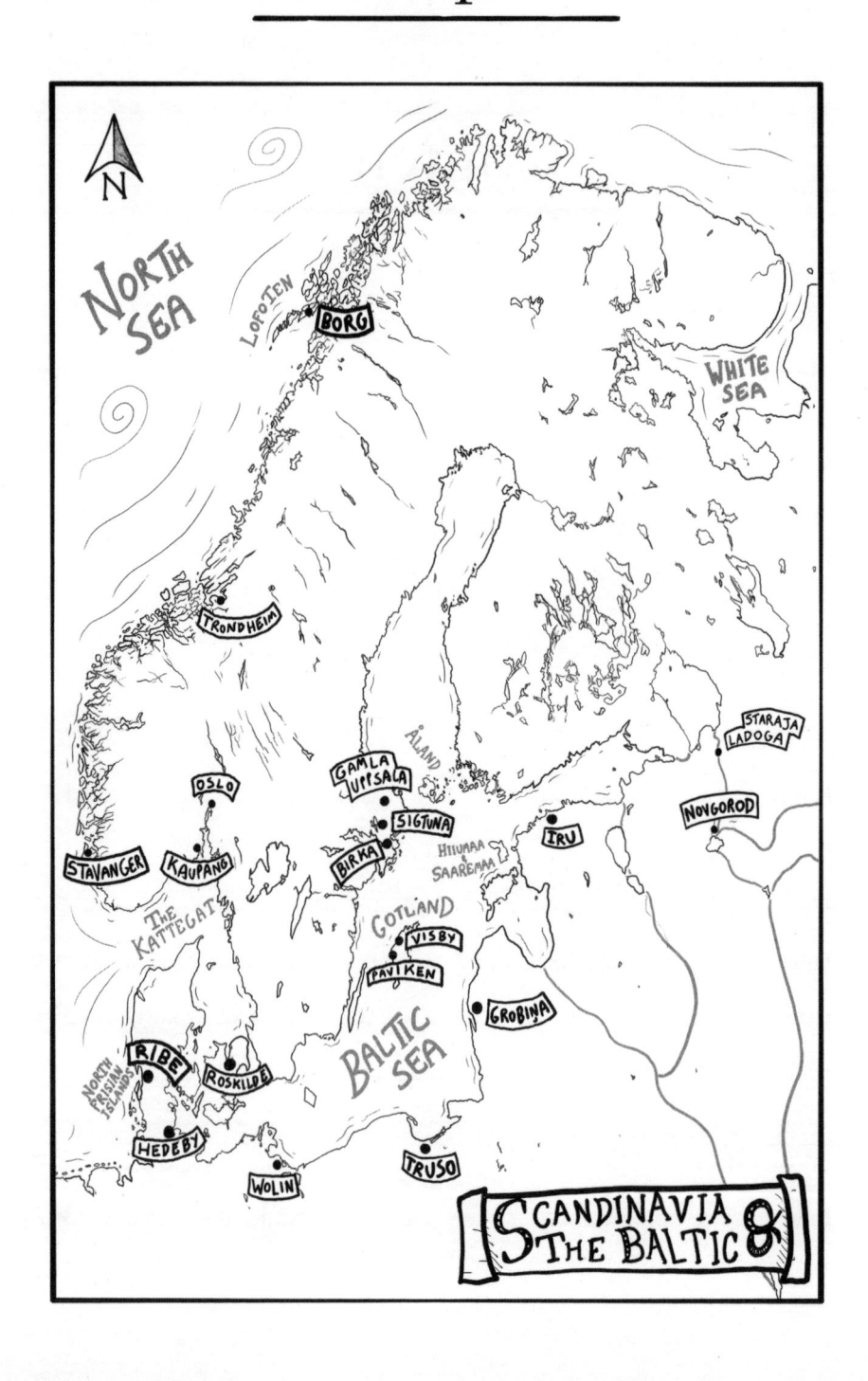

Maps

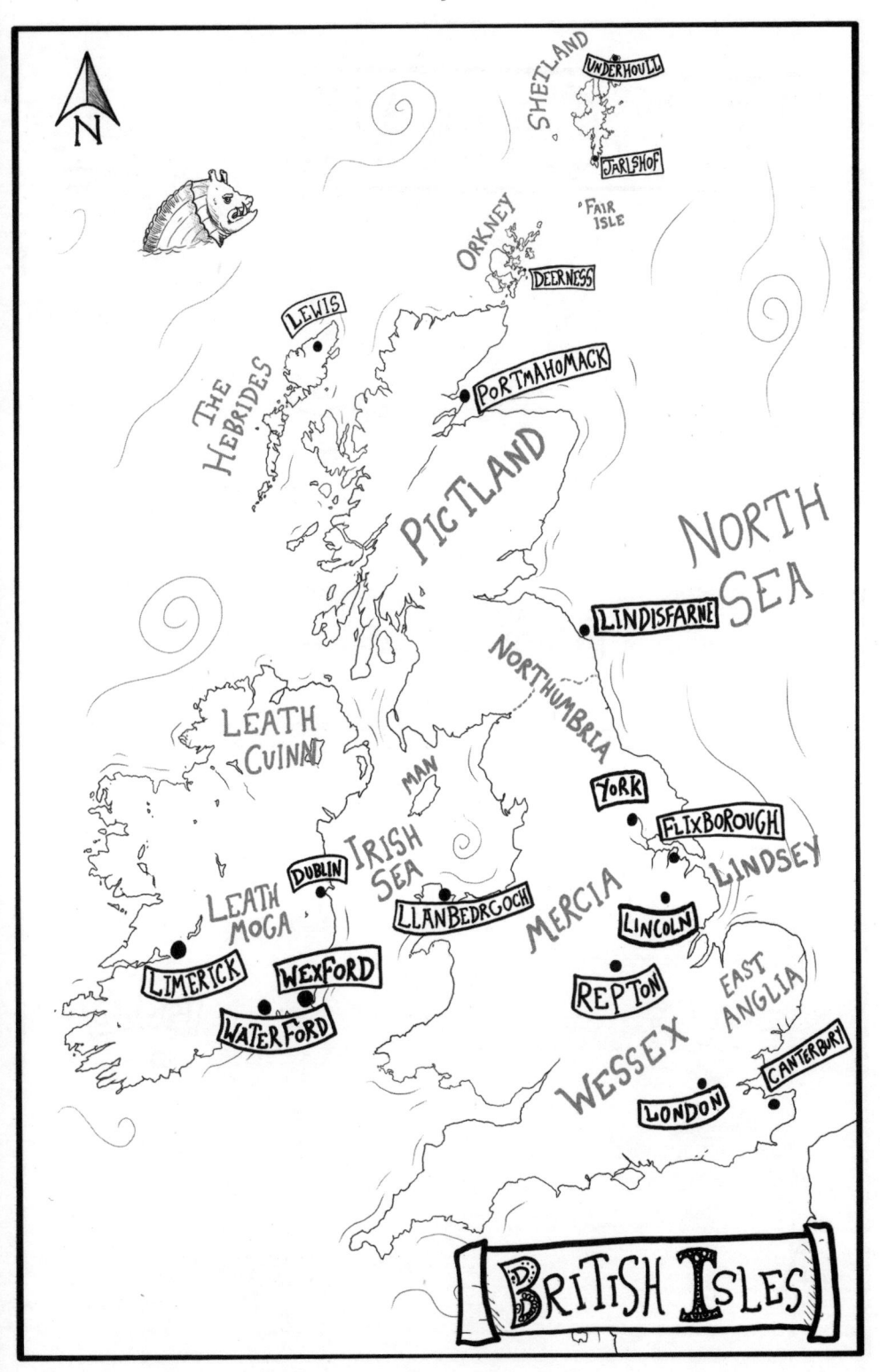

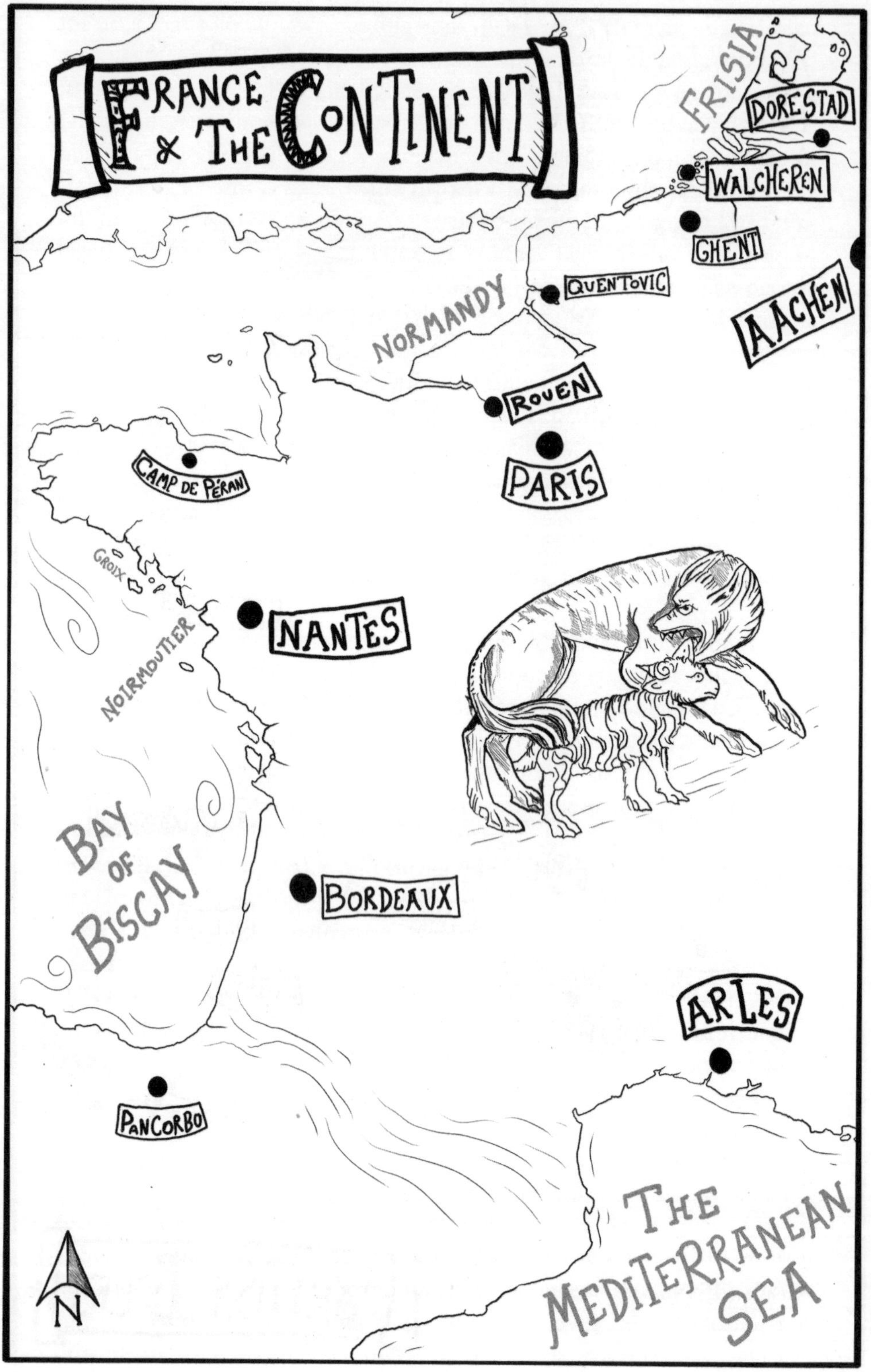
France & The Continent
Frisia
Dorestad
Walcheren
Ghent
Quentovic
Normandy
Aachen
Rouen
Paris
Camp de Péran
Groix
Noirmoutier
Nantes
Bay of Biscay
Bordeaux
Arles
Pancorbo
The Mediterranean Sea
N

Maps

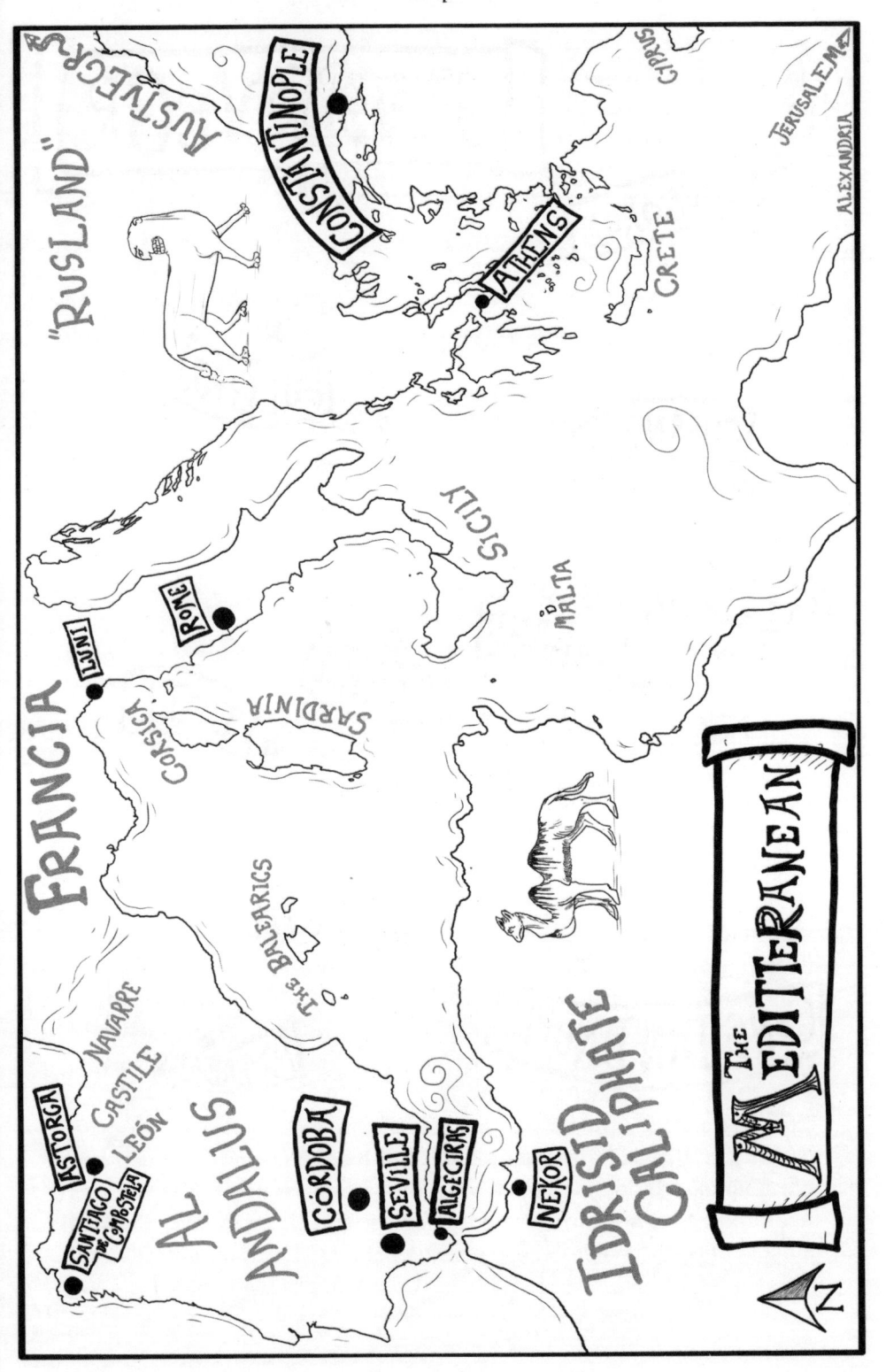

The Mediterranean

"Rusland"
Austriega
Constantinople
Athens
Cyprus
Crete
Jerusalem
Alexandria
Francia
Luni
Rome
Corsica
Sardinia
Sicily
Malta
Navarre
Castile
León
Astorga
Santiago de Compostela
Al Andalus
The Balearics
Córdoba
Seville
Algeciras
Nekor
Idrisid Caliphate

N

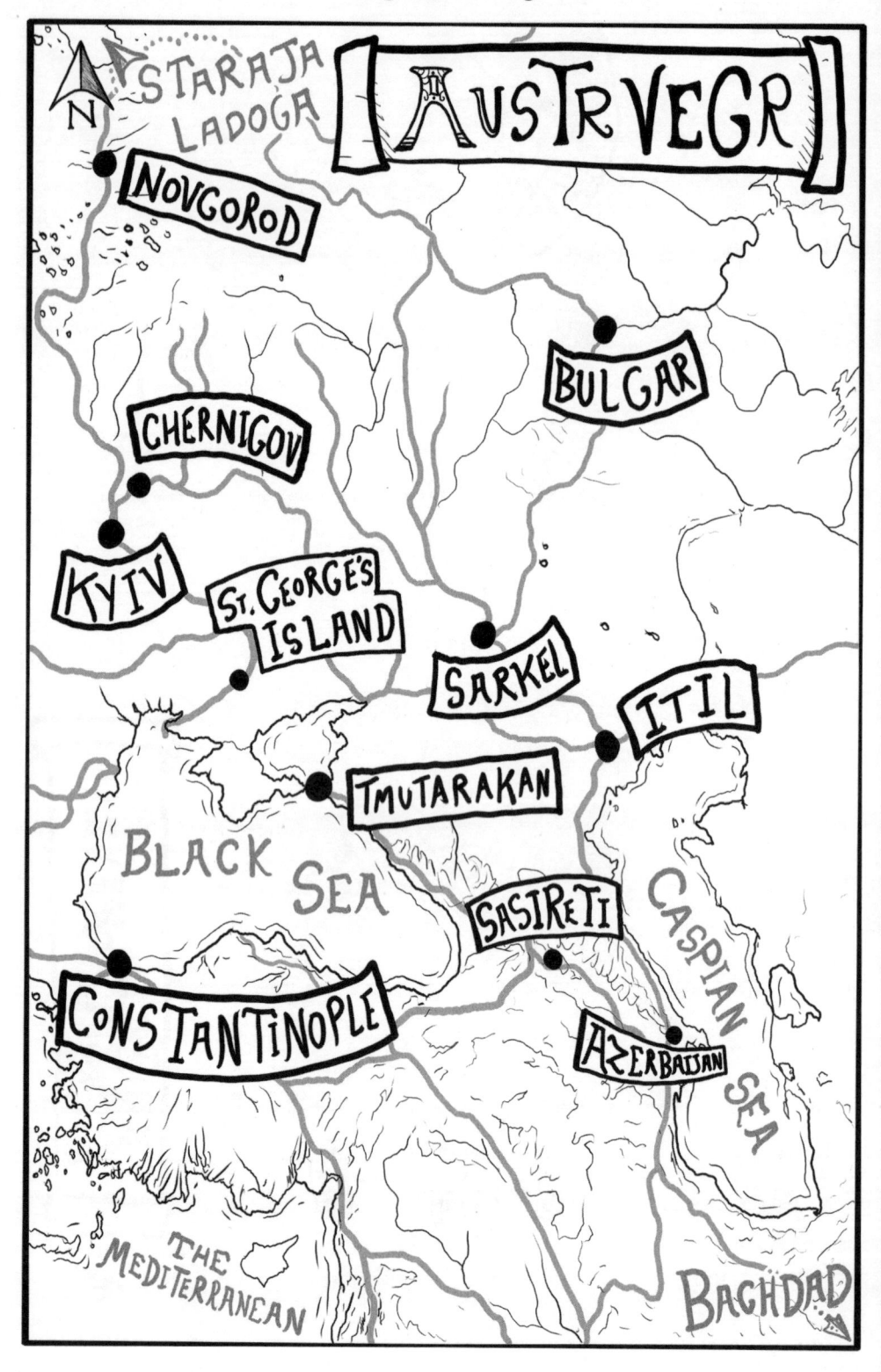

Forgotten Vikings

Austrvegr

- Staraja Ladoga
- Novgorod
- Bulgar
- Chernigov
- Kyiv
- St. George's Island
- Sarkel
- Itil
- Tmutarakan
- Sasireti
- Constantinople
- Azerbaijan
- Black Sea
- Caspian Sea
- The Mediterranean
- Baghdad

10

Maps

byrja; To begin

The perception of the Viking Age has changed over generations of scholarly evolution; from an era of bloodthirsty raiders to one of peaceful profiteers, the latest lens on the Viking Age is one that highlights the weirdness of the time, the sometimes uncomfortable differences that separate us from them (and some uncomfortable similarities). I wrote this book because it is the Viking Age book that I have always wanted to read. I am a student of the latest generation of Early Medieval researchers, as the authors that I once read (and still read) were once students of the previous generation. *Forgotten Vikings* is the product of several years studying under some of these great scholars. Like those before and after me, I hope to contribute something new to this field, and my first contribution is this book.

In the footsteps of giants, *Forgotten Vikings* aims to provide a chronological narrative starting in 536 and ending somewhere in Greenland a thousand years later. This is the story not just of 'the Viking Age' between 793-1066 but also the period before *and after*.

Forgotten Vikings opens in around 536 CE with *Dawn*, setting the scene for the Viking Age and explaining the climatological and psychological origins that made the Vikings so different to their contemporaries. Why did they raid? Did something happen in the world to prompt such a mindset? And where did they go? *Rise* details the economic and technological reasons for raiding, mapping the long road to the 793 Lindisfarne raid. While it may seem a watershed moment, the Lindisfarne raid was just one of many from the perspective of Scandinavian pillagers. The act of raiding is highlighted over the following two chapters; as the *Storm* of Viking activity increased across the North Sea in England, Ireland, and Francia, even as far as Spain. The description of the *Shadow* left behind by these raids, and then the full-

byrja; To begin

scale invasions and conquests that were soon to follow is based upon a variety of linguistic, archaeological, and textual sources, but there are also shadows *within* the shadows, elements of the Viking Age which history books take for granted. The fifth chapter briefly abandons chronology to explore the vast Scandinavian diaspora between the eighth and eleventh centuries through the Nine Realms of Norse mythology, equating real places with those of the mind. The *Power* of the tenth-century heyday of the Viking Age is interrogated in the sixth chapter, from Roman Period Scandinavia to the Battle of Brunanburh, and the ever-changing nature of kingship, status, and influence. With power comes pushback, and *Nemeses* to face; the Early Medieval world was filled with conflict and much of that involved Scandinavians, operating either as insurgents, mercenaries, or kings. A pragmatic people, Scandinavian raiders and traders were always in *Flux* throughout the final centuries of the first millennium. To what degree would they alter their identity? The book takes a step back through time for the penultimate chapter. In order to explore the spread of Christianity (and thus the end of the Viking Age) one must first the examine the previous belief system and the relationship between the two. What is 'Ragnarok'? How can it be explored through archaeological evidence? What can we learn about Odin and Thor? Finally, the *Fate* – or rather fates – of the Viking Age will be laid bare. History books on the Vikings often end in 1066 and dedicate a footnote or two to the aftermath; *Forgotten Vikings* hopes to explore further.

Interspersed throughout the chapters are my illustrations of artefacts and sites. Any errors with the drawings, and indeed any part of *Forgotten Vikings*, are my own.

All this wouldn't have been possible without the breadth of scholarship I had access to throughout my research: Neil Price, Marika Mägi, Judith Jesch, Søren Sindbæk, to name a few, historians, archaeologists, linguistic experts, literary analysts. Superscript numbers throughout refer to further reading on the subject being discussed.

I have written most of the names and terms in their original Old English and Old Norse using the letters ð (eth) and þ (thorn), pronounced like *th-* from '*there*' and *th-* from '*thin*' respectively. However, to avoid confusion, where names are repeated (and this happens a lot) I have slightly amended the spellings or anglicised a few for the sake of accessibility. For instance, one Harald is just Harald, but his son Harald Haraldsson will only be spoken of as Haraldsson, rather than as a second Harald. One Olaf might be Olaf, whereas his contemporary namesake will be written as Olafr.

Principally, *Forgotten Vikings* aims to shed light on aspects of the Viking Age that have received less than their fair share of popular attention. To people interested in learning just a little more about the subject, I hope you enjoy reading this work and thank you for buying it. Or perhaps you simply stole it from a coastal monastery; now that would be fitting.

Chiefly, I would like to thank all researchers on this subject either in the text or in the bibliography for their valuable contributions to the wider corpus, be they academic or 'mainstream' in nature. While I cannot list every single academic, I would like to draw special attention to Dawn Hadley and Steve Ashby, with whom I have learned much about the Early Medieval Period, and Carolyne Larrington for her much needed suggestions about the initial draft. My academic journey started at the University of York in 2018 through the tutoring of John Schofield, Nicky Milner, Jim Leary, Carl Savage, Ian Armit, and others, though I must also thank my secondary school teacher Adam Woodland for encouraging me. Thanks to my good friends Jonah Walker, Hilbert Vinkenoog, Harry Ellerd-Cheers, and Paul Stein, who have all served as useful sounding boards. Thank you to Hilbert, especially, for your knowledge on Frisia. Hayden Ashby, an unparalleled source of wisdom for the fifth and ninth chapters of this book, knows how helpful he has been – my sincere gratitude to you. Alison Owen and Bianca Chiaccia sent me their relevant essays, and Nathaniel Dargue imparted much knowledge on the topic of corvids. Chance and pre-planned conversations with scholars Bob Fish, Michael Drowt, David Brear, David Fletcher, and David Castriota were invaluable.

The Icelandic author Þórunn Valdimarsdóttir has sent me many kind emails since 2020 and she is ultimately responsible for one of the more outlandish and interesting portions of the fifth chapter, Icelanders in Mexico. My grandparents encouraged me to keep writing, especially my grandmother whose interest in history was clearly inherited, and my parents always ensured that I had the means to do so. I must also thank Amberley Publishing for facilitating this project in the first place, principally Connor Stait, Shaun Barrington, and Philip Dean, not only for tolerating my relentless emails but for all the advice and edits along the way.

My wife Dettori has listened to me drone on about *Forgotten Vikings* (and the next project and the one after that) for many months and has been a font of wisdom and advice throughout its creation. Thank you very much for your support.

Dawn

> Men will know misery,
> adulteries be multiplied,
> an axe-age, a sword-age,
> shields will be cloven,
> a wind-age, a wolf-age,
> before the world's ruin.
> A description of Ragnarok; *Völuspá,* from the *Poetic Edda,*
> translated by Ursula Dronke

When you read the word 'Viking', what do you picture? Horned helmets? Screaming victims? Perhaps you're not thinking of the 'Vikings' themselves but what they left behind; burning towns and churches, or maybe something gentler; the 'Vikings' as peaceful émigrés, profiteers and wealthy traders as discovered through the famous Coppergate excavations. Perhaps you are indeed thinking of York, the English city that even now keeps one foot in the past. Or you're thinking of other locations that were touched by these people: Dublin, Reykjavik, Istanbul, Newfoundland, Paris, London, Seville. Maybe you are thinking of more local examples, place names like *-toft, -thorpe,* or *-by,* clear indicators of an Old Norse presence. Perhaps you're even thinking of the traditional Viking Age homelands: Norway, Denmark, Sweden. But what language did they speak? What people are we even talking about? Vikings? Did such people even exist as we would recognise them today? Was a 'Viking' an ethnic or cultural marker of identity, or was it neither? Are the 'Vikings' who were trading Baltic amber and Shetlandic soap stones in the markets of tenth-century York the same 'Vikings' who were ravaging the Balearic Islands en route to Italy?

The 'Viking Age', that period of coastal massacres, international economic expansion and heathen barbarism, lasted, as the history books will tell you, from 793 to 1066. Why those dates? According to near-contemporary sources, 793 is the year when a hitherto unknown force of pagans struck the British Isles, raiding the Monastery of St Cuthbert at Lindisfarne and shocking the world. The people of the kingdoms of England prior to the raid did not wake up the morning after and suddenly realise that they were in the Viking Age, just like the Norwegian soldiers fleeing the Battle of Stamford Bridge in 1066 did not put down their 'Viking' heritage and evolve overnight into 'Medieval Scandinavians'. To understand and learn about our shared past, rightly or wrongly, we segment it into recognisable and neat sections; first came the 'Celts', then the Romans, then the 'Anglo-Saxons', then the 'Vikings', and finally the Normans, before the Medieval Period began in earnest. We segment these periods because of dramatic societal differences between them, differences that would not occur overnight but over generations, only really apparent with hindsight. And this is just in Britain.

The world that the 'Vikings' interacted with in 793 when they appeared out of the blue, blundering onto a shore of a country they had allegedly never visited before, was a different world to the one they supposedly fled in 1066, never to return. The dramatic changes that swept across England, France, Scandinavia, and beyond were, in many cases, direct results of the activities and actions of these 'Vikings', but they also changed themselves.

What's in a Name?
The origins of the word 'Viking' are confusing. We have Sir Walter Scott's writings in the nineteenth century to thank for our English definition.[1] The father of historical fiction borrowed an earlier word from Old Icelandic – *viking* – and used it both as an adjective and a noun in his 1817 poem *Harold the Dauntless*. Sir Walter's 'Viking' could be used to describe an individual, or a group of individuals (a group of 'Vikings'), who took part in 'Viking raids'. What separated them from other literary villains like pirates, bandits, and Saracens, who also raided coastlines both real and fictional, was their origin: Scandinavia. To be a raider was one thing, but to be a 'Viking' meant that you were specifically of Scandinavian origin participating in raids from the eighth to eleventh centuries.

Within most modern academic and mainstream circles, the word 'Viking' is now used to describe anyone of Scandinavian heritage between the dates of the 'Viking' Age. You'll hear no complaints from now on about this broad usage – nobody can turn back time and prevent such a moniker from becoming universal, and it certainly does fulfil a need. However, this seems like a good opportunity, perhaps just this once, to move away from the modern usage. And to do that, we must find the origin. While the English word 'Viking' is a borrowing from Medieval Icelandic sagas, it has a slightly different meaning to its forebears. There, on the vellum of thirteenth and fourteenth-century tales of blood feuds and heroic journeys, 'Viking', or rather *víking* (pronounced 'vee-king'), describes the activity of going raiding. One could not *be* a 'Viking', one could *go* viking. Usually, these individuals are described negatively, but these sagas were written down long after what we deem the end of the Viking Age. An individual going viking would be described as a *vikingr* (pronounced 'vee-king-er'), or if they were in a group then they would be a group of *vikingar*, from the earlier Old Norse words. We can build a clear etymological picture of what the words viking/vikingr/vikingar meant during the Viking Age (793-1066), but not what they meant beforehand, as stated above, these neat historical periods are inventions. A Scandinavian raider in 792 was just as much of a vikingr as his counterpart in 793. These words originated long before their age traditionally began; people of Scandinavian heritage were engaging in long-distance trade and violence across international borders long *before* the Viking Age.[2]

Does 'viking' come from Old English, a language very similar to Old Norse but across the North Sea? Does it come from *wicing*, to travel and trade across coastal markets and emporia (known as *wics*)? This would certainly be a more peaceful origin for the word, but still in keeping with the maritime travelling and profiteering so associated with the Viking Age.[3] '*Wicing*' was used by an archbishop of York to mean 'pillager' at one point. The phrase '*northeska wizsegge*' from Old Frisian, means 'northern raider', a reminder that not all vikingar hailed from Scandinavia. Perhaps it is, however, a geographic descriptor, emerging from across the mists of The Kattegat strait in the bay of Viken, Norway, where there is archaeological evidence for pre-Viking Age farmsteads.[4] Was a vikingr someone from Viken? And then did this cognomen become retroactively applied to *anyone* from *any* bay or fjord? Were vikingar just 'bay-men'? Was a vikingr an identity recognised by the subject, or was it only imposed upon someone by others? Would Harald Haraldsson of Norway view himself as a vikingr one day, and then a farmer the next? Perhaps he would not even recognise such a distinction. The clunky but nonetheless accurate descriptor 'Early Medieval Scandinavians' is a 'safer' term to use, though this excludes all the Baltic, Frisian, and Finnish people undoubtedly going viking.

We will leave behind the traditional start and end-dates of the Viking Age, and instead attempt to view the phenomenon as a series of successive events, linked but distinct. The 'Viking Age' that ended on British soil in 1066 was not the same 'Viking Age' that was doomed to fail in the fifteenth century in Greenland. Surely we cannot describe those Greenland farmers, who had likely not raided for generations, as vikingar. But we're getting ahead of ourselves; the colonies of Greenland did not meet their fate until the same century as the Battle of Agincourt, the Wars of the Roses, the European discovery of the New World, and the fall of Constantinople, long after the invention of gunpowder, a few decades before Michelangelo's painting of the Sistine Chapel. To find an identifiable origin of the 'Viking Age' is to go back long before 793. Before history.

Pre-Viking Scandinavia

The Scandinavians of the Viking Age were shaped by their geography, topography, and heritage that extended back into the mists of time over thousands of years. The elements we so often associate with the Viking Age – Odin, axes, shield-walls, longships, ritual sacrifices, and masses of silver – did not emerge out of the blue in 793 but were in place for quite a long time beforehand, gestating and evolving until they reached the point where we can say, 'That was the transition.'

In fact, in some halls of Scandinavian academia, the Viking Age is still classed as prehistory. For we Brits, this is not the case, for our definition of prehistory ends when the Romans arrived in the first century. Just over the North Sea, then, are countries with a prehistory apparently lasting for a further eight centuries. What was happening in this 'pre-Viking' period? Due to the scarcity of written information, we are not entirely sure. However, we can be confident that many of the tell-tale characteristics we associate with the Viking Age were present long before the traditional start date. For many, the Viking Age is personified by bloodshed and warfare, but specifically, warfare far removed from the well-organised (and neatly dressed) Roman cavalry units. This was 'barbaric' warfare; savage, merciless, or at least that is how contemporary writers put it. It was Roman and Greek authors who first described the Eruli in the third century, one of many sub-divisions of the north European peoples they frequently waged war against (and employed in their auxiliary forces).[5] That very status, of northerners fighting for and against contemporary Greco-Roman armies, aptly describes Scandinavians in the tenth and eleventh centuries. The Eruli are described as hailing 'from the most ice cold deep sea' – this was likely *Scandza*, Scandinavia, although there has been some scholarly debate over separating the Eruli into a western and eastern grouping, the latter based around the Black Sea.[6,7] We know absolutely nothing else about the Eruli save for the fact they were likely similar to other adversaries of the Roman legions described collectively as 'Germanic'. The Empire never touched Scandinavia to any great extent; an impact far less than that left behind by *Romanitas* in Britannia.[8] They were thwarted along the way by numerous population groups like the Frisii in the Low Countries, though Roman material did indeed end up in the far north, and likely influenced the people who were already there.[9,10] Were these people, these pre-Viking Age Scandinavians, all called the Eruli? Or are we already running into a similar etymological nightmare as with the word 'viking'?

In describing non-literate societies, their identities only come down to us through the lens of others. As a result, we only hear of the Eruli as a villainous force renowned for their hardiness, social and geographic isolation, sacrificial rites, and skill in battle. We have no idea, none given by the Byzantine writers Procopius[11] and Sidonius Apollinaris,[12] of their ideas of the world, religious beliefs, or their culture. We do know, however, that the Eruli sacked Athens, Argos, Sparta, Corinth, and a slew of other places across the Mediterranean world, either on their own or acting as mercenaries for others. Archaeologically, there are similarities between pre-Viking Age burial mounds in Scandinavia and those across The Danube, which gives us some indication of the international spread of similar people, or perhaps just similar ideas.[13,14] Similar people would indeed be found across northern Europe throughout the Roman Period.

The alleged progenitors of various 'Anglo-Saxon' dynasties, and some of their principal pre-Christian deities, are akin to those found in the traditional Old Norse pantheon.[15] When we think of the Viking Age today, we might be influenced by popular culture; the gods Thor and Loki, as quip-cracking aliens in *Avengers: Endgame* (2019) or as unseen bloodthirsty overseers in *The Northman* (2022). The enduring motif of a central cosmic tree, which anchors everything around it, forms a key part of the world depicted in *Elden Ring*, just as one example. These elements are, like the Viking Age itself, neatly defined for modern audiences like logos or as specific characters with defined traits. Thor is normally the strong-willed muscleman of the group, while his counterpart Loki is a wily trickster. The pair of them served under Odin, usually positioned as an equivalent to Jupiter or Zeus from earlier pantheons; a classic God-King, who is always at the top of the food chain.

Our modern perception of the Old Norse deities is coloured by later writers like Snorri Sturluson, who transformed oral traditions of legendary characters into a narrative populated by heroes and villains written for Christian audiences. These thirteenth-century works (the *Prose Edda*, written by Snorri, and the *Poetic Edda*, dated slightly earlier) are some of our best windows into the cosmology of the Viking Age. Because of their lateness, we cannot be sure that the Óðinn (pronounced 'Ou-thinn') portrayed on ninth-century runesticks in Sweden was the same 'Odin' discussed in the thirteenth century by Snorri, but we can make a few guesses.

Prior to the Viking Age, the people travelling up and down the coastline of the North Sea were worshipping, among other deities, Wōden, Tiw, Thunor, Frīcg, and Fosite, relatively synonymous with Óðinn, Týr, and Þórr (pronounced 'Tor'). This is consistent even further eastwards. In pre-Christian Slavic and Baltic pantheons, which lasted for quite a while longer than their Norse counterparts, we hear of Perun and Perkūnas, hammer-wielding brutish gods associated with trees and thunder.[16,17] Are we looking at equivalents to Þórr, perhaps? In Frisia, sometime in the eighth century, the Christian missionary Boniface dared to strike at 'Donar's Oak', a sacred tree allegedly associated with a Frisian equivalent of Þórr.[18,19] Heligoland, one of the North Frisian Islands off the coast of Denmark, shows some evidence of the ancient veneration of Fosite, a possible (though uncertain) equivalent of the Old Norse god Forseti.[20]

There are innumerable deities lost to us completely that were perhaps not worshipped as openly as Týr and Freyr, and thus never copied down into the vernacular. It is highly doubtful that figures like Loki were ever worshipped, given the negative connotations, and yet this beguiling figure dominates a wide array of Old Norse tales, so maybe Loki was worshipped. We just can't be sure. For this really was a belief *system* and not a religion. There was no top-down hierarchy or dogma instructing Early Medieval Scandinavians or wider groups to worship certain gods in certain ways. The Old Norse pantheon and the veneration of the gods was inherently individual and localised. Certain farmsteads along the coast of Norway might, for instance, favour Þórr or Njǫror, gods associated with the sea, while to the south in the boglands of Denmark, their cousins might prefer to worship the war-god Týr, due to the prevalence of border conflicts. Indeed, up to a certain point, Týr appears to have been the chief deity among the Old Norse pantheon, above even Óðinn.

So the belief systems of the Viking Age already existed to some degree long before that. Tacitus, writing in the first century, even alludes to similar governmental structures being present[21] and others mention human sacrifice, also long associated with the Viking Age.[22] Such Roman accounts are of course all biased.

To better identify *when* the deities worshipped by the precursors of the English became the Old Norse deities worshipped by the Scandinavians, we must analyse their differences as best we can. And to do so takes us even further back in time, to the Nordic Bronze Age.

Spear Dancers and Horse Prancers

Ask the average person if the 'Vikings' had horned helmets and, having seen them on pizza vans and in Wagner's *Der Ring des Nibelungen* they will probably say yes.[23] We have Swedish artist Gustav Malmström to thank for this ahistorical trend. It was his paintings of horned heathen heroes – inspired by real archaeological finds from the Nordic Bronze Age – that so influenced Wagner's costume designer, Carl Emil Doepler, to adorn the stage with spiked and winged helmets.

Anyone with any deeper interest in the Viking Age will confidently correct you. 'No, they did not have horns.' The truth is, rather annoyingly, somewhere in the middle. Viking Age warriors would never be seen wearing horns on the battlefield, but in specific ceremonial situations embellishing a cap or helmet with horn-like adornments was an identifiable practice. Long before the Viking Age, we see evidence of this in the form of petroglyphs; the very things that inspired Malmstrom.

In the Nordic Bronze Age (2000-500 BCE), the recurring motif of what we call 'the weapon dancer' or 'the spear dancer' began to appear on granite panels and standing stones. Carved, and sometimes coloured, the figure is locked in a strangely warped pose, one foot raised off the ground, holding one or more spears, with a horned head. There is a long and vigorous argument associating this Weapon Dancer figure with the later veneration of Óðinn; the following summary will attempt to bridge the gap between the two, though it is possible that these two figures merged at one point preceding the Viking Age.[24] On the Kirkby Stephen cross, in Cumbria, a variation of Loki is depicted with similar horns, though these curve downwards. Loki and Óðinn are 'blood-brothers' in the mythic corpus; perhaps they were occasionally artistically interchangeable?

Regardless, thousands of years before the Lindisfarne raid and the carving of the Kirkby Stephen cross, individuals were painting 'The Dancing God' on the Järrestad panels, in Sweden, and this was clearly not a depiction of either Óðinn or Loki.[25] This is not the sole example; Bohuslän, in Götaland, features similar petroglyphs[26] and the Kungsängen figure from elsewhere in Sweden appears to also be depicting the Weapon Dancer. So, too, do certain Iron Age bracteates and foil fragments from the centuries immediately before the Viking Age.

The tantalising, murky gap between the Roman Period and the Viking Age has many names in popular culture and academia. These three centuries are usually referred to as the 'Migration Period' or the 'Dark Ages'. What followed the withdrawal of Roman administration from much of western Europe was supposedly a time of unfettered travel across the North Sea, though such movements were undoubtedly happening already during the Roman Period. This period is also referred

A Bronze Age rock carving from Tanum in Bohüslan, Sweden, depicting two 'weapon dancers' in motion. This depiction is remarkably like a contemporary rock carving from Bro Utmark nearby, reflecting a wider Bronze Age tradition associated with this figure.

to as the 'Germanic Golden Age', a poetic era associated with works like *Beowulf* and *Widsið*; tales from the early years of the 'Anglo-Saxons' (a later moniker describing various Germanic-speaking groups). *Beowulf*, a story allegedly taking place in the 500s, though first written down in the 1000s, features raiding up and down the North Sea between Geats (Beowulf is a Geat) and Danes from Sweden and Denmark respectively.[27] A significant part of the story centres around Frisia in what is now the modern Netherlands, the important 'middleman' of the North Sea economy. A fragmented copy of another near-contemporary manuscript describes a *freswael*, a slaughter of Frisians, at the hands of Danes.[28]

Through literature and legend, we can observe a well-attested continuity between the pre- and proper Viking Age. Before and after 793, individuals from Scandinavia were raiding the neighbouring coastlines and their social structure was based around a warrior elite. We see this most clearly in the Weapon Dancer motifs, but also in how they appear to evolve between the Nordic Bronze and Iron Ages. The *Dioscuri* from

Greek mythology are animal-human hybrids who sprout bullhorns from their foreheads as they transition from man to beast.[29] The Weapon Dancer, similarly horned in Iron Age depictions, is often depicted alongside animal-human hybrids, as on the Torslunda Die Matrix from 600 CE (see the front jacket). These half-man half-beasts have historically been observed as representations of the *berserkir* or *ulfheðnar*, bear- and wolf-skins, berserkers (there is also a theory that boar-skins existed, the *jöfurr*) mentioned by Tacitus as key components of 'Germanic' military groups.[30, 31] Contrary to popular depictions, the 'berserker' was never a formal military unit. In later Icelandic sagas, individuals demonstrating animal-like tendencies are often seen as antagonists, or at the very least social pariahs.[32]

The Iron Age is when this Weapon Dancer became clearly associated with some form of physical hybridity. Some have argued that earlier Bronze Age depictions represent not necessarily a horned individual but one with two birds atop his head (likely waterfowls, due to their prevalence in later Iron Age artwork; the Gundestrup Cauldron, found in Denmark, is a great example).[33] Over time, however, as one moves into the Iron Age, this artistic tradition blended the two birds into horns.[34] It is also worth mentioning the prevalence of two ravens within the Odinic corpus. The debate regarding religious and artistic similarities between contrasting periods will come into play once more in a later chapter on the Christian conversion of Scandinavians.

Did these believers in Óðinn associate him with the Weapon Dancer motif? By the Iron Age, the two may have become one and the same. The Weapon Dancer appears on sixth- and seventh-century material like the Vendel and Caenby Helmets,[35] as an artistic foil fragment, and on personal adornments like the Finglesham buckle.[36] Contemporary with these depictions are the aforementioned bracteates[37, 38] depicting a hybridisation of man and beast, notably the horse, as also seen with the later myth of Óðinn and his eight-legged horse, Sleipnir.

From at least 1700 BCE, then, we have evidence of a figure venerated in various parts of Scandinavia (though most notably Sweden), a figure made distinct by his large phallus, his single sandal, and weaponry. Via comparisons with other Indo-European societies, it is likely that such a figure represented the top echelons, the dominating warrior elites. This is not just the case in Scandinavia but in much of Rome's northern periphery.

If all these temporal and geographic similarities exist between the 'Viking' gods and their forebears or counterparts, then what makes the 'Viking' gods distinct? Can we identify when they evolved from their antecedents? And if so, what would have caused such a change?

A Certain Doom

To return to our earlier discussion on what made individuals of the Viking Age so distinct and so 'Viking': was it their technology? The development of the traditional longship will be discussed in the following chapter, but it is worth noting that similar ships were utilised by North Sea people during the preceding centuries, and Bronze Age petroglyphs from across Scandinavia depict rowed vessels filled with armed men thousands of years before a religious community on Lindisfarne was even an idea.[39] Perhaps the attire and weaponry of the Viking Age were notably distinct from what came before? Not exactly. Artefacts like the Vendel Helmet (dated to 600 CE, so named for where it was found in Sweden) show clear links with the few Viking Age helmets we have (and indeed their English counterparts),[40] and the classic 'Viking' sword[41] is a natural typological evolution of Roman and earlier craftsmanship. Warfare and looting were endemic in the Early Medieval Period, both before and after the Viking Age, so merely the act of *going* viking wasn't unique to Scandinavians. It was really a combination of all the above factors that led to the dawn of the Viking Age – but one could argue that the defining trait of the 'Vikings' was not their physicality but their worldview.

Where did that worldview come from? In the sources we have from the period, Scandinavian *vikingar* are always portrayed by Christian writers; they are heathens, foreigners, and utterly hateful. Their belief system is alien to the people of Christendom. Later Icelandic sagas, our best vernacular portal into the mindsets of Viking Age Scandinavians, do demonstrate certain unique elements that characterise the Old Norse cosmology as distinct from other, similar faiths. One is the predetermined nature of life, both the lives of the gods (the Æsir and Vanir) and the mortals who do not necessarily worship them but live according to their whim. These deities were supra-natural beings; they existed in some form but did not need to be worshipped like the Christian God. The Æsir and Vanir, the two opposing but since-united families that made up the Old Norse pantheon, are believed by some to have very early Proto-Indo-European origins, linked to the population movements of the post-Roman period. A character who appears in some of these tales, Atli, is a literary counterpart of Attila the Hun in the 400s.[42] It is possible that these legendary figures – Wōden, Óðinn, Thunor, Þórr – all originated from real people, and that these tales of inter-family strife and warfare (so similar to the *mortal* struggles of *Beowulf*) are memories from a time long past.[43] There is no scope to dissect this particular train of thought, but what united both the lives of mortals and the gods above was predetermination.

Ragnarǫk is the certain doom that awaits both man and god at the end of all things. There was no escaping this fate, as much as characters like Óðinn and Loki desperately try. Descriptions of *Ragnarǫk* and its equally dismal prelude all come from stanzas and lays compiled *after* the Viking Age, but the cosmological motifs these works were drawing from exist across the true Viking Age diaspora, from the Isle of Man to Gotland, from Yorkshire to Denmark. One of the most extensive descriptions of *Ragnarǫk*'s first act comes from Snorri Sturluson, which he based on an earlier source; it was a time of wolves, axes, swords, and war. Brother kills brother and the rivers run red with blood. Nothing grows, everything decays. This dire period is known as *Fimbulvetr*, merely the introduction ahead of the great doom.[44] *Ragnarǫk* dawns: the legendary and long-dead warriors from every mortal battle throughout history will be resurrected to form an army of corpses, hand-picked by Óðinn and his valkyries – not beautiful women as popularised by Wagner, but terrifying harbingers – to face off against Loki, this comically evil and beguiling figure, and his own legion of monsters. It is a 'battle of the Gods' scenario but is nevertheless distinct. As far as we can tell, the western pantheons of Wōden, Thunor, Tiw, and Frīcg, so like Óðinn, Þórr, Týr, and Frigg, had no predetermined doom awaiting them. Granted, this might just be a result of the paucity of evidence for Old English paganism. *Ragnarǫk* isn't just the final battle of the gods, but one that has been long-coming, foretold by a seeress to Óðinn millennia in advance. It is an awaited event, a prophesied cataclysm; if the gods cannot change their fate, then neither can man.

Such an important part of the Old Norse worldview may have originated from a real event, so scholarly thought suggests.[45] It is this worldview that could be argued to be the real impetus for the Viking Age, the real change that separated 'the Vikings' from their ancestors. A belief system that prioritized glory in death, and a recurring theme that the future could not be changed no matter what – man's fate has already been decided, so if a raid on the Irish, Spanish, Moorish, or English shore is where a man will die, then that is where a man will die. This belief is of course at complete odds with Christianity. Some event, somewhere, at some time, had such a long-lasting impact on the top layers of Scandinavian society (the warrior elite, so dominant already in the Iron Age) that a new altered pantheon was born. An altered belief system. An altered way of life. One that would shake the world.

The Dust Veil

536. Almost 250 years before the Lindisfarne Raid, and 150 years before our earliest possible evidence of international Scandinavian raiding,

there was a devastating climate event. The cause is unclear, though evidence points towards a chain of volcanic eruptions leading to winters particularly damaging in northern climates. While 536 is the likely first date for these eruptions, as ascertained through dendrochronological dating[46] and Greenland ice cores,[47] it is possible that this climate catastrophe continued until at least 542, affecting the ensuing decades and generations.[48]

In Greece, part of the Roman Empire at the time, we have accounts from Procopius and Michael the Syrian: 'The sun became dark and its darkness lasted for one and a half years.'[49] The poet Cassiodorus wrote in his letters, 'The heat from the sun was feeble... Prolonged frost and unseasonable drought... Frosts during harvest, which made apples harden and grapes sour'.[50] This was a 'dread portent'. In the affluent and marble-lined streets of Constantinople, the once golden skyline became grey and dim. The lights were snuffed out. The sprawling web of trade was fractured, and this was only in the south.

A Chinese source, so far away, talks of a 'dense, dry fog'[51] in 540 and there is archaeological evidence of shrinking agricultural yield throughout the Americas and in Siberia.[52] Irish sources like *The Annals of Ulster* describe a 'failure of bread' for 536 (and again three years later)[53] and the Welsh *Annales Cambriae* mark this same year as the moment when the legendary Arthur fell in battle against Mordred. The anonymous annalist wrote that there was 'great mortality' across the land.[54]

All these sources are from literate societies and importantly are from no further north than the Giant's Causeway. For more northerly climes, the situation could have only been worse; a localised temperature drop predicted to have been between 2-4°C, which would demolish the usual seasonal cycle, affecting the harvest and yield, devastating local economies and leading to fear, panic, anger, and hate: then to violence and bloodshed. It is easy to see how this chain of events could play out, starting as a series of volcanic eruptions and ending with a total restructuring of society. For Sweden and Norway, the years between 536 and 600 saw a transition from what we would call the Iron Age into the Vendel or Merovingian Period. In Sweden, 75% of identified pre-Viking Age farmsteads and homes were abandoned, and around the Lake Mälaren region and on the island of Gotland there is evidence of layers of ash telling of times of conflict and burning.[55] All in all, over a thousand individual sites were left to rot, never to be reinhabited. The site of Valhagar on Gotland is a window into the turmoil of these dark days; whole communities uprooted and forced elsewhere as roaming bands of survivors desperately searched for food. The production of pottery across most of Scandinavia ceased for a time, and pollen analyses across

Norway, Denmark, and Sweden indicate vast swathes of uncultivated land turning barren and cold.[56,57]

An agrarian society without any agriculture would be changed irreversibly after even a short while (5-15 years). This would place greater emphasis on those with the means to enforce power; no longer would the economy be centred around farms, but roaming war bands who took, rather than earned their wealth.

Archaeological evidence also reveals an increase in votive deposits and hoards around 536, but not always of precious metals, food and fabrics too.[58] In this age, perhaps bread *was* more valuable than gold. The abundance of ostentatious gold and gilded material from the ensuing Vendel Period adds weight to such a theory. In the aftermath of a societal restructuring, a new warrior elite wanted to demonstrate their power and control over the land. An increase in barrow mounds and tomb burials is seen, as if to say 'Look over those hills, traveller, for they are lined with the tombs of my forebears. We have always owned this land!' Material evidence also points towards a focus on gold over silver, a more valuable form of wealth that is comparatively scarce in later Viking Age deposits.[59]

The 536 'Dust Veil' event would have irreparably changed the lives of Scandinavians and those living in already cold areas of the world. Without suitable farming terrain or crops, population centres would move to warmer southerly regions, further displacing population groups, which would create a knock-on effect. The battles in *Beowulf* and beyond are now brought into clearer focus – a rich warrior culture that emerged out of the struggle for survival.

Shortly after the initial volcanic eruptions, the onset of famine led to plague. Named after the contemporary Roman emperor, the Justinian Plague swept across Europe in 541 from its origins in the east[60] and, like the famine before it, was catastrophic. Written descriptions of *Ragnarǫk* now seem very apt indeed. One of the most famous, from the poem *Völuspá*, contained within the *Poetic Edda*, warns of a 'wolf age', conjuring images of those three successive winters. This trilogy was *Fimbulvetr* – described in another poem, *Vafþrúðnismál* – a dreadful prelude to an even worse event: the destruction of mankind and the gods above. The aftereffects of modern volcanic eruptions, such as Krakatoa, leave us with tantalising glimpses into the mindsets of the people of 536. Wherever these eruptions were, perhaps the initial boom could be heard as a reverberating soundwave, perhaps the sky over the ensuing days was tinted yellow and orange, even blood-red. Then it became grey, sunless, the temperature would start to plummet. Watch any predictive documentary on the approaching Yellowstone eruption and you'll be able to taste just enough of such 'an axe-age, a sword-age ... before the world's ruin'.

A disaster so devastating, affecting so many people across Scandinavia (a large area, but with sparse population centres), would have not only affected social stratification but also worldviews. If the gods above couldn't prevent such a disaster, with red skies and acid rain, then how could man ever hope to change his fate?

Wōden became Óðinn, a figure newly associated with self-torment, concepts of determinism, and an insatiable lust for knowledge, traits all attested in the very same stanzas that reference *Ragnarǫk*. Is the Dust Veil Event the underlying root behind this myth? Is it the forgotten cause for the artistic differences between these pre-Viking Age and Viking Age gods? Perhaps not in isolation; Óðinn's ritual hanging and spear wound on the branches of *Yggdrasil* (the world tree) evoke images

Type B bracteate from De Valom, The Netherlands, dated sometime between 475-550. The figure depicted has been argued to be *Óðinn* on his horse *Sleipnir*.

of Christ's wound, and near-contemporary depictions of a deity in Frisia also feature a one-eye motif.[61] The recently discovered Vindelev Hoard from Denmark contains a bracteate depicting a one-eyed god inscribed with the Proto-Old Norse runes *Wodnas* or 'he is Odin's man', and this is dated a full century *before* the Dust Veil. All these differences may be entirely superficial; 'Wōden' became 'Óðinn' through linguistic evolution, not through an official name-changing ceremony to distinguish new from old.

Whatever the case, *Ragnarǫk* and a belief in some form of determinism do appear to emerge as some kind of boundary between the pre-Viking Age and what came next. This sense of eschatological determinism became weaponised by the warrior elite; if they and their men were to fall in battle, then it would not matter, not only was it already destined to happen, but they would be remembered.

Going Viking

We neatly sub-divide the Viking Age (793-1066) into a few smaller periods. Historian Peter Sawyer once delineated a 'Second Viking Age'[62] for England, separating the Ælfredan wars of the ninth century from Cnut the Great's conquest in the eleventh, and he was not alone in making such bridges and barriers. The traditional narrative of the Viking Age is that following the Lindisfarne raid (and a few rarely mentioned preceding incidents), the attacks from Scandinavian marauders grew from isolated monastic assaults to coastal village pillaging, and then inland with river raids, and finally raiding grew into military invasions and permanent occupation.

The arguments for the push-and-pull factors leading to this surge of violent young men will be discussed in the following chapter, but it is worth reiterating that this society, this mindset, had been growing long before 793. Even prior to the Dust Veil, warrior societies throughout Europe were on the move. Rising sea levels and the slow decline of state-funded Roman militaries led to population shifts; the original inhabitants of Frisia were ousted by an incoming wave of Germanic-speaking settlers, the people of Britannia had to fend off raids from the Scotti in Ireland and also immigration from the east – even the 'Huns' are an example of these fifth- and sixth-century archetypes. The decline of the Roman Empire from the late 300s had been a consequence of roaming warrior groups, among other factors, and with the infrastructure and state management of Rome gone, this provided an opening for new powers and new hierarchies.[63]

Even before 536 there is evidence of international exports at the site of Helgö, in the Lake Mälaren region of Sweden. Prior to the 700s, there were no real functioning towns or areas of even proto-urban nature throughout Scandinavia. They were in fact quite rare in post-Roman Europe for a time, as life shifted away from regulated commerce to local subsistence. Seasonal market centres or 'central places' existed, but these were not village communities, more hosts. Like a travelling circus, large groups of people would set up temporary tents and structures, only then to leave in a fortnight. Helgö was an example of one such central place, situated on a small island in the centre of a lake, easily accessible via boat in summer or via sleigh and skates in winter.[64] There were parallels to Helgö all across the post-Roman world; Flixborough, a well-known excavated site in Lincolnshire, England, began as a seasonal beach market.[65] What makes Helgö stand out are the most famous finds from the site: a buddha figurine, a crozier, and a Coptic scoop. These finds were from Afghanistan, Ireland, and Egypt.[66]

How they ended up in Scandinavia is probably via the same route later Viking Age treasures found their way there, by the 'Eastern Way' or *Austrvegr*, a series of riverine routes centred around the Dnieper and Volga cutting through modern-day Ukraine and Russia, connecting Finland in the north to Constantinople in the south. It is doubtful that all these items were brought to Helgö by the same people, making one exhaustingly long voyage from Ireland to Egypt and Afghanistan, but it isn't entirely out of the question. What is much more likely is that goods like these, exotic goods, were traded and carried via middlemen; a craftsman in Gujarat sold to a travelling Arabic merchant who then took the figurine with him along the Silk Road until he arrived at Constantinople. There, in the city of cities, *Mikligarðr* as the Scandinavians knew it, this small figurine was bartered between Roman and Bulgarian hands, before finding its way on raft and canoe up the Dnieper and Volga rivers, changing owner from town to town, perhaps traded for a slave here and some beeswax there, before eventually arriving at the site of Staraja Ladoga, one of the earliest of these international emporia in the north.[67] From there, it was a short sail westwards across the untrustworthy and fog-ridden Baltic Sea to Helgö.

This journey, and others like it, were a common occurrence before the Viking Age and they certainly continued throughout it, as best illustrated by the Indian carnelian bead found near Repton investigated by Cat Jarman.[68] The period after the decline of Rome is often popularly presented as a time of separate peoples living in mud huts barely talking to one another. This couldn't be further from the truth. Even in one of the least Romanised corners of the world – Scandinavia – home to the Eruli the contemporary author Procopius so slandered, the people were receiving goods from the very city he was writing in, Constantinople.

The bronze Helgö Buddha, probably manufactured somewhere near northwestern India in the seventh century, 8.4 cm tall. When first found in 1956, it was adorned with a few leather straps obscuring the neck and left hand, and initial reports describe it as having copper inlays.

Indeed, the very fact Procopius could speak of the Eruli indicates cross-cultural awareness.

The Eruli were not the only pre-Viking Age raiders;[69] *Saxones*, Frisians, Angles, Jutes, Scotti and Franks harried the coasts of England and Gaul prior to the decline of Rome, as did the Picts to the north.[70] These terms likely describe overlapping cultural identities. Raiding was not unique to

Viking Age Scandinavians; they were simply the best at a long-established form of profiteering.

But Scandinavia was not monolithic, unique identities had emerged throughout the sixth and seventh centuries just as they had in England. As the multi-ethnic polities of Wessex, East Anglia, and Kent formed over the North Sea, so, too, did the identifiable territory of the Danes, the Geats, and the many *smákonungar* ('small kings') who occupied territories up and down *Norðvegr*, the 'Northern Way' – Norway.

Also inhabiting Scandinavia were the Saami in the Arctic Circle, with a long tradition of hunting and gathering across Norway, Sweden, and Finland dating back centuries before other settlers even arrived. The Saami, as we will see, were intrinsically connected to the wider world through trade, and while ethnically distinct, there was a certain amount of cultural overlap between Viking Age Scandinavians and the Saami; both groups shared a focus on animal hybridity and shamanism, though to different degrees.[71] One could be ethnically Danish but *culturally* Norse, as an example. It is incredibly tricky to piece together how people in the past viewed themselves using only archaeological material and historical sources. Just because someone buried near the trading town of Birka, in Lake Mälaren, is found alongside a bow and arrow does not necessarily mean that they were an archer. Likewise, the many sixth-century cemeteries found throughout England could conceivably be either of native or immigrant origin. One way to work this out is to analyse grave goods and grave orientation, though the truth is always more complicated than we like to assume. To continue with the example from Britain, it was in one of these sixth-century cemeteries that genomic evidence for a Scandinavian presence in England was discovered at the site of West Heslerton, Yorkshire.[72] One has only to listen to the similarities in the dialects of Old English, Old Frisian, and Old Norse to see further connections. As Matthew Townend noted, there was a certain degree of 'mutual linguistic intelligibility'[73] across the North Sea in the ninth and tenth centuries. It is highly likely that in the fifth, sixth, and seventh centuries, this mutual intelligibility was even greater.

The Frisians are the unsung heroes of the Early Medieval Period, as we will see in the next chapter, and their importance as a cultural middleman between the populations in England and those in Scandinavia at the dawn of the sixth century cannot be overstated. There, on the windswept tidal marshes, was a people linguistically and culturally like both groups – a foot in both camps. The Frisians would go on to play an immensely important and similar role to Scandinavians in the ensuing centuries, though they have gone largely unnoticed by popular culture. The entire North Sea was a nexus of cultural, linguistic, and material exchange.

Dawn

Do these monikers even matter? Does it matter if one individual was what we would call an 'Old Frisian' or an 'Old Norse' speaker? While archaeology can usually only give us a snapshot of an individual at the very end of their lives – in the grave goods their kin chose to bury them with – we can through legend and some documentary sources get another glimpse into the mindsets of the time.

The wife of King Ælfred, Ealswitha, whom he married in 868, was an 'Anglo-Saxon' like him, but from another kingdom, Mercia. She was, as Ælfred's biographer Asser says, a member of the 'tribe called *Gaini*'.[74] So Ealswitha is first and foremost an 'Anglo-Saxon', an ethnic and political label for countless Germanic language groups merged into one following several generations of settlement in England. She was a member of the kingdom of Mercia, therefore a Mercian, whose identity may have been shaped through border conflicts with rival groups, as 'Mercia' hails from Old English for 'border' or 'march folk'. Then, at the most intimate level of identity observable to us, she was of the kin group of the *Gaini*, probably centred around *Gegnesburh* (Gainsborough). Asser's depiction of Ealswitha gives us as a figure with three layers of identity; one national, one regional, and one local.

As already mentioned, while the fledgling kingdoms of sixth-century England were in their infancy, so were similar states over in Scandinavia, and they must have also been developing layers of identity. Identity and belonging are what make an individual and also what allow him or her to claim elements from their own heritage. We see a glimpse of this tendency to cling onto kin groups and tribes from the Old English poetic catalogue, *Widsið*:[75]

> I was among the Huns and the Hreth-Goths,
> among the Sweonas and among the Geatas and among the South-Danes.
> I was among Wenlas and among the Wærnas and among the Wicingas.
> I was among Gepthae and among Winedas and among the Gefflas.
> I was among the Saxons and the Sycgas and among the Sword-men.
> I was among the Hronas and among the Danes and among the Heathoreams.
> I was among the Thyringas and among the Throndas,
> and among the Burgundians, where I received a ring –
> there Guthhere gave to me a resplendent treasure,
> as requital for my song. That was no sluggish king!

Widsið's 143 lines, contained within the *Exeter Book*, are grouped into three catalogues called *thulas*, each describing a different section of society: ancient figures of renown, miscellaneous people the narrator visited when travelling, and then figures of myth. All these descriptions are steeped in the poetic pseudo-history of the pre-Viking Age; a rich corpus of interwoven elements recognisable to people of the time, repeated in smoky mead halls.

Often in modern depictions, we find heathen zealotry, pagans deliberately targeting Christian centres because they are an affront to their own identity. Aside from one or two examples, this was almost definitely not the case. Really, a desire to cling onto a religious identity and enforce it upon others was more of a Christian game, though it is plausible that there was some pagan 'pushback', so to speak.

The truth of the matter is that by the late sixth century, the nameless territories within Scandinavia and their various inhabitants had been forged into a culturally unique cluster of petty polities on the northernmost rim of the North Sea trade zone and placed *just* close enough to take advantage of international economic growth. Scandinavia had never been geographically isolated from the rest of the world, as Roman writers would so often claim, the archaeological evidence runs counter to this. Nor had Scandinavians been living in a Dust Veil bubble for several centuries – they had experienced changes in the world after the decline of Rome like everyone else, just in different ways.

It would be misleading to suggest that by 'going viking', Early Medieval Scandinavians were simply following the chain of events that led to so many population movements in the preceding centuries. The reasons for the onset of raiding at the dawn of the ninth century and the reasons for mass-migrations in the fifth and sixth centuries are different. Nevertheless, certain events that took place throughout the immediate post-Roman period did have long-term effects that would only show themselves to the world – in brutal fashion – at the end of the eighth century. While the raiders of Lindisfarne did not, as contemporary accounts suggest, appear like a bolt from the blue, they did come from somewhere, and that somewhere was, arguably, the *Ragnarǫk* of 536.

We will never know if pre-536 Scandinavians would have developed a cosmology and belief system like that of the Old Norse one had the Dust Veil not transpired, nor will we ever know for certain if the two are even linked. Archaeological and literary evidence make it very tempting to suggest that they are. While there has always been a Scandinavian element to the character of the North Sea and its territories before and after the Roman Period, we would never call this a 'Viking' element, but should we?

'Vikings': New and Old

Gildas, a sixth-century British cleric lamenting in his *On the Ruin and Conquest of Britain*, described the immigrating and invading population of Germanic language speakers as one homogenous entity, the Saxons, borrowing from the earlier catch-all Latin term *Saxones*, which may have simply meant 'North Sea pirates'.[76] In Gildas' worldview, one was either a Briton ('shameless', and thus to blame for the perceived dire straits) or a Saxon ('fierce and impious', and thus an agent of change). Unlike other near-contemporary sources, Gildas drew no distinction between Saxon, Angle, Jute, Frisian, or Frank, or others, despite the fact we can nowadays realistically assert that different dialect groups migrated to different areas of the British Isles. In its description of Scandinavian raiders, traders, and farmers, Gildas's work is surprisingly similar to later tenth-century accounts. At the height of Ælfred the Great's wars, one was either a member of an *Ænglisċ* (English) kingdom, or a *Dene* (Dane).[77] To the Carolingian annalists, the threat came unanimously from *normanni* (Northmen) with no account for individual geographic origin,[78] nor did Arabic sources move beyond describing all vikingar as *madjus* ('fire-worshippers', or simply 'heathens'). Irish sources go a step forward with first a religious identifier as *gentiles* and then an ethnic identifier as 'foreigners'. To the victims and enemies of Viking Age Scandinavians, one was either kin or alien. There was no room for all the grey areas and cross-cultural transfer we see today in academic analyses.

This sums up quite a lot of Viking Age research. Outside of archaeological and linguistic evidence, our best 'windows' into the time are almost exclusively from the perspective of others. These *others* viewed the Scandinavian raiders and traders *as* others, thus creating a perpetual loop of imposed identity. This bleeds into a lot of older and modern studies of the period, even though we now know conclusively that there was a Scandinavian presence in the British Isles ahead of Lindisfarne, some still tend to depict the Viking Age as a shock, a coup de main, where mysterious threats that were only partially understood by contemporaries uprooted everything. The Viking Age and its characteristic viking activities was actually the latest and greatest example of the hit-and-run kin-based warfare of the Early Medieval Period, and Viking Age deities the final evolution of a long-recognised polytheistic pantheon. And their ships were the result of centuries of technological advancement. But these people were unique, call them Early Medieval Scandinavians, Viking Age raiders, or simply 'Vikings', they had a distinct character that was built on centuries – if not millennia – of cultural transformation, miscellaneous world events, and cross-cultural mixing and matching. The Viking Age, whether it started in 536 or 793, was real.

Dawn and Dusk

It is tempting to view the Viking Age as a cyclical story mirroring the myths of *Ragnarǫk* and the Æsir and Vanir. Such coincidences are mostly superficial. What began in 536 as a horrifying winter that lasted for at least fifteen years (with ongoing after-effects) changed society and formed the emerging warrior elite so associated with plundering and portable wealth. Almost exactly one thousand years later is the date of a fictitious account of a Danish ship stumbling upon the abandoned coastline of Greenland,[79] their ancestor's colonies having left decades prior, and finding the body of a red-haired man face down in the snow. Upon turning over the individual, the Danes stumbled upon the usual accoutrements one would expect of an Arctic European, along with a peculiar pendant in the shape of Þórr's hammer, seemingly calling back through the ages to a time of heroes and warriors. This story, which is certainly at the very least embroidered, is dated to the year 1540, in a world completely alien to the people of 536, and yet still there is a tenuous link, which shall be returned to in the closing chapter.

One thing that connects this broader 'Viking Age', if such a term can be applied, is the mindset of these people. Be they sufferers and refugees of a climate crisis in Norway, fleeing their homes and joining bands of squabbling warlords, or desperate farmers attempting to hold out in Greenland during the fourteenth-century Little Ice Age, resilience is the common trait. A warrior's stoicism, possibly, born from a mutual cultural memory of death and destruction: a fate that not even the gods could prevent.

A man's glory was measured in gold, silver, cattle, slaves, and *deeds* – to succeed in this world was to be a powerful warrior, with an armed band of men to sing your praises. It did not matter if you died this day or that day, on a raid in Ireland or on the trade routes of the *Austrvegr*, for it has been foretold, and when you fall you will rise again in *Valhöll* (Valhalla), and the cycle will repeat. But before that glorious and long-foreseen death, life presents its own challenges; to succeed one needs wealth, lots of it, and where better to look than the trade routes of the seventh and eighth centuries? It is to those routes we now sail.

Rise

'My brother Peada and my beloved friend Oswy began a minster, for the love of Christ and St. Peter: but my brother, as Christ willed, is departed from this life; I will therefore intreat thee, beloved friend, that they earnestly proceed on their work; and I will find thee thereto gold and silver, land and possessions, and all that thereto behoveth.' Then went the abbot home, and began to work. So he sped, as Christ permitted him; so that in a few years was that minster ready.

Entry for the year 656 in *The Anglo-Saxon Chronicle* Manuscript [D]. Cotton MS. Tiberius IV.

In researching the pre-Viking Age, it is difficult to identify any real figures of importance for Scandinavia. *Beowulf* refers to several rulers and their retinues across the North Sea area, such as the Danish king Beow, the Swedish Eadgils, and Ingeld, king of the *Heaðobards* ('warbeards'). Many of these figures are referenced in other manuscripts, chief among them being the Geatish king Hygelac, who is likely one and the same as the figure referenced by Frankish Gregory of Tours as 'Chlochilaicus' in the third of his sixth-century *Ten Books of Histories*.[1] Hygelac has a brief genealogy referenced in *Beowulf*, but it is difficult to attribute much weight to it, let alone suggest that Hygelac was a real figure. Rather, Hygelac might be best seen as an idealised version of an Early Medieval chieftain. As said numerous times in *Widsið*, people in charge were best respected and could best maintain their power if they bestowed wealth via a trickle-down economic system, if they were 'most generous in the sharing of rings'. Hygelac is one such figure, and even if entirely fictional, the oral tradition that *Beowulf* is based on maintains that ever-present link with warrior heroes and wealthy elites, as seen throughout the Iron Age and Vendel Period of Scandinavia. In the aftermath of the Dust Veil, as northern Europe healed and steadied, this fledgling elite society present around the North Sea rim was rich and primed to take advantage of the post-Roman twilight. There were no dominant powers just yet, but they would come, and along that road would, in time, follow raiders a-viking.

Wealth and Power; Kings and Connections

To fully understand the driving force behind the Viking Age is to get a grasp on what the state of the surrounding world was on the eve of raiding. If we use the 8th of June 793, the Lindisfarne raid, as the end-date for this period of build-up, then we must consider the following factors: the economy of the North Sea, and how it affected Scandinavia and influenced the people; the religious conflicts between Christianity and those unwilling to convert; and the formation of polities within Scandinavia itself. We must look for the first kingdom, and first recognisable king, of the Viking Age.

Mentioned above is Chlochilaicus, though he isn't a particularly noteworthy historical figure outside of literature. The eighth-century English *Book of Monsters*[2] and Gregory's *Ten Books of Histories* both describe Chlochilaicus as 'king of the Geats' and 'king of the Goths' respectively, claiming that he was Danish and that he raided in Frisia. Chlochilaicus's corpse was remarked upon as being significantly taller than contemporary men (a recurring literary trope in these descriptions of Scandinavians), which gives the whole mention an air of mysticism, of legend. He was someone 'whom no horse could carry from the age of twelve'. The author even compares Chlochilaicus with the classical Colossus. There were indeed powerful chieftains operating in the North Sea in the sixth century. Chlochilaicus, or Hygelac, appears as an idealistic composite of these rulers; being allied with him was itself worthy of note – 'Higelac's mates are we' – and prizes won by Beowulf throughout the narrative are often sent as gifts to Hygelac. Several of the figures in *Beowulf* are named alongside their deeds and generosity, with the villain Grendel – an exiled kin-killing marsh-dweller – appearing as the antithesis.

Because Hygelac/Chlochilaicus is referenced by Gregory of Tours, historians have been able to date him and, by extension, the events of *Beowulf*, to the sixth century. While there is no archaeological proof Chlochilaicus existed, there is some evidence for organised manpower and border consolidation in contemporary Denmark; the first layers of the Danevirke were established in this same century.[3] The Danevirke is an immense earthwork like Hadrian's Wall or Offa's Dyke, which runs along the old border between the Frankish territories and what could conceivably be called a 'Kingdom of the Danes'. The structure now lies in Germany, but Early Medieval Danish territory extended this way and covered parts of Sweden, too. The name Denmark, though it first appears in the vernacular in the 900s, stems from the root words of *Dene* (from Dane, an ethnic and cultural identifier), and *-mark* (from 'march' or 'borderland'). The Kingdom of the Danes, then, emerged as a recognisable polity through strife with another, perhaps the people of France and Germany. This phase of Danish history is difficult to discern, for we have few reliable historical sources, and the archaeological evidence is, as ever, open to interpretation. The textual evidence for pre-Viking Age Scandinavia is slim overall and so to better build up the picture of the wider 'road to Lindisfarne' we must turn once more to the British Isles.

Of the many Anglian, Brythonic, and Saxon warlords of *The Anglo-Saxon Chronicle* (ASC), the first historically recognisable individual that we would call a 'king' is probably Æthelberht of Kent, who reigned during the late 590s into the 600s, and was the first notable convert to Christianity following the missions led by Paulinus.[4] Æthelberht of Kent would later be joined in the historical record by such figures as Rædwald of East Anglia, Æðelfrið the Twister, and Kings Edwin, Oswald, and Oswiu, not to mention the pagan warlord Penda of Mercia. These people and their kingdoms, as described by near-contemporary sources (chief among them eighth-century author Bede's *Ecclesiastical History of the English People*),[5] appear in the two centuries following Imperial administrative decline in Britannia. We don't know who the forebears of most of these early kings were, but they existed at the same time as the first warlords of pre-Viking Age Scandinavia. Contemporaneous with Chlochilaicus in Denmark or Sweden were semi-legendary English ancestors like Ida the Flamebearer, Ælle of Sussex, and Cædbæd 'Battle-Crow'.[6] At the onset of the Viking Age, England was divided into kingdoms, many with recognisable names like Wessex, Mercia, and East Anglia, but these were only the extant and most-powerful from a much larger collection of smaller states and even tinier polities. The same situation was undoubtedly happening in Scandinavia with the emergent nations of Norway, Denmark, and Sweden, which were once also clusters of smaller territories.

Any genealogical research that goes beyond the Norman Conquest will eventually lead to semi-legendary figures; heroes and dragon-slayers from an unknown golden age. For Scandinavia, there are various dynasties like the Ynglings, allegedly buried at Gamla (Old) Uppsala, in Sweden, and the Danish Scyldings mentioned in *Beowulf*. These dynasties, like the Old Norse gods themselves, might never have existed, but the important thing for us is that Viking Age Scandinavians *identified* with them and claimed a somewhat mutual heritage. With masses of land taken and reoccupied following the archaeologically identified population movements of the Dust Veil, new elites with reasons to claim that they had 'always been here' emerged. This is likely the same impetus for the abundance of *-ingas-* place names[7, 8] across the British Isles, from Old English for 'the kin of'.[9] Names of communities were identified with long-dead or semi-legendary figures like Winta, Finn, or Wōden. They proudly referred to themselves (or were referred to by others) by that name. 'The people of Winta' is one example. Thus, their heritage became baked into the landscape, recognised and legitimised. This worked on both a small and large scale; if a tiny farmstead in North Lincolnshire became known as Winteringham ('the estate of Winta's folk'), then this identity became known to others as a specific identifiable territory, much in the same way that the origin of the name for Denmark emerged as a larger political identity through opposition to others. With a greater and renewed sense of identity, kin-groups could lay claim to their surroundings, compete with others, and eventually this competition would generate wealth and status.

To understand raiders is to understand the hierarchy aboard the raiding vessel, the longship. Christian Cooijmans neatly describes these small-scale internal power structures as hydrarchies;[10] polyglot maritime-based social hierarchies, unaffiliated with landed realms, where many self-governed men served common interests, akin to pirate crews in the 1700s.[11] In pre-Viking Age Scandinavia, we see through archaeology the emergence of individuals who wore the Vendel Helmet (rich and powerful men of status),[12] and through literature characters like Sigurd the Dragon Slayer[13] and Halfdan 'The Generous'. These are the types of people who would benefit from wealth generated by roaming raiding hydrarchies.

Halfdan is a particularly interesting example, a Norwegian king who allegedly lived in the eighth century according to Snorri Sturluson's *Ynglinga Saga*. 'It is said that he paid his men as many gold coins as other kings gave silver, but he starved them of food.' This was the trickle-down economics so vital to a lord demanding loyalty from his subjects, so Halfdan (if he was real at all) was respected: 'He was a great warrior and went raiding for long periods and gained property.'[14] Let us hope his successor was a little more generous at the dinner table.

Such demonstrates the power struggles at the core of the murky histories of pre-Viking Age Scandinavia. Even once we are into the Viking Age proper, the warlords and 'kings' of Scandinavia are a confusing and difficult-to-discern bunch, but more on that later.

Rise

The rise of vikingar is intrinsically tied to the rise of kings and the growth of individual status; with gold-rich men of wealth on the horizon, growing more and more powerful with each generation, so, too, would the desire of other men to take that status from them. In the 600s, the activities of pagan and Christian kings in England were not far removed from the land-based raiding of the Great Heathen Army in the ninth century. Æðelfrið the Twister, so-named by his enemies for being duplicitous, slaughtered a group of monks at Chester in 616, and once he himself was slain, his successor Edwin gathered loot and portable booty from his enemies' forces into assemblages we sometimes unearth today, like the Staffordshire Hoard.[15] This hoard is, again, not dissimilar from many Viking Age examples, such as the Bedale Hoard.[16] Both are collections of glorious wealth, with pieces of equipment chipped up to be melted down for scrap, to further boost local economies. King Oswald, a later Northumbrian king, was dismembered and paraded as a gory trophy by his adversary King Penda of Mercia in 642[17,18] – these are not the actions of a people far removed from perceived Viking Age brutalism. But what separates them is time. The warmongers of the seventh century are trapped in their era; after the 650s, the institution of the church became a main enforcer in the consolidation and security of secular power in England. It would take until the late 900s, and even beyond, for Scandinavian counterparts to reach that same position.

But this then becomes a conversation about what really distinguishes a 'king' from a mere warlord, a jarl from a king, even. Once again, the post-Roman Period gives us a few tantalising clues. Gildas, the Nennian compiler, and Bede each distinguish between different tiers of monarchy; *subregulii* or 'under-kings', *duces bellorum* or 'battle-leaders', and *regulii* for genuine kings.[19,20] Even above the 'true kings' there are unmentioned overlords or people of higher status; the title of *bretwalda* is first mentioned in the *ASC* for the year 827, the 'wide ruler' over all Britain. Æthelberht of Kent may very well have been subservient to a Merovingian (Frankish) overseer, with vested interests in his state, judging from artefact similarities between Kent and the continent. In the Viking Age, before the countries of Norway, Sweden, and Denmark were formed, there existed many smaller polities, all with their own rulers and their own inter-regional links and alliances. This, in Scandinavia, as across the British Isles, would have led to peer-polity competition between rival chieftains, jarls, warriors, warlords, kinglets, and kings. But what would they have been fighting over, exactly? Not simply land, but what land could produce.

Access to arable land and the associated livestock could make or break a society. We often view the Viking Age as being all about stealing silver, and while silver undoubtedly played an important role in later economies, the most dominant elements of wealth were food and flesh, livestock and slaves. Near-contemporary sources from Early Medieval Ireland talk about cross-territorial cattle raids,[21] and it is likely that such a practice was occurring all over northern Europe; small-scale border invasions over boundaries to accrue capital for use in generating new internal economies. We see this best with the campaigns of Godfrid, king of the Danes, in the early 800s.[22] There was a variety of reasons for his assault into modern Germany, but chief among them appears to have been the destruction of the Frankish town of Reric in 808[23] and the replacement of its economic centre with a market town based in Godfrid's lands: Hedeby. Not only did this weaken the competition (the Carolingian Empire), but it strengthened Godfrid's economy. We see this in Early Medieval England, and so it is plausible that similar activities were occurring over the North Sea in Frisia and Scandinavia, too, hundreds of years before the Viking Age.

A key difference between these countries is of course geography. Where England and Frisia are flat and boggy, Norway is mountainous and segregated by fjords. Where England would have been better traversed via the Roman roads on foot, Sweden was segmented by impassable barriers like unending forests and swampland, better suited to boats. Denmark's central landmass, Jutland, is very similar to the Low Countries, but its storm-washed eastern archipelagoes couldn't be more different. And so, to be a successful raider, and thus a successful *duces bellorum* (battle leader), one must learn how to best traverse that terrain.

'Someday I will buy a galley with good oars, sail to distant shores'

Egil's Saga, transcribed in the thirteenth century, preserving earlier oral traditions, expresses this somewhat wistful yearning.[24] One of the most recognisable motifs of the period, the evolution of the Viking Age longship was a multi-faceted chain of events; never was it a clear and clean process of step-by-step improvement, but fittingly, more of an ebb-and-flow. The ship developed differently in different parts of Scandinavia, as it did across the rest of the world, but eventually, it was the longship that would push the Viking Age forward and separate Scandinavians from their counterparts. Technologically speaking, they were ahead of the curve.

But this was not always the case. Ships powered by sails had been around for quite some time, used by many different societies around the globe. In Ancient Egypt, Greece, and Rome, sail-power was a key facet of both commercial and military might. Granted, this was in the calm Mediterranean waters, but it is still worth mentioning that long before the Viking Age, vessels were powered by both oars *and* sails. So, what made the Viking Age longship so special? It is even possible that Scandinavians had sail-powered ships in the preceding Nordic Bronze Age, judging by comparative technology elsewhere in the world at the time, though the vast majority of these prehistoric vessels must have been rowed, as depicted on petroglyphs.[25] Our earliest piece of physical evidence for the development of ship technology within Scandinavia does indeed come from a vessel remarkably similar to these early carvings; the Hjortspring boat, dated to 400-300 BCE.[26] As the petroglyphs date from nearly a thousand years before, it is likely that the Hjortspring boat was simply continuing earlier trends. But which trends?

The Hjortspring boat is possibly the oldest existing clinker-built vessel in the entire world.[27] Made of overlapping wooden planks and animal sinew, this vessel was not simply built to carve *through* water but to glide over it. There is no evidence for a sail; the likelihood is that it was far too thin to support one, only capable of housing a small handful of men armed with weapons. This boat, found alongside deposited weapons and metalwork, was the home of a hydrarchy; sword and shield bosses influenced by continental Iron Age designs were excavated alongside the vessel itself, and all seem to have been purposefully deposited in a bog in Jutland. The act of Scandinavians depositing important material (and people) in bogs is well attested through the study of 'bog bodies', but the fact the practice has also been applied to a boat here is of particular interest.[28] Was the Hjortspring boat purposefully sunk beneath the marsh to trap the vengeful revenants of troublesome rival soldiers? Or was it a commemorative deposition of fallen loved ones and valiant heroes?

The Hjortspring boat is an exceptionally well-made vessel, made of local material like lime tree planks and thin hazel limbs, bound together as one clean and compact knife to cut between coastal islands. It was likely rowed along coastlines or between the eastern archipelagoes of Denmark and beyond. The hundreds of islands of the Baltic Sea would have seen their fair share of similar vessels throughout the pre-Viking Age.

A reconstruction of the Hjortspring boat (400-300 BCE). About 19 metres long and housing ten internal thwarts, around twenty crew members could have propelled the boat across the waters of The Kattegat and beyond.

Perhaps later examples, like the ship fragments from Halsnøy (200 CE)[29] or Nydam Mose (200-400)[30] were also bog boats purposely buried with warrior accoutrements. These vessels and their earlier Bronze Age petroglyph depictions point to a very well-established maritime military society that not only placed great emphasis on strength and victory, but also mastery of the water. Despite their impressive construction, none of these boats would last very long out on the open ocean, but they were beginning to develop the unique characteristics of the archetypal longship. It was not simply the addition of a sail to these thin boats, but the keel, perfectly cut from a single tree so that it could bend with the waves but never break, allowing for a comparatively high speed when sailing.

The boats discovered at Sutton Hoo (600 CE)[31] in the 1920s, like later longships, were keeled boats, designed to withstand the force of the waves of the North Sea, though importantly there is minimal evidence these vessels had sails. It is doubtful that sails were an unknown entity to Germanic-language speakers of the time, they were perhaps just not yet adopted – there was no need for a sail when only rowing along coastlines. Eventually, however, as raiding and trading intensified, sails would follow. Or perhaps they came first and facilitated such an expansion? A 'chicken and egg' scenario.

Ultimately, what set the 'Vikings' apart from the rest of the world was their well-established lifestyle; anyone who had grown up on the fjords of Norway or the islands of the Baltic would have *needed* to master sea travel, and with such an emphasis on martial prowess and status, it is no wonder that effort was dedicated to ship development and maritime technology. This was distinct from contemporary cultures, though would see some parallels with the Frisians, as discussed later. It was not simply the keel that made Viking Age longships 'Viking', for we see keels on boats elsewhere, nor was it just the sail, nor necessarily a combination of both. According to the *ASC*, King Ælfred oversaw the construction of his own fleet in 896 'not shaped either after the Frisian or the Danish model', and yet it saw no tremendous success defending the waterways, nor did later monarch Æthelred the Ill-Counselled two centuries later.

The sail, the keel, and the clinker-built overlapping wooden planks all combined to form a vessel that could travel the seas at speed. It didn't bob along in the water like Irish coracles or Ælfred's boats.

The turning point of ship technology[32] would either be the Kvalsund Boat, from Norway, or Salme I and II,[33] found on the island of Saaremaa off the coast of Estonia. All three of these vessels are near-contemporaneous, though importantly only the second of the two Salme vessels shows signs of a sail, as suggested by archaeologist Juri Peets.

Kvalsund, on the other hand, could plausibly have held a sail, though all evidence again points to it being powered by oars. Kvalsund is dated between 700-800, just before the much more famous Oseberg and Gokstad ships were built, which are both firmly from the Viking Age and feature the capacity for masts. These three vessels, then; Salme I and II, and Kvalsund, are in transition between oar and sail power.

Something happened between the seventh and eighth centuries that saw multiple strands of maritime engineering collide; the clinker-built rowing vessels of the Danish bogs, the arched keel of boats from the Norwegian fjords, and the royal Swedish sails found on Saaremaa. Wind power and manpower melded; Scandinavians had created longship power. This is not to say that viking activity was not already happening prior to this development. As previously mentioned, the act of raiding and obtaining loot and status was endemic across the Early Medieval world, and even a naval element would be seen before 793. Be it the documentary evidence for war bands in boats off the coast of Britannia, or the definite presence of weapons and military evidence in the Hjortspring burial, maritime warrior societies were already in place before the Viking Age. Can we identify a true precursor?

Raiding or Trading?

By the tenth century, the difference between a 'raid' and a 'military operation' becomes blurred. The activities of the Great Heathen Army shocked the native 'English' when they conquered kingdom after kingdom in the 860s, however, this was no longer necessarily 'viking' activity but arguably rather military occupation on a large scale. Likewise, Godfrid's invasion of Frisia in 810 was, in the first thirty years of the Viking Age, an example of a large, state-organised fleet targeting specific economic hot-spots, not merely a bunch of disorganised raiding parties. What is the difference? The result for local populations will have been the same; death and destruction in the worst cases, peaceful exchanges of goods in the best. It was not until Scandinavian war bands started permanently to settle areas of Europe that the impact changed significantly.

In 2008, construction workers unearthed seven burials and what resembled a classic Viking Age longship in Salme, Saaremaa, mentioned earlier.[34] In 2010, another ship was found and the discoveries included 41 skeletal remains, a large selection of iron weaponry, evidence for hawking, hounds, and military strategy, and a possible sail. The Salme boats are archetypal Viking Age longships. We can surmise they would have been rowed and sailed to Saaremaa, the small island near modern Estonia. We can safely posit that the boats were not local due to some of the grave goods found amongst the burials. The dead were reasonably respected, considering that it is likely these boats contained men of war intent on violence. Or did they? Are these boats, dated between 700-750, the first evidence of viking activity – raiding – anywhere in the world? Or are they perhaps evidence for something else entirely?

Of the 41 skeletal remains, many were isotopically analysed, revealing that most of them came from somewhere over the Baltic Sea in Sweden.[35] Well-armed and armoured men, with ornate gold-inlaid iron swords, a sign of prestige compared to spears and axes, as were their gaming pieces, which also indicate some degree of planning and strategy – all of this evidence points towards an elite Swedish war band of some capacity travelling across the Baltic Sea to engage with Estonians. But for what reason? Was this a diplomatic mission sent by the semi-legendary Yngling dynasty to open trade routes? Estonia sits right in the maw of the Gulf of Riga to Constantinople, and it is known that in later centuries, people called the 'Oesellians' would periodically raid Scandinavia from the Estonian coast and Saaremaa, so it is reasonable to assume that they presented a problem for the vital eastern trade routes. Or these 41 individuals could have been sent specifically to pacify another warlord, maybe not even an Oesellian but a fellow Scandinavian.

Most importantly, would we call these people *vikingar* in the same sense that the Scandinavians who fell upon Lindisfarne 93 years later would be known? Ultimately, the aim of viking activity was to generate status and wealth, and such was the aim of many if not all military operations in the Early Medieval Period. The distinction between a raid like the 793 attack or a 'military encounter' like the 700-750 Salme incident is not a particularly clear one, and as mentioned earlier, these lines will only become more and more indistinct as the Viking Age progresses.

Also blurred is the distinction between viking activity and trading activity. Both generated immense wealth and both seem to have increased in scale at the dawn of the ninth century. We have near-contemporary written accounts of The Kattegat, the straits between Jutland and Norway, being 'infested by pirates'. 'Vikings' did not just raid other societies, but Scandinavia, too. In contrast to piratical activity, we have archaeological evidence of the development of early market towns and temporary 'trading posts'. The earlier example of Helgö was founded sometime between 200-400, and had its heyday in the 500s before later being replaced by a larger town, Birka,[36] elsewhere in the Lake Mälaren region. Helgö is but one example of these Scandinavian nodes on a larger trading network of exchange economies. Ribe, located in central Jutland, is another equally important cog in this wider Early Medieval trade nexus. Just as emporia up and down the North Sea

Rise

were increasing in scale and wealth, so too were comparative sites in Scandinavia, exchanging goods from the north with the west and east. Staraja Ladoga, a site with Slavic and Finnish origins in the 500s,[37] saw a widespread Scandinavian presence long before the Viking Age,[38] as the river routes of the Dnieper and Volga opened. So did sites all along these routes; Novgorod, Kyiv, and Gnezdovo. Their beginnings were possibly in the Viking Age proper, but it is plausible to assume they, too, started as seasonal markets long beforehand – the towns and proto-urban centres that dominated northern Europe from 800-1000 did not come out of nowhere. They, like the 'Vikings' themselves, were a product of a long chain of events and evolution.

The merchants and craftspeople in Ribe, in Jutland, judging by artefacts like soapstone and worked antler, were in contact with Arctic Norway from 710-725, if not earlier.[39] We can imagine the magnates living at the gargantuan lordly estate on Borg, Lofoten, trading with the Arctic Saami for antlers, which they then redistributed with local farmers or the magnates at Avaldsnes, near Stavanger,[40] who in turn travelled further down 'the Northern Way' all the way to the market towns of Kaupang, near Oslo, and Ribe farther south, before sailing all the way back with new goods like Baltic amber or fur. Perhaps this journey would even continue; westwards from Ribe along the Frisian coastline to Dorestad and Quentovic, contemporary sites of the North Sea rim. Eighth-century Quentovic and its buildings, workshops, and markets was already separated by drainage ditches, evidence of a local coastal elite.[41] Journeys like this, described by scholar Sorin Sindbæk as a 'small world' economy,[42] were distinct from the later trading and bartering of the ninth and tenth centuries, for it appears from the distributions of artefacts (like worked antler, combs, amber, soapstone, and quernstones), that there was no 'inter-hierarchical' trading, meaning the poorest farmers were only bartering with other poor farmers, and not trading material with warrior elites. This was to change as the eighth century drew to a close, however, as more and more wealth began to circulate through the North Sea. Individuals in state-of-the-art longships, with a violent warrior culture and a sense of predetermination, were primed to take advantage. It would not take long.

Sceattas and Saltmarshes

A *sceat* is a relatively thin silver coin minted at various sites across the North Sea between the seventh and ninth centuries.[43] This transferable currency was not a shilling with a specific embossed monarchal figurehead but a generic lump of standardised value, probably referred to as a 'penny', though with a different pattern according where it was minted. *Sceattas* are found by metal detectorists all over the British Isles, The Netherlands, and Denmark, where they are most common, but they were undoubtedly circulating in wider areas of the North Sea.

Between the sixth and seventh centuries, after the turmoil of the Dust Veil and the consolidation of kings and kingdoms in France and England, not to mention Scandinavia, local economies started to grow and prosper and their interactions with one another increased. This is the same era as the opening of the Eastern Way – the *Austrvegr*, the time of the Salme boat burials, of ship development and of trade between the farmers of Norway and the markets of Denmark, of Kings Æðelfrið, Edwin, Oswald, and Penda. *Sceattas*, in some ways, fuelled this development in the west, and despite slowly being superseded by regionalised coinage in England and France, the necessity for a standardised form of silver wealth remained. The usage of *sceattas* in tandem with the direct bartering of goods is unclear. They appear to have had minimal usage east of Denmark into the Baltic regions, nor did they spread southwards significantly into and beyond France. Their presence seems to be largely based on North Sea trade, and at the heart of this trading zone were the Frisians.

The Frisians emerged out of the post-Roman period as a Germanic-speaking group inhabiting the *terpen* (artificial mounds) and marshes of the Low Countries, serving as a natural buffer between the lands of the Merovingian (and later Carolingian) Empire and the turbulent North Sea. Theirs was a world of tidal flats and stormy weather, of lost horizons and liminality. Extensively researched by Nelleke IJssennagger[44] and John Hines, among others, Frisians represent arguably *the* most important puzzle piece in the picture of Early Medieval North Sea economies, and thus an impetus for the Viking Age. While one would not necessarily say that without Frisians, there would be no Viking Age, it could be reasonably argued that the Frisians played a much more significant role than any other group in the spread of raiders and portable wealth throughout the preceding centuries.

The Frisii[45] were named by Roman sources as early as the second century, and amidst the rising sea levels, climate downturn, and turmoil of the fifth and sixth centuries it appears that this original population was forced to flee its homelands, its material culture becoming replaced by a new one, closer to what might be called 'Anglo-Saxon'. Either that, or the original Frisii simply assimilated into a new migrating identity pouring out of Angeln, Saxony, and Jutland.[46] This territory was to some degree formalised in the late 700s with the *Lex Frisionum* law code,[47] following annexation by the expansionist Carolingian ruler Charlemagne. Prior to this, out of the gloom of legendary history, two pagan rulers Aldgisl and Redbad exercised dominion over Frisia in the seventh and eighth centuries, themselves only a few steps removed from unverifiable figures like Hygelac. Whatever the case, there *was* some degree of political centralisation within Frisia in this period, forming a unique social and economic identity through the natural geographic isolation of the Low Countries' tidal marshes. The 896 entry from the *ASC* mentions Frisian seamanship, indicating that these people were known to be as adept on the water as Scandinavians. Indeed, 'Frisian' appears to become synonymous with 'maritime trader' in later periods, and there is emerging evidence that there was a not insignificant number of Frisians or 'Friso-Danes' in the Great Heathen Army.[48, 49] We assume that Frisians were in Fishergate, York, from as early as the eighth century, trading and selling wares, judging by a trans-North Sea pottery typology present in the site's earliest layers – Ribe was also likely founded by Frisians. Several place names across the British Isles like Friesthorpe and Frieston in Lincolnshire point to permanent settlement.[50, 51] The Frisians made up a segment of the various Germanic-speaking culture groups migrating to England during the Late Roman decline and would have undoubtedly played a major role in the development of this North Sea economy, stretching between England and Scandinavia.

Speaking of Lincolnshire, it was legendary numismatist Mark Blackburn who first identified that, of all *sceat* finds across the Portable Antiquities Scheme (PAS), the vast majority by far were found in Lincolnshire. Over four hundred,[52] almost double that of the second most plentiful county (Yorkshire). Prior to industrial drainage, Early Medieval Lincolnshire, like Frisia, would have largely consisted of a few raised plateaus encircled by a tremendous tidal wash. As the petty kingdom of Lindsey,[53] Lincolnshire saw immense wealth circulating in the marshlands.[54] Why is this, compared to other contemporary kingdoms? Why do we not see the same number of *sceattas* in Kent, which was very wealthy in the seventh century?

The reason might be the topography of coastal marshes. Both Lindsey and Frisia were beholden to the whim of the sea; liminal zones made up of swampland and bogs, like Jutland in Denmark. These territories would have been natural barriers to people on foot, but to people in boats (like the Frisians and Scandinavians) they would have been motorways affording quick access to various trading points and productive sites, serving as inland frontiers of the North Sea. There are material and stylistic links between burials in Lincolnshire (like the Caenby barrow dated to the 600s)[55] and those in Frisia and Denmark. The three territories appear to have been linked when this North Sea trading zone was steadily growing. In short, areas with easy access to water would become prime spots for trade, and prime spots for trade would become generators of immense wealth, either to be distributed between merchants and craftspeople or reinvested into local economies and power bases, be they secular or religious. Coastal and marshland environments facilitated easier maritime travel, which led to increased 'footfall', thus increased cultural, material, and linguistic exchange, linking all similar nearby territories.

The opening quote of this chapter is from the [D] manuscript of the *ASC*, probably written in Worcester in the tenth century. It speaks of land, provisions, and wealth in tandem with the development of a monastic community. Wealth and kingship were one thing, but having one's power consolidated by the institution of the church was another. King Oswald of Northumbria (633-642) was the first monarch in England to combine secular and religious power; his state outlasted him after his death because of the stock he had placed in his religious communities through 'book-land' (land given to the church separate

A pressed foil fragment depicting the 'Weapon Dancer'. This is one of the only remaining fragments of the Caenby Helmet, recovered from Caenby in the Lincolnshire Wolds in 1849 by antiquarian Edwin George Jarvis. There are visual similarities between this foil fragment and pieces from Sutton Hoo, along with examples from Frisia.

from royal inherited wealth). The church was powerful and ultimately, very wealthy. And many of its establishments were situated right on the rim of the North Sea.

Overlords

With the development of economies came the rise of 'high kings', as seen in Ireland, England, and beyond. While Oswald (and his brother and successor Oswiu) maintained some degree of recognised status above other nearby kings, it was not until Offa, the great king of Mercia (757-796), that such a powerful central ruler can be identified archaeologically. Offa seems to be a similar figure to whoever was responsible for the development of the Danevirke on the Merovingian-Danish border. Offa, like the unnamed rulers of Denmark between 500-600, was responsible for overseeing a large earthwork designed to control trade and to increase security, or perhaps to act as a springboard for border raids into neighbouring territories. Like the Danevirke, Offa's Dyke, situated in modern Wales and Shropshire and extending between the Severn and Mersey thanks to the additional Wat's Dyke, was first and foremost a demonstration of power and authority.[56] Like barrow mounds, Offa's Dyke said 'Look upon me at what I can do. You are in my kingdom now. Pay me taxes!' Such grandiose displays of power could not be achieved without funds, some to pay subservient war bands. While a ruler over a landlocked kingdom, Offa could not have existed without the development of North Sea trade, which continued throughout his reign in the eighth century, The effect this had on external territories like Frisia and Scandinavia was negligible; trade still existed, and Frisians and Scandinavians were still active in the British Isles. Offa was not all-powerful, however. Through letters and insular coinage comparisons,[57] we can infer that Offa, to some degree, was styling himself on a much more powerful ruler, Charles the Great, Charlemagne.

Charlemagne is one of the most important and recognisable figures of the age.[58, 59] To England, he was an idealised ruler, an exceedingly powerful character, an exemplar of Christian virtue and statehood. To the Carolingians (residents of his empire, following from the earlier Merovingians of the sixth and seventh centuries), Charlemagne was the second coming of Rome. By 800, he had been awarded the title of Holy Roman Emperor.[60] Charlemagne, though a modern name meaning 'Charles the Great' (from Charles *Magnus*), was undoubtedly recognised as great in his time as well. The growing economy of the North Sea and the political consolidation of various kingdoms in England, France, and Germany had eventually led to the point where one man could emerge as more powerful than all those beneath him. As seen in England with the annexation of petty kingdoms like Lindsey, the Hwicce, and Wreocansæte to become a greater Mercia, so too did Charlemagne extend his influence and strengthen the Carolingian Empire through the conquering (and conversion) of neighbouring territories. Chief among them, in the decades preceding the Lindisfarne raid, were Frisia and Saxony, right on the very borders the Danevirke may have been built to protect.

While dendrochronologically dated to the sixth century in its earliest phases, the Danevirke was repaired and extended numerous times by later rulers. One Oengendus (or Angantyr) of the early 700s, described by missionary Willibrord as 'more savage than any beast and harder than stone',[61] was responsible for developing portions of the Danevirke. The fact Willibrord and his mission were able to roam across Oengendus's heathen kingdom and return unhindered tells us what Christian writings will not; that he ruled over a relatively centralised realm. This is an insight into what was expected of – and more importantly *respected in* – contemporary rulers. Strength, determination, and resilience in the face of opposition.

Opposition to the nebulous 'Kingdom of the Danes' came in the form of direct military pressure from Charlemagne and through Christian conversion. Would Oengendus, a powerful king amongst Danes, respect an even *more* powerful king like Charlemagne? An overlord? Figures like Offa, Charlemagne, and Oengendus characterise the burgeoning political hierarchies of the time, though Oengendus was outside of that previously mentioned Christian sphere of influence. Unlike Offa and Charlemagne, if he was to die, there would be no recognised authoritative figure to cover the interregnum between him and a possible successor, his territory would be up for grabs. While, indeed, succession conflicts and disputes did occur in Christian nations, it is telling that the aftermath of Christian King Oswiu's reign compared to pre-Christian King Æðelfrið's was very different in terms of strife. Oengendus is best compared with Æðelfrið, not Oswiu nor Offa, as a strong pagan ruler; a member of this military elite borne out of resistance to foreign powers, strengthened by growing maritime power and fuelled by the rich resources of the North Sea. Oengendus and his ilk, then, were temporally displaced, about 100-150 years 'behind' the ecclesiastical and governmental developments of England and the Carolingian Empire. And there would be pushback.

The Resistance

While it is very unlikely that the early targets for viking activity were specifically chosen because they were Christian, for Christian militaries there very much *was* a concerted effort to damage paganism.

Rise

Charlemagne's religious crusades against Frisia, Saxony, and Denmark are hailed in contemporary sources (written by Christians *for* Christians), but when observing them from the perspective of the persecuted pagans, they appear like bloodthirsty rampages, not too far removed from the war-bands of pre-Christian Europe.

On the very eve of the Viking Age we find a relatively consolidated network of states. But in the east, things were very different. Our evidence for pre-Medieval rulers in the Baltic and Slavic regions is even murkier than for Scandinavia, but undoubtedly there was no consistently recognised 'overlord' as there was for England and France. Overlords needed to demonstrate *why* they were overlords, through conquest and conversion.

The people of Saxony felt the brute force of Charlemagne in the late eighth century, converted or executed.[62] They had no choice in the matter.[63] Whoever was ruling the Kingdom of the Danes at the time, looking out over the Danevirke to see smoke rise on the far horizon, would have known that a great enemy was approaching. If Frisia and Saxony had fallen to Christianity and the Carolingians, then it was only a matter of time before Denmark would feel the wrath of Charlemagne.

This was not just a one-and-done military campaign. There is evidence on both the large and small scale of religious and secular pushback from Frisia. After their annexation into the wider Carolingian world in the 780s, rebellions led by pagans like Widukind[64] occurred continually, likely drafting in Scandinavian spears to face Carolingian swords. Archaeologically, this period of pushback appears in Frankish jewellery purposefully 'vandalised' to represent Óðinn; an eighth-century pendant once depicting Jesus has one eye blotted out, changing the 'White Christ' into the one-eyed war god. Designs like these are in evidence across pagan England (which held out until 686 when the kingdom of the Wihtwara, on the Isle of Wight, was disestablished) and contemporary Denmark; symbols of Wōdenic or Odinic cults in direct opposition to the spread of Christianity.

As we will see later, there are some examples of anti-Christian zealotry and militant paganism throughout the Viking Age, but these are rare. The immediate threat to eighth-century Scandinavians was probably not felt through a possible erasure of their sacred groves and highly individualised belief systems (like those who worshipped Týr at Lake Tissø, Denmark), but through a danger to their own economies and power structures. Rich Scandinavian warlords and kinglets up and down the coast of Norway would not be too bothered by Charlemagne's aggressive conquests hundreds of miles to the south, but those living by the Danevirke in Denmark would. Sweden is difficult to assess this early in the pre-Viking

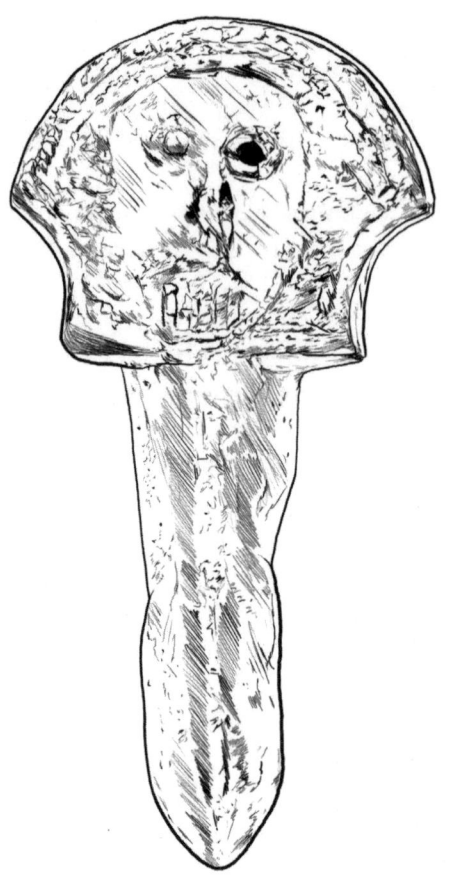

A niello-eyed silver-gilt buckle of Frankish type that has been rewrought to represent Óðinn.

Age, but some continuity of the ostentatious designs like those on the Vendel Helmet, and the isotopic evidence of Swedes on Saaremaa in the 700s, indicates that there may well have been 'kings' in the great lakes and forests, but their focus would have most certainly been eastward. It is east central Sweden which has the densest clusters of richly adorned graves, indicating wealth and status shared by a militarised elite in the seventh and eighth centuries.

One thing that would have united Scandinavians at the dawn of the Viking Age was this desire for wealth. As in all martial societies, where there is a top layer of warrior elites and little opportunity for one to ascend the ranks, the options available require a broader outlook. If direct military action within Scandinavia simply took the form of small-scale cattle raids then one must look elsewhere for options to accrue riches. And if the trading networks of the North Sea don't allow for much inter-hierarchical movement, then the available options become two: one can either corner the market and sell sell sell across England, Frisia, and Scandinavia, or one can raid.

Blood in the Water

Where exactly *would* one raid? How would targets be selected? As discussed, Lindisfarne and rich monastic communities on the coast of England would have been well known within the countries themselves and beyond. Scholar and clergyman Alcuin of York resided in Charlemagne's court at Aachen in 793 and heard immediately about the overseas attack. While the appearance of foreigners on the coasts of Holy Island on 8 June 793 must have been a shock to the resident monks, there is absolutely no evidence to suggest that, as the contemporary sources claim, these people came out of nowhere making hitherto unheard-of 'inroads'.[65] What was shocking was not the arrival of the Scandinavians but their violence; the gall to strike at a monastic community. Even the letters that lament the raid, and later sources like the writings of Symeon of Durham,[66] attribute some of the blame for the attack and later events on the people of the time *dressing* like the heathens that attacked them. Genomic, linguistic, and archaeological evidence – and now also textual – all point to Scandinavians already being in England prior to the Lindisfarne raid. Not as vikingar, but as traders – though if these traders and merchants were travelling up and down England scoping out locations for easy portable wealth to later steal, then is there really a distinction between the two?

The development of the North Sea economy had created trading sites all up and down the coastlines and river routes of Europe that were flooded with continental goods, international tradespeople, and transferable currencies. Silver could be gained in the form of bullion, which would also be generated in the east in later centuries, but it is worth remembering the chief item of commerce in the Viking Age was slaves. From Ireland, it was largely people that were kidnapped and sold abroad by crews of vikingar, not individual items, though of course who could resist some shiny croziers or spoons from an undefended chapel? While warfare was common in the Early Medieval Period, outside of a few examples religious sites were normally excluded and were viewed as outside the normal sphere of conflict. This was not the case for pagans, notably with King Æðelfrið in the seventh century and again with Scandinavians in the eighth.

While we can now view these people from the comfort of our time as multi-faceted, the horror that the raiding element of their society would inflict on their victims is always worth remembering. It would not matter to the average monk if his murderer was also a peaceful trader or farmer for the winter months. His murderer had defiled a religious site, something few other contemporary armies would dare to do. Such was the shock and awe generated from the Lindisfarne raid.

In the entry for the year 787, the ninth century [A] text of the *ASC* references sailors appearing on the shores of King Beohtric's Wessex, on Portland. A later twelfth-century chronicler, John of Worcester, added that they were rebuffed by the local authority figure (a reeve named Beaduheard), and that they committed some acts of violence and swiftly left. While not a raid, the *ASC*'s annalist claimed that 'These were the first ships of the Danish men that sought the land of the English nation.' We have no idea where these people came from; a much later recension of the *ASC* states 'Hordaland' in Norway, but we cannot be certain that this is true.[67] It is possible these 'raiders' included Frisians, or were predominantly Danish, maybe even continental Saxons. The multi-ethnic nature of *vikingar* is a point overlooked by contemporary sources. There was no monolithic 'Danish' or 'Norwegian' raiding army; national identities of this scale in Scandinavia would not form for quite some time.

Weak kingdoms presented an opportunity for raiding. Unfortunately for foreign interlopers, Offa and Charlemagne ruled over well-established and secure nations, give or take a few border disputes and external conflicts. It wouldn't be until both of their deaths that opportunities arose for hit-and-run attacks. Comparatively, Ireland in the eighth century was a mosaic of petty rulers, split into hundreds of *túatha* (political territories), each ruled over by an individual king-like figure called a *Rí*, occasionally subservient to an overlord or *Ruiri*. It is no wonder, then, that Ireland, the Hebrides, and the wider Atlantic coast of Scotland saw the first waves of raiders and settlers following (and perhaps before) Lindisfarne. These were territories outside of organised state control and security, with minimal portable wealth but rich in populace and livestock. Many viking raids undoubtedly returned with cattle and slaves.

What was the result of these raids? In 845, we hear of one Reginherus (or Ragnar) who, after successfully extorting 7,000 lb of silver from Paris, returned to Denmark to give quite a substantial amount of that sum to his overlord King Horik.[68] This is perhaps an example of a formalised tribute-based economic system. There are multiple attested 'kings' leading the Great Heathen Army in the 860s – which one of them was the most important? How would this even be gauged? At the very dawn of the Viking Age, it has been suggested that the impetus for raids was for young men to 'get rich quick' and thus compete with other local warrior elites. The result of such a process would, inevitably, mirror the result of the seventh-century conflicts of England: overlords and high kings. Certain individuals would become richer than others and would thus become able to fund larger war bands. They would eventually reach a point where they could not realistically be challenged by others. King Horik may very well have once been an opportunist raiding the shores of

Rise

Frisia in the late 700s before making a claim to the throne of Denmark. While external sources refer to Horik and others like him as 'kings', it is not clear whether they would be seen as kings as we would identify them in England and France, or simply as the most powerful warlord present at the time.

The long-running and probably endless argument amongst academics as to the reason for the onset of raiding normally settles on it as a symptom of the developing North Sea economy of the time and the abundance of available wealth. In tandem with this was the development of localised kin-based territories up and down Scandinavia which would engage in peer-polity competition and land-grabbing; after-effects of the restructuring of society following the Dust Veil. This was the long road to the Lindisfarne raid; two-and-a-half centuries of economic, societal, spiritual, and technological development that all occurred just at the right time. Odinic cults and worshipping grounds dedicated to Týr were visited en masse, as sailors trading soapstones across Lofoten and Denmark wore one-eyed pendants around their necks, while Frisians scrawled defiant graffiti against Christianity. Silver, slaves, and goods flowed in and out of the Baltic from the North Sea, moving further east between the small towns along the Dnieper and Volga en route to Constantinople, the journeys made ever faster by the development of ship technology. Warriors, warlords, and war bands, seeing and seeking greater opportunities on the horizon, and perhaps fearing threats from greater international powers, were well-placed to take advantage of all the above.

This was the time of the Viking Age. Well, not quite. We've still got to hit that arbitrary boundary of 793. Before Lindisfarne, there are just a few more stops along the way.

Pre-Lindisfarne

Early Viking Age grave goods across Norway include items looted from Irish Christian sites.[69] While difficult to date, we can safely assert that croziers, reliquaries, and generic silver goods such as spoons and candlesticks come from the very early ninth century or possibly before. It is not out of the question to think that some of them were looted before 793. Really, this date appears most important to us because we are viewing the Viking Age retrospectively; we *know* the Viking Age ramped up in ferocity from 793 onwards, so the Lindisfarne raid appears like a very natural start point. But, of course, the Viking Age is not always characterised solely as a succession of violent attacks; traditional narratives will include the consolidation of power in Denmark under Harald Bluetooth in the tenth century, the prospering of York thanks to

Anglo-Scandinavian merchants, and the discovery of new uninhabited lands in the North Atlantic. These separate elements of the period are, like the arbitrary temporal boundaries, much more linked than they first appear.

Take, for instance, the first Scandinavian inhabitants of Shetland. The pre-existing population (responsible for the famous Mousa Broch) were joined by new arrivals in the late eighth probably from Norway, based on geographic proximity – thus these migrations will be referred to as 'Norse'. The homes where these warriors and farmers and traders would be based for most of their lives were predominantly farmsteads. Later, we see evidence of urbanisation in towns and marketplaces, but in the eighth century our examples are mostly rural building groups or isolated magnate residences. Borg, on the Lofoten islands, is the greatest example of the latter, or perhaps Lejre in Denmark; these sites feature monumental longhouses that would have housed dozens of inhabitants and livestock around the central hearth. Borg, and other sites like it, would have maintained its status and the wealth of its owner via taxing satellite farmsteads and (in the case of Borg specifically) the nomadic hunter-gatherers of the Saami, in return for offering them protection and economic opportunities. Ring giving.

For the average person, however, life would have been based around a modest farmstead. The average Viking Age farmstead consisted of a central dwelling structure, normally a longhouse, one or more outhouses for the storage of cattle, a pit-house for either ritual purposes or crafts production (or perhaps to function as a slave dwelling), and a handful of shielings, which are best described as seasonal task-specific locations.[70] All of these structures apart from shielings existed within the 'infield' of a farm;[71] where animals would be housed for the winter months. Shielings would be situated in the 'outfield', on the edge of a farmer's territory, to watch over grazing animals throughout the summer or to store tools.* A lot of these buildings were multi-purpose.[72, 73] Viking Age architectural research was pioneered by Bjørn Myhre in the 1980s and 90s,[74, 75, 76] however, earlier antiquarian scholars must also be credited, the initial excavations of Viking Age sites were led by iindividuals in the nineteenth and twentieth centuries, such as the famous Oseberg burial. While our image of the Viking Age might be overwhelmingly dominated by images of longships like that from Oseberg, and shield-wall warfare, for much of

---

* This settlement model was not strictly a 'Viking' one. It sees parallels all over Early Medieval Europe. The famous 'Ribblehead longhouse' discovered in the Yorkshire Dales fits the model of a 'Viking hall' and yet is almost certainly a native residence.

the time life for Early Medieval Scandinavians would have simply been farming in homesteads like these.

It was this model of agropastoral subsistence that was common across Scandinavia, with some minor regional variations between the different areas. Norway, for instance, had boat houses (or *nausts*)[77] near farmsteads located along fjord networks, while in Sweden and in eastern Denmark pit-houses demonstrate some continuity with earlier Slavic houses (perhaps these 'Slavs' were the origin for the 'slaves' of the pre-Viking Age; it can be confidently said that there was pre-Lindisfarne raiding and trading in the Baltic and Slavic regions). The boundaries between where one farmer's land ended and where another's began were probably demarcated by landscape features like earlier Bronze and Iron Age burial mounds or shielings, mirroring the border conflicts of kings and kinglets. Many of these small kings would have been farmers themselves, of course. Silver and gold could not grow anything or feed livestock. Agriculture was the backbone of Early Medieval Scandinavia.

The Viking Age farmstead model was ported from Norway to a number of locations across the North Atlantic, and at each location we can observe through architectural changes[78] the adaptations of the farmers to new environmental and societal challenges.[79] For instance, in Shetland, farmsteads appear relatively consistent with those in Norway, however, a unique trait of these early Shetland settlement sites is that some are built atop the pre-existing native buildings. In the case of Jarlshof in the south, likely a ninth-century magnate's residence, certain outhouses were built on Atlantic wheelhouses of the native population (who were close to what we would call 'Picts').[80, 81, 82] Old Scatness displays evidence that the initial Norse settlers reused local buildings prior to constructing their own habitations,[83] removing building material to use as foundations. Dating these sites is relatively difficult, for while the artefacts are certainly Scandinavian in origin, there is nothing to say a spindle-whorl is specifically from the 780s or the 820s.

On the northernmost isle of Unst, at the site of Underhoull, is a cluster of around thirty largely unexcavated longhouses.[84] Only two[85] have been researched, and they have been classified as relatively simple longhouses compared to their predecessors in Norway. Where the average Viking Age longhouse was primarily for human habitation, with the outhouse reserved for cattle, in the preceding Scandinavian Iron Age simpler longhouses were used for both humans and livestock. The dwellings of Underhoull, then, represent either a much earlier start date for the Scandinavian settlement of Shetland (in the pre-Viking Age) or an adaptation of the settlers to the environmental difficulties of their new home, notably the scarcity of available timber. Instead of being partitioned into multiple rooms with corner posts and wooden framing, the longhouses at Underhoull feature one central supporting log propping up a turf and stone roof, with a floor split between packed earth for heat retention and stone flags for the run-off of animal waste. Positioned so far north on Unst, almost equidistant between Norway, the British Isles, and the Faroe Islands (which has some evidence for similar simple dwellings as at Ergidalur and Kvívík),[86] we have what appear to be very early Norse settlements.

Recent radiocarbon dating places these settlements no earlier than 805, close to the Lindisfarne raid.[87] It is possible that reports of Shetland and viable unclaimed land reached Scandinavia at the same time as rumours of rich, undefended coastal monasteries.

The evidence for raiding in Atlantic Scotland sites might also predate Lindisfarne, or be broadly contemporary. The monastery at Burghead, mentioned only briefly by contemporary documentary sources, would have been a beautiful structure acting as a beacon of Christian veneration in the far north of Scotland.[88] People often referred to as the 'Picts' had a power base in the kingdom of Fortriu, centred around Moray, and shared an artistic culture with neighbouring southern polities like Atholl and Strathclyde. This unique Pictish expression was to disappear from the archaeological record in the later ninth century, a loss largely put down to Scandinavian invaders, however Scotland at the time was awash with conflicts between native Brythonic-speaking people. Vikingar would have an important part to play in these conflicts, though not just yet.

Reconstructed Viking Age turf-house. Buildings such as this would be commonplace on the average Early Medieval Scandinavian farmstead, constructed from a stone foundation and turf bricks. Wooden planks began to be used in the Late Viking Age. They were preceded by wooden strakes, wattle, and daub woven together with some thatch.

Rise

For now, attention was focused on raiding. A layer of black earth dated to the ninth century indicates that Burghead met at least a temporary end as a well-populated Christian community at the hands of violent attackers or through abandonment. The same for Portmahomack nearby, a Pictish site excavated by Martin Carver, raided around 800 CE.[89] Whether these raids were perpetrated by Scandinavians in longships or warriors from another kingdom is unclear,[90] but their proximity to the coast does give us a clue, as does a shattered cross slab, possibly having felt the wrath of a pagan. So too the skulls of buried brothers discovered at the site. While these raids are dated to the ninth century, the locations of these monasteries were probably known to raiders long before Lindisfarne. We can imagine crews of vikingar, either launching from Norway or perhaps the farms on Shetland and the Faroe Islands, working their way down the Scottish coast before reaching Lindisfarne, eyeing up monastery after monastery along the way, looking for the easiest, richest target. Perhaps it ran deeper than that; direct attacks on Pictish power centres, like Portmahomack, to destabilise insular governance, so that these raiders could carve out new territory.

The entry for 794 in the *ASC*, a year after the Lindisfarne raid, states that 'all the isles of Britain were raided'. Some have argued this to be evidence of semi-permanent Scandinavian habitation of the Hebrides and Orkney, which we know was occurring around this time as evidenced by the 1963 discovery of a female burial on Westness, the grave exhibiting both insular and Scandinavian attributes. However, it could also be said to be a bit of retroactive correction by the West Saxon chronicles. Chroniclers of the *ASC*, writing in southern England, would have cared tremendously about the damage done to the prestigious Monastery of St Cuthbert on Lindisfarne, founded by King Oswald and Aidan in the 630s. Pictish monasteries, however? Far removed from the politicking and ecclesiastical world of the south, the destruction of these sites would never be 'big news'. That is, of course, until an important site was raided, and then suddenly, the knowledge that raiding had been ongoing *beforehand* became relevant. A letter from Offa of Mercia in 792 to Kent describes a need to 'strengthen churches against roaming heathens'[91] – the road to Lindisfarne is signposted.

These early raiders, hungry for wealth, had set their eyes on the best target yet. Groups of vikingar pouring out of Scandinavia, using information gathered from generations of North Sea trade, knew exactly where to go for quick portable loot. It is likely that these groups were competing indirectly with one another; in-fighting was inevitable. A perfect target at the edge of the North Sea, Lindisfarne was next on the list.

Dragons

The words from the *ASC* for the year 793 that state 'ill omens' were seen prior to the heathen raid, that 'forked lightning' split the sky asunder and that 'dragons' were witnessed in the distance, are well-known. Fanciful images, and later author Symeon of Durham also tells us of a sinner buried at the site who was possibly responsible for such fear. All these comments were written *after* the raid, with the hindsight that dire times were coming.

On the 8th of June 793, on a summer's morning, sails were seen in the distance. These sails were the latest and greatest addition to the keel-based clinker-built ships of Scandinavia; they cut through the waves en route to the prestigious monastery, established by saintly King Oswald in 635 and monks from Ireland and Lindsey,[92] built in the shadow of the fortress at Bamburgh. The home of gorgeously illuminated manuscripts like the *Lindisfarne Gospels* and St Cuthbert himself, this was not just any old monastic site; this was the eastern parallel to Colm Cille's Iona in the west. To strike at Lindisfarne was the equivalent of terrorism. And yet dragons did come.

Lindisfarne was not decimated, however. We should not underplay the fear of the time and the bloodshed caused but let us also not get carried away with any alleged devastation. While undoubtedly many brothers were enslaved or drowned on the beach, and many treasures were taken and books defiled, this was not the end of Lindisfarne. The community would suffer more raids, as would many other resilient monastic and trading sites. Eventually St Cuthbert's remains were moved across the north of England. Excavations led by David Petts and the University of Durham partnered with DigVentures[93, 94] have revealed continued habitation of the site into the eleventh century – pottery from international connections, evidence of local smithing, and a coin of Edward the Confessor (1042-1066).

This was the last hurrah of the Early Medieval Period, and it would affect all of Europe and beyond. But as we have seen, this 'new' age was never a bolt from the blue, it was a long time coming, and there was still a long way yet to sail.

Storm

> Wolves attacked and devoured with complete audacity the inhabitants of the western part of Gaul. Indeed, in some parts of Aquitaine they are said to have gathered together in groups of up to 300, just like army detachments, formed a sort of battle-line and marched along the road, boldly charging en masse all who tried to resist them.
>
> The entry for 846 from the *Annals of St Bertin*, translated by Janet Nelson.

Like Óðinn, large military forces existed in Scandinavia before the Viking Age. How else would the Danevirke have been constructed without a well-organised militia? The Eketorp hillfort[1] on the island of Öland hints at a substantial Iron Age military presence, though it was abandoned sometime after the Dust Veil. It is certain that like other countries around the world in the Iron Age, Scandinavians prior to the 500s lived in communities under the shadow of nearby hillforts, which were bases for powerful elites. Hillforts are not intrinsically entirely military structures, often they were simply communal refuges locals could travel to during times of crisis. The individuals who lived on Öland, called the Auviones by Roman sources and the Eowlanders by Wulfstan of Hedeby in the tenth century, likely hid behind the walls of Eketorp hillfort during times of conflict and famine. There are fourteen other Danish examples like Eketorp, more in Norway and even more spread across the bogs and forests of Sweden.[2] Most of these hillforts seem to have been abandoned in the seventh century, their functions replaced by large earthworks like the Danevirke and the typical longhouse and magnate's hall; perfect communal spaces for telling tall tales and sharing treasure. Where once there were stratified tribute zones and sedentary elites, now there were hydrarchies and an emphasis on the *familial* nature of the hall, its shape, size, and function reflecting the society that created it. Hierarchies and warfare had been altered, the culture of warriorhood had changed.

By 793, these warriors of the various petty kingdoms of Scandinavia were no longer simply fighting amongst themselves or with the eastern people around the Baltic and river routes, but westward into Christendom. Principally, these early westerly raids were against the northernmost sections of the British Isles, Ireland, the Hebrides, Orkney, Atlantic Scotland, and the kingdom of Northumbria, though they would also occasionally spill southwards. In 795, the [D] and [E] manuscripts of the *ASC* record raiders who 'plundered Ecgfrith's monastery at *Donemuðan*' at the mouth of the River Don, in the Humber Wash. As discussed in the previous chapter, areas impassable by foot (marshes, bogs, swamps) would be highways for sleek boats capable of traversing both the deep open ocean and shallow rivers. This would not just be important for trade but also for raiding. Areas like the Isle of Axholme, a raised promontory above the tidal wash of the kingdom of Lindsey, would have acted as an enclave for naval-based raiding groups – pit stops between assaults on nearby estates.

On a much larger scale, we have the territory of Frisia, similarly marshy like Lindsey but situated right on the edge of the rich and well-defended Carolingian Empire. Viewed as a liminal zone by the footsoldiers and cavalry units of Francia, Frisia became a springboard for coastal incursions. Frisia is intrinsic to understanding how Viking Age raiding went from hit-and-run attacks on coastal sites to large-scale military invasions.

Evolution of Raiding

The anonymous chronicler of the *ASC* for the year 794 did indeed mention that 'all the isles of Britain were raided', but what does this mean? Does it relate to widespread marauding as seen at Monkwearmouth-Jarrow and across Ireland and Aquitaine in the years following, or does it instead relate to a burgeoning Scandinavian presence in the Atlantic region of Scotland, principally around Orkney and the Hebrides? To understand the early years of viking activity in the British Isles, the routes taken by raiding parties from Norway towards their targets must be considered.

We have already introduced the archetypal longship, though the longships used by these first waves of enterprising raiders in the eighth and ninth centuries were different to the later types used by kings and their armies in the tenth and eleventh. In later sagas, we hear of ships like *The Long Serpent* or *Bison*; dramatically lengthy vessels with rowing benches capable of housing almost a hundred armed men. But longships came in many varieties. The Oseberg ship, previously mentioned, found in a barrow mound having been ceremonially 'tethered' to the ground along with associated grave goods – a cart, dress accessories, tools[3] – was a royal vessel, a pleasure barge, sailed between the calm waters of the Hordaland fjords by the two individuals interred within. Often equated with Åsa Eysteinsdottir, semi-legendary grandmother of Harald Fairhair, the 'Oseberg lady' was clearly a wealthy person who, in about the year 830, was put to rest alongside another woman, a slave or servant, or an equal, it is difficult to say, though isotopic evidence points to at least one of the individuals having travelled from Arabic regions.[4] The grave goods, on the other hand, simply tell us how the individuals doing the act of burying saw the individual being buried, not how the individual saw themselves while they were alive.

The correlation between the Oseberg lady and Åsa Eysteinsdottir is based entirely on conjecture in a remarkably similar way to an earlier bog body, said at first to be the legendary figure of Queen Gunnhild, though now known to date from a time before the Viking Age.[5] Neither of these burials are the figures people once thought they were. On the topic of bog bodies in Iron Age Denmark, it is possible some of them

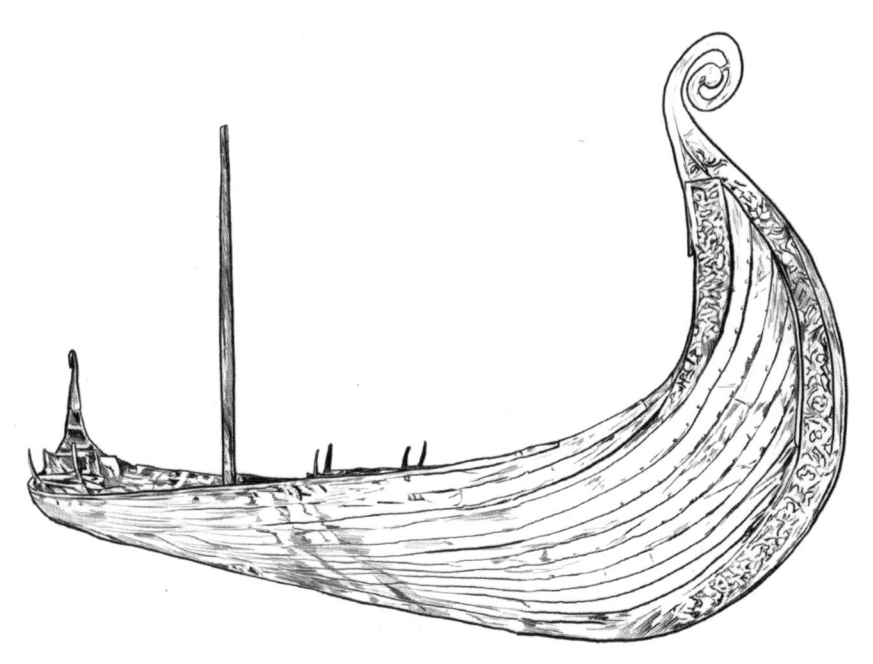

The Oseberg ship reconstruction. Excavated 1904-5, the ship was found alongside four elaborately carved sleighs and a four-wheeled cart, with silks, textiles, and wooden tools. Most interesting was a yew bucket adorned with cloisonné enamel work in the style of Irish gospel artwork and a Buddha-esque figure, and a fragmented tapestry depicting a processional scene.

were submerged into the silt as battle sacrifices. Like the votive deposited weapons accompanying the Hjortspring boat, warriors and social outcasts may have been sunk into the bog as punishment, to trap them even after death.

Bog burials all but disappeared beyond the fifth century in Scandinavia, again marking a change in martial culture and belief, but roaming bands of armed men controlling or functioning within certain strata of society remained. Moving beyond the Dust Veil, there appears to be a greater emphasis on those with the power to hold agriculturally viable territory. Of course, farms and farm-owners were important before such a climate disaster, as they are now, but in times of strife and stress, it was these landowners who would hold all the cards. Landowners, like the magnates at Borg or Lejre, would need weapons and manpower to secure their status, and wealth to secure their weapons and manpower. The wealth would come from agricultural surplus, taxation of local estates, and through the spoils of war. Without war and raiding, the elite would not be able to continually bolster their status and wealth. Perhaps the reasons for raiding outside of Scandinavia are the same as for raiding *within* Scandinavia.

Early Medieval Scandinavians were different. While the previous chapter did describe the onset of the Viking Age as a chain of events, there is an observable distinction between the people they were raiding and the raiders themselves. For one, Scandinavians were playing by different rules of military engagement. While the average ealdorman of England and his *here* (army) would be based around local estates and defending a land-based economy on foot, their enemies emerging from the North Sea and penetrating rivers in the late eighth century were not interested in the long-term protection of land yield. They were after portable wealth; gold, silver, slaves.

The longship provided vikingar with the ability not only to penetrate sites that would be more difficult to reach for an army on foot or horseback, but also gave them a fast getaway. In a heist, *escaping* the scene of the crime is just as important as getting the goods to begin with. Tactical withdrawal was as large a part of the Scandinavian military mindset as the initial assault and shock-and-awe factor.

We see no great difference between the on-foot military strategies of Scandinavians and the European societies they fought against, nor do we see any clear victor. In the ninth century Ælfredan wars, the chronicles paint a back-and-forth between defenders and aggressors. It wouldn't be until later in the Viking Age that other societies caught up with Scandinavian maritime technology, so for a while the longship served as a 'cutting edge'.

Early Medieval warfare was not based around cavalry or specialised units, nor was it, for the most part, engaged in by always-active state-sponsored military forces like the Roman legions. Unlike the Imperial machine, armies of the fifth to ninth centuries were largely farmers who took up arms, when necessary, levied in England to form the *fyrd* (and similar continental examples). There would be a landed elite specialised in combat – who as discussed dominated society – the *gesith*, the thegns, the warriors. Both warriors of the Scandinavian and *Ænglisċ* varieties were armed with spears, axes for both throwing and hacking (tools as well as weapons), shields made of lime wood and leather with an iron boss, and in some cases the bow and arrow.

Spears make up most of the weaponry found across England and the Low Countries. They were cheap to produce, required less skill to hold and wield in the frontline, and could also be lobbed to inflict damage from afar.[6] Give a man a sword and he might not know how to use it. Give any man a spear and he becomes a threat. The longbow would not see widespread use in the British Isles until the later Middle Ages. The sword was common among the elite. So often are we used to the image of the 'Viking' armed with an axe and nothing else, but it is likely the Scandinavian warrior elite would primarily be using swords (forged from iron rods beaten and pattern-welded over one another) like their counterparts in the British Isles and in Francia.

The *seax*, and Scandinavian equivalents, was important. In the claustrophobic hell of the shield wall, without the space to swing a weapon, the ease of access provided by a short gutting knife was useful. One's shield brother would hook down the opponent's shield, allowing one to stab overhand with the *seax*, or underhand to disembowel from beneath. That is unless an opponent was wearing a *byrnie* or mail coat. Not available to the average Early Medieval conscript, the *byrnie* would make an elite warrior stand out in the crowd, so too would headgear like the English Coppergate helmet[7] and the Scandinavian Gjermundbu helmet.[8] Helmets in the British Isles were larger and more often found with cheek-guards, 'Viking' helmets feature eye-guards similar to the Sutton Hoo example and appear to have been worn with a lower-face covering of mail. Mail, or chainmail, would have been expensive and time-consuming to produce. The two thousand interlocking rings found alongside the Coppergate helmet would only cover the breadth of the back of someone's neck. One can only imagine the length of time and energy required to repeat that process for an entire mail coat or shirt, which would then be worn over padded leather and cloth in the shield wall.

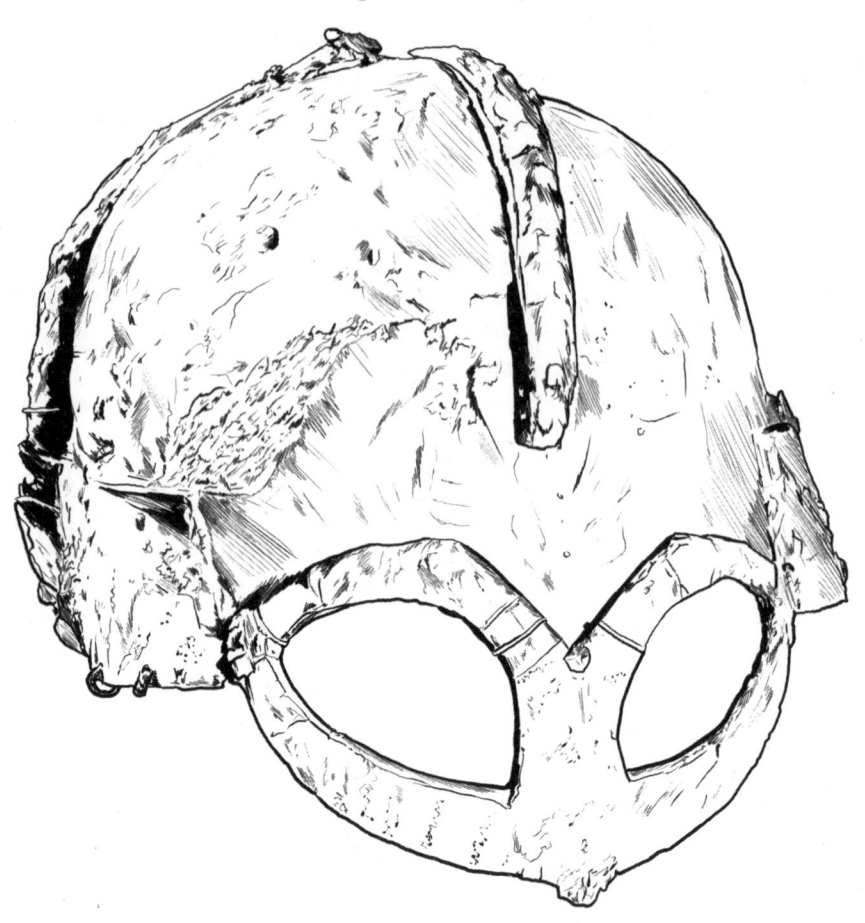

The Gjermundbu helmet, a rare example of a Viking Age Scandinavian helmet, dated between 950-975.

The shield wall or *skjaldborg* was the latest in a long line of military techniques that had evolved out of sheer common sense, combatants hiding behind brass, iron, and bronze defences to prod at the enemy. The Battle of Aquae Sextiae (102 BCE) and of Vercellae (101 BCE) between 'barbarians' and the Roman legions are precursors of Viking Age battles using a similar technique. To break an enemy's wall was to form a *svinfylking* ('swine wedge': a boar's snout formation) and rush with enough momentum to topple over the front row of the opponent's forces. Then it would be a case of hacking and slashing through the backs of those who had previously been on the defensive. This was, in essence, the Early Medieval warfare that Scandinavian vikingar and their foes were engaging in.[9] Footwork, terrain, and balance were as important as weapons.

Shield walls would not characterise every battle; there is reason to believe that their status has been exaggerated and that many military engagements were fought as smaller scale duels. The shield wall that we think of is a composite of numerous poetic kennings describing general warring and people cowering behind iron-banded discs of wood. This new foreign threat to British shores was much more grievous because of the attackers' ability to target and rush sites by water that would not have a resident guard presence.

Early Medieval warfare was not always about killing the opponent. In a battle, taking out the elite figurehead of the enemy with minimal collateral damage may have been the ideal outcome, rather than a mass slaughter. Again, this was another factor that may have distinguished the Scandinavian vikingar from their English counterparts; the northerners had no interest in making sure enough of the enemy were alive to plough the fields of conquered territory.

What did these raids look like? There are lists of looted locations available, but there is one possible eyewitness account from 843 which sheds more light on the brutality of the time. Contained within the *Chronicle of Nantes*[10] are a gruesome few paragraphs describing how, on the day of the holy festival of St John the Baptist, pagan raiders disembarked from their ships, scaled the walls of the town of Nantes using ladders and broke down the doors of the church to commit mass slaughter. Monks and nuns were killed in prayer, church silverware was ripped from the altars and stored away in sacks, the 'stone flags of the church ran red with blood'. The church was burned and the town was pillaged before the raiders left in their longships with dozens of slaves captured. It is believed the *Chronicle* was written in the 1050s, though it is preserved in a late fifteenth-century translated manuscript, so its description of events in the ninth century cannot be relied upon.

In the aftermath of the raid, blame was attributed to numerous parties; the former count of Nantes, Lambert, was said to have led the vikingar to the town to capture it for him. From this we see that raiders used local information to strike targets at times when guards were preoccupied (holy festivals), that they immediately dealt with the largest collection of wealth on-site (the church), and only then proceeded to massacre everywhere else, obtaining slaves in the process. But we can infer even more, by considering historical parallels. During the sixteenth century, Portuguese colonists were attempting landfall at numerous sites in Morocco, establishing their own bases along a polyglot coastline. We hear accounts of select groups from these wider crews who were hand-picked as 'ambassadors' to speak to local officials, to broker deals and to gain information ahead of any military endeavours. Via a process of 'creolisation' intelligence gathering by the would-be aggressors was made possible; where important sites were, the routines of guards, how much wealth was on display, and so on. We can reasonably assume that the first stage of many viking raids involved days or weeks of 'intel gathering' ahead of a larger military offensive: one that was timed to meet as little resistance as possible for maximum gain. The objective was never to slaughter, but to make a profit; a burned building here, a looted treasury there, that would quite often be enough.

Sea Wolves

The first few decades of widespread raiding were only the first few decades from a western perspective. While documentary sources from the *Austrvegr* are scarce, evidence from the Salme burials and the burgeoning of trade sites like Birka and Staraja Ladoga do tell us that long before 793 there was prolific piratical activity up and down the Volga and Dnieper, and across the shores of the Baltic. This raiding wouldn't have been dramatically different to the activity occurring across the North Sea in the British Isles and Frisia; attacks on riverine settlements out in the wilds between modern Russia and Ukraine could probably be just as orchestrated as on the coastal monasteries of England and Ireland. Modern scholarship, however, tends to characterise viking activity in the eastern world as being predominantly trade-based, and all our best guesses show us that this theory holds good. The types of portable wealth on display across the riverine routes of the *Austrvegr*, such as amber and furs, would not be the same class of 'loot' as the silver items in a seaside chapel. Those kinds of bulk items would be best dealt with via trading and traditional exports and imports, rather than smash-and-grab attacks. Nevertheless, there would still be a few examples of concerted military activity in the East, raids on native hillforts and market centres, though from what we can tell these would occur later in the Viking Age.

The eighth-century West was about to face the brunt of the *skjaldborg* across the beaches of Frisia, England, Ireland, Francia, and possibly Al-Andalus, Spain. These attackers would be known by many names: heathens, *gentiles*, Danes, Northmen, *finngail* and *dubgaill* (fair and dark foreigners respectively), and the enigmatic *Majūs*. First translated in 1923 by E. Fagnan as 'Northmen', the term *Majūs* appears in Arabic sources[11] in the western world predominantly in relation to Scandinavian attackers. 844 is the widely accepted date of the first major raid on Al-Andalus – the so-named 'Sacking of Seville' – but the term *Majūs* appears decades earlier in 793, the year of the Lindisfarne raid.

> In 177 [Islamic calendar], Hisham put Abd El Melik Ben Moghith at the head of the summer expedition against the Christian countries. This campaign ... went as far as Ifrandja [Francia], in front of which he laid

siege and opened a breach in the walls with the help of war machines; he threatened the country of the Majūs, travelled through the enemy territory and for several months remained burning the villages and destroying the fortified castles: he even attacked the town of Narbonne.

This conflict, at the frontier of Islamic expansion beyond the Iberian Peninsula into the Pyrenees, is placed somewhere around the Aquitaine and Gascony area in southern France. Later Arabic sources, predominantly based on the Iberian Peninsula, only used the term *Majūs* to describe Scandinavians, and not other pagans like the Basques or Zoroastrians (in eastern Arabic sources composed around Baghdad, things are slightly different). Academically, these early mentions of the term *Majūs* have been long debated, most recently between Stephen Lewis[12] and Joel Supéry.[13] One camp views it to be unlikely that there was a sustained Scandinavian presence in a 'country of the *Majūs*' (near Gascony and Pamplona) prior to the middle of the ninth century, the other views it as a possibility.[14] Viking activity occurred most prominently throughout the 700s and 800s in areas where there was a certain amount of political tension. Logistically speaking, the ongoing border strife between the Christians and Muslims of the Iberian Peninsula and the Basque caught between them would be a prime area of opportunity; not to mention the old Roman roads and trade routes running through Spain into the Mediterranean, out of the reach of powers in the Francian heartlands, which would be very attractive. We even hear for 795 a mention of these same *Majūs* fighting on behalf of insular kings in Asturias, acting as mercenaries.[15] 'In the year 179 [795], Abd El Melik Ben Moghith marched with a large army to Astorga. Alfonso gathered an army; he was helped by the king of the Vascons [in Pamplona] who was his neighbour and the Majūs who lived on the coast of this region.'

By 700-750 Swedish warriors were on the coasts of Estonia demanding tribute or raiding. By mid-century, central places in Scandinavia played an active role in the international trade of the North Sea economy. By the first decade of the ninth century, Charlemagne imposed trade restrictions on Scandinavians attending markets, so it is conceivable that they then sought mercantile opportunities elsewhere. It is the 793 'start date' for the Viking Age that is the biggest obstacle to equating the *Majūs* mentioned in the above sources with Scandinavian profiteers. It is possible these *Majūs* are simply Basque pagans as described by Ibn Hawqal, but the descriptor is only ever used in later entries to refer to non-Christians of Scandinavian descent, so the jury is out. Regardless, the end of the eighth century was a period of increased military activity for these roaming sea wolves, and they would travel far from their homelands. Later twelfth-century

Danish sources like Saxo Grammaticus's *Deeds of the Danes* and the *Chronicle of Lejre*[16] describe a Scandinavian presence south of Aquitaine as early as the 770s, though the veracity of these particular documents is unsubstantiated for any events before the eleventh century. In Astorga and the surrounding region archaeological research has been thin.

Elsewhere across western Europe, things couldn't be clearer. We have the already-mentioned layers of burnt ash at Portmahomack and Burghead in Scotland, as well as contemporary mentions from Ireland of further raiding. *The Annals of Ulster* and *The Annals of Inisfallen*, both near-contemporary with the events they describe, record Scandinavian attacks into the ninth century. A place called Rechru suffered 'burning by the heathens' in 795 and the hugely important site of Iona, in the old sea kingdom of Dál Riata, was attacked successively. The Rechru incident appears to be the first recorded Scandinavian raid on Irish shores, though the exact location is debated, either Rathlin Island (which faces Iona and the Hebrides), or Lambay. Iona's suffering parallels Lindisfarne's. Both sites were immensely wealthy ecclesiastical centres which acted as areas of political and evangelical administration over surrounding religious sites. There is a chance that Lindisfarne and Iona were targeted purposefully not solely due to their wealth but for the damage to morale that such contemporary terrorism would inflict.

While the principal targets for raids on religious sites would be portable treasure, the most frequently stolen piece of Ireland would be freedom. Almost archaeologically invisible, the enslaved were the single most significant aspect of Viking Age economies. From these hit-and-run raids in Ireland, longships filled with slaves would take their cargo to markets like Hedeby and Dorestad to sell to middlemen. These middlemen, or perhaps the original raiders, now acting as traders, would then sail eastwards into the Baltic towards the *Austrvegr*, or perhaps via southerly routes through the Loire and Seine until they reached the Mediterranean. Even in the eighth century, these trade routes stretched across much of the known world; by 801, Islamic dirhams (coins) started to appear in Swedish hoards, the prize at the end of these long inter-continental slaving routes.[17, 18]

In western France, the monastery of Philibert of Jumièges was raided by vikingar on the island of Noirmoutier in 799,[19] lending more credence to the idea that they may well have penetrated even further south. Normally, the Noirmoutier raid is mentioned alongside the Irish ones as part of a growing momentum that had only increased post-Lindisfarne, but these longship crews were operating independently from one another. The foreigners appearing on Irish shores were most likely launching raids from bases in the North Sea, whereas the enterprising vikingr who first spied an opportunity on Noirmoutier may very well have already been trading in the Bay of Biscay. The spread of information across these international waters would be just as important as the goods themselves. We must not lose sight of how connected this increase in raiding appears. While it would be unreasonable to assume the same raiding parties were perpetrating all the damage, the evidence in the previous chapter hopefully provides the basis for a larger picture and explanation for the origin of the Viking Age and the outbreak at the end of the eighth century. Northern England, Ireland, France, and Spain, and innumerable unmentioned places around the Baltic Sea and along the *Austrvegr*, were the first targets of raiding, but other military activity was growing.

War Machines

There is a need to distinguish between the actions of these 'sea wolves' and disparate raiding parties and the military campaigns of kings and armies. In the year 800, it is mentioned in Frankish sources[20, 21] that King Godfred 'of the Danes' strengthened the Danevirke, that expansive earthwork reminiscent of Offa's Dyke. The creation of Offa's Dyke[22] indicates the state was rich and powerful. Slaves, servants, tenants, and warriors would need to work around the clock for months on end to build and then man such an immense structure. The same must be said for the Danevirke. Dendrochronological dating places its beginning sometime in the mid-500s, contemporary with the Dust Veil, but the bulk of the work appears to have commenced during the 700s, possibly under Oengendus. King Godfrid's additional ramparts, palisades, and staffing of the earthwork tell us what the Frankish annals do not; that Godfrid was a powerful ruler with a considerable degree of political and military strength. To best understand Viking Age Scandinavia, both its internal and external activity, is to read between the lines of the annals. The near-contemporary Carolingian accounts in the *Annals of St Bertin*, the *Annals of Fulda*[23, 24] the *Annals of Xanten*,[25] or the *Annals of St Vaast*[26] never reveal the strength of the enemy, nor do our principal sources for Arabic and Christian Spain, such as the *Chronicle of Sebastian* and *Codex Albeldensis*[27, 28, 29, 30] speak positively about the military tactics of the northern heathens.[31] Almost all textual sources from the Viking Age have undergone several centuries' worth of mistranslation and forgery. The quotes throughout this book are simply our best modern attempts to read these already edited accounts. We are quoting from layered and successive opinions written with preconceived biases.

Scandinavian activity in other countries must be discerned with some interdisciplinary deduction; we cannot simply read off a list of raids perpetrated against different locations. Godfrid's reign over Denmark in the eighth and ninth centuries is a prime example.

Godfrid's lineage is obscure, but he is the first Danish ruler with any significant historicity attached to him. As an opponent of Charlemagne, it was Godfrid (or an unnamed predecessor) who would have watched from the borders of Saxony and Frisia as territory was annexed and people were crucified in the late eighth century. It was Godfrid who exerted some degree of political centralisation to face this oncoming storm. In 798, envoys of Charlemagne were slain en route back from Danish territory by rebels living in the wilds at the edge of Francia. The envoys were originally to meet one Sigfrid, an unidentifiable figure who may have been a king before Godfrid (literary depictions of him are remarkably like Oengendus, so they may have been equated at some point). Godfrid comes into the Carolingian picture in the first decade of the ninth century, and leaves it shortly after, at the same time as other raiders still were inflicting hardship at Hartlepool and Tynemouth.

Godfrid and his Danes must be viewed as a separate entity. As the Viking Age moved into its latter half – the 'Second Viking Age' identified by Peter Sawyer – we start to talk not of raiding parties motivated by portable wealth but of state-funded militias with long-term economic incentive. There is a lot of overlap here that begs the question, what distinguishes a raiding party from an army? For the victims on the coast of Frisia, not much. It was Frisia that sat between the interests of the Carolingian Empire and Godfrid's kingdom. Godfrid's domain was probably not what we would nowadays call Denmark, but it principally included the Jutland peninsula, swathes of northern Germany, and possibly also parts of Sweden and the other Danish isles. Denmark as a term first appears in the vernacular in the tenth century during or shortly before the reign of Harald Bluetooth, widely heralded as the first true king of the country, though before his dynasty there was some degree of state centralisation. Call it Denmark, *Denemork*, *Denemearc*, or just the Kingdom of the Danes, it does not matter – King Godfrid had a kingdom. His actions, then, of raiding and invading across the Carolingian territory of Frisia at the dawn of the ninth century, were in part done out of self-defence. In 808, Godfrid's forces are said to have destroyed Reric (a Carolingian trading site) and moved the merchants to Hedeby (a Danish one). In this, Godfrid appears as a very intelligent leader, able to drive both military and economic interests.[32] This is a far cry from the sporadic raiding of Irish monasteries to steal slaves for a pre-existing trade network; this was the action of a monarch wishing to strengthen his *own* trade network. While Arabic dirhams started to flow into Sweden and the Baltic, so, too, did migrants into Danish territory. We can infer from an 801 mention of Carolingian border territory being given to the Obotrites that Charlemagne was displacing people up and down the territories neighbouring Denmark. Saxony was being annexed and split by mercenary groups and insular troops working on Charlemagne's behalf. These were the villains at Godfrid's door, and they were knocking. The Obotrites were a confederation of tribes that probably spoke Slavic dialects, their territory pre-annexation extending eastwards into modern Poland.[33] As of the late eighth century the Obotrites had fallen under Charlemagne's wing and in the 790s there appear to have been active Obotrite leaders pushing Carolingian interests. Drożko was one such, a tribal leader or petty king fighting on behalf of Charlemagne against Saxons, Frisians, and later Danes. He is mentioned in the Frankish *Annals of Lorsch* as a leader of the Obotrites. It was Drożko's trading port of Reric that was the target of later Danish attacks.

We build up a picture of the all-powerful Charlemagne tactically manipulating the migrations of people in northern Germany against what would be his chief adversary on that frontier, the Kingdom of the Danes. Eighteen campaigns were led by Charlemagne into Saxony between 774 to 804, and the result was the nominal conversion of the Old Saxons. One can imagine refugees from the territory pouring over the Danevirke, perhaps, into more tolerant areas of the world. It is these conflicts that add some weight to the idea that viking activity was specifically targeted at Christian sites *because* of an aversion to the religion. Charlemagne's conquests and his endorsement by the church in Rome must have been terrifying to non-Christians. Their choices were either to convert, at least outwardly, or to fight. It is likely Christian missionaries were probing into the Kingdom of the Danes in these years. If some viking raids were indeed 'pushback' against Carolingian Christian zealotry, then it was not widespread or shared across the rest of the Scandinavian diaspora. The shattered cross-slab at Portmahomack, in Scotland, may very well have been an isolated incident, a raider taking satisfaction from dismantling what a fallen Christian brother had held so dear, to put the survivors in their place. As will be seen in a later chapter, the process by which Scandinavians and their nations converted to Christianity seems to be on an individual level disconnected from the military politicking of enterprising warlords like Charlemagne. People converted if they wanted to, not if they were forced. These 'Saxon Wars' that ended in 804 can be seen as a precursor to Godfrid's later invasion of Frisia. It is 804 when Godfrid first appears as an antagonist in the Carolingian record, but we are of course reading these events from only one perspective. Godfrid was merely responding to a rival king, and with fire and fury, too.

A modern reconstruction of an Early Medieval palisade. Based on excavations along the modern Danevirke earthworks, it would have resembled something like this during the early ninth century but would be expanded and refortified in the tenth.

The Kovirke was allegedly added as an extension to The Danevirke in 805, following a series of territorial raids into Obotrite lands over the border. Kovirke literally means 'cattle wall' so we can hypothesize, again using Offa's Dyke as a parallel, that these raids were to steal local livestock from Saxony and Obotrite territory to weaken the enemy and enrich the rustlers. Or perhaps the opposite? This 'cattle wall' was to stop other raiders from escaping with *Danish* cattle? It is possible further gates and towers were added to the perimeter, though it is difficult to assess which military additions were built before or during the later reign of Harald Bluetooth. Certainly, his dominating presence in the history of the tenth century has made these earlier Danish rulers appear less important. King Godfrid, however, was going up against Charlemagne, *the* ruler of the post-Roman world, so he certainly deserves attention.

While there is no record of a direct attack from Obotrites or Carolingian vassals against the Danevirke, like other earthworks, there is evidence of turrets and archer-posts. Offa's Dyke, and the earlier Hadrian's Wall, were not simply barriers. These were economic checkpoints to keep a watchful eye on the movement and exchange of people and goods, not necessarily roadblocks to prevent movement altogether. It is worth placing the Danevirke and Godfrid's kingdom in the wider North Sea economy at this point; this was a proto-Denmark trying to stake a wider claim in the international trade of the rest of Europe. Harald Bluetooth would later realise that to do so would entail conversion to Christianity, but these early rulers were doing their best with what they had; such as the redirection of trade from Drożko's Reric to Godfrid's Hedeby.

By 806, all ambitions Charlemagne had to invade the lands beyond Saxony were thwarted by a plague. This pestilence likely affected all parties involved in these 'Danish Wars'; without the surplus to feed armies, military endeavours would be unwise. In the meantime, however,

Iona had been raided again, and the bishop of Lindisfarne, Higbald, who had probably witnessed or at least heard of the 793 attack, passed away in 803. Higbald had been communicating with Alcuin of York, sat with quill in hand at Charlemagne's court at Aachen, aware of the news of Scandinavian raiders in his homeland of the British Isles and an aggressive Scandinavian king in his new home of Francia. For Europe, there was seemingly no escape from such barbarism.

A glimpse of this fear is seen in a fascinating tale about Charlemagne's final days in Notker the Stammerer's *Deeds of Charles the Great*, where the Emperor looked out over the beaches near Narbonne and saw ships on the horizon.[34] Unable to believe that the sails were Scandinavian, after queries as to whether they were Saracen or Jewish in origin, Charlemagne shed a tear: 'He is asked the reason for his grief and Charlemagne explains that if these pagans dare to challenge him on these shores while he is alive, he fears the worst for his descendants.' This literary episode allegedly occurred in 814, in the last year of Charlemagne's life, and the mention of Narbonne places these Scandinavian ships in the Mediterranean. This account might be falsified. Notker is often viewed as unreliable due to his signature injection of humour and allegory to historical frameworks, and so scholarly thought has relocated this anecdotal episode to the North Sea. Perhaps there is still some truth here; maybe vikingar *were* in the Mediterranean this early. In the twilight of his life, Charles the Great foresaw widespread raiding in the years to come, wolves ravaging all his empire, not just the northern limit.

The Elephant and The Duck

Frisia would continue to play a significant role in Godfrid's raiding activities. Like the old kingdom of Lindsey in England, marshy enclaves with rivers and tributaries that linked distant trading ports would be shortcuts for raiding parties in longships. Max Adams provided a brilliant visualisation of this in the form of a Viking Age 'tube map'; Scandinavians would not see the river routes and coasts like cartographical charts as we would, but as abstract thoroughfares.[35] 'This line for Dorestad, that river for Eoferwic!' Frisia, Lindsey, East Anglia, and other marshlands would be the equivalent of Charing Cross.

These routes and an abstract view of them would be useful not just for raiding but for trade: Abul-Abbas was an elephant given to Charlemagne via returning envoys from Baghdad, the largest city in the world.[36] Charlemagne's envoys had probably received Abul-Abbas as a calf, but it wouldn't be until 802 that Charlemagne would receive his gift at his palace in Aachen. Either from India or Africa, Abul-Abbas had probably been born in Baghdad to elephants that had travelled via boat or silk road from the jungles and savannahs of the far south, and then overland or in the belly of a cargo ship westwards to the rainy gloom of northern Francia. Such an animal would of course have been difficult and expensive to feed and maintain. We can never know if Abul-Abbas was used in battle as a war mount as seen so frequently in the battles of the historic Mediterranean and Persian worlds. We can only imagine the astonishment of a Saxon or Danish warrior in Carolingian territory, looking upon such a mighty tusked and bejewelled beast, a symbol of Charlemagne's immense power and the gigantic international exchange network to which he had access.[37]

Scandinavians had access to it as well. In 807, Northumbria, Connacht, and Scotland were raided, and in the following year so was the port of Reric. It was this year, or perhaps 809, when Godfrid's adversary Drożko fell in battle. Now this war would be fought between the main players, Charlemagne and Godfrid would go head-to-head on the grand stage. Perhaps Abul-Abbas would be on the frontlines of Charlemagne's army, towering over the infantry, looking over the turrets of the Danevirke as arrows whistled past, frightened, maddened.

The immediate precursor to the 810 invasion of Frisia was the construction of greater coastal defences by Charlemagne's delegates and the foundation of a fort at Itzehoe to watch over Danish interests. These frontlines were becoming dangerous badlands, and it is likely there were many small skirmishes happening up and down both Carolingian and Danish territory, as these two worlds came head-to-head in dramatic fashion. The record of Frisia is punctuated by small-scale 'pushback' against Christianity on behalf of the marsh-dwellers. While we use monolithic terms like Frankish, Carolingian, Old Saxon, Frisian, and Danish, it is highly likely that sides in this conflict included elements from one another. The *Royal Frankish Annals*, the document which later Carolingian accounts follow on from, remarks that 'a leader of the Northmen, called Halfdan, submitted to the great Emperor, accompanied by a host of others and strove to keep lasting faith.' This Halfdan, otherwise unknown, would be the first recorded Scandinavian to change sides. What were his motives? Did he and his men have a personal vendetta against Godfrid? Had Godfrid perhaps annexed some of Halfdan's own territory in his first years as king? Did Halfdan just believe he could earn more money and wealth serving under Charlemagne, after seeing his glorious elephant, than he would under Godfrid? We cannot know, but Halfdan serves as a demonstration of the multi-ethnic nature of these armies. The Great Heathen Army that went on to ruin England's fortunes in the closing years of the ninth century would be made up of Danish, Norwegian,

Abul-Abbas as depicted on a twelfth-century fresco in San Baudelio, Spain.

Swedish, Frisian, and British components. Godfrid's own forces, returning from the burning of Reric in 809 led by his son Reginfrid, would be in part composed of the *Veleti* (or Wielzians), another Slavic tribe like the opposing Obotrites.

Itzehoe, and forts like it, were occupied by Charlemagne's new vassals from annexed Saxony and Obotrite lands. Count Egbert was one such, hailing from a new formalised bloodline brought into the Carolingian and Christian fold following the conquest of Saxony. He served at Itzehoe, the fortified encampment: 'it was occupied by Egbert and the Saxon counts', watching the approaching Danes. This was a declaration of Charlemagne's fear of the Danes: war was coming.

In 810 Godfrid extorted 100 lb of silver from Frisia as part of his invasion. He had at his disposal an immense fleet of longships, filled with warriors and raiders.

In the later Viking Age, we will see how kings like Sweyn Forkbeard and Cnut the Great commanded armies of insular warbands (each with their own sub-rulers) operating as one unit. Upon the death of their overlord, in this case, Sweyn in 1014, his sub-groups would all disperse, not content to stick around to wait for the next-in-line to prove himself. Godfrid's armies likely acted in much the same way; these were state-sponsored and organised militias, but they were not held to the same discipline as contemporary armies. On both the small and large scale, aboard both the longship and in the court and kingdom, when Scandinavian rulers died their powerbases would evaporate, and new players would enter the game.

Godfrid's end would come on a hunting trip with one of his sons, shot with an arrow. Notker says Godfrid's adultery led one of his sons to kill him while they were out hunting ducks, a doubtful tale. Whatever happened, arguably Charlemagne's most fearsome foe had fallen. It is likely the latter breathed a sigh of relief, and there would indeed be a brief period of calm on the Carolingian-Danish border. The Kingdom of the Danes now had no king, but it still had chieftains.

For Power and Glory

'Word-fame' is a concept that comes down to us in post-Viking Age writings like *The Lay of The High One*.[38] In short, word-fame concerns one's posthumous reputation, how someone is remembered for deeds in battle, but also for their behaviour in the hall.

> Cattle die
> kinsmen die
> all men are mortal.
> Words of praise
> will never perish
> nor a noble name.

This lay is one of many Viking Age poems contained in the later *Poetic Edda*[39] compiled in Iceland. Earlier copies of these poems acted as the foundation for Snorri Sturluson's *Prose Edda*. The 'noble names' were the top dogs of the ninth century; the most enigmatic, wealthy, and violent men standing at the prow of their longships as they entered foreign waters. They were also the most generous, they were 'ring givers', sharing out looted wealth to foster loyalty and respect. It is likely that some of the most famous names started out as humble raiders themselves, but over time grew to lead their own men; Haesten, Ubbe, Ragnar of Paris, Ganger-Hrolf, and Ivarr the Boneless, to name a few. It was word-fame, wealth, and manpower that propelled a young man upwards through the social strata. In the power vacuums after such deaths as King Godfrid's in 810, the opportunity for advancement was for the taking. We hear in Frankish sources of several pretenders vying for the Danish throne by the following year. Peace was made between the Carolingian Empire and one Hemming, a possible son or relative of Godfrid, but other relatives like Reginfrid and Anulo/Ale, and Sigfrid and Harald Klak all became embroiled in a war for the country not long after. Godfrid's territory had likely also covered areas of southwest Norway and Sweden, as evidenced by conflict in 813 in which Reginfrid and Harald, now joint kings of the Danes, attempted to reimpose control over the area near Kaupang, modern Oslo. Their attempts were thwarted by Horik and other sons of Godfrid, the former then becoming the sole ruler of the territory.

By 813 Kaupang, or *Skíringssalr* as it would be described in the late ninth century, was a major trading port and the principal market centre of Norway. Such a country as we would recognise it today did not exist at this time. The name may derive from *Norðvegr*, meaning 'the Northern Way'. Like its Eastern equivalent, *Austrvegr*, the moniker was in reference to a long trade route that wound up into the Arctic Circle into the territories of the Saami. These pale lands were home to valuable goods like furs and reindeer antlers, harvested via tribute, and then sold southwards at markets like Kaupang and smaller sites. The impetus behind Reginfrid and Harald's invasion was simple; to consolidate another corner of the trade economy.

Previous scholars have been tempted to correlate Kaupang's archaeological findings with the scant history and legends of Scandinavia's prehistory. Situated around Lake Tjølling since the Iron Age, there is evidence of sporadic settlement in the form of timber walkways, houses, and at least one hall, though nothing on a par with the markets at Hedeby and Ribe. Site expert Dagfinn Skre[40] has argued Kaupang was the home of local kings who live on as legendary characters like Halfdan 'Whiteshanks' and Halfdan the Black. However Kaupang operated, it may very well have had a local magnate who styled himself as a 'king', controlling trade and overseeing international relations with the Danes. If Matthew Townend's phenomenal work tracing the linguistic development of Old English and Old Norse is anything to go by, then it is likely that in the Viking Age there was a high degree of intelligibility between Old Norse speakers from *Norðvegr* and Old Norse speakers from *Denemeorc*.

Between 1998 and 2003, a series of archaeological digs revealed a mass of material from Kaupang: copper-alloy metal mounts made on-site by local smiths, ornamental brooches and jewellery from both home sources and international looting, gemstones, jet, Baltic amber, glass from local crafters, pottery, whetstones and grindstones, and the debris of everyday life like food waste and shells. Kaupang, when it was occupied, was a very busy site, seeing a lot of footfall and with a population of about a thousand people. It would not be occupied for very long, though, falling into disuse in the following century. Situated as it was near modern Oslo, Kaupang sat on what was likely the border between warring territories; their margins determined by geography. These territories had kings and kinglets who wanted sole access to international goods and status, power and glory. It is likely the earliest 'kingdoms' of Scandinavia were quasi-nomadic, based around the pecking order of the longship and roaming sea rulers, who exacted tribute from sites like Kaupang. Ribe and Hedeby are other examples of these intersections.

The stories of viking raids are only told to us through written sources, not every place vikingar looted and razed has a tell-tale layer of ash like at Burghead or Valhagar. The markets and central places of Scandinavia and places Scandinavians occupied, however, couldn't be more different. The archaeological records of Ribe were published in a brilliant overview by Stig Jensen[41] in 1991, and decades more work has since been undertaken in the area. Ribe started life as a seasonal market of tents and stalls in the middle of the Jutland peninsula positioned on a vital naval trading route. Later, it was demarcated by a small ditch. This ditch was likely not for defensive or run-off purposes but to mark where untaxed land ended and taxed land began; Ribe was generating wealth, and like the English examples, someone collected payment for facilitating this trade (recent arguments have placed the ditch in the tenth century, though clearly by the ninth Ribe was generating serious profit).

The Scandinavian equivalents of an English port-reeve (*portgerefa*) are mostly nameless, but we can argue with reasonable confidence that they existed. By the first decades of the eighth century, Ribe was well on its way to resembling some limited form of proto-urbanism; it was a busy place, with wattle-and-daub houses next to one another in sporadic timber tenements. Craftspeople, travelling from afar every year or perhaps based at local farms nearby, created beautiful necklaces from coloured glass beads, repurposing older material like Roman mosaic tesserae. Locally made goods, like these beads and antler combs, appear to have been out-competed by items from the Arabic world as the ninth century progressed. These wide-ranging trade routes that Scandinavians had been engaged in now started to bear fruit; the first Arabic dirhams to enter Sweden in 801 line up very neatly alongside Ribe's archaeological layers.[42, 43] On the ground, we can imagine Ribe as a noisy and smelly place; farmers travelling from the silty shores inland may have been shocked to see a metalworker weaving gold and silver together as if it were some kind of magical force.

These proto-urban centres were not the norm for Early Medieval Scandinavians. As stated earlier, for most of the Viking Age everyday life was tied to the farm. Places like Ribe and Kaupang, then, and Hedeby too, emerged as distinct areas of abundance in an otherwise relatively static world. These were the areas most affected by the trading and raiding of the Viking Age. The comb provides a kind of trope; traditionally made of antler, often carved with beautiful patterns and zoomorphic designs, the Viking Age comb was a thing to behold, a treasure. Comb-making was big business. Comb-makers travelled to Ribe to use red deer and reindeer antlers to create designs informed by international ideas. The bulk of the work on identifying and following the spread of Viking Age combs and the urbanisation that so often came with it has been led by Steve Ashby.[44, 45]

Hedeby would be familiar to any marketgoer who travelled from Ribe or Kaupang. Perhaps they had travelled over Carolingian territory in the aftermath of the 'Danish Wars' to trade, or they had sailed in from the east via the Kanhave Canal on the Danish island of Samsø. This canal was constructed sometime in the eighth century, probably by the same

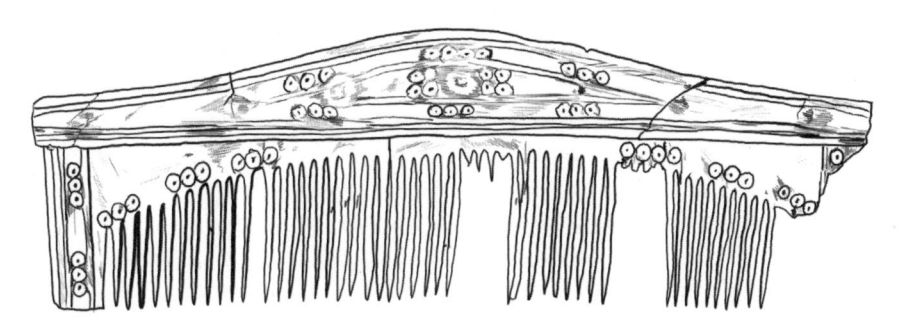

An early Scandinavian type comb found in Ribe, dated to 720-740. This example was made from reindeer antler and thus likely imported to Ribe from Arctic Norway, while most locally made combs were created from red deer antler.

powerful individual who had facilitated repairs to the Danevirke or, perhaps, a competing warlord from a rival kingdom based not on Jutland but the surrounding islands. Longships docking at any of these markets, small or large, for cargo or for warfare, would be greeted by sights, smells, and sounds unfamiliar to rural farmers but familiar to those well-travelled *vikingar* who had been occupying the towns elsewhere across the Early Medieval world. The population of Hedeby (or *Haithabu*) would live and trade there in the busy streets and then perhaps be buried in the nearby cemetery. Hedeby was a border town, looking east into the Baltic Sea, encircled almost entirely by the Danevirke and subsidiary extensions. Many of these extensions and defences came in the later tenth century; in the ninth, Hedeby was still growing, kickstarted of course by the economic injection of new traders from Reric in 808. At least one street, timber jetties and a few pit houses along with a cemetery existed by the ninth century.[46, 47] It is likely that all of these Scandinavian market centres were raided by *vikingar*, a reminder that 'Scandinavian' was not an identity that prevented in-fighting, much in the same way that 'Anglo-Saxon' didn't.

Indeed, in 814 and 815, Reginfrid and Harald Klak both made attempts to restore their hold on the Danish throne, being thwarted by coastal defenders from Jutland. These visits to the changing Kingdom of the Danes were funded by Charlemagne. Reginfrid and Harald Klak were loyal to him and had shared interests in mind. If Charlemagne could put two individuals on the Danish throne whom he could trust, then the danger would be allayed at least for a short while. In 814 Charlemagne died, four years after his elephant. He would be succeeded by Louis, later 'The Pious', who would continue the Carolingian defence against the Danes. He would never escape his father's shadow, but it wouldn't be until the reign of his own sons that the absence of *Karlo Magnus* would be felt the most. Harald Klak was likely an exiled dynast from Danish territory who sought powerful allies. His ally Reginfrid, if he had similar plans, had died in 815 on another sponsored attempt across Jutland. Harald's lineage is nebulous; he first appears in the *Royal Frankish Annals* as a nephew or grandson of someone called Anulo/Ale, who was allegedly a son of King Godfrid. Harald Klak may have had 'royal' heritage, but it is equally likely he was simply another warlord. The gargantuan semi-fictitious genealogical work *European Family Trees*[48] published in the 1900s by Wilhelm Karl linked Harald Klak to other less attested figures like 'Whiteshanks', the Saxon rebel Widukind, and the wider Yngling Dynasty from Sweden. True or not, figures like Harald would have likely claimed descent from such lofty ancestors to provide backing to their claims.

Whatever his ancestry, Harald Klak was another who had lofty goals and would use whatever means necessary to achieve them. He was baptised, nominally converting to save face before his new Frankish allies, which no doubt made him even more unpopular in the Kingdom of the Danes. The nameless individuals leading raiding parties to the shores of Ireland and England between the years 811 and 816 were probably also power-hungry chieftains. Limerick was looted in 812, and so were the monasteries across Mungret, Mayo, Killarney, Connaught, and Cork. A local Irish Rí (*Rí* meaning 'King'), one of about a hundred dwelling on the island, by the name of Cosrach, was killed in a raid the following year. Ireland, split as it was between so many petty territories, had no central seat of government or any agreed upon 'main site', so conquering such a wide area involved the constant attritional defeat of *túatha* after *túatha*. England, in comparison, had between seven and twelve nominal kingdoms at the time, much larger and much more consolidated than Ireland's.

While we do not know the name of the chieftain who led his men to victory in the raid against Inis Cathaigh in Ireland in 816, we do see the name *Ṣaltān* – 'the best knight of the *Majūs*' – appear in Arabic sources describing the Battle of Pancorbo in the same year. Fought between Emir al-Hakam of the Umayyad Caliphate (based at Córdoba) and Prince Íñigo Arista of Asturias (a Basque Christian), the Battle of Pancorbo is said to have lasted thirteen days, a form of trench warfare with both sides digging rough dykes fortified by logs and poles, culminating in a last charge by the Basque before they were defeated and thrown off the nearby cliffs by the Arab invaders. Íñigo Arista would escape and go on to rule Pamplona, a Carolingian-allied area of Basque territory right on the southern border of Louis the Pious's territory. This *Ṣaltān* who appears in the written record with the same descriptor of *Majūs* used to describe the earlier 793 and 795 incidents was possibly a 'Halfdan', considering etymological interplay between languages. One might recall it was a Halfdan who switched sides over to the Carolingians in 809. Are these two people the same? It would be foolish to attribute much weight to that theory, but it is possible. The Battle of Pancorbo marks another possible instance of Scandinavians fighting Arabs and Berbers before the traditional 844 origin of their relations.

Unlike the farmers and warriors of England and France, who fought with a mixture of shield wall and cavalry, or the Irish who flung spears from afar, Arabia had a standing army; the *Ahl al-Sham* ('the people of Syria')[49] in the east, and so it is likely contingents would be seen on the flanks of the western frontier. Uniquely, in Spain, Umayyad forces included vast numbers of Berbers, their presence understated in Arabic accounts. These soldiers would be a fearsome threat, their armour-piercing arrows could make short work of the Scandinavian *byrnie*. They were paid like Roman legions, divided into military contingents called *junds* based around urban centres. This rigidly organised fighting unit was one of the most formidable forces of the ninth century. It is no wonder that viking activity in the Arabic world was so often mercenary in nature rather than attempts at conquest, though there would of course still be attempts. In 825, Arabic sources describe a battle by *Djabal al-Majūs* ('the mountain of the *Majūs*') which has been argued by some to detail a not insignificant Scandinavian presence in the region by the Urdaibai Estuary. This location, joined to the Bay of Biscay in the Guernica region of Spain, is also known as Mundaka Guernica (first written in the vernacular in 1070 as *Mondaka*). The prefix *Mund-* has likely Latin origins but *Mund-* also means 'mouth' in Danish, in this case it would refer to the 'mouth of the River Oka' that flows from the bay through Santa Catalina and Laida. Unlike Hedeby, Ribe, and Kaupang, any archaeological work that has ever been conducted in the Urdaibai Estuary is scant and poorly published.[50]

For the ninth century, at the outbreak of this raiding storm, all we can conclusively say is that western Europe felt the brunt of the damage according to vernacular sources, but it is likely the *Austrvegr* felt a similar surge of activity, and possibly other places, too; expeditions led by chieftains seeking power and glory.

Raid Leaders

In the poem *Rígsþula*,[51] preserved in a fifteenth-century manuscript folio alongside a version of Snorri's *Prose Edda*, we catch a glimpse of Viking Age hierarchies. The deific figure Rig (either Heimdallr or Óðinn in disguise) wanders through the land seeking shelter and hospitality with a variety of people. His first hosts were Ái and Edda, great-grandfather and great-grandmother, who let him stay for three nights, offering food and warmth. Nine months later, Edda gives birth to Thraell, or *Thrall*, who goes on to sire the race of serfs and servants. Rig then goes to the home of grandfather and grandmother, hard at work fixing things as the world goes on around them. Their son is Churl, or *Ceorl*, the peasant. Sunburnt, exhausted, and desperate for more shelter, nine months later a tired Rig walks to a new home, as Churl's wife gives birth to characters like Hero, Youth, Thegn, and Warrior. Rig's new abode was the home of father and mother, and the story repeats itself. Earl, or *Jarl*, is the product of this final union, and his sons go on to be King, Kinsman, Inheritor.

Here we see not only another example of High Medieval poems codifying the manners and attitudes respected in the Viking Age (offering hospitality, food, and having a good time), but also how society was structured and seen through the eyes of the gods. At the bottom of the tier are the un-free, relatively archaeologically invisible, making up the vast bulk of Scandinavian society who tend the fields, feed the animals, and dwell in shielings on the edges of farms. Above them are free-men or *ceorls*, also observed in contemporaneous England; farmers and labourers who would serve a lord through obligation but not necessarily desire, unless they were loyal warriors hoping for promotion. They would be aiming for the highest stratum of society, the warrior elite responsible for so much dramatic change before, during, and after the Dust Veil. It was this warrior elite, the chieftains, raid leaders, and kinglets, who would all be competing for the ultimate title of king. The word 'Rig' has the same root as the Old Irish term 'Rí'. Whoever the stranger of *Rígsþula* was, he was royal. All the names of the elite class in the poem are male; there was little room for women in the highest layer of society outside important dynastic marriages. The differentiation between cognomens like chieftain, jarl, and king is perhaps meaningless for the ninth century. These early raids were perpetrated by chieftains and jarls, but the Great Heathen Army was led by kings. What is the difference between the titles? Access to more men? Better goods? Better equipment? More land?

One jarl, Glum, was the first to attack Count Egbert's Itzehoe fortress on the edge of Danish territory in 817. He failed. Was he acting in his own interests or under the thumb of the new king of the Danes, Horik, the son of Godfrid? The following year, a period of iconoclasm, assassination, and political infighting in Anatolia[52] witnessed the first recorded raid in the eastern world by vikingar. These vikingar, given the name *Vaerangoi* or Varangians (meaning by this point 'pirates'), were probably only partially Scandinavian in heritage, having intermarried with the Slavic peoples along the river routes between the Baltic Sea and Constantinople. Or perhaps they were entirely Scandinavian, specifically Swedish or Gotlandic. Whatever their ethnic makeup, these eastern vikingar are normally named the *Rus*. Emperor Leo V of the Roman Empire (now the 'Byzantine' Empire) was amid regnal turmoil in 818. He would be overthrown by his avaricious general Michael the Amorian two years later. This was a politically weakened target with a lot of wealth on display. The Eastern Roman world was a juggernaut compared to the Christian spheres of northwestern Europe but the impetus for these raids remains the same; blood in the water ... and the sharks would come.

In 819 Leinster was raided[53] while further border strife between the Danes and the Carolingians involved the murder of a Dane-allied Obotrite leader called Sclaomir and the installation of a new Carolingian-allied individual, the son of Drożko. The politicking would continue, for in 820 Harald Klak was made the 'official' King of the Danes though likely had not even set foot in the territory for some time, instead ruling from afar as a vassal of Louis the Pious. For all intents and purposes, the Kingdom of the Danes was still ruled over by Horik and other surviving sons of Godfrid. The political tensions and conflict that were so often used as an opportunity for viking activity abroad were now happening in their homelands. In this same year, vikingar exploited Louis' diverted attention by sailing down the coast of Flanders and then the Seine to the village of Bouin in Aquitaine, which felt the heat shortly after. The Bouin raid is described in Carolingian sources as being perpetrated by a 'fleet of longships', and so here we start to see that evolution of scale. From small groups of vikingar to moderately sized fleets operating as mercenaries and pioneers – the pirates in Anatolia in 818 were probably a conglomerate of multiple crews rather than just one. From chieftains to jarls, from kinglets to kings, the Viking Age was giving violent men a boost. These raid leaders from both Danish and Norse territory would mostly focus on Ireland in the ensuing decades. There were probably as many differences between the Norwegians living in the Arctic Circle near the Lofoten islands and those living in the southwest as there were between Norwegians and Danes. Many of these raiding groups and roaming hydrarchies would have fought one another, competing for spoils and word-fame.

As vikingar were using others' political weaknesses to their advantage, so, too, would their foes. In 823, Louis the Pious sent one of the first waves of Christian missions into Danish lands to convert the masses. Had Scandinavia still been made up of hillforts and isolated farmsteads, these conversion attempts would have been much slower, but Scandinavia was now on the road to urbanisation. And with urbanisation, bolstered as it was by international economies and loot, came cultural melting pots and the opportunity for evangelism. Vikingar were indirectly funding Christian missionaries to change their own way of life very gradually: from roaming heathens to Christian militaries. This first mission, led by Archbishop Ebo of Rheims, was both spiritual and political. Hedeby would make a nice location for a new church, but the real impetus it seems was to reinstate Harald Klak as the King of the Danes yet again. This was another failed attempt, but these 823 missions were an early example of the Christian/European sphere attempting to expand into Denmark.[54] For now, Denmark was enjoying new economies without needing to Christianise, but as opportunities would start to wane, the need to convert would become greater.[55, 56, 57]

Bangor and Skellig Michael were raided twice in two years. By 824, *The Annals of Ulster* and other Irish chronicles become catalogues of raids, almost as repetitive as Carolingian-Danish treaties, like the one

Coins found and minted in Ribe dated 800-840. They represent a transition between the earlier sceatta designs and later truly 'national' currencies.

in 825 which coincides with early evidence of an increase in locally minted Danish coins. These were a national coinage to some extent, slightly different to earlier *sceattas*; another example of Horik's kingdom attempting to break into that wider European sphere.[58]

Ireland continued to suffer the vast majority of attacks. Was it due to the abundance of cattle and undefended farmsteads, easily looted and with individuals sold to the growing slave economy that connected Ireland to Constantinople? To sail between Norway and Ireland regularly would be a sizeable undertaking and fraught with risk. Raid leaders would need bases closer to home, perhaps Shetland, or perhaps even closer to Ireland, like Orkney and the Hebrides.

The Eye of the Storm
At the heart of early viking activity in the British Isles are the Scandinavian settlements at *Orkneyjar* and *Suðreyjar*, Orkney and the Hebrides. While

it is plausible that Shetland was the first location outside of Scandinavia in the North Sea to be settled, it is likely that within a few years after reaching Underhoull and Old Scatness Scandinavians were travelling further south. Like Shetland, the Hebrides and Orkney were already home to a pre-existing population, the people the Romans referred to as the Picts. During the time of Claudius's invasion in the first century, there was a 'king of the Orcades'. Some kind of Brythonic population existed in the far north of the British Isles and they were of some importance. Neil Oliver put it best when he suggested one should turn a map of the British Isles upside down so that Orkney sits where London usually does, to give a greater sense of its Neolithic and Iron Age significance.[59] Orkney, as an independent kingdom or as a vassal of Fortriu, clearly held some power, so how could the Scandinavians seemingly completely dominate the local populace and culture?[60] Genomic evidence[61] has suggested that up to 30% of all male genomes in the area are from Scandinavian settlement. The greatest question attached to Viking Age Scotland looms; was the situation on Orkney and the Hebrides an example of genocide or integration? Did the natives of Atlantic Scotland put up a valiant fight against invaders only to be wiped out? Or did they assimilate pragmatically into a new and dominant culture?

Archaeological evidence for these new settlers across the Hebrides[62, 63, 64] and Orkney, principally at sites like South Uist and Buckquoy,[65] date the longhouses and reoccupied local wheelhouses to the dawn of the ninth century, or slightly earlier. There is a certain architectural continuity between the farmsteads and raiding bases of these locations and those previously mentioned for Shetland. At a certain point, the Scandinavian army camps in Ireland became the westernmost link in this long chain that would later be known as a 'Kingdom of the Isles'. Not only were Orkney and the Hebrides placed geographically at the centre of so much raiding turmoil, but their many excavated farmsteads are also a perfect exemplar of that farmer-raider dynamic of Early Medieval Scandinavians. To the sheep farmers and church looters of Orkney and the Hebrides, life was life; one could farm one day and raid the next. The storm of ninth-century raiding activity was just getting started, and Ireland was at the heart of it all.

From farmers to warriors, chieftains to jarls, raid leaders to kinglets, and from kinglets to kings; the act of raiding facilitated societal development and the rise of a military elite through Viking Age society. Loot and slaves generated a stronger economy in the Scandinavian homelands, providing kings with stronger tools of governance. Charismatic leaders like the Ṣaltān who fought the Arabs in 816 or the Turgesius (Thorgest) who sowed havoc in Ireland in the 830s, or perhaps the famous Haesten and Bjorn Ironside and their daring voyage from 859-861 into the Mediterranean, or the Ragnar responsible for besieging Paris in 845 – these leaders were as important as the peaceful traders making combs back in Ribe or Birka, as important as the fur traders between Staraja Ladoga and Constantinople. The ninth century saw a huge boom in the fortunes of Scandinavia and Scandinavians. Trading would become raiding, raiding would become invading, and invading would become settling. The traditional narrative of the Viking Age must still be followed to interrogate the immediate impact of these pirates and their legacy.

By the middle of the ninth century, the activities and actions of these sea wolves had coalesced to such a point where grandiose armies made up of individual war bands led by charismatic rulers could ravage the landscapes of insular kingdoms. These violent warlords were now no longer there to plunder and leave, they were there to stay. Be they armies launched from Scandinavia or from Irish and Frisian shores, the vikingar of the late ninth century would increase the scale and scope of warfare considerably. The reasons for the change from raiding parties to raiding armies will be considered in the following chapter. Much in the same way that the Viking Age can be seen as a response to the stimuli of the North Sea economy, Charlemagne's conquests, and Arab expansion, so would others respond to the Viking Age. Enter stage left: King Ælfred of Wessex.

Shadow

> After this battle King Harald met no opposition in Norway, for all his opponents and greatest enemies were cut off. But some, and they were a great multitude, fled out of the country, and thereby great districts were peopled.
>
> Extract from *Harald Harfager's Saga*, written by Snorri Sturluson, contained within the thirteenth-century *Kringla* manuscript, which later became known as *The Chronicle of the Kings of Norway*.

For the British Isles, the impact of the Viking Age diaspora on the language, social structure, and eventual unification of polities is well documented; vikingar helped to shape the idea of *Anglalond,* England. Elsewhere, the evidence is similarly spread across a variety of disciplines though has seen less intensive study. It is known, for instance, that areas around Rouen were settled in the early tenth century by Scandinavian war bands, setting the keystone for the Duchy of Normandy in later generations, and there was an archaeologically visible Scandinavian holdout in Brittany. Where things become murkier, however, is how these settlers assimilated into their new cultural and political environments. For England, both Scandinavian and *Ænglisċ* (English) folk influenced one another to form a mutual identity based on pre-existing regional politics and cultural differences (the original North-South divide, if you will).

For Normandy, within one or two generations the Scandinavian settlers became, for lack of a better word, 'Frenchified', resembling their surrounding neighbours but with a few hardwired psychological differences, discussed later. Raiding evolved into military invasions, which in turn evolved into waves of settlement. The *ASC*, in astonishment, refers to these initial settlements as 'wintersetl' ('winter camps'), though they would not just be bases to outlast a season, but strongholds for years and years.

King Ælfred would not be the only resistor to this Scandinavian staying power; powerful rulers like Charles the Bald and Count Odo of Francia tried their very best to build bridges to block the riverine routes of viking crews, or to destroy their siegeworks on the walls of Paris. There would also be canny Scandinavians playing both sides, like Rorik of Dorestad, arguably the most intriguing figure of the ninth century, and Oleg the Wise, who would strengthen a united dynasty of multi-ethnic origins along the *Austrvegr*. But there are also characters mentioned by history books who may not have existed, like Harald Fairhair and Erik Bloodaxe, sandwiched between forgotten and perhaps more intriguing people like Guthred, Sigfrøðr, and Knútr, who all ruled York for brief periods between 885-905, or the unnamed individuals responsible for creating the campsites some argue were in Portugal. Viking armies would roam Europe for a while, not just in England but Frisia, Francia, and Spain. They would reach a great deal of the known world and would leave behind a variety of consequences.

Gifts and Benefits: Agents and Entrepreneurs

Harald Klak spent his entire career in the first half of the ninth century attempting, with the backing of Charlemagne's son Louis, to enforce his claim to the Kingdom of the Danes. He was unsuccessful, barring a few nominal obligations to the throne in the mid-to-late 810s. We view Harald Klak through the sources as a bit of a fool; he was a cowardly double agent, perhaps, not sticking true to his homeland but abandoning it for foreign intervention, only for his people to turn to others to bear the crown. His epithet, *Klak*, may mean 'Complainer'. We do not know if Harald Klak was a great warrior or a canny politician, we can only infer that he was attempting to some degree to play both sides of the Carolingian-Danish confrontation that by the 820s had somewhat cooled.[1] Principally, the exiled dynast lived in Carolingian territory, possibly in Frisia if later land grants are anything to go by. What Harald Klak may not have realised is that he, like the Halfdan who defected to Charlemagne in 809, was paving the way for a widely observed motif of the Viking Age; raiders being given lands in payment to prevent further viking incursions.

The most famous example of this is also from Francia, with the granting of Rouen to Ganger-Hrolf (or Rollo) in 911 through the Treaty of Saint Clair-sur-Epte,[2] but Rollo was only the latest in a long line of enterprising Scandinavians who knew when to accept bribes from their opponents. Harald Klak may not have played the game particularly well, but he was still playing it. 826 saw the first recorded baptism of a Scandinavian; later there are many examples of *prim-signing*, a nominal baptism that required little commitment other than a promise that they will be fully baptised later. Harald's baptism must have been an official one, done as it was in the grandiose palace of Louis the Pious at Ingelheim. Ingelheim was an imperial residence established by Charlemagne, but obviously had been populated earlier.[3] Perhaps this blending of religion and culture between Scandinavia and Christendom was deliberately performed at a place likely once known as Ingill's Home; a heathen redoubt of the sixth century.

Harald's reward for Christian commitment was lands in Rüstringen, in modern Friesland, very close to Denmark. Rüstringen was a *gau*, an old term for a slice of Germanic-speaking territory, and likely extended into the North Sea much more than it does today. Frisia was a recently annexed territory by this point and it was prone to tidal flooding. Rüstringen, while the first benefice ever to be given to a Scandinavian warlord, may not have been the best of locations, but it was in a useful tactical position for Harald and his men[4] to harry the coasts of their former home, as they would do in 827. These 'anti-vikingar' parties likely involved Carolingian soldiers, Frisians, and Obotrite mercenaries too, but what they did not involve was any success. Be these intrusions into the Kingdom of the Danes military or religious endeavours, the new-King Horik expelled them all the same, so the annals tell us. Harald and Louis' foreign policy towards Danish territory continued to stagnate, though it clearly had some mild breakthroughs with an increased Christian presence at Hedeby, and even farther north in Birka in modern Sweden.

Birka's archaeology is tantalising, not only was it another rich trade site that had grown from a seasonal market centre into proto-urban capital, but it also had a formidable hillfort with later tenth-century examples of Scandinavian armies; the *hirð*. Birka looked out over the Baltic Sea with several inlets and estuaries leading into the wider Lake Mälaren region; it was very well positioned, with specific bays for specific types of ships. One such was Kugghamn, perhaps from 'kogge-haven' – the *kogge* (or cog) was the principal Frisian maritime vessel. One of the first Christian missionaries to reach Birka that we know of was one Ansgar, and his journey likely started aboard a Frisian *kogge*. This journey would have taken him through The Kattegat and the dangerous pirate-ridden waters of the Danish isles, out into the mists of the Baltic Sea before finally settling into the great lakes of Sweden, the land of the *Svear*. Founded in the middle of the eighth century, Birka was the successor to the earlier trading site at Helgö, home of the Buddha figurine. Why Helgö did not expand to accommodate burgeoning trade requirements is unclear, but perhaps the geography of the region played a part. Birka was well positioned on a much larger island, with room to spare. There is similar archaeological evidence as at Kaupang; timber tenements and jetties extended into the clear waters along with a parallel administrative centre on the island of Adelsö.[5] Adelsö would be mirrored by elite residences like Erritsø, in Denmark. Wooden breakwaters were placed off-shore to create areas for docking. Finds from Birka's long excavation history include over two thousand graves of local residents and visitors and many ship's clench nails.[6] Anchor ropes have been found and also ice-skates, for when the waters froze over.

These lakes were sheltered extensions of the naval trade routes of the Baltic Sea, free from piracy, and taxable by a resident elite. The ninth-century *Vita Ansgarii*,[7] written by a later Archbishop of Hamburg-Bremen, describes Birka from an outsider's perspective, a version of what Ansgar himself may have seen in 830 when he arrived after a long and arduous journey, partly overland and partly in a cramped boat. The result, after a seemingly peaceful meeting with the local king Bjorn, was at least one church built in the area for an individual named Herigar; 'A little later he built a church on his own ancestral property and served God with the utmost devotion.'

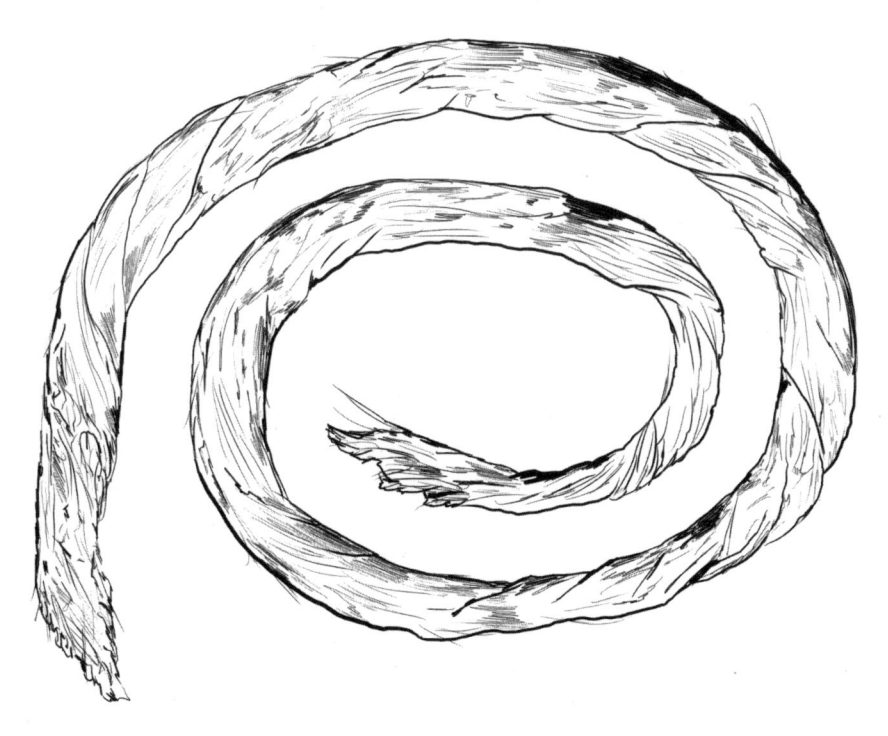

A ninth-century anchor rope excavated at Birka; one of many well-preserved examples.

This Herigar is described as a 'prefect', a word that Bede had used earlier to describe the first converted officials in the kingdom of Lindsey in 625. There, in the crumbling walls of *Lindum Colonia* (Lincoln), the prefect named Blaecca was the first to convert; later baptised in the River Trent. Ansgar, experienced in converting Danes, had converted the first Swede. In 831 he would return to Carolingian territory and his conversion efforts would continue, but during that decade a terrifying pagan threat emerged in Ireland: Thorgest.

Through reading *The Annals of Ulster* the picture one builds of Thorgest (rendered as Turgesius) is one antithetical to Harald Klak. This was not a politician partially converting for material gain, nor does he appear to have inserted himself into the larger game of thrones played by kings and courts. Thorgest was an agent of destruction, a charismatic chieftain or jarl for Ireland to deal with, his goals to obtain wealth and word-fame. In 832, Thorgest and his raiders unleashed themselves upon Clondalkin and Armagh, the latter perhaps the most important religious site in all of Ireland, raided three times in one month that year. Thorgest has a few later fables attached to him, some connected to High Medieval Irish foundational myths such as those collected in the *Cogad Gáedel re Gallaib* (*War of the Irish with the Foreigners*),[8] which describe how he and his vindictive wife Otta took up residence in the cathedral at Clonmacnoise and began using it as an anti-Christian outpost for human sacrifice and pagan veneration. There is no archaeological evidence for such heathen zealotry on this scale anywhere in the world. The exaggerations probably originate with Gerald of Wales or earlier writers. The twelfth-century *Topography of Ireland*, written by Gerald, preserves such myths, but none of the near-contemporary Irish annals do.[9]

The unreliable account in the first translated volume of the *Annals of the Four Masters*[10] associates Thorgest with further raids on Connacht, Mide, and Clonmacnoise, though without the zealotry. It is possible that Thorgest was one of those rare *vikingar* whose motivations were driven by his pagan beliefs, but it is more likely he was simply driven by the desire for treasure.[11] Thorgest captured Clonmacnoise and other ecclesiastical sites to use as base camps or springboards for future raids. These could be seen as prototypes for the army camps established by later Scandinavian raiding parties in Ireland, such as Dublin, as will be discussed later. Loughs Ree, Neagh, and Lene fell under his control according to the annals. In 843, an equally charismatic ruler of men, Rí Niall, met him in battle and won. Thorgest was said to have been ritually drowned in Lough Owel by Rí Niall, perhaps mirroring earlier bog burial traditions.[12] After 843, Thorgest, the terror of Irish monks, disappears in the record, but he lingers as the first recorded example of the threat in Ireland.

Having been targeted more than anywhere else in the western world, Ireland saw a huge increase in raids in the ninth century, as raiding fleets grew in size. Thorgest's camps were a precursor to the later *longphuirt* (slave trading bases) established along the southeastern coast by even more powerful rulers with larger forces at their disposal. Amongst the later legends and myths attributed to Thorgest it is said local ruler Máel Sechnaill governed *under* Thorgest. If true, that would make Thorgest another first; the first Scandinavian to exercise recorded dominion over an insular ruler.

The Isle of Sheppey was raided for the first time in 832. Perhaps enterprising crews were tempted by the prosperous trade further down the Thames at *Lundenwic* (London), which may well have been raided earlier in an unrecorded attack, as indicated by a layer of burnt ash. The targets of these viking raids were becoming larger. King Ecgberht of Wessex, who had spent his youth at Charlemagne's court, was said to have been defeated in 833/836 by a viking fleet off the coast of Dumnonia, modern Cornwall. In 838, Ecgberht struck back. Dumnonia had finally fallen, clearly not helped by the Scandinavians employed by the Britons as mercenaries; maybe they should have been offered a bigger bribe? The following year the Pictish kingdom of Fortriu probably collapsed, crushed by the *gentiles* according to the Irish annals. By 847, Frankish sources hint at the implosion of the nearby Dál Riatan sea kingdom, as vikingar 'got control of all the islands around Ireland'. These conquests (no longer raids) may have been the work of Norwegians, launching attacks from bases in Ireland like the ones established by Thorgest. As for Danish interests, they were for the time turned back on the Carolingian frontier into Saxony in response to further religious incursions in 833. Louis The Pious's sons were about to rebel against him. A wound had opened in the most formidable family in Christendom, and the Danes could smell it from afar.

mycel hæþen here

Just as the 'Vikings' did not appear out of thin air in 793, neither did the Great Heathen Army – the *mycel hæþen here* – appear on English shores in the year 865 with no forewarning.[13,14] *Mycel hæþen here* is a term given by the chroniclers of the *ASC* – we do not know what name, if any, these people gave themselves (*here* perhaps more correctly means 'raiders' rather than 'army', in 934 it is used to describe an English raid against Scotland). The Great Heathen Army was really just another, larger example of the viking armies that had been ravaging Carolingian territory for the better part of two decades. This army was not the first nor the last *hæpen here* to rampage through foreign territory, but it would be one of the most successful and well-documented. To analyse the damage and aftermath of the army's invasion of England we must look again to Frisia.

Viking Age Frisia was the site of many 'firsts' for the period; it was the first area to see such large-scale invasion and army activity in the form of Godfrid's assault in 810, it was the first to be parcelled off as a benefice to Scandinavian warriors as payment to characters like Harald Klak and Rorik of Dorestad, and it was likely the launchpad for the invasion of England in 865. But over thirty years prior to that we see Frankish sources noting a significant increase in the size of Scandinavian activity; gone were the days of isolated raids, Frisia was now home to armies. Nothing captures this better than the later *Vita*[15] attributed to Frisian missionary Liudger. Like Charlemagne, he too had a dreadful portent of times to come.

> In a dream I saw the Sun soaring over the earth, [fl]eeing[?] from the north, followed by dreadful clouds. In its light it passed me by and disappeared from sight, allowing darkness to cover all places along the coast. Large scores of Northmen are coming, bringing war and unimaginable destruction with them, leaving this friendly land bereft of life.

But would the actions of these 'Northmen' be quite so devastating as first assumed by Liudger (or his hagiographer)? The entry for 834 in the *Annals of St Bertin* mentions that the lands between Utrecht and Dorestad were ravaged. Dorestad, like Birka, Ribe, Kaupang, and *Lundenwic*, was another vital emporium along the North Sea trade routes and a prime target for viking raids. Dorestad was attacked again in 835 and in 836, prompting King Horik of the Danes to send emissaries to Louis' court to apologise (here we catch a glimpse of Horik playing both sides), but they were apparently killed. The language used in the annals to describe these attacks on Dorestad would lead one to believe that nothing would ever grow there again: '[they] burned the surrounding region'. The sheer frequency of the raids gives the impression of absolute devastation in Dorestad, and ultimately its annihilation. We must read between the lines. The fact that Dorestad could be 'completely destroyed' repeatedly, implies that in between these attack, it was being completely rebuilt. Dorestad's fortunes (as assessed through archaeological excavations of Wijk bij Duurstede)[16] appear to have dipped only slightly in the 840s and trade continued to some degree until the very late ninth century.[17] Dorestad would later be given as a valuable benefice to a Scandinavian warlord and continued to mint coins throughout that time,[18] so the emporium could not have been on its last legs as the annals suggest. Rather, the very fact of Dorestad being nominally ruled over by Scandinavians led annalists to exaggerate its destruction and to tarnish its reputation. Excavations in the 1970s revealed a series of jetties, workshops, and buildings facing the slow-moving river. Clearly, Dorestad continued to function to some extent for several decades after its 'destruction', regardless of who was in control. Christian Cooijmans has offered an alternative theory[19] that the gifting of Dorestad to Scandinavians was a long-term strategic move on behalf of Carolingian monarchs, a 'poisoned chalice'. Dorestad had not been defended by the coastal blockades established in 838, nor was it particularly economically important in the grand scheme of things. By turning the leader Rorik into 'Rorik of Dorestad', Louis had pacified one enemy and brought increased trade to an already fading market centre, one which would eventually disappear entirely in the 880s due to the silting of the Lek. Though Rorik of Dorestad still appears to have been a successful player of the game Harald Klak had failed to win.

The *Annals of Fulda* mention 'Northmen constructing ships' in 837, possibly off the coast of Walcheren, an island near Dorestad (now no longer an island but part of the Dutch province of Zeeland) and home to another vital trading point at *Walichrum*. The island had likely become a launchpad for raids by this decade. Harald Klak's son Hemming was killed attempting to repel these same raiders. Amidst border strife with Obotrites and King Horik, Louis the Pious would die in 840, and his empire was then split three ways among his squabbling sons. The people of Francia must have looked on in trepidation. Lothar, Louis II, and Charles all succeeded to subdivisions of Charlemagne's once-mighty territory, as did Louis' nephew, Pepin, in Aquitaine. The duty of dealing with the Danish threat now fell to them.

Lothar attempted to bring one Harald into his forces in 841. It is unclear if this was the now-ageing Harald Klak or another warrior, but they were offered Walcheren all the same (which leads one to believe it was a separate Harald, given that Klak's own son had died failing to recapture the island). Rorik, another Dane, was given lands in Friesland this same year. West Francia, the territory of Charles, appears to have borne the brunt for a time (possibly raids launched from Dorestad or Walcheren), but in 845 Hamburg was attacked, and Dorestad several more times, leading to Rorik's temporary imprisonment. Why Rorik was specifically blamed for these attacks on territory that he had just been given is interesting, but there was conflict observed among the three sons of Louis the Pious at this time.[20] By Lothar parcelling off land to a

Harald in Walcheren, and by Rorik being given land in Friesland, these brothers were basically passing the buck.[21, 22] Rorik, given Dorestad by this point, would try to prevent raids on his own territory by telling raiders to 'try over there'. It was a black comedy that lasted a decade or more. Only the smartest warlord could navigate the constant politicking and double-crossing. Skill in cunning, as seen in later skaldic verses, was highly valued.

In 850 this same Rorik had allied with a son of Harald Klak, Godafrid, to raid wider swathes of Frisia upon the death of King Horik of the Danes. Despite owning land in the region, Rorik would not waste an opportunity to take advantage of border strife. Two years later, Ghent was raided, and the same Godafrid returned with a fleet of '252 ships' to strike at Frisia.[23]

Dorestad seems to have enjoyed a long period of peace from this point on, under the watchful eye of Rorik. Likely he became very rich from the port activities there. Rorik was even granted more lands along the River Elbe near Saxony (which was raided in 858) as part of his supported claim to the throne of the Danes against King Horik II. This claim had the backing of Lothar in a way that echoes the earlier relationship between Harald Klak and Louis the Pious, but in a manner that seems much more beneficial to the Scandinavian claimant. Rorik largely disappears from the annals for a time, but it is known he maintained control over Dorestad until 879. He may have suffered a few temporary setbacks due to rival claimants and in 867 at the hands of the *Cokingi* (probably 'the people of the cogs'), but large swathes of Frisia were, by the 860s, under the control of one or more Scandinavians. These rulers may have officially been under the thumb of Carolingian monarchs, but clearly, they exercised their own power.

It was Rorik's Frisia that Bjorn Ironside (*járnsíða*) allegedly returned to in 862 following his dramatic voyage across the Mediterranean, according to William of Jumièges writing in the eleventh century.[24] In Saxo's *Deeds* and the earlier (unreliable) *History of St Cuthbert*, Ubbe, a leader of the Great Heathen Army, is described as a *dux Fresonum*, a 'leader of Frisians', or *Ubbe Fresicus*, 'Ubbe the Frisian'. Frisia was a staging post, a launchpad; increasingly large armies rallied at territory owned by their kinsmen. The Great Heathen Army that was about to land on English soil was composed of independent warbands, each led by their own 'king', working towards similar goals: conquest, wealth and power. They had to temporarily put aside their own differences for the greater good. It is unknown where the viking army launched from, but the political evidence leading up to 865 points to Frisia just across the water. Perhaps contingents also came from Ireland, home to several military bases by this point, and Scandinavia itself. It was not a monolithic force that came to England and then remained until it was defeated; it was reinforced repeatedly by raiders, traders, and family units travelling from elsewhere to the British Isles to camps like Torksey[25] and Aldwark.[26] Contingents splintered off to plunder elsewhere around the world. In 870, a *micel sumorliði* ('great summer fleet') joined the rogues already occupying England. Ælfred's defeat of this army in 878 was only the defeat of the most immediate threat; these *mycel hæpen heres* would threaten Europe for the remainder of the ninth century.

While York was captured in England in 867, Lothar was rallying forces against Frisia. While the camp at Torksey was established in Lincolnshire in 872, King Charles of West Francia was engaging in peace talks with Rorik of Dorestad and the Friso-Dane Rodulf[27] over territorial issues. In 876, as it seemed the invaders were about to overwhelm one of the last redoubts of leadership in England, Wessex, a revolt by Frisians against their new Scandinavian conquerors occurred in an unknown location over stolen treasure. While this 'Viking world' was connected, it also contained individual parts – Frisia has been highlighted here to illustrate the links between the Great Heathen and other armies, and how the invasion of England was a long time coming and the result of various land grants and larger forces just over the North Sea. However, the rest of Europe and beyond were also suffering at the hands of the Scandinavians to various extents; the Earn and Tay Valleys of Pictish Scotland were ravaged in 836, a fleet of *Rus* attempted to besiege Constantinople in 839, Noirmoutier saw the first Frankish army camp in 843, Seville was sacked in 844, Paris in 845, Brittany in 846; and in England, there was a gargantuan battle in 851 which saw King Æðelwulf of Wessex triumph over his opponents.

One thing that unites all these areas, from Ireland in the West to Constantinople in the East, was that viking activity was increasing. More wealth brought greater reputation, and greater reputation brought more warriors. Armies like the *mycel hæpen here* were an inevitability.

Sceadugenga

England would not drown in this flood. It is tempting now to shift the perspective of this Viking Age narrative to the eyes of King Ælfred and the loyal *fyrds* who came to his aid in the sweeping campaigns of 871-878. The research by Dawn Hadley and Julian Richards in their seminal work on the Great Heathen Army cannot be surpassed; the impetus then is to view these conflicts in a new light. Think not of Ælfred as a noble English hero beating all odds, nor of the army leaders – Guthrum, Halfdan, Ivarr, Bacsecg, and others – as villainous, squabbling jarls. Instead, flip the perspective: these Scandinavians were conquering new territory in a way not too far removed from Charlemagne's land grabs of Saxony and Frisia a hundred years before. We view the the army through a Christian lens and so are predisposed to see it as a bloodthirsty beast that stalked the land, but the archaeological record leaves only a faint shadow of this supposed violence. We saw with Dorestad that there was no significant destruction, the mint never stopped creating coins, and the surrounding countryside did not see a reduction in trade. After an initial short-term calamity, the invasion of a foreign force, life for the merchant and farmer would have continued as normal. Nowhere is this more apparent than at the well-documented site of Flixborough, near the Isle of Axholme in the old kingdom of Lindsey.

We have Henry of Huntingdon to thank for the depiction of 'Anglo-Saxon England' as a heptarchy, a land of seven kingdoms.[28] Wessex, Sussex, Essex, Kent, Northumbria, East Anglia, and Mercia. At the time of the army's invasion, Sussex and Essex had long since lost their political independence and would have been no better or worse off than the territory of the Middle Angles further east. Northumbria, too, which we nowadays view as a singular entity, had only been a discrete unit a few times in the past, notably under Kings Edwin, Oswald, and Oswiu in the 600s. Northumbria in 867 was in the middle of a bloody civil war fought between rival claimants to the throne, Ælle and Osberht. Ælle was said to have been 'blood eagled' by the sons of Ragnar Loðbrók Sigurdsson, who, according to *Ragnarssona þáttr* (*Tale of Ragnar's Sons*),[29] a story found in the fourteenth-century Icelandic manuscript *Hauksbók*, cut open his ribs and pulled out his lungs. The term 'blood eagle' may be a distorted reference to one of the traditional Old English and Old Norse beasts of battle, the eagle, which roamed the battlefield after a fight and pecked and clawed at the backs of fallen foes.[30] Eagles are not carrion feeders. The literary concept of 'blood-eagling' within skaldic poetry is grisly and sometimes associated with Óðinn: 'the figure of an eagle' was 'carved on the back', followed by cutting 'the ribs all from the backbone' drawing 'the lungs there out'. All the sources that mention the 'blood eagle' were written after Scandinavia was converted to Christianity, half-remembering (or imagining) a bloody heathen past. The phrase is a hybrid of the most vilified heathen tropes, misunderstood and then dialed up to shock Christian audiences. Contemporary mentions of eagles and scavenging birds in skaldic verses are employed as alliterative kennings; being given a 'blood eagle' was to be killed and left for bird food. An 'eagle of blood' might just mean a raven.

The story of the 'blood-eagling' of Ælle and not Osberht suggests that King Ælle was killed separately to his rival, perhaps in a pitched battle outside of York and not in the city itself where Osberht was supposedly felled. Like Ælle's literary ribcage, Northumbria was split in two, with these two claimants representing its two parts, Deira (based around York) and Bernicia (based around Bamburgh) – two more kingdoms to add to Henry's seven. Lindsey must also not be forgotten, a sizeable territory east of Mercia and south of Deira, situated around what is now the Humber Wash down to Lincoln.

This was where Flixborough was located, a wealthy site with both ecclesiastical and secular features. Thanks to the excavations and reports of Christopher Loveluck and others, we know of uninterrupted occupation of the site from at least 550 into the mid-1500s.[31, 32, 33, 34] We can pinpoint exactly when a likely Scandinavian presence reached the location and assumed ownership. Place names of local suburbs like Conesby (Old Norse for 'king's farm') confirm this. Between Phases 3 and 4 of the occupation layers, dated tentatively to no earlier than 860, there is a layer of burnt ash above the already prosperous ninth-century settlement and its rectangular wooden buildings, encircled by a run-off ditch and with a kingly hall positioned right in the centre of what was an earlier entirely different building.

It could be that this layer of burnt ash is evidence of an industrial fire, but the dates point to Scandinavian intrusion; the later renovations of the middle of the site also add weight to this theory. Though this appears to have been the only change for the residents of Flixborough. Prior to the 860s, they would have been paying taxes to a local magnate, after the 860s, they would have been paying taxes to a foreign magnate. Fortunes dipped for a short while, for the material record shows less evidence of inter-regional and international trade, but that is to be expected, for the 870s and 880s was a time of warfare across England. By the end of the tenth century, however, this new Anglo-Scandinavian Flixborough

Reconstruction of a typical Viking Age magnate's hall, a far cry from the average farmstead. Many new Scandinavian residences were erected across England in the wake of the Great Heathen Army.

was ready and roaring to go; richer than ever before, with evidence of a significantly prosperous whaling industry on-site.

The hinterlands of Flixborough would have played a key role in the development of the site, the Isle of Axholme included, a marshy archipelago with good arable yield and fisheries. The PAS record for the Isle is dominated by lead net-sinker weights; all appear to have been made in Flixborough. For the more famous site of York, by 930 we have the 1970/80s Coppergate excavations to thank for bringing 'Vikings' into the spotlight once again, not as raiders, but as traders. Coppergate, just one small market corner of *Eoferwic* (the name *Jórvík* emerged slightly later), was very close to becoming cosmopolitan, with planned timber tenements and market stalls backing onto residences occupied full-time by local Anglo-Scandinavians.[35, 36] We do not currently know how *Eoferwic* went from a marginally successful trading settlement situated around modern Fishergate in the 860s to the wealthy maritime hub based around Coppergate in the 930s.[37, 38] There is a transition period missing, but it is likely the process on the ground was similar to Flixborough. The top layer of society, the military and economic elite of *Eoferwic*, was replaced by foreign usurpers or turned into puppet rulers, while for everyone else life changed little; there were new dialects on the streets, and new trade goods in the markets, but they still paid taxes.

The Scandinavian occupation of the north of England in this period was marked not just by the occupation of rural and proto-urban sites but also by army camps. Aldwark, Repton, and Torksey are the chief examples, and the work of Jane Kershaw and Jane Harrison has revealed a military enclosure in the Coquet Valley, Northumberland,[39] probably from the northern contingent of the army which split in the 870s, and there is emerging evidence of fortlets around York. These 'D-shaped camps' as they are sometimes known are seen not just across England but also in Ireland with the *longphuirt* and, surprisingly, in Portugal.

Viking army camps were not strictly just camps. They display variable archaeological signatures. Some, like Torksey, resemble the earliest layers of seasonal central places like sixth-century Flixborough and eighth-century Ribe, emerging centres of trade and production. Others, as seen across Pocklington and Repton, appear to have been earthwork headquarters for roaming military crews. Repton may have been only a small section of a much larger camp, revealed through burial excavations at nearby Heath Wood; likewise, 'Howe Hill' near Aldwark might reveal the burial site of leaders who camped there.

There was a grander narrative at play here. Scandinavian vikingar and their families and merchants did not *peacefully* reoccupy England – there was an elite class already living here and the agriculturally based society of the locals did not take kindly to their arrival. King Ælfred led the resistance, first through peacekeeping following the footsteps of contemporary ruler King Charles of West Francia, and then through guerilla warfare. Insular sources for the Ælfredan wars refer to repeated instances when Ælfred was forced to sue for peace (or *frið*) with the enemy.[40] Felix Liebemann translates the Old English word *frið* not as 'peace' but as 'legal order'.[41] This term *frið* (pronounced 'frith') only occurs in relation to the peacemaking between insular and Scandinavian armies, not other kingdoms. Ælfred was following the earlier work of Charles, who had essentially been creating an unofficial guidebook on how and how not to sue for peace when faced with viking incursions. After the siege of Paris in 845, seven thousand pounds of silver were given to the invading army in exchange for peace, but later Charles would demonstrate extreme cunning by fortifying his rivers with bridges *after* crews of longships had already sailed down them, forcing them to then pay him on the way back upstream.[42, 43] The international connections between the West Saxon and Frankish courts are well observed, so advice was probably passed to and fro.

Ælfred's peace-making attempts truly shone in the 870s when, through successive meetings with leaders of the army between battles, he appears to have shifted tactics from merely paying bribes to insisting on the swearing of oaths. An oath represented the reputation of a man, and word-fame lasted longer than gold and silver. *The Lay of Völund* from the *Poetic Edda* emphasises the importance of oaths.[44] Exemplifying the communications between Wessex and West Francia, in 873 and 882 Danes were forced to swear on oaths to not 'damage [the Frankish kingdom] nor anyone in it'.

Several of these oaths (such as the peace recorded on arm rings in 876) were immediately broken, but what we are seeing here is perhaps not a betrayal of a sacred promise by Scandinavian leaders but their bending of the rules. In 876, according to Asser's *Life of Ælfred*,[45] the rings the king of Wessex requested Guthrum to swear on were gifted alongside Christian relics. Breaking an oath overseen by a foreign deity was not such a bad thing. That would be, of course, until God *became* a Scandinavian deity.

From the perspective of the army leaders, these mighty jarls and kings who had made their fortune in smaller raids between 830-865, we must view King Ælfred as a *sceadugengan*, a 'shadow walker' from Old English folklore.[46] He was a ruthless politician who played the game as well as Scandinavian *vikingar* could; reading between the lines and bending the rules to suit himself. East Anglia, Deira, Lindsey, and large swathes of Mercia all fell to the Great Heathen Army but not Wessex.

A golden arm ring found in Wendover, England, dated to the tenth century. Arm rings like these were both portable wealth and symbols of trust and loyalty. They are frequently mentioned in skaldic verses.

Every time conquest was attempted, Ælfred slipped through their fingers. From the Athelney marshes in 877 and 878, there is an obvious irony in Ælfred's raids into Danish-occupied territory. From a marshy enclave, a West Saxon king was raiding beyond enemy frontlines, looting goods, and disappearing before the forces could do anything about it.

Force meets force, and King Ælfred was the first in a long line of West Saxon opponents who would test the Scandinavians across the British Isles.

Once and Future Kings

In 876, the *ASC* mentions how army ruler Halfdan 'shared out the land' in Northumbria between his men to settle and plough. This fits with the recently discovered Coquet Valley site, overlooking the Cheviot Hills. Perhaps this split in the army was between a northern contingent happy to settle their already vast conquests, and the more entrepreneurial (perhaps younger) warriors still keen to conquer more territory, unhappy with what they had already achieved.

As will be discussed later, the identity of northern England shifted gradually because of this army's occupation, eventually creating an Anglo-Scandinavian milieu. The reasons for land grabbing are obvious, the natural next stage after raiding; land was a more valuable target than slaves and silver. To own land in a foreign country and to become ruler of that country was to set yourself up for life. But why was this not possible in the Scandinavian homelands? King Horik II is one of the last few Danish kings to appear in the historical record for a while. It wouldn't be until the tenth century when the Kingdom of the Danes, now as Denmark, would reemerge as a centralised polity. Norway and Sweden for this century are even more obscure; *Vita Ansgarii* mentioned a King Bjorn resident in Birka, but it is highly improbable that this individual extended dominion over all modern Sweden. The country did not exist in the Viking Age as we know it today, and neither did Norway. There was undoubtedly a Norwegian element in England, just as there were Frisians and Danes; were these raiders and kings leaving *Norðvegr* to obtain wealth to then send home or were they leaving their home altogether? And why would they have to do that in the first place? It is clear some degree of political centralisation occurred in southwest Norway in the second half of the ninth century, around the modern provinces of Agder, Vestfold, and Vingulmark for example. Territories which had previously had their own kings were becoming minor polities governed by higher rulers. Why was this? Was there a historically identifiable figure uniting large swathes of what had previously been territory owned by the Danes? The answer is complicated, and to best analyse it we must look at another national figure from another country's foundation legend; his name is Arthur.[47]

King Harald Fairhair was the son of Halfdan the Black and Ragnhild Sigurdsdottir. He would father, according to sagas, the equally legendary Erik Bloodaxe and, supposedly, Haakon the Good who would be fostered in a court in Wessex at the behest of his father.[48] Harald's story is one of unification, strength, of dynastic marriages to secure bloodlines and fantastical stories filled with whimsy. He was 'Fairhair' because he refused to cut his hair until he had united all the petty kingdoms of The Northern Way under his own banner. Such a character would go on to reign into the middle of the tenth century, dying at the exceptional age of eighty-two.

We have no contemporary sources that mention Harald Fairhair, king of all Norway. We do have later sagas, of course, compiled in the High Medieval Period about three hundred years after the events they are describing, and Fairhair is a recurring character spread across the 'genres'. The *Fornaldarsögur* or 'legendary sagas' mention him as the latest and greatest in a heroic bloodline stretching back to times ancient even from the perspective of the ninth century; on the other hand, the *Íslendingasögurnar* or 'sagas of Icelanders' usually refer to Fairhair as a shadowy antagonist lurking in the background. He is chiefly the main reason for the mass exodus to Iceland, which saw such a passionate anti-monarchist republic form over the ninth and tenth centuries, characterised by blood feuds and regional assemblies. It is dangerous to take the sagas at face value, as it is difficult to take even earlier historical sources (such as the annals we have analysed thus far). Perhaps our only piece of vernacular 'evidence' for Harald Fairhair's existence comes from skaldic poems, praise-chants for kings in their courts, written down after the Viking Age but composed from earlier oral readings. *Hrafnsmál*,[49] *Eiríksmál*,[50] *Hákonardrápa*,[51] and *Hákonarmál*[52, 53] have all been dated by Old Norse poetry experts and linguists to the tenth century, but none of them mention Harald Fairhair.

Hrafnsmál, however, mentions an individual called Haraldr *Lúfa*, and the others describe his sons (these being Haakon the Good and Erik Bloodaxe). All we know of this figure is that he won a military engagement at Hafrsfjord (traditionally dated to 871) near modern Stavanger in southwest Norway and that he took a Danish wife. It is possible this Haraldr is also the 'Haraldus' who gave King Æthelstan of England a gilded longship in 939, as mentioned by William of Malmesbury,[54] but it is just as likely that this Haraldr is Harald Fairhair, who is for all intents and purposes a legendary figure.

Like Arthur, Harald Fairhair emerges from the mists of time to fill the gaps where the written record falls short. He is the ultimate king, a unifying force of divine wisdom who crushes the bad habits of pre-existing and petty under-kings. Like Arthur, Fairhair embodies the virtues that make real kings supposedly so great (gift-giving, a stable and peaceful rule, luck in battle), and Fairhair has a long and well-attested series of myths relating to him marrying scores of beautiful women. Fairhair lacks the thirteenth-century heraldry and fairytale escapades that have solidified Arthur in popular culture today, but he is certainly closer to King Arthur conceptually than any real identifiable person who lived and died in the Viking Age. There very well may have been a Harald/Haraldr/Haraldus who pushed out rival warlords in southwest Norway in the ninth century,[55] but this figure never exercised any visible dominion over central and northern Norway, nor Jämtland on the border of Sweden, or the western fjords of modern Oslo. The *idea* of Harald Fairhair lies in a different history entirely, in the need for an Icelandic origin story amidst thirteenth-century fears of royal overreach.[56] The Battle of Hafrsfjord, such an important part of Norway's own foundation story, may have not even been a battle of unification, but a defence against enemies attempting to invade.

The archaeology of the Agder region indicates a series of halls yet to be excavated that may have functioned as part of a royal network of taxation, but this is just one small region in the southwest, not the entire Northern Way. As with Arthur, Fairhair is presented in some histories as an undisputed fact, but there is far more evidence to support him not having existed at all than there is to prove his existence.[57] Even his famous epithet of 'Fairhair', written in the earliest sources as *Hárfagri*, is originally used to describe Harald Sigurdsson of Norway, better known as Harald Hardrada (*harðráði*), a real person. Such a figure would have been at odds with the long-standing non-monarchist tradition on the island.

Such a *Hárfagri* would become, over time, *the* traditional enemy, much in the same way that King Arthur has become *the* traditional king for English, Welsh, Cornish, and British identities. The final similarity between fictitious kings Arthur and Harald would be that both were likely based on a composite of several real people. Arthur, for instance, is an idealised hodgepodge of Ambrosius Aurelianus, other legendary characters like Urien of Rheged, and probably some contemporary Brythonic warrior fighting on the Mercian border in the ninth century.[58] Fairhair, like Arthur, is a hybrid monarch, a composite created in the High Medieval Period and transported back through time, blending other *real* Haralds together in the process. It is highly unlikely, though not impossible, that the ruler of southwest Norway who allegedly fathered Haakon and Erik Bloodaxe lived to be eighty-two. If he did, then he would have almost lived to see his son eclipse him in fame: but can his *son* even be attested as a real person?

The Always Army

What we do know for certain is that the victory in 878 of King Ælfred and Wessex at the Battle of Edington was an end for large swathes of Guthrum's forces; a significantly more 'real' monarch than Fairhair. Guthrum was forced into baptism and to swear oaths of legal order on rings and relics that now – crucially – meant something to him and his men. Guthrum was given territory in East Anglia that had by 878 probably already fallen under total Scandinavian dominion anyway. So, too, had most of England apart from Wessex and Bernicia, which both exercised some degree of independence, though fraught with difficulty. It is tempting to view Edington as an ultimate defeat for the invaders, but it was merely a temporary setback; both the *Annals of St Bertin* and the *Annals of Fulda* describe a sizeable force arriving in Ghent in 879 which went on to plunder the town of Deventer three years later. This attack, well attested by archaeological remains, was likely orchestrated by some warbands or contingents that were not content to share out the land as Halfdan's northern army had in England. It is unknown which warlord or king was leading this viking army, but they were likely as wealthy and respected as the ones who had charged headlong onto British shores in 865. Layers of black earth found in both Zutphen and Deventer in The Netherlands and dated to the last quarter of the ninth century are most likely from these incendiary raids, which can almost be seen as a 'last hurrah' for the stragglers of these armies. At Wapse, an island by Zutphen, lead gaming pieces were found matching those uncovered from the army settlement at Torksey in Lindsey.[59]

Across the North Sea, viking armies were utilising islands and marshlands to their advantage in military campaigns against fortified settlements. At least one skeleton has been identified from the attack on Zutphen, and the possible remains of a child – a sober reminder that these events had very real and terrible consequences. While thus far we have attempted to ground the Viking Age in the politics and behaviour of the time, as we will soon see, Early Medieval Scandinavians were from a world that was – as Neil Price puts it – 'very different, very old, and very odd'.[60] The mindset of the vikingr separated them from those they were attacking.

The armies temporarily repelled from England by the political and military recovery of Ælfred's Wessex were now fixed on new targets. Paris was besieged for a second time in 885-886, and the weak peace-keeping attempts of new ruler Charles the Fat were only attracting further raiders, huge payments of silver drawing them like flies to a corpse. A *coup d'état* occurred amidst this military activity which saw a new, stronger, ruler by the name of Count Odo take charge. West Francia had pushed back against the viking armies; they now had their own Ælfred. Between 886 and 890, just as the real Ælfred of Wessex and Guthrum (now baptised with a Christian name) formalised the territorial and legal divisions previously agreed in the Treaty of Wedmore in 878, separating English and Danish-ruled areas of the country by rivers and Roman roads, the viking armies operating in Frisia headed back over the Channel. They were a cluster of large raiding groups moving between territories whenever they became weak enough to strike. The spread of information between these advanced maritime contingents was rapid; they knew when West Francia was well-defended and when it had political weaknesses, just as they did for Wessex.

In 892, an army perhaps even larger than the original arrived on the shores of southeastern England, establishing themselves at a fortified coastal base at *Beamfleot* (Benfleet). This army was likely made up of the stragglers who had been expelled from Francia the year before by King Arnulf. The leaders of the army, Gudfrid and Sigefrid, had been slaughtered along with so many of their men that the River Dyle 'filled with bodies'. Francia was a no-go area, so why not try England? Unfortunately for these new leaders, one being Haesten, the West Saxon government was no longer unfamiliar with viking tactics. An aged King Ælfred passed on what he had learned from the 860s and 870s to his son, Eadward. We see Eadward's name on charters in Kent from 895 onwards,[61] and it is in that same year that he presumably exercised some degree of military oversight in recapturing *Beamfleot* from the invaders, alongside his father. Much has been written on King Ælfred's health, but nobody can deny that according to the *ASC*, the charters, and the archaeology of the later *burhs*, he was a conspicuously strong-willed man. It is a shame he appears in no sagas. Nor does this conflict, apart from an imagined drama involving the legendary Ragnar and King Ælle's death at the hands of his sons. Ragnar's eulogy appears in the twelfth-century poem *Krákumál*; this mythical composite met his end in a Northumbrian snake pit (the very idea makes little sense), which served as the vengeful motive for the Great Heathen Army, who went on to storm Wessex. From the perspective of real raiders, southern England was not an arena in which to wreak revenge, but an opportunity to gain wealth. These opportunities were dwindling.

In 898, however, the scales tipped in the other direction. Odo of West Francia had perished, and during the interregnum new viking armies struck, sailing down the Carolingian waterways. The year before, King Ælfred's new fleet of warships defended the Sussex coast from raiders just as a another viking force appeared on the banks of the Loire. These large warbands were presumably communicating with one another, sharing tips and expertise – but also quite possibly lies. These Scandinavian warlords and raid leaders were not pig-headed brutes hell-bent on destruction, they were operators in a very complex political network. And they were very good at it. For the vikingr mindset, there was no shame in running from a fight for richer, easier pickings elsewhere.

As with the death of any great ruler, Ælfred of Wessex's demise that year left a power vacuum, A succession dispute began between his heir Eadward and his nephew Æthelwold. Æthelwold exemplifies the ever-changing allegiances of armies and mercenaries. He was a West Saxon, and by 901 an exile. His army which lost at the Battle of the Holme the following year would be made up of East Anglians (now ruled over by someone called Eohric or *Haruc*), raiders from afar, and most probably Deirans and Northumbrians. The idea of 'England' did not exist in the minds of most people in the ninth and tenth centuries – it would be forced upon the north through violent conquest. Those in Deira (Yorkshire), based at this point on a multi-ethnic urban centre of Scandinavians and *Ænglisć* in York, may well have felt a greater tie to the Danes than the West Saxons so far south. Above Watling Street, the traditional boundary that seems to have marked the split between Ælfredan and Anglo-Scandinavian territory, the country was just that, Anglo-Scandinavian. The magnate's residence excavated at Goltho, near Lincoln is a fine example of this.[62] This was a wealthy estate with a sizeable hall, and the site was occupied continuously from before Scandinavian settlement to the eleventh century, and there is no suggestion from the toponymy or archaeology that the reigning elite was ever displaced. As at Flixborough, just a few miles north of Goltho, throughout 'Danish territory' were the locals. England was, prior to the ninth century's foreign invasions, already a multi-ethnic collection of polities. This would continue.

The final clause of Ælfred and Guthrum's treaty states that 'no slaves or freemen might go over to the [Danes]'; in so doing, a dichotomy was imposed upon the British Isles. To be one with West Saxon reforms was to be 'English', to be an enemy was to be 'Danish'. Upon Ælfred's death, the *ASC* states that he was 'king over all the English race except that part which was under Danish control'. In the other corner, there was Æthelwold, whom the twelfth-century *Annals of S. Neots* describe as *rex paganorum* and *rex Danorum*.

Æthelwold's 'pagan-Danish' army was defeated in 902, and four years later East Anglia had nominally fallen under the control of Wessex, its ruler Eohric, dead. The final attempt by any sizeable Scandinavian army (or perhaps, by this point, an *Anglo*-Scandinavian army) appears to have been the Battle of Tettenhall of 910. Here, Ælfred's progeny King Eadward and Lady Æthelflæd of Mercia asserted further dominance, crushing an alliance between new villains Eowils, Ivar, and Healfdene somewhere in the Midlands. England, once a territory of divided hostile kingdoms with a *fyrd* (levy-based) army system that could not respond fast enough to the rapid raiding of Scandinavian fleets, was now becoming more and more consolidated. In Ælfred's time, and largely through the reigns of his children, the system funded by the *Burghal Hidage*[63] saw the widespread creation of fortified earthworks and defensive towns up and down West Saxon and English-Mercian territory. These *burhs* acted as roadblocks for any enterprising raiding force attempting to cross borders and steal, and they each had a standing army of trained warriors. The *burhs* are perhaps the most visually conspicuous aspect of the English resistance to the ninth-century onslaught. Like Charles the Bald's bridge-building, the West was now facing up to and answering the challenge posed by Scandinavian warlords. So was Ireland.

New Haunts

Ireland had been raided and settled more than anywhere else in the western hemisphere throughout the ninth century. In 837, just as Walcheren was being juggled between Danish and Carolingian control on the continent, the Irish annals record one Soxulfr leading a fleet of sixty (and later over a hundred) longships down the River Liffey towards Dublin.

Duibhlinn had been a small monastic site on the east coast of Ireland since the eighth century, named after the black pools of water of the Liffey. It was not until the middle of the ninth that it truly started to grow into a proto-urban centre, as best seen through the brilliant Woodquay excavations documented by Patrick Wallace and others.[64, 65] *The Annals of the Four Masters* record activity in Dublin from as early as the third century, but such ancient references should be used only in tandem with archaeological evidence, and by far the greater part of Dublin's material record appears no earlier than the middle of the ninth.

Dublin's importance only started with a Scandinavian presence; by the seventh century, the area around the modern church of St Michael le Pole near Chancery Lane and Ship Street has been identified by some as the ecclesiastical centre of the Uí Fergusa, a minor religious polity with ruling abbots.[66] The last of these Abbots, Fergus, was likely one of many victims enslaved or killed following the Scandinavian takeover of the site in 841, if not twenty years earlier, when nearby Howth was raided. The reason would, of course, be the black pool; ideal for naval inroads further west into Ireland but also across the small but dangerous Irish Sea to Scandinavian holdouts in the Hebrides, Orkney, Scotland, Wales, and later, Mercia. But Dublin was not the sole Scandinavian encampment in Ireland. Two years prior, one was established at Lough Neagh, called in modern terms a *longphort*, essentially a part-military camp, part-slave market, and part-production centre, and there is emerging evidence that the earthworks identified at Woodstown predate Dublin. The archaeological record associated with *longphuirt*, principally in Dublin, reveals that these were comparatively urbanised areas, very wealthy centres of local trade.[67] The Dublin record chimes with the Coppergate excavations of York; both were multi-ethnic proto-urban centres with a tightly packed street layout and a variety of buildings and shops. People worked beads, tanned leather, and turned wood on lathes to make bowls and cutlery; they made combs, bred livestock, led slaves onto longships, and lived, loved, and died in situ. Dublin, like York, was a world unto itself.[68] As in Scandinavia, there was the rural sphere, and the urban. It is likely the rapid proliferation of the latter in the later Viking Age played a significant role in the evolution of that 'very different' mindset.

In 839 the final frontlines of Pictavia were all but erased by Scandinavian forces. The Pictish kingdom of Fortriu, centred around Burghead and Moray and led by Kings Eoghann and Áed, had more or less been conquered.[69] As seen with England further south, it is likely the top layer of society was all killed or enslaved, with everyone else falling into line shortly after. It is worth noting the language barriers (or bridges) present at the time. Old English and Old Norse were both dialect groups composed of numerous different subdivisions that would have been mutually comprehensible. Many excellent scholarly pieces have been written (and performed) showing how conversations between Old English and Old Norse speakers would have flowed.[70] At some point, these languages probably mingled to create an insular hybridised dialect in Northern England, if they hadn't already, prior to ninth-century settlement, through frequent mixing across the North Sea. Importantly, all these North Sea Germanic languages derive from a common root and thus shared certain similarities. The languages spoken in Atlantic Scotland, Wales, Cornwall, and in various pockets across the remainder of the British Isles were from Celtic linguistic roots; the Britons and Picts spoke variations of Brythonic, closer to modern Welsh. The Irish, the Scotti, were likely speaking Goidelic variations of the same language group. There were far fewer crossovers between Celtic languages and Germanic, so communication between those with Scandinavian and Brythonic heritage would have been more difficult.

In central England, the Brythonic kingdom of Elmet (based around West Yorkshire) likely remained a firmly identifiable ethnic polity judging by toponymic evidence (like the villages of Sherburn-*in-Elmet* and Barwick-*in-Elmet*), so it is possible these linguistic issues occurred further south as well. Language plays a huge role in how societies function, and large swathes of Scotland had been reoccupied by an entirely new population speaking a new dialect: Old Norse.

Things were different in Ireland. Based in their *longphuirt*, Scandinavians formed enclaves of resistance on the east coast against the native Irelanders. Ireland, as mentioned, was made up of many more polities than England, and so there would be no easy chain of conquest as seen with the Great Heathen Army's annexations. There, East Anglia fell, and then so did Deira, and then so did Mercia and Lindsey. With Ireland, while the kingdoms were smaller and subservient to a cluster of peripatetic overlords, there were many more of them, with no identifiable seat of government or centralised authority to overpower. The Scandinavians in Ireland would borrow elements of this insular culture, and vice versa. L*ongphuirt* like Dublin were very important not just for the Scandinavians but also the Irelanders. Dublin, in fact, would be juggled between the two for quite some time. The work of Clare Downham[71] has identified a plausible link between one of the leaders of the Great Heathen Army, Ivarr *beinlausi* (commonly known as 'the Boneless', which probably means 'detestable') and the progenitor of the Uí Imarr dynasty centred around Dublin, which went on to become one of the main players in the first half of the tenth century. This dynasty saw Dublin reach unparalleled wealth and prosperity, with well-attested trade links over the Irish Sea to sites like Llanbedrogh,[72] on Anglesey, Chester, and down the Rivers Dee, Ribble, and Ouse into Yorkshire.

The Uí Imarr dynasty represents the evolution of scale we have been seeing thus far. This was, nominally, a royal enterprise that generated extreme wealth via the ownership of land and trade ports and the taxation that came with them. Ivarr and his kin were no longer simply thieves or occupiers, they were residents. It wasn't just the elite of course. As observed through Torksey's material record, most people travelling with the armies and other such forces were not soldiers, not kings, but merchants, family groups, and everyday folk, a significant proportion of them enslaved.

The first recorded Irish-Scandinavian alliance occurred in 842 in Donegal, but this wouldn't be the last coming together of cultures. The Bedale Hoard, discovered in the eponymous village in 2014, included hacksilver ingots, gold sword rings, and silver jewellery. There was a giant torc (neck ring) made up of thousands of melted-down coins. This torc, and a few of the brooches alongside it, were made in the style of other material from western England and eastern Ireland; a Hiberno-Norse artistic blending.

The hoard was buried in a small village in North Yorkshire which would have housed the ruins of a Roman villa. It also contained goods from the Arabic and *Rus* worlds. The Bedale Hoard delineates the economies and trade routes of the 'Viking world'. So too does the Cuerdale Hoard,[73] probably buried about three decades later following the expulsion of the elite of Dublin. In 902, the Irish had seized control from the Uí Imarr dynasty, at least temporarily. Dublin, passed back and forth thanks to its inordinate wealth generated by the slave trade, became the core of late ninth- and tenth-century activity in Ireland.

There would also be Scandinavian versus Scandinavian conflict among the bogs and heath plains of this westernmost isle. In 848, Irish sources describe the arrival of the *dubgaill* (the dark foreigners) who immediately started battling the resident *finngaill* (fair foreigners) for supremacy of the *longphuirt* along the coast at sites like Cork, Wexford, Limerick, and Waterford. The naming conventions here appear to be in relation to the length of time the Scandinavians had been in Ireland; those who

The neck ring from the Bedale Hoard, created in a unique 'West Viking' style blending Danish and Hiberno-Norse styles to form something entirely new.

had arrived with Thorgest or earlier raiders of the first half of the ninth century were the 'fair' foreignerss. The new arrivals, with their own claims to Ireland's wealth, were the 'dark' foreigners; a new and perhaps more dangerous problem for both Irish and Scandinavian alike.[74] The Isle of Man and parts of Wales were also part of this Irish Sea economy, mirroring as it did the larger North Sea just beyond England. This 'sea kingdom' (a thalassocracy) was spread between the waterways of Orkney in the north all the way down to Cornwall and was ruled over by autonomous hydrarchies and pirate lords.

There was resistance, of course, as there was in England and Francia. By 852, the royal Mael Sechnaill was attempting to unite the disparate *túatha* of Ireland in league against the new invaders, and Rhodri Mawr of Gwynedd (in northwest Wales), probably originally from Man, landed significant blows on raiders like Orm, who in 855 raided between Ireland and Wales only to be defeated both times. Likely, though, these raiders did not split their world into 'West' and 'East' as we do now when discussing

Shadow

the Viking Age. The opportunities down the *Austrvegr* in Novgorod and Kyiv were likely just as enticing (and reachable) as those in Ireland.

To look ahead slightly, this movement is best demonstrated by the expulsion of the Hiberno-Norse from Dublin in 902, only for them to reappear immediately occupying land around Chester in The Wirral in the same year. Certain factions led by one Ingilmundr emerged as a new threat following the defeat of Æthelwold at the Holme. The English became stuck between two separate waves of armies in the first quarter of the tenth century, with some overlap. Eadward The Elder dealt with Scandinavian incursions in East Anglia while Lady Æthelflæd and her husband Æthelred of Mercia tackled the incoming wave of exiled elites from Dublin in Danish-Mercia. It is likely some Hiberno-Norse made up a segment of the enemy force at Tettenhall, in 910.

If it was not Dublin being striven over, then it was York. The two centres (and innumerable nodes between them) formed a very useful artery that cut through England for both military and economic purposes. As West Saxon hegemony started to extend upwards into Mercia and Lindsey, so too did Hiberno-Norse dominion extend over Northumbria. Regional identities, not national, would play the biggest role moving forward.

North and South

Even today, there is a North-South divide in England. Use any cross-country train connecting, say, Leeds-Manchester or York-Lancaster and you will see the difference between the money invested in these transport links and those available to Londoners. London, with its gravity-distorting pull on the map of England, feels like it has always been the centre of everything. It hasn't. In the first few decades of the tenth century, attention was split between the many peoples of England, and at the centre of much of the conflict and trade was York.

As stated, the average farmer of Deira, Lindsey, or Mercia, or even those with more local identities, like the average Islonian (from the Isle of Axholme), would have likely cared not whether they were paying taxes to a foreign or an insular lord, provided they could understand what they said and were left alone to till the soil. The violence left off the page when the *ASC* talks about the 'victorious' reconquests of 'lost' territory by Eadward and Æthelflæd obscures the truth that many everyday folks living in 'the Danelaw' were probably quite content to remain in it. Being brought into the fold of Wessex and this new alien idea of *Anglalond* meant sacrificing, to some degree, a sense of local, tribal, and regional identity, something that had not happened with the Great Heathen Army's invasion in the 860s. These enemy groups which Eadward and Æthelflæd faced as they conquered town after town further north, and established *burh* after *burh*, were likely made up in no small part by local people who, for generations, had lived in England. The identity we now call Anglo-Scandinavian had formed following the widespread immigration of new foreign people to these shores.

Matthew Townend has put forward a brilliant case using place names and back-mutation to hypothesise that the way in which the pre-Viking Age rural sphere worked had changed. Where there had once been farming villages with orbital farmsteads, there were suddenly poly-focal farmsteads that all served as their own nucleus; there were now more farms, but fewer *big* farms. Each of these Scandinavian farms was, like their earlier equivalents, composed of a small hall and a few rectangular buildings (we see no grandiose longhouse in England as is seen in Scandinavia), and they likely functioned as workshops as well as residences. Resident farmers now had to travel slightly different routes to trade, and the markets became inhabited with new accents and loan words, but this was not a drastic change. This was not, for instance, anywhere near the scale of rapid change seen by the Norman Conquest.

As far as material culture goes, which in many ways is our only method of determining how the *Ænglisċ* and Scandinavians saw themselves in this period, we see in the tenth century a rapid adoption of art styles across both spheres. Christian cemeteries and grave markers became adorned with the inter-twining snake-like structures of the Jelling style that so beautifully demonstrated how artisans perceived the living world. We see this same style in jewellery, knife handles, combs.[75, 76] Residents of England in proto-urban centres now had access to trade items from much further afield than they had previously. Prior to 867, York was only a marginally prosperous settlement, with access to items from across the North Sea and European spheres. By 930, the Coppergate excavations led by Richard Hall and others revealed Baltic amber, silk caps from Arabia, quernstones from the Rhinelands, and many more items. With new trade came new opportunities, new visitors, new ethnicities, and new cultures.

England had always been a hubbub of international visitors and many ethnicities, but this would have been multiplied after Scandinavian residence, owing to their wider trade routes and superior maritime technology.[77] And with an increase in urbanity and cultural cross-pollination came religious blending, new religious ideas and cultural norms percolating in ninth-century minds. The Gosforth Cross, in Cumbria, is a four-sided cross shaft caught between two worlds: it depicts Jesus Christ and the wolf Fenrir, the resurrection of Christ and *Ragnarǫk*.[78, 79] Found beneath York Minster during restorative construction work was a gravestone from a Christian cemetery depicting Sigurd *Fafnisbani*, the heathen dragon slayer. Sigurd fought and killed

Shadow

The four faces of the tenth-century Nunburnholme Cross, adorned with later Scandinavian and Norman additions. Of interest is the bizarre hybridity of the Sigurd and Regin story with Christ's blood in a chalice (bottom far right) and a clearly unorthodox depiction of the Christ Mother motif (top far left). The plumed figure on the innermost right face is armed with a Petersen-type Viking Age sword, displaying late-ninth century Norwegian influence. The reference images for these faces were kindly provided by Melanie Hutchinson, and Peter Halkon has advised that the cross itself has been erroneously reconstructed in modern times. Like so many elements of Old Norse myth, we are working with reorganised fragments.

a mighty serpent, and echoing the Eucharist, consumed its blood. In a pagan twist, he could suddenly hear the voices of birds, which he then used to deduce that his foster-father Regin was about to betray him. One can see how that story ended.[80]

Like Guthrum, Scandinavians adopted Christianity through a mixture of pragmatism and, eventually, genuine devotion. The leaders of the 'Kingdom of *Jórvík*' (a section of Deira centred around York) became Christianised under Guthred in the late ninth century, who was placed on the throne by the cult of St Cuthbert in a bizarre blending of Christian veneration with second-generation Scandinavian raiders. Following Guthred, we have two rulers who have only been identified through coinage: Sigfrøðr and Knútr. York then became part of the Hiberno-Norse sphere under the leadership of the Uí Imarr dynasty, Ragnall in the late 910s and his kinsman Sigtryggr soon after. Perhaps the most famous Scandinavian ruler of York, however, was Erik Bloodaxe.

The 'Truth'

Did Erik Bloodaxe, ruling until 954, really exist? The world he inhabited certainly did; his dwindling Kingdom of *Jórvík*, which barely extended into wider Yorkshire, still functioned as part of a key trade route of greater England, and the farmers who tilled his soil viewed themselves as *Ænglisċ*, Anglian, Saxon, British, Danish, Scandinavian, Anglo-Scandinavian, or none of the above. Throughout this book so far, and indeed in the following chapters, the Viking Age and its themes have been explored through the main characters, the names referenced in annals and chronicles and sagas. Most people are invisible, people whose names we will never know, whose lives we can only guess at based on what their families buried with them. They thought of the past, their childhood, their parents, their brothers and sisters, what they would have for dinner, and their worries about the future. Like us, they disliked paying rent and taxes. Erik Bloodaxe was not one of these people.[81]

Erik Bloodaxe first appears, like his alleged father Harald Fairhair, in a thirteenth-century Icelandic Saga, though it contains a skaldic poem of earlier origin, *Words About Eirikr*. *Egil's Saga* depicts Erik as ruling York (though it gets a lot of the politics and geography of England wrong) with an iron fist. He is a hot-tempered and violent man prone to aggression, so, of course, Egil Skallagrimmrson, who has more of a claim to reality than Bloodaxe does, decides to put together a few verses about him. Fearing execution, Egil creates the most scintillating and flattering praise poem, and so Bloodaxe spares his life. The whole tale is immensely entertaining but reads just like that: entertainment. We know that around 950 coins minted in Eirikr of York's name were circulating across Deira, but this was just on the eve of the West Saxon takeover. In 954, this same Eirikr was killed on Stainmore, thus ultimately uniting England under a single ruler.[82]

It would only be after the Viking Age when this shadowy Eirikr and the idea of Erik Bloodaxe would be conflated into one being. Even then, the sources can't really agree on certain elements. Twelfth-century histories of Norwegian monarchs describe him as a 'brother-slayer', and the work known as *Ágrip*[83] places Erik's final hours in Spain, though it is possible this is a conflation with *another* dubious figure – Ulf the Galician – who is attested in a thirteenth-century saga as having 'scorched and sacked' areas of the Iberian Peninsula at roughly the same time Erik fell on Stainmore. Roger of Wendover, writing in the thirteenth century, added that Erik was betrayed by his confidant, Maccus. *Eiríksmál*, a poem likely composed in the tenth century (and thus one of our few contemporary sources about Eirikr), depicts him arriving in *Valhöll* following his death, welcomed by Óðinn, Bragi, and Sigmundr, pagan heroes and gods. *Eiríksmál* reveals how Eirikr of York was perceived in elite circles as the brightly burning final candle of Scandinavian Northumbria. It was this rendition of Eirikr that likely formed the foundation for Bloodaxe, but ultimately, we can't be sure. There will always be more to know.

Scandinavian raiders, traders, farmers, and settlers operating across Europe in the late ninth century had changed the landscapes they inhabited, principally the east coast of Ireland and northern England, but they were also being changed themselves by their new environments. Ireland and England were somewhat familiar territory. There was the mutual linguistic intelligibility and similar pre-Christian belief systems. But Scandinavians did not, of course, simply travel to Francia and the British Isles. The scope of the Viking Age diaspora was massive, unparalleled by any population movement of contemporary times. The scope of this book will now expand dramatically, to explore further themes of the Viking Age. For now, England and the evolution from raiders to kings to armies to settlers will take a backseat, as we explore the many alien worlds these people visited on their travels around the globe, but also, perhaps more importantly, the alien worlds they already lived in.

Journeys

But so it befell at last that they were ware of land; a great land it was, but they knew nought what land. Then such rede took Gudleif and his crew, that they should sail unto land, for they thought it ill to have to do any more with the main sea; and so then they got them good haven. And when they had been there a little while, men came to meet them whereof none knew aught, though they deemed somewhat that they spake in the Erse tongue. At last they came in such throngs that they made many hundreds, and they laid hands on them all, and bound them, and drove them up into the country, and they were brought to a certain mote and were doomed thereat. And this they came to know, that some would that they should be slain, and othersome that they should be allotted to the countryfolk, and be their slaves.

From *Eyrbyggja Saga* translated by
Eiríkur Magnússon (1833-1913).

What is most inspiring and interesting about the Viking Age for many people will not be the violence or the conquests so typical of the time but the sheer distance these people travelled. It is true, other peoples and kingdoms were fighting and raiding, but it seems only 'the Vikings' were discovering at such speed the same amount of unsettled territory. Of course, not all of the lands Scandinavians would explore *were* unsettled; there would be many threats still to face, but for the most part, this chapter takes a break from the politicking and military campaigns of the ninth and tenth centuries and seeks to explore the world and worldview of the Scandinavians from the perspective of *landnám* – land-taking; the act of claiming virgin territory, in part through the lens of the Old Norse cosmogony and cosmology. Out of the confines and complexities of international warfare and trade routes were a few locations, some inhabited, many not. Scandinavians would see them all. The epic literary voyages of Bjorn *járnsíða* and Haesten in the 860s, and of Yngvar the Far-Travelled in the 1040s, temporally removed from one another by so many religious and political changes, but thematically very similar, will be considered along with smaller trade journeys like Wulfstan of Hedeby and Ohthere's travels to the court of Wessex in King Ælfred's time. These journeys, and others like them, saw Scandinavians cover the continents of Europe, Africa, Asia, North America, and perhaps even beyond. These alien landscapes and their mysterious people came home through garbled stories and fantastical reimaginings to form a core part of that already unique Viking Age mindset. The many realms of *Yggdrasil*, the world tree, no longer seem so otherworldly.

Other Worlds

The mind of the Early Medieval Scandinavian was shaped by the dramatic scenery of the Norwegian fjords, the Danish bogs, and the Swedish forests. Now, we can see all the world on a screen. We can observe the passing of time on our phones, can tell the weather with the push of a button, and can experience cultures from the other side of the planet with a click. Our Earth, our *Miðgarðr*, is a world no longer alien to us. Sure, you may feel overwhelmed when stepping foot in a foreign country, but you are grounded in the knowledge that we are on a planet orbiting the Sun, and we have been here for several hundred thousand years in some shape or form, and before us were other lifeforms going back a further four-and-a-half billion years. When we look up at the stars, we know that they are balls of gas burning in perpetuity, occasionally blotted out by satellites or black holes thousands of light years away. We know that the Moon is a satellite that controls the tide and is a desolate rock.

In the long centuries before and during the Viking Age, when people in Scandinavia and the Baltic looked up at the sky, they may have felt similarly confident in their beliefs. Possibly, they were confident they were looking at the branches of the world tree, extending through multi-coloured abstract forms like the *Aurora Borealis*, with the stars acting as gaps in the leaves, letting light in from an even more alien sky above our own. When they looked over the sea, they saw the 'whale road', a means to travel, and a barrier and bridge between realms. They saw birds, insects, creatures, men, wolf-men, bear-men, mountains, fjords, forests, rainbows, clouds, trolls, dwarves, light elves, dark elves, ogres. They also 'saw' dragons, serpents, land spirits, water spirits, forest spirits, giants, gods, ancestors, *draugar*; things dark and terrible and deadly, perceived as real.

The *Miðgarðr* that Scandinavians inhabited was the home of man – *Manheim* – but it was only one of many realms that existed, accessible via rivers and oceans. One would not be able to necessarily walk to *Jǫtunheimar*, far to the north, or *Útgarðr* beyond even that, but they could get into a longship and sail the whale road to get there. They could even sail to the hot place, to *Muspell*, or to the fertile plains of *Vanaheimr* or the glistening lights of *Ásgarðr*, or to *Hel*, which Snorri placed north of everywhere else. All these places, as far as we can tell from High Medieval vernacular writings on earlier cosmological thinking and contemporary skaldic verses, existed in the same way that York existed, that Dublin existed, that Scandinavia itself existed. They were very real but also abstract and non-linear; worlds within worlds, perhaps the modern obsession with 'multiverses' might do the idea justice.

Most of our knowledge about this comes from Snorri Sturluson, whose thirteenth-century manuscript we call the *Prose Edda*.[1] The *Prose Edda* consists of four parts: three form a sort of collective handbook for would-be poets, with the first containing earlier oral traditions about the creation of the cosmos and Snorri's euhemeristic rationalisation of Iceland's pagan heritage. The *Poetic Edda* is a collection of poems describing various elements of the Old Norse mythological corpus by an earlier unknown scribe. It is found in the Codex Regius manuscript and contains works which influenced the *Prose Edda*.[2] Both were written hundreds of years after the events they describe.

The settlers who first visited Greenland around the dawn of the eleventh century did not think 'This is the year 985, and I have settled the southwestern tip of the largest island in the world.' Perhaps they thought it was *Niflheim*, or a place even colder still, *Niflhel*, below even the afterlife. The Nine Realms, first described as '*Níu Heimar*' ('nine worlds') in the *Poetic Edda*, are in truth a modern idea. 'Nine' as a number was certainly sacred in Germanic-speaking pagan circles, and its frequent usage across Old Norse literature point to it more broadly meaning 'a dozen' or 'a couple'; not specifically 'nine' but simply a quantity. Realms beyond the Nine are hinted at in occasional stanzas, and ultimately 'The Nine Realms' may have just been 'the other places' – abstract locations, some real, many not, that existed out there in the beyond. We will attempt to sail through some of these places, using them as a visual backdrop to discuss real locations.

These realms existed, in some form, to Viking Age pagans; *hugr* (inner self, thought, and memory) was shaped by the turmoil of the Dust Veil and a martial warrior culture. This was a universe that man dwelt in, but he was joined by Æsir and Vanir and all manner of things we will never know the true names of. Each realm housed its own populace and each realm had individuals travelling between them all. The first to be created, out of the shell of the giant Ymir's skull and bones, was *Miðgarðr*.

Miðgarðr

Miðgarðr was encircled by a massive wall, giving us some idea of the concept of 'inside' and 'outside'. To *dwell*, to live in a hall, was to be a functioning and normal member of society, no matter if the hall was built of wood, turf, or gold. There was something inherently different about having a place to call one's home and not having a permanent abode; to wander was the lot of wolves, others, Grendel from *Beowulf*. Miðgarðr in Christian writing from after the Viking Age[3] is as normal as our own lives; people farm, people fight, people love, people die. Outside the walls, outside our normal lives, there are those people without settlements, who roamed unceasingly. We get a glimpse of what may have inspired this train of thought through the interconnected world of the Arctic Circle, where the lands of the Saami and Scandinavians met. Theirs was a relationship of mutual understanding, it seems, which became more strained with the adoption of Christianity in Norway and Sweden. Though initially the Saami and certain magnates in the northernmost provinces appear to have traded.

A window into this relationship is found in the Old English translation of *Orosius*,[4,5] transcribed sometime during King Ælfred's reign. In the 890s, a Norwegian named Ohthere visited Ælfred's court and described the journey he had taken to reach England, along with some of the sights and people of his homeland. Ohthere, was not the only wayfarer in Wessex, the other was Wulfstan. Wulfstan's heritage is unknown, but the wording of *Orosius* suggests he was possibly of West Saxon origin. He was not content to stay there.

> Wulfstan said that he went from Haethum to Truso in seven days and nights, and that the ship was running under sail all the way. Weonodland was on his right, and Langland, Laeland, Falster, and Sconey, on his left, all which land is subject to Denmark. Then on our left we had the land of the Burgundians, who have a king to themselves. Then, after the land of the Burgundians, we had on our left the lands that have been called from the earliest times Blekingey, and Meore, and Eowland, and Gotland, all which territory is subject to the Sweons; and Weonodland (the land of the Wends) was all the way on our right, as far as Weissel-mouth.[6]

'Wulfstan's Voyage', as this passage is now called, describes a journey through The Kattegat and into the Baltic Sea, observing the various polities and proto-urban centres along the way. *Haethum* is Hedeby,[7] that impressive and by then well-fortified trading settlement on the borders of *Danemearcan*: Denmark. Truso was another such trading site, extending the web of international economies further eastward, acting like its northern counterpart Staraja Ladoga. Archaeological excavations in Truso on the edge of the Vistula basin have revealed a multi-ethnic cluster of Scandinavian objects and trade goods and also Slavic residential structures and Arabic coin deposits. Marek F. Jagodziński who discovered the site has interpreted several of the postholes and outlines in Truso's strata as being Scandinavian-inspired longhouses.[8] This was not just a site of trade, however, for there are those tell-tale layers of burnt ash and dark earth – the former an indicator of fire, and the latter of urban sprawl – along with weapons and arrowheads. Truso may have been occupied by military groups on a few occasions. As early as the eighth century, Truso's core was inhabited by traders and merchants, probably expanding into the wider Courland and Livland areas. Truso's hinterlands, however, appear to have only been inhabited by the natives. All this was on Wulfstan's right-hand side, the southern shores of the Baltic Sea, or *Weonodland*. The Wends inhabited an area covering most of the Baltic shore; not one ethnicity, but instead a multitude of different dialects and groups. Like the term 'Anglo-Saxon', Wend was describing several tribes and peoples. The Obotrites on the Carolingian-Danish border were one such. West Wendland, coterminous with Poland, has only slight evidence of Scandinavian settlement and occupation.

To Wulfstan's left, he describes lands we would nowadays associate with Sweden, which he mentions as still being under a Danish ruler. By this time, we cannot conclusively identify who that would be. He also talks of Eowland and Gotland, islands off the coast of Sweden with their own rulers, discussed in the next chapter.

Wulfstan of Hedeby's voyage is useful for calculating the time distance between locations. We are so used to measuring journeys in miles or kilometres, but the core measurement is time. A seven-day voyage from Jutland to the Vistula Lagoon could become a month-round trip if there was some shore leave. Much has been written on the topic of Viking Age navigation but the likelihood is that a healthy dose of common sense and inherited knowledge was all it took for Scandinavians in their longships to cut across so much of the world; saga descriptions of voyages between Norway and Greenland remark how crews kept at least one landmass to their left (or right) at all times, or followed the migratory paths of whales and birds, or even looked up at the branches of *Yggdrasil* – the stars – for guidance. For Wulfstan, his geography of the Baltic Sea was based upon knowledge of what landmasses (and their peoples) lay to his left and right, so he always knew where he was going and who he could trade with. We can imagine a similar mindset was present for vikingar too.

Wulfstan's voyage was only a small section of a much larger trade route, the *Austrvegr*, or 'the Eastern Way'.[9, 10] Through the Gulf of Finland, the Daugava River, the Velikaga River, and other tributaries throughout modern Estonia and Latvia, silver flowed into and out of the Baltic Sea towards the Byzantine and Arabic worlds to the east. These routes changed over the Viking Age, with old ones closing or silting up and new ones taking their place, like the Gauja, the Narva, the Emajõgi, the Võrtsjärv, and the Pärnu. Along the way were pre-existing centres of power such as the indigenous hillforts at Iru, Tartu, and Viljandi, home to their own militarised societies who no doubt put up quite a fight when confronted by river-raiders. In Grobiņa, Latvia, there is evidence of Scandinavian settlement and occupation from as early as 650, mixed with the resident Slavic and Baltic inhabitants as at Truso.[11, 12] Grobiņa may have been some kind of early military encampment established by Gotlanders before it was captured by the locals. It sat in a landscape peppered by hillforts like Daugmale, Sengals, Jersika, Apuolė, Impitils, Eketė, and Imbarė.[13]

All these bases sprung up around the rivers, indicating that the Baltic and Slavic societies were naval-based and connected to the wider world up and downstream. Lithuania appears to have been outside of the *Austrvegr* trading routes, with far less evidence of Arabic coin hoards and silver deposits between 800-1100 than its neighbours. Though Eketė Hillfort in Lithuania was so large it was more of a timber city than an encampment. Excavations in 1972 revealed the people of Eketė were smelting metal goods on-site, making jewellery from amber, and processing lumber from beyond the walls.[16]

The area of the modern Baltic states was once the land of the Oesellians, the Livs, the Sels, Latgalians, and Chuds, and others, groups with their own material cultures. The cross-cultural relations along this Eastern Way were likely not always based on trade. We associate raiding with the west and trading with the east, but there was probably an equivalent amount of both in either direction: but Baltic societies were not recording such attacks. (Though *Vita Ansgarii* does describe a Swedish raid on *Seeburg*, normally identified as Grobiņa, in 845). Iru Hillfort, for instance, in Harju County, Estonia, displays evidence of at least four instances of being burned to the ground.[14, 15] Material deposits indicate that the waterways were, for the most part, dominated by Scandinavians.

In the west, one of the most interesting areas of Europe the Scandinavians encountered was Brittany, which during the eighth and ninth centuries was a multi-ethnic home to a significant population of Brythonic-speaking peoples who had migrated from Britannia during the post-Roman decline.[17] Called Bretons, between the 830s and 840s they were ruled by people like Nomenoë, vassals to more powerful Carolingian rulers. On the death of Louis the Pious in 840 and the ensuing breakdown of his empire, Nomenoë became an independent ruler, separating his land from West Francia via the Breton marches. His successor, Salomon, would employ Scandinavians in his armies to fight against Francia. From 843, Noirmoutier, an island slightly south of Brittany in the Bay of Biscay, became a raiding launchpad for Scandinavians, and almost a century later between 915-919 there was a concerted military campaign to take Brittany from the Bretons. It is likely the campaign was fought by warriors based at Noirmoutier and those who had just been given land around Rouen, in modern Normandy, by Charles the Simple in 911. We will return to these 'proto-Normans' later.

By 936, the Bretons had overthrown their new occupiers leaving only the evidence of their military camps behind. Brittany did not become linked to the wider trade routes that connected Ireland and the rest of the Viking Age diaspora. Slaves who entered the network may have been Bretons, but there is no evidence for any markets or *longphort* equivalents this far west on the French mainland. There is, however, evidence of burning. Le Camp de Péran, Vieux M'Na, and the site at Île-de-Groix display the violence of the time, the latter site being one of the famous Scandinavian ship burials.[18, 19] The individual interred within had been killed sometime in the tenth century, but they had lived a long life beforehand. Isotopic tracing revealed that the Groix warrior had spent some time in Birka, along the banks of the River Elbe, in the wider Rhinelands, and in Norway. He was, like all these people, a man of the world, of *Miðgarðr*.

Miðgarðr was also populated by other, inhuman beings. One need only look briefly at the Icelandic sagas or even visit Iceland today to hear of the *huldufólk* ('hidden people') – not supernatural beings but *supra*natural.[20] They were as real as the rocks, the rivers, and the sky above. One day you might see a frog, the next you might encounter a troll. In the eddas, the distinction between a 'troll' and a 'giant' is unclear. Perhaps they are best interpreted as representing dangerous aspects of the natural world, or unwanted character traits. In Icelandic sagas, particularly villainous characters or social pariahs were described as 'half-trolls' or as *helljarmenni*.[21, 22] To be a 'troll', or any of the other beings, was to demonstrate behaviour that went beyond the human. (Being ugly was sometimes enough.) Pronounced 'neath', *níþ* was the worst of all status-based insults, used to describe men who broke from their role in society.[23] A *seiðmaðr* (a man who practised sorcery) ran the risk of being called a *níþing*. It is difficult to express how insulting the term is with a modern translation.[24]

Journeys

Even though Óðinn and Loki were known to practise sorcery, male practitioners of *seiðr* were, like trolls and *berserkir*, social pariahs. In the fourteenth-century *Laxdæla* saga, both male and female characters are bound by societal gender norms: one character divorces her husband because he dressed in a low-cut top, while another male is slashed and has his right arm disabled by his wife, who is dressed in male clothing. Much Old Norse literature concerns gender roles and sexual normativity. When Þórr disguises himself as a woman to retrieve his stolen hammer from giants in a lay from the *Poetic Edda*, he laments that the other Æsir will mock him.

A huge stone wall encircled *Miðgarðr* to keep these in-humans out. One can only wonder what lingered in the *hugr* of Scandinavian sailors as they took shelter near great monuments like Maeshowe, Orkney,[25] or as they sailed around Shetland using the crumbling Iron Age tower of Mousa Broch as a reference point.

Mousa Broch, Shetland. The tallest extant broch anywhere in the world, thought to have been built no earlier than 100 BCE. Mousa Broch was – and still is – a landmark guiding sailors along the shores of Shetland.

Travellers may have even asked 'Who built these things?' Whether the people they asked knew the answer will forever be unknown. *Miðgarðr* was the land of men, but before that it was inhabited by gods and giants.[26] While post-Roman people had a clear understanding of extant Roman monuments, prehistoric remnants were very much a mystery, recognised as old but that's it – the work of gods?

Jǫtunheimar

The other voyager to grace Ælfred's court was Ohthere, who travelled from the Arctic north of Norway. Long argued to mean 'The Northern Way', it has been postulated that the original spellings of *Norðvegr* (or *Norge*) indicate that the prefix is a possessive word, meaning that the *-vegr* or 'way' *belonged* to someone. In this case, Nór, from Saxo's *Deeds of the Danes* and the fourteenth-century *Flateyjarbók*.[27] It does not matter if a king called Nór really existed, what matters is where these names came from and how people perceived them. The cosmology that the Viking Age inherited had been around for quite a long time. We might have the Dust Veil to thank for the more destructive and dramatic elements of the pantheon, but major elements existed before. The concept of other worlds and other beings has precedent in most European folklore. Chief among these villainous entities were the giants, or *jotnar*; the classic nemeses of the Æsir and Vanir.

Jǫtunheimar is a plural descriptor of multiple peripheral realms that were bizarre and dangerous, though not desolate. Jämtland, the Swedish county on the border with Norway today, was once its own polity that resisted the unification attempts of Haraldr *lúfa* and existed outside the trade networks of 'King' Bjorn of Birka. There is evidence of human habitation there dating back as far as 6,600 BCE. These original inhabitants hunted moose and painted their likeness in bright red on the boulders of the countryside.[28]

These monuments from the ancient past would have sparked wonder in later travellers. By the seventh century, barrow mounds like those across the rest of the Germanic-speaking world started to appear in Jämtland, built near to the earlier painted stones, and by the eighth and ninth centuries, rural farmsteads and settlements joined them.[29] What appears to have been the centre of activity was a rural estate on Frösön ('Freyr's Island'), associated with nearby painted runestones. In an area so cold and isolated from overseas trade, venerating a god of fertility and harvest was prudent.[30] So, too, were the regional assemblies, like the one preserved through the place name *Jamtamót*, an eastern equivalent to Iceland's *Alþingi*. Jämtland is mentioned in relation to the semi-legendary Harald Fairhair as one of the areas people migrated to following his reign over 'all Norway', which does to some degree align with the archaeology, but the only historically identifiable king we can connect to Jämtland and Frösön would be the eleventh-century Norwegian monarch Olafr Haraldsson. Olafr is credited with converting most of Norway to Christianity, as described on the Fröso stone raised a few years after his death.

Jämtland was also inhabited by the Saami, who principally roamed the parts of Norway, Sweden, and Finland in the Arctic Circle, *Sapmi*, their land. It was Ohthere who first described the Saami. Like Wulfstan, Ohthere described two journeys that he had made prior to his arrival in Wessex. The first was from his home, Hålogaland, 'the farthest north of all Norwegians', to the White Sea and then back to the port of *Skíringssalr*, and the second from there to Hedeby and then onto the British Isles. Again, we find distance measured in time, Ohthere described the first voyage as taking a month, one spent weaving through the fjords and islands of northern Norway travelling past all the petty kings and isolated farmers of the late ninth century (importantly, Ohthere makes no mention of Harald Fairhair). Ohthere's main source of wealth was his reindeer herd, through which he extracted tribute from the Saami.[31] He was, in essence, a landlord, and an inordinately wealthy one. Later, *finnkonge* (Saami kings) emerge. Richer individuals had to pay more tribute to Norwegian landowners than their poorer kin.[32] The Saami and their southern neighbours had been interacting and borrowing elements from one another's culture long before the Viking Age. Often described as *finnas* ('Finns'), several archaeological deposits in northern Norway indicate that the Saami appreciated and desired certain elements of the southerners' material culture. The idea of shapeshifting seems to have been borrowed from Saami *noaidi* shamanism and painted skin drum rituals. In one tale, Óðinn is accused by Loki of dressing like a woman and beating a skin drum. The name of 'Finn', a legendary character mentioned in *Beowulf*, may have derived from some early acknowledgement of the Saami.

The Saami, despite sometimes called *finnas*, were different to the inhabitants of Early Medieval Finland, though their worlds were similar. Parts of Norway and Finland have similar ecosystems, with dense pine forests encouraging a nomadic hunter-gatherer way of life amongst the snow, tundra, and taiga. Häme, in southern Finland, shows some degree of settlement. This coincided with the abandonment of sites by the native peoples following the influx of Scandinavian migrants in the eighth century.[33, 34] The site of Karjaa, dated to 800, displays this.[35] Hiittinen, on the other hand, farther north and inland, shows the exact opposite; here, the residents were actively trading and profiting with pirates sailing

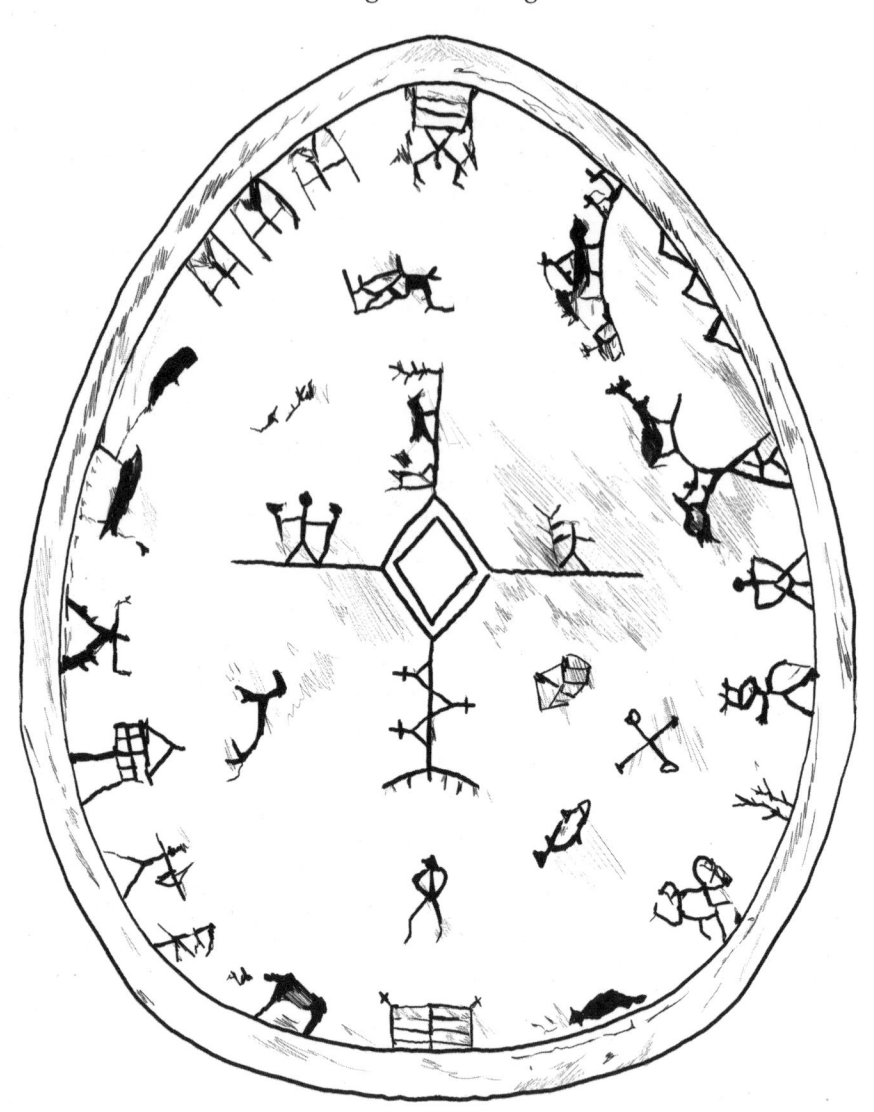

A noaidi skin bowl drum, decorated with elaborate characters and patterns. Drums like this still exist today, and in the past played a significant role in Saami rituals. Noaidi may have employed runic divination.

past the Gulf of Finland along the *Austrvegr*. An Icelandic saga about the character of Burnt Njal references the lighting of beacons along the coasts of Finland as crews of longships sailed past to trade and to raid. Finland adapted to viking activity.[36] The Åland Islands appear to have been settled by an incoming autonomous community similar, but far less rich, to those on Gotland. Across these islands, Swedes manned archipelagic outposts well situated in the Baltic Sea to watch over the Eastern Way, to monitor the spread of silver, slaves, and information.[37,38]

Journeys

Across the mythical regions of *Jǫtunheimar*, one is described as *Járnviðr* – the Iron Wood – home to troll-wives and their wolf spawn. Snorri reckoned the Iron Wood to be the birthplace of Fenrir's counterpart, the flesh-eater, the Moon-swallower, the 'mightiest of all': Mánagarmr. The apparently infinite taiga forests of Finland and the people who roamed there may have been perceived as alien to those who did not. Nevertheless, there was communication. Saami people further north were paid to skin and freeze-dry reindeer hide and were renowned for their trapping ability. Likely, magnates like Ohthere employed their services in hunting specific animals, for a price of course. If southern Finland parallels descriptions of *Járnviðr*, then the regions around the White Sea could be associated with another world of *Jǫtunheimar*: *Útgarðr*. This was the 'Outside' – outside *Miðgarðr*: a fortress of giants. Described as a 'wasteland' by Ohthere, the White Sea rim was inhabited only by the *finnas*. So it was not a wasteland.[39] It was just settled in a manner markedly different to the sedentary lives of *Manaheim*.

Around this icy rim, at sites like Kainuu, Kuusamo, and Salla, trade reached the Saami via the Dvina River,[40] and across the polar country, there is emerging evidence of deposits of weapons and goods.[41] Walrus and seal were hunted here by Norse and Saami alike, and probably other people like the *Beormas* from *Bjarmland* described by Ohthere. Walrus tusks, most notably harvested from Greenland later in the Viking Age, were a prestige item sold at a high price, not in bulk.

Finns of the seventh and eighth centuries lived in log-panel houses made of woven wood panels and branches, smaller than longhouses but echoing the same design, either through convergence (not unexpected, as Scandinavian-like pit-houses appear across the Slavic world, too) or through emulation. They also cremated their dead in boats and had a silver bullion economy, though importantly, Finnish boats were not clinker-built nor anywhere near as large as Scandinavian examples. Though this does demonstrate that *vikingar* were not the sole masters of the freezing waters. Rivers in Finland would have been lower than today, so land travel may have been preferable. Bothnic skis and sledges were used, bound to an individual's feet and richly carved out of antler and bone.[42, 43] Perhaps the skiing deity Ullr was invoked by these nomads.

Perhaps these individuals were hunting bears, martens, squirrels, foxes, wolves, or harvesting honey from bee farms, claws from beavers or fish from the coast, keeping a watchful eye out for sails on the horizon. There were pockets of Finland that appear to have had more of a 'Swedish' character than a 'Finnish' one (if such a thing can be observed through material goods). There are over forty coin hoards filled with Arabic, European, and Asian coinage, along with an abundance of

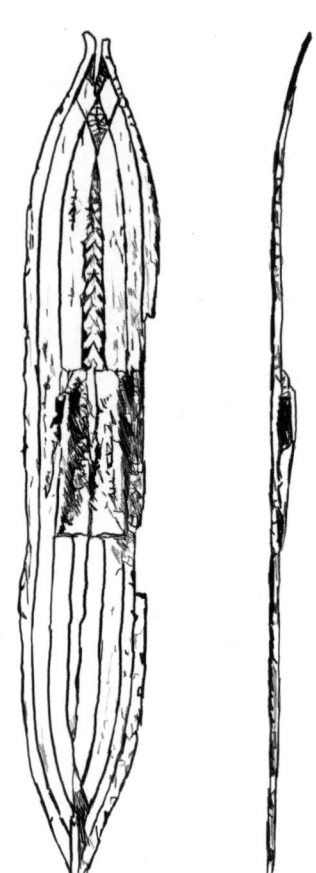

A Bothnic or Bothnian type ski from Kinnula.

sword and weapon deposits from the Byzantine world dated to the tenth and eleventh centuries, probably reflecting the homecoming voyages of Varangian Guards. In Birka there is substantial evidence of a transient Finnish population who were creating pottery on site,[44] and one of the most interesting items from the Bedale Hoard is a Permian arm ring, its style borrowed from those of the peoples of the Gulf of Finland.

These natives were deeply engaged with the forest and the natural world. Like the Saami to their north, Finns and Balts were always on the move, bar a few exceptions like the residents of Karjaa, and their world was shared with Scandinavians, but it seems on their own terms. These foresters could, if they wanted, stay within the thick woods of *Járnviðr*, and let raiding parties get lost amongst the darkness, or they could emerge and make many a profit at their seasonal beach markets. There appears to have been some degree of veneration or respect in the upper strata of Scandinavian society for their Saami neighbours, at least in Norway and Sweden. Of the many legends of Harald Fairhair, perhaps the most famous is his marriage to Princess Snæfríð, a match made to unite territories. The very inclusion of a Saami princess, the daughter of a *finnkonge*, indicates that the Saami's world – *Sapmi* – was viewed as such an intrinsic part of Norway that it could not be excluded if one wanted to rule over the entire nation.[45] Even outside the Viking Age world, in our hypothetical *Útgarðr*, the Saami were still ever-present and important.

Muspell

We associate the Viking Age so strongly with blizzards and icy seas, we forget that significant military activity and exploration occurred in warmer areas. *Muspell,* or *Muspellsheimr,* was one of the other primordial realms; not forested and home to giants and shapeshifters like *Jǫtunheimar,* but to the crucible of fire. Such fire was primal, powerful. Fire could spell doom for all, but it could also bring life and prosperity. After all, it was a volcanic eruption that may have created the impetus for the Viking Age back in 536.

In Iceland, Scandinavians would discover volcanoes and caverns that went deep into the earth to pockets of magma and brimstone. Imagine the heat from a lava flow, pouring over a farmstead on the shores of Iceland;[46] the dust cloud from an eruption; imagine the monsters emerging from the burning forests, encroaching upon civilisation.

Scandinavians reached Iceland around the beginning of the ninth century, though large-scale migration would not take place until after the so-called 'tephra layer' of 871 (a layer of volcanic ash, which sits under the settlement layers). The first inhabitants were probably fishermen from Norway, though some believe that Irish monks in Iceland arrived before them. Dicuil, a Hebridean geographer writing in the ninth century, stated in his version of the *Measurement of the World* (compiled from Roman geographical sources) that he knew of brothers from a place called 'Thule'. There is no archaeological proof for such early Icelandic monks, though carved crosses in the Seljaland cave system do indicate that there was at some point Christian veneration in the area, as do place names in the southwest. A layer of sediment in caves has been tentatively dated to the ninth century, but this is not necessarily indicative of a pre-Scandinavian Christian presence.[47, 48] What we *do* know about the earliest settlement of Iceland is that a wealthy magnate and his retinue were inhabiting a large longhouse at Stöðvarfjörður, Fjarðabyggð. This longhouse, excavated in 2015, was dated to no earlier than 800, showing signs of an on-site smithy, bead-working, walrus and fish processing, and tucked in the walls was a small sandstone pebble carved with the likeness of a longship.[49]

This carved sandstone pebble from Fjarðabyggð, is the oldest extant drawing from Iceland. It was discovered in the Stöðvarfjörður longhouse. It is possible this pebble was placed in the walls of the longhouse deliberately, invoking safe sailing and good landfall; or perhaps as a 'thank you' following the successful voyage to Fjarðabyggð.

Early settlements were probably only occupied seasonally. Iceland is associated with the sun-bright sparks of *Muspell*, but it is not an entirely barren expanse of basalt and cooled lava. Greenery covers Iceland because of subterranean volcanic activity. The Stöðvarfjörður excavations revealed a smaller longhouse built inside the ruins of the previous one, from above the tephra layer of 871. Perhaps in the later mass migration to Iceland, the next generation of the family who had inhabited the first longhouse came over to maintain their foothold on these verdant volcanic plains. Or perhaps the original longhouse was purposefully abandoned and left to rot, and newcomers reused the material to build their own home. Two important sites in Hafnir and Reykjavik, Vogur and Aðalstræti, also date from this period, especially the former, which might have been founded as early as 770.[50] The settlement pattern appears to follow that which we have already observed on Shetland; tentative transient lodgings which were occupied seasonally ahead of widespread and permanent immigration. After the first settlers arrived in Iceland, news of the discovery spread. By the 870s, the island was swamped with refugees seeking new opportunities, likely fleeing southwest Norway for a fresh start following the annexation of their lands by mysterious long-haired chieftains.

It is likely that a significant percentage of the first settlers in Iceland came from the Faroe Islands and Ireland, based on genomic evidence.[51] The Faroe Islands, stretching into the Atlantic Ocean like the fingers of a petrified god, with steep inclines and verdant ash-enriched soil, were formed fifty-five million years ago by subterranean volcanic activity. Like the mythical *Hel*, this archipelago was covered in streams that sprang from wells beneath the earth; *Hvergelmir*, with its daughter rivers of *Élivágar*, *Svol*, and *Gunnthro*, are placed in both *Hel* and *Niflheim* by Snorri. These rivers and the mountains they carved through had existed since the dawn of the universe, since the great void; Ginnungagap. *Muspell* was also one of the oldest realms, placed south of Niflheim and inexplicably intertwined with it through the dichotomy of fire and ice. An observed phenomenon of the Faroe Islands farmsteads is that quite a few of their doorways face eastwards.[52] In later *drapur* poems and skaldic verses, the East is described as the home of other beings, the Æsir, the Vanir, and worse.[53] Jǫtunheimar is often located in the nebulous north and east – elsewhere, far away, but reachable. It is possible that this orientation of the doors reflects some form of veneration or at least acknowledgement of these other worlds. It is equally plausible that it was simply an architectural adaptation to the topography.

Echoing *Muspell*'s many rivers, some Faroese farmsteads featured irrigation ditches and attempts to enrich the soil, owing to the steepness of the place. At the site of Toftanes, a longhouse, outhouse, pit-house, and possible early water-mill were all segmented and built atop a series of run-offs and dykes carved into the hillside, heading towards the sea.[54,55,56] Toftanes is a typical Faroese dwelling; a wealthy if small estate, whose owners lived in cramped conditions breathing in acrid smoke in their dimly lit halls, sharing their shelter with sheep.

Sheep were the main source of subsistence for these settlers. The name of the island chain, *Faereyjar*, means 'sheep islands'. But this name did not originate with the Norse themselves. It is said in later sagas that the semi-legendary figure Grimur Kamban, whose epithet denotes Gaelic origins, discovered the islands completely abandoned in 825, home only

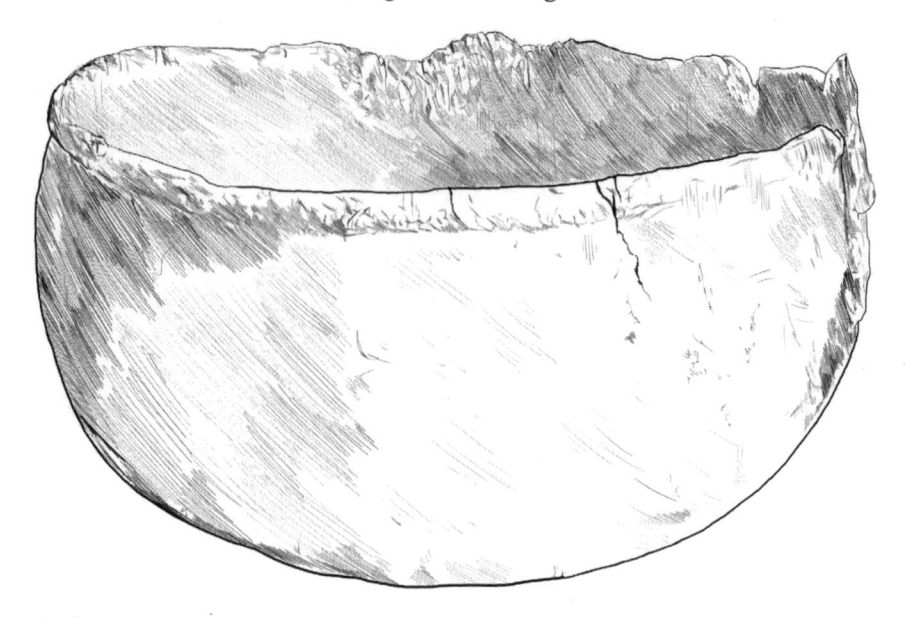

Cooking and serving implements made from steatite (soapstone) were commonly used across the Viking Age diaspora. Much of the raw material was sourced from Shetland or Norway, like this bowl from Gjestad.

to roaming sheep.[57] Dicuil, however, wrote a plausible earlier description of the Faroe Islands:

> Many other islands lie in the northerly British Ocean. One reaches them from the northerly islands of Britain, by sailing directly for two days and two nights with a full sail in a favourable wind the whole time... Most of these islands are small, they are separated by narrow channels, and for nearly a hundred years hermits lived there, coming from our land, Ireland, by boat. But just as these islands have been uninhabited from the beginning of the world, so now the Norwegian pirates have driven away the monks; but countless sheep and many different species of sea-fowl are to be found there.

Unlike Iceland, there is undeniable evidence that the Faroes were inhabited before Scandinavian arrivals. Lying under the ninth-century butchery shielings of Argisbrekka, a layer of burnt earth dated to 500 CE was found by Lorelei Curtin and her team, containing pollen kernels, cereal cores, and sheep droppings.[58] As Dicuil states, it is likely these initial farmers and discoverers of *Faereyjar* were Irish monks, either that or Shetlanders.

Scandinavians brought their own building styles, as they did on Shetland. Their settlement model had so far seen minimal adaptations between Norway and the Faroes. The farmers had yet to adapt too much to their new environments, though the irrigation ditches do indicate that this first wave of Faroese settlers had to make some quick changes.[59, 60] The archaeofaunal deposit found at Undir Junkarinsfløtti on the island of Sandoy gives further clues.[61] Routinely used for the disposal of animal bones or on-site slaughter, Undir demonstrates the change in the diet of Scandinavian farmers from the first settlement of the islands in the ninth century to the end of the tenth. The bones tell us that while there was initial consumption of pigs and cattle, eventually goats and sheep took over. There was also an increased reliance on seals and fish. Within a century the Faroese had changed their lifestyle, further demonstrating the innate pragmatism of the Viking Age. Here, on what was the edge of the known world, or near enough, people were preparing for the future.

Iceland was of course next on the roadmap. By 871 a mass migration of Scandinavians from Norway and Ireland had reached the island. This was the period of *landnám*, land-taking, with many great myths and semi-fictitious characters emerging, all escaping the tyranny of the equally dubious Harald Fairhair. Archaeology reveals the truth of the matter, an abundance of farmsteads, far more than across the Faroe Islands and Shetland. These farmsteads were established in such great quantities that it is clear a socially stratified hierarchy like that (but not identical to) in Norway had been transferred overseas. While in the previous locations mentioned one can expect to see shielings marking the outfields and borders of farmsteads, in Iceland they disappear from the archaeological record.[62, 63] Place name elements like *Sel-* or *-saet* do indicate that they still existed, but the fact remains that out of all excavated Viking Age rural sites across the entire island, only one shieling has so far been identified, at Pálstóftir.[64] So where were animals being sheltered? What buildings were being used to demarcate where one farmer's land ended and another's began? Amidst the mass migration to Iceland these matters would be important.

Animals were stored in the outhouse still, but also in turf rings that archaeologists have identified as pens. The abundance of new settlers probably also solved the problem of the lack of shielings; with so many farms, both large and small, perhaps a small farm sandwiched between two larger estates could function *as* the shieling.[65]

Society was structured differently in Iceland. For one, within a generation or two of settlement, the *Alþingi* was created, a much larger national version of the 'thing sites', the assemblies, seen across Norway and Sweden. This was distinct from kingly authority, and it is interesting to speculate on why exactly among this land of fire and ice the many petty kings of Norway were not attempting to claim that *they* were the true king of this new home. Perhaps a mutual agreement was reached. Iceland would remain in the firing line of Norway for centuries to come, and even the quasi- democratic *Alþingi* would eventually be dominated by a small handful of powerful landowners, like Snorri Sturluson himself.

In *Vatnsdæla Saga*, we read our first description of the purpose of an outhouse; 'used for the storage of fine goods', and the same story describes the interior of a shieling, despite there so far being minimal evidence that they existed on the island: 'The shieling was constructed with a single roof beam, which reached from one gable to the other and protruded at the ends, with a thatch of turf.'[66] Besides such quotidian descriptions, what the Icelandic sagas share is an atmosphere of otherworldliness. Trolls who lurked inside magma boulders, *draugar* who dwelled in the ravines and glacial crevices, *alfar* (elves) who bestowed wisdom to those who sacrificed. There is nowhere else in the Viking Age diaspora with such a high proportion of identified 'cultic sites' as Iceland.[67] These *blót* houses came in many shapes and sizes, pit-houses on the periphery of farms, in their own enclosed spaces and also isolated in the wild ashen countryside, as well as monumental longhouses like Hofstaðir where over thirty cattle skulls were found buried at equidistant intervals around the exterior.[68, 69] These sacrifices, known as *blót* rituals, blended the spiritual and physical world together: *hamr* (the physical shell of a person) and *hugr* (the mind) became one. Animals were slaughtered en masse in a display of wealth rivalling the kings in the homelands. Perhaps this was a demonstration of power, 'I can kill thirty of my valuable livestock, now you see how much wealth and power I have', or done in times of crisis to facilitate a bountiful harvest the next year, courtesy of the fertility siblings Freyr and Freyja.

Iceland was a wealthy place, in terms of material resources and cosmology. The island sparks our imagination today – no wonder the sagas describe such a wide cast of mythological characters.[70] Iceland was a land of contradictions, home to flames and belching mountains, but also serene star-filled skies, home to hundreds of farms, but also death, and undeath.

It was the heat of *Muspell* that so inflamed Snorri's imagination when compiling the *Prose Edda*. He turned the destructive and regenerative properties of fire and magma into a physical plane associated with the outrider sons of the flaming Surtr. Earlier versions of *Muspell* may have started out not as a place but as an event, the act of burning. No single place properly parallels *Muspell*. For argument's sake, look at a map and try to find somewhere volcanic, dusty, once-burning: the Canary Islands spring to mind.

A necessary preface is that there is no proof that vikingar ever visited this southerly archipelago, but viking activity did extend across North Africa and along the borders of the Sahara, and the Canaries can be sighted on a clear day from those shores. The isles were for a very long time home only to the native Macaronesians.[71] The volcanic islands of grey beaches and rocky cliffs are high-yielding agriculturally. Several beaches in Lanzarote are home to a unique green stone called olivine. It may have found its way to the markets of the Roman world, for in 1997 some evidence of international trade was detected in an excavation at El Bebedero.[72] Here were found Mediterranean potsherds, pieces of metal, and a few fragments of worked glass, all dated within the first to fourth centuries, either from a visit or shipwreck.

The Canaries were described by Greek historian Plutarch (46-120) as the 'Gardens of Hesperides', Elysian lands that lay beyond the Pillars of Heracles. The Mediterranean was the only sea to exist in the minds of authors; beyond it was the edge of the world. Later, these 'gardens' were described by Lucan and Ptolemy, and they subsequently appeared on maps as the 'Fortunate Isles'.[73,74,75] The Roman world knew of the Canaries, and the odd amphora did indeed wash up on their beaches, as evidenced in 1964 and in the El Bebedero excavation. There is no evidence at all that Scandinavians visited here. The Canaries may have been sighted, though, from the bows of a longship, en route through the Gibraltar Straits to raid Spain and Morocco. We know that at least one shipload of cargo arrived in the more northerly Macaronesian island of Madeira sometime in the tenth or eleventh centuries due to the isotopic origin of mice bones recovered during excavations; they were from a cold and northern location that was probably Scandinavia.[76,77] These mice perhaps hopped from a longship as a crew stopped overnight to replenish supplies; the towering ash pillars of Madeira's scraped cliffs and vistas would have been eerily silent, inhabited by nobody. Scandinavians would not attempt to settle Madeira, but they may have visited at least once.

'The islands are said to be two in number separated by a very narrow strait and lie 10,000 furlongs from Africa. They are called the Isles of the Blessed.' So Plutarch knew of Madeira and Vila Baleira.[78] Madeira is connected to the Canaries by a volcanic fault line of over 250 miles. If vikingar could travel 1,250 miles between Africa and Madeira, then they could certainly cover 250. The Canary Islands and Madeira are in the 'firing line' of Scandinavian incursions. Vikingar did, almost certainly, traverse a world of fire and brimstone, and they would indeed leave layers of ash in their wake. Their presence on the Canaries however is limited only to hoaxes* and speculation. Onwards to new shores, new lands, new carnage.

Niðavellir

Snorri's *Prose Edda* mentions *Svartálfaheimr*, the land of the *svartalfar*, the dark elves, and the *Poetic Edda* describes *Niðavellir*, or *Myrkheimr*, the 'dark dwelling' of the dwarves. Long have these two mythological locations been conflated. In the *Poetic Edda*, *Niðavellir* is said to be home to the golden hall of Sindri and his folk; a legendary dwarven smith. This was the forge that would produce Draupnir, Óðinn's self-duplicating ring; the golden boar Gullinbursti; the sun-bright blade Tyrfingr; and Þórr's hammer, Mjǫllnir. But even these items were created to match far more legendary treasures like Óðinn's spear Gungnir and Freyr's ship Skíðblaðnir; older items created in older forges. Many of these items were associated with war. The sword *Dáinsleif* mentioned by Snorri Sturluson 'which must cause a man's death every time it is bared' was forged by dwarves. It was one of many fictional swords which inspired the blade *Draugr* from *The Northman* (2022), modelled on an archaeological find from Valsgärde, Sweden.†

Svartálfaheimr is also mentioned by Snorri as home to 'dark elves', who lived alongside certain dwarves. It is unknown when it became synonymous with *Niðavellir,* but it is not clear if they were viewed as one and the same in the Viking Age, nor even when Snorri compiled his *Prose Edda*. Likewise, the dwarves, *svartalfar*, *dökkálfar*, and the *myrkálfar* may either be synonyms for the same breed of shadowy burrowers or entirely separate. All these myths were perceived differently by different people. While Snorri's writings codified much of these diverse tales, and invented unnecessary distinctions, there was never an 'official' handbook to the Old Norse cosmogony. One farmer may have believed *Niðavellir* to be a region within *Svartálfaheimr*, while a sailor thought they were entirely separate worlds. It is worth reiterating that even the Old Norse language did not exist as it does today through the phenomenal work of Jesse Byock, Carolyne Larrington, and others.[79] It was split between several dialects with regional variations, some entirely lost to us.

---

* The discovery of a longship on Tenerife was once used as an *inocentada* by local newspaper *Diario de Avisos*, a kind of prank played on 28 December, the 'Day of the Innocent Saints'.
† Thank you to Neil Price for the information, and Robert Eggers, and the team behind *The Northman*.

Journeys

Mistranslations, differences in interpretation, and contradictions abound all these imagined elements.

Svartálfaheimr and *Niðavellir* were associated with darkness, dwarf smiths, and gilded halls. this was surely and expression of an innate appreciation of the important role blacksmiths played in Early Medieval society, not just in Scandinavia but elsewhere prior to Christian conversion. *Niðavellir* 'stood to the north' in the *Prose Edda*. The character of Wayland the Smith (in Old Norse, known as Vǫlundr) from European folklore is credited with such momentous forging deeds, and the character of Sindri/Eitri was just one of many talented dwarves capable of creating the finest goods.[80] Lime-washed halls like those excavated at the magnate's estate at Tissø, in Denmark, likely shone brightly white over the surrounding fields like the sun-sword of Surtr. Tissø's was not quite a golden hall, so to speak, but it echoed that sentiment.[81, 82] The lordly residence identified at Avaldnes, near Stavanger, has long been argued to be one of the residences of Harald Fairhair, or earlier pre-Viking Age 'sea kings', but really all we can say is that it was a militarised dwelling of immense scale.[83] Then there is Lejre[84] and Borg,[85] two archaeological sites from Denmark and Norway which have evidence of multiple grandiose longhouses, and also the pagan 'temple' mentioned by Adam of Bremen at Gamla Uppsala[86, 87] in Sweden. Gamla Uppsala was perhaps the only true 'golden hall' in Scandinavia, something supported by both textual references and archaeology. The internal birch and ash pillars of the hall were lined with gold foils, shimmering in the smoky flames rising from the central hearth. Pools of blood stuck to the boots of travellers as they walked beneath the giant statues of Þórr, Freyr, and Óðinn, dripping from sacrifices dangling above their heads down into the deep well below. Such travellers must have felt like dwarves themselves, in a world of giants.

Even Gamla Uppsala would have paled in comparison to the sights encountered by enterprising *vikingar* in the Arab-Berber world of Spain: Al-Andalus.

By 711, the Umayyad Caliphate had begun its violent conquest of the Iberian peninsula, led by the Berber leader Ṭāriq ibn Ziyād, governor of Tangier.[88] By mid-century, the emirate of Córdoba had been established as a judicial and political capital of the Caliphate in its newly acquired territory.[89] Al-Andalus was not coterminous with modern Spain, there were Basque and Asturian holdouts along the northern borders, which Scandinavians may have occasionally roamed. Al-Andalus and its borders were a warzone, fought over by the aggressive Umayyad Caliphate and the remnants of an earlier Germanic-speaking kingdom. Place names across Portugal, Leon, and Galicia such as Lormano, Lordemanos, and Lodimanos indicate that the Latin root word of *nordmanni* was used

Forgotten Vikings

Some examples of the gold foils found in abundance across various Viking Age sites in Scandinavia, including at Gamla Uppsala. These foils are tiny but adorned with impressive detail likely stamped onto the thin metal sheets with dies. The many motifs seen across the foils share similarities with ones elsewhere on runestones. They are also known as *guldgubbar* and *guldkoner* ('little old men of gold' and 'gold wives'). These are from Aska and the islands of Bornholm and Öland, near Lofoten in Norway, and from Västra Vång and Uppåkra in Sweden (clockwise from top left).

to describe some degree of 'north-man' settlement across the peninsula, though from what century we cannot be sure.[90]

Córdoba was a centre of learning for Europe and the western Arabic world, filled with palaces both new and old; one of the rulers of the caliphate, Abd ar-Rhaman I, would even take up residence in an old Roman villa previously occupied by mercenaries. He called it Ar-Ruṣāfa. Soon after, merchants would flock to the sandstone streets and plazas; open spaces ready for bazaars and entertainment from all around the world, home to spices, exotic animals, mercenaries, traders, landowners, peasants, and slaves. The winding streets would become hotspots of urban crime. This new world, lit by candles and braziers, was irrigated

Journeys

in part by water wheels (*noria*)[91] which used the flow of rivers like the Guadalquivir to funnel water to the palm-tree adorned private gardens of Alcázar de los Reyes Cristianos. But all this splendour and majesty was dwarfed by the building at the centre of Córdoba, its own golden hall, the Great Mosque: column after painted column connected via double arches of marble and stone, alternating horseshoe patterns of red and white brick extending to the heavens, high and low passages, secret courtyards and huge balconies, gates for all cardinal directions and private *maqsurah* for the intimate prayers of the Caliph and his entourage, oriented through the ornately adorned *qibla* wall towards Mecca. The Great Mosque of Córdoba still stands today, truly a testament to the splendour and engineering of the Arabic world. For it, there was never a decline as observed in the western world with the slow withdrawal of the Roman Empire.

The Arabs would of course meet resistance. The people of the Basque country and the resident Christians of the Spanish kingdoms were soon on the offensive. Arabic armies combined loyal Muslim warriors with mercenaries from the Berber lands far to the south beyond the desert sea, hailing from the ancient Silk Roads that ran between fortress cities. In 844, an army like this would suffer vikingar in the so-called 'Sacking of Seville'.[92]

On 25 September, a sizeable fleet of Scandinavian raiders launched an attack down the Guadalquivir River on *Išbīliya*, modern Seville, an impressive Arabic city comparable to Córdoba. The *hajib* (chief minister) of the city, Isa ibn Shuhayd, is said to have immediately mobilised his own troops along with the larger forces of the emir in Córdoba and the converted local dynasty of the Banu Qasi, and within two months *Išbīliya* had been retaken, the vikingar leaving in dribs and drabs. These raiders had sailed down the waterways of southern France into Asturian Spain. Before reaching *Išbīliya*, crews of longships were defeated by a Christian named Ramiro at the still-standing Roman lighthouse known as the Tower of Hercules. Lisbon was next on the hit-list, occupied by Arabs and Berbers led by their own *haqib*, Wahballah ibn Hazm, who alerted his emir to the threat. The military mobilisation and skill in defeating these raiders is proof of the organised and interconnected strength of Al-Andalus. By using the Banu Qasi, a newly Muslim frontier territory, Umayyad leaders were mirroring the practices of Charlemagne and his Obotrites. Nevertheless, whichever forces were initially guarding *Išbīliya* had been defeated by the *madjus*, the heathens.

As observed in the rest of Europe, these vikingar had harried *Išbīliya* from the surrounding Guadalquivir marshlands, creating a base at Isla Menor as a launchpad for raids against the city's defences. *Išbīliya* had no walls, and so according to Arabic sources 'terrors of imprisonment or death' were put upon the city, where 'not even the beasts of burden were spared', but still the central citadel held out during the siege. This *was* a siege, akin to the attack on Paris the following year; a massive invading army camped on the perimeter of an ancient city, doing their best to break in. This type of warfare was the antithesis of fast hit-and-run longship raiding. The vikingar were put to flight by mid-November of 844, defeated in a pitched battle outside *Išbīliya* and then again amongst the crumbling Roman ruins in the old city of Italica, by then no more than a graveyard inhabited by pilgrims. At this second battle, Arabic sources recount the use of what is most likely a variation of napalm to burn over thirty longships and a thousand raiders to ash. The tools at the disposal of the Arabic armies rivalled those of Constantinople. Nearby, at a place known as Talyata, the survivors of the Scandinavian forces are said to have been allowed to return unhindered to their fleet sheltering near the Algarve, in southern Portugal. Their raid leaders, however, were hanged on the palm trees that lined the streets.[93, 94]

Immediately in the aftermath of 844, a naval force (*dar al-sina'a*) was created by the emir, along with a network of messenger stations, checkpoints, and beacons between all the major cities and military outposts of Al-Andalus, all of which were commissioned with outer perimeters and walls. Within fifteen years, this new anti-raiding network, like Ælfred's *burh* system, made Al-Andalus into one massive fortress. We will see later how similar strategies were employed in Eastern Francia and, surprisingly, Denmark, to quell raiding parties. Though similar in concept to *burhs*, the craftsmanship and resources on hand for the Umayyad Caliphate were unrivalled in the western world. But the Caliphate was not invincible.

The eleventh-century compilation called the *Fragmentary Annals of Ireland* states that by 862, 'blue men' were appearing in *longphuirt*, captured by raids in the far south.[95] Recently, the skull of an African girl was discovered in the tenth-century cemetery at North Elmham, in Norfolk.[96] This was indeed an international and multi-ethnic world, though not always through settlement or conquest. In fact, the idea of *longphuirt* would spread across the Scandinavian diaspora. Llanbedrgoch in Anglesey preserves the name *Llongborth*, also found in the thirteenth-century Welsh poem *Geraint, son of Erbin*.[97] In Scotland, there are place names like Longformacus. We tend to associate the idea of *longphuirt* with Ireland, but there were sites with evidence of insular production, external trade, and slave processing all over the Early Medieval world.[98] This becomes a matter of definition, of course, for a *longphort* is a term which overlaps with sizeable army sites, such as the one on Oissel in Francia used in the ninth century, or le Camp de Péran in Brittany.

Even in Spain, Arabic sources mention how the first harrying of *Išbīliya* was launched from a marshy encampment based on the neighbouring island of Isla Menor. The twelfth-century *Chronicle of Iriense*[99] records a fleet of one hundred ships arriving in Galicia in 859 and the eleventh-century *Chronicle of Sampiri*[100] says the same for the year 968. These expeditions across Al-Andalus and Asturias were not isolated raiding parties but fully organised military endeavours, armies against armies. Or at least, this is what the sources claim, often prone to exaggeration to enhance the prowess of their heroes and perfidy of their villains. These armies would need camps, to process slaves (like the 'blue men' later found in Ireland), generate income, and to act as a defence against the formidable Umayyad forces.

The work of Irene García Losquiño and Jan Henrik Fallgren has been instrumental in reassessing the evidence for viking activity on the Iberian Peninsula. Now we have evidence for an abundance of longship anchors, 'D-shaped camps' up and down Portugal and Galicia, and topographic and geographic assessments as to their likely routes and usage of the hinterlands surrounding towns and fortifications.[101, 102, 103] Ultimately, viking activity in Spain was closer to the well-published campaigns in England than anything else, especially in the tenth and eleventh centuries where military endeavours would be launched over long periods, such as between 968-971 and 1047-1066.

Vikingar would travel beyond the reaches of Al-Andalus into even deadlier territory: North Africa, by then Moorish land inhabited by myriad peoples from around the world. The ethnic groups of North Africa, often homogenised as 'Berbers' or the Amazigh, had seen their lands frequently the target of the political machinations of various empires throughout history: Carthage, Greece, Rome, and then the caliphates. By the eleventh century, this was a desert rich in ancient ruins and crisscrossing cultures. Following the latest Arab conquests, the North African coastline became a launchpad for raids and invasions of the Iberian Peninsula. It was a vital core of the Islamic world, split between the caliphates of the Umayyads and Idrisids. The Straits of Gibraltar were dominated by two imposing bastions of Arabic power: their architecture immense, their weapons formidable, their armies unstoppable. When a viking fleet left the Mediterranean in 861 for the Atlantic, it was an Arabic naval contingent they had to push through. It is likely these ships were stationed as a preemptive force, following a raid two years prior.

For the year 859, the tenth-century *Chronicle of Alfonso III* describes how '[Northmen] sailed the sea and attacked Nekur [Nekor], a city in Mauretania, and there they killed a vast number of Muslims.'[104] Nekor was an emirate in Morocco. This is the same location described by inventive historian Ibn Khaldun[105] writing two centuries later, who added (or forged) details like the names of the individuals captured, enslaved, and in some cases ransomed back to the emir, along with the total amount of time the *madjus* spent in the city, eight days. This was enough time for the vikingar to allegedly capture significant numbers of the population, one of whom may have been discovered in the River Coln in Fairford, England, in 2013.[106] The *Fragmentary Annals* give details about viking activity in Spain, including the 'king of Mauretania' losing his arm in battle followed by the slaughter of many of his men. These opposing forces meeting the Mediterranean viking fleet in battle were likely cosmopolitan troops reflecting Morroco's diverse nature, Amazigh warriors, hardened by a lifetime in the Sahara.[107] Archaeological evidence from Nekor, however, indicates that the town was well out of reach of the international trade routes that passed through the Mediterranean and over the deserts; locally made ceramics dominate the artefacts rather than foreign goods, and a century later the town may have been abandoned. These textual sources are perhaps adding some spice to whatever truly transpired amidst these dunes.

The vast Sahara would have been completely otherworldly to people familiar with the snow-capped peaks of Scandinavia or the wet boglands and forests of the Baltic and the Low Countries. A sea within a sea, a world within a world, an endless barren ocean of dust that stretched across the infinite horizon. And yet, people were crossing it on camels, watered and fed at conveniently located checkpoints, and making their way out of oblivion and onto the battlefields near Nekor in Morocco. If this desert was so inhospitable, then how did these people cross it with ease? What world did they hail from, beyond the infinite waste? What lay further south?

As far as we know, Scandinavians would never figure that out, and this land of golden architecture dotted by ancient Roman ruins, bazaars, wooden golems, and strange folk, and guarded by the most formidable foe ever to face viking armies in battle, would be the last stop on their southwards journey. A land of darkness and dust, but also beauty and wonder, wealth, and opportunity.

Ljosalfheimr

Bjorn *járnsíða* and Haesten's voyage is one of two dramatically long semi-fictitious raiding expeditions which took place during the Viking Age. While it may have really happened, over the years the events have become infused with legend, despite being corroborated to some degree in various Mediterranean annals. Beginning in 859 along the banks of Frankish rivers, Bjorn and Haesten's immense fleet of longships reached the Iberian Peninsula through the Bay of Biscay. They would be defeated at Neibla, in central Spain, but were victorious in burning the mosque at Algeciras. They would then raid the Idrisid Caliphate around Nekor, only to be repelled from Orihuela in Alicante. This far-flung voyage was a rollercoaster of defeats and victories. A site near Roussillon in southern France was attacked and used as an overwintering camp; Narbonne, Nîmes, Arles, and Valence were all in the firing line, as was the land that would become Italy. There is a tale about Bjorn believing the phrase 'all roads lead to Rome' to be accurate and so, intent on raiding Rome and securing his reputation, his word-fame as the man who raided the Christian capital, he headed down a random road and raided the first city he found. This was not Rome, but Luni. To achieve victory Bjorn (or Haesten, for tales differ) faked his own death and posthumous conversion to Christianity, and then his men took him inside the walls to be buried, only for him to spring out from the casket fully armed, ready to wreak havoc. Such a tale is best for entertainment only,[108] and indeed, it inspired the finale of *Vikings*' third season in 2015.

There is no archaeological evidence for a Scandinavian raid in Luni, though it is attested that the area was constantly disputed by various military groups – the Saracens, the Lombards, and the Carolingians – lying as it did on the borders of various polities. Bjorn's supposed involvement originates in the eleventh century and earlier accounts all contradict one another; all we can really be sure of is that there *was* a viking fleet active in the Mediterranean between 859-861. Haesten and Bjorn are comparable to Harald Fairhair, legendary figures who serve as exaggerated composites of multiple real individuals.

By the sixth century, Luni's Roman forum had succumbed to nature; public buildings had crumbled, and the administrative infrastructure had shrunk. Decrepit, but not abandoned. In the 1970s, evidence of postholes indicating wooden residences was found within the area of the forum; perhaps a new community had sprung up in the Imperial shadow. An amphitheatre and theatre were found, along with a segment of an ancient pre-Roman road linking Luni to other urban centres across Italy and beyond.[109, 110] Luni had passed from the Goths to the Romans, then the Lombards by the seventh century, falling out of favour with the latter thanks to better trade routes offered by towns like Lucca on the coast. By 774, Lombard rule fell to the Franks, and later the Muslims. The Lombards came from a similar part of the world to Old Norse speakers. There may have been an intelligible word or two passed between the guards at Luni and the raiders at their gates.

The character of the Roman Empire – or rather the *idea* of Rome – had not left Italy by the time of the Viking Age. While there were no legionaries roaming the streets, Rome still had its glory and splendour. The Colosseum would have awed any visitor, as it does to this day. While a shadow of its former self under the Republic and Empire, Rome by the ninth century was still a sight to behold; it remained the seat of the Catholic church and was a site of pilgrimage. Wilfrid, a seventh-century Northumbrian monk, visited Rome on no fewer than four occasions. The city's character would have changed between each of Wilfrid's visits, as marble pillars were repurposed for public repairs, wooden constructions were built to take advantage of new market spaces cleared by the demolition of old ruins, and treasures were unearthed from the winding labyrinth beneath the Palatine Hill. In many cases, the facades of ancient buildings were restored, as if to say 'Rome has not fallen, we are still here.' Ælfred's visit here as a boy may have inspired his desire to restore Roman learning, virtues, and state-craft to and beyond the bounds of his English kingdom. *Romanitas* was inherent; new residents in wooden villas attempted to emulate their earlier counterparts. Later 'imperial' figures of tenth- and eleventh-century Europe would consciously refer back to the values of Ancient Rome.[111, 112, 113] In this regard, the alluring realm of *Alfheim* or *Ljosalfheimr* – home of the light elves – bears some similarity. The *Poetic Edda* describes 'Alfheim' as property given to Freyr on the arrival of his first tooth; was it a realm, or just a hall? Snorri in his *Prose*, expands the scope of this glistening domain significantly:

> Many places are there, and glorious. That which is called Álfheimr is one, where dwell the peoples called Light-Elves; but the Dark-Elves dwell down in the earth, and they are unlike in appearance, but by far more unlike in nature. The Light-Elves are fairer to look upon than the sun, but the Dark-Elves are blacker than pitch.

Other parts of Snorri's *Gylfaginning* could be describing the shadow of Rome:

> It is said that another heaven is to the southward and upward of this one, and it is called Andlangr; but the third heaven is yet above that, and it is called Vídbláinn, and in that heaven we think this abode is. But we believe that none but Light-Elves inhabit these mansions now.

Imagine the ghosts that inhabited the empty halls of Rome, the superstitions of the new residents, caught somewhere between paganism and Christianity as the Catholic church asserted or reasserted itself. In the streets were pilgrims and beggars wishing to see the Pope. In the gilded majesty of the post-Roman palatial complexes were people in coloured togas, harking back to a better time. The 'third heaven' mentioned by Snorri might even hint at hierarchies above even *Ásgarðr*. It is in *Víðbláinn* that the survivors of *Ragnarǫk* await the new dawn; it was in Rome where infrastructure was rebuilt following the fifth-century sackings.

Pisa was also allegedly raided by *vikingar*, along with Fiesole in Tuscany. Unlike Rome, Pisa had seen a far less dramatic dip in fortunes following Imperial decline.[114] Thanks to its extensive river networks and coastal defences, Pisa remained a wealthy port straddling the Lombard, Roman, and Frankish worlds for several centuries before falling to the latter in the eighth, just as Charlemagne was gearing up to annex Frisia. Pisa was a prime target to raid. Fiesole, further inland, had been the site of a battle won by Stilicho's legions against the 'barbarians' in 406, though like many areas of the empire it would eventually fall to new occupiers. Razed by Byzantine forces in the sixth century, Fiesole must have resembled a ruin by the ninth, its baths dry, its forums empty, its walls unmanned.[115]

There is a possibility that Bjorn and Haesten's fleet then went on to raid more territories around eastern Italy and the Adriatic Sea, but they disappear from the historical record for a time. We do know, however, that they raided the Balearics, the island chain off the south coast of Spain and France, Mallorca, Ibiza, Menorca, and Formentera.

Conquered in 539 by Emperor Justinian, the Balearics had been seized by the eastern Roman Empire from the Vandals. Today, the Balearics are home to the greatest number of basilicas anywhere on the Iberian Peninsula. These were huge structures, visible for miles from both land and sea. An earlier Roman fort at Formentera may have acted as a lighthouse for weary travellers as they approached this entrepôt between Toledo, Carthage, and Constantinople; equidistant between the great powers of the ancient world and, by the ninth century, the Umayyad, Idrisid, and Byzantine realms. Perhaps these travellers were pilgrims, to be baptised in the decorated and coloured fonts at Son Peretó, Mallorca, or Son Bou, Menorca.[116, 117] Germanic speakers, Greeks, and Arabs all inhabited these islands, along with the natives.[118] As the Balearics would suffer continual warfare from the first century BCE onwards, the islanders likely had to adapt fast. Arabic accounts record a need in 902 to prevent further piratical raids from being launched from the islands. Launched by whom, we do not know.

There were older structures here, from before the Phoenicians. Talaiots, which lend their name to the otherwise unknown people who built them, are large Bronze Age megaliths found all over Mallorca and Menorca, dated between the second and first millennium BCE. A series of cemeteries include the awe-inspiring Necrópolis de Son Real in northwest Mallorca, perhaps at one point holding jewellery and bronze blades from the distant past as found at nearby Puigpuynent.[119]

The Mediterranean was bordered on all sides by a truly ancient series of civilisations that had existed since long before the Dust Veil and some of their their structures remained in the landscape, inspiring and haunting the minds of later travellers. The Old English poem *The Ruin*, allegedly composed in and describing *Aquae Sulis* (Bath), captures this wonder.[120] Did vikingar have an idea as to who built these marble towers, these huge stone faces? Did they know who was responsible for the waterways of Pisa, the Etruscan walls of Fiesole, or the lighthouse on Formentera? Perhaps the most experienced and well-travelled among them saw similarities between the architecture in Constantinople and the ruins in Italy and the Balearics, and perhaps they would have then thought about the passage of time and the fall of even these most powerful empires.

Bjorn and Haesten's legendary voyage would end in 861, limping out of the Mediterranean past the bronze towers of the Pillars of Hercules and an Arab fleet, back into the Atlantic Ocean. Far away from the turmoil they had caused across the old lands of Rome, and more rooted in observable history, was a community living a peaceful life in one of the greenest places on Earth. The Azores.

In 2015 a team of researchers led by Jeremy Searle noticed a connection between the genomes and bones of mice on the Azores, an archipelago in the middle of the Atlantic Ocean, and those from Scandinavia, the same as the evidence for a Madeiran-Scandinavian link.[121] A few years later, Pedro Raposeiro and others revealed layers of sediment dating back centuries before Portuguese dominion over the uninhabited islands. Between 700-850, someone had made their way to the Azores.[122] What these visitors found, by the inland lakes of Pexinho and Caldeirão, sheltered from the bracing Atlantic winds by grassy slopes and thin forest canopies, was a pristine landscape. Trees were cleared for livestock, cattle and sheep foraged on the emerald grass, and the farmers who watched over them thought of their colder homelands. So far, no identified settlements have been found on the Azores, but Scandinavians were here during the Early Medieval Period. Out in the middle of a gargantuan body of water, farming, and feasting, sleeping, and singing, telling tales.

Niflheim

The many monsters that dot Old Norse mythology were, like other fantastical creatures of Antiquity, probably loosely inspired by real animals. They fill the pages of Isidore of Seville's *Etymologies*, the

Journeys

vellum of Icelandic sagas, and myriad maps (like the ones in this book, sketched from the *Physiologus*). In the sixth century, a 'sea monster' called Porphyrios harassed ships for a fifty-year period in the harbours and offshore fisheries of Constantinople.[123] During Justinian's reign, Greco-Roman writer Procopius mentioned Porphyrios many times in the *History of the Wars* and *The Secret History* as a genuine nuisance that needed to be removed. Allegedly, Porphyrios met its end on the shores of the Black Sea when it beached and was bludgeoned to death by a mob. It is unknown what exactly Porphyrios was, but some species of whale is most likely; a very large orca perhaps, due to their tendency even today to attack yachts for fun, or a sperm whale, known to rise rapidly from the deep, with their battering-ram heads. The fear that the ocean instils in us today, that portal to the abyss, is a primordial one. It has been with humanity for thousands of years, but Early Medieval Scandinavians mastered the sea, carving through island chains and over the tops of waves with their ships which, by the tenth and eleventh centuries, had evolved into war machines. *Drakkar* and *busse* types, longer and sturdier, capable of fitting more warriors than earlier variants like the *snekkja*, were used for raiding and military expeditions across Europe and beyond.[124] The bulk of oceanic travel, however, especially deep sea voyages, would be sailed in *knerrir*, big-bellied mercantile vessels.[125] These were the ships capable of storing slaves and livestock and which transported families of migrants to distant locations; the backbone of the Viking Age economy. These were the ships whose sailors first sighted the shores of Greenland.

Greenland was probably known about shortly after the mass migration to Iceland in 871. It is sometimes visible from the tallest peaks on the northwest coast of the latter, above the fog. Greenland's winters are deathly cold, and in the Early Medieval Period this was no different. Contrary to popular belief, the settlement of Greenland was not significantly boosted by the so-called Medieval Warm Period, which saw a marked increase in temperature globally for a few centuries.[126] By the end of the tenth, the first Europeans were travelling from Iceland to Greenland, but this is well before the temperature reached its highest, and after the boulders shifted by glacial expansion had been raised. The Greenland that the first Scandinavians inhabited was a freezing expanse of ice and rock, with only a few pockets of greenery – much like it is today.[127]

The first settlement of Greenland occurred around the same fifteen-year span as the adoption of Christianity in Iceland in the year 1000, and sagas mention the original family being partially Christian. Erik the Red's wife, Thjodhild, asked for a church to be built within the first few years of arrival. The adaptations of Greenland farmsteads were not

An example of a knarr (or knǫrr, pl. knerrir). This example is based on the Skuldelev I vessel recovered from the Peberrenden waterways near Roskilde, Denmark, dated to 1030.

only responses to environmental challenges but also social stimuli; for the first time across these North Atlantic migrations, we see evidence of churches, small things that seem to dominate the archaeological record in the place of pit-houses, which all but disappear. But Greenland was not an overwhelmingly Christian colony, at least not at first.

Niflheim, the land of mist and cold, indeed the very coldest realm, is first mentioned in Snorri's *Gylfaginning*, though the bulk of its idiosyncrasies come from *Hrafnagaldr Óðins* ('Óðinn's raven song', or 'prelude'), a heavily disputed and likely seventeenth-century poem.[128] As a result, there is very little we know of *Niflheim*, just that it was located *below* all of the other realms, often associated with the idea of 'Hel'. Even its position can be doubted, for Snorri may have been referencing a Christian creation framework when he wrote that realms were created by being lifted above *Niflheim*. It was a frigid, misty abyss, a yawning void at the base of all things; the deep sea, perhaps, where so many sailors would meet their end. Whether or not *Niflheim* was an afterlife or some kind of purgatory is unknown. *Jotnar* were frequently sent to *Niflheim* by swings of Þórr's hammer, and the rivers of *Hel*, like *Hvergelmir* and *Élivágar*, also carved courses through *Niflheim*. The two realms were linked, like the settlers of Iceland and Greenland.

From the latter half of the tenth century, Scandinavians were not just settling unknown Atlantic islands, but they were also travelling further and further northwards up the Norwegian coastline. The localised spatial analyses undertaken on Lofoten isles like Vestvågøy[129] indicate that new farms were being created with new borders and new shielings to house animals in the outfields. These shielings situated on Arctic archipelagoes could take advantage of a variety of marine fauna. Subsistence in these polar regions was initially based around cattle, pigs, and caprines, but as seen with the Faroese archaeofaunal record, farmers soon adapted their diet to include fish, shellfish, whales, and seals. These 'marine shielings', to borrow a term coined by Christian Madsen,[130] would become core components of the farmstead model in Greenland. In fact, despite the possible reduction in shielings in Early Medieval Iceland, they reappear shortly after in Greenland's archaeological records.* Various ruins dot the coastlines and fjords of Greenland's southerly regions, spread across the three identified settlement areas of Scandinavian farmers from no earlier than 985.[131] These settlement areas, collectively forming the Greenland colonies, were known as Eystribyggð, Vestribyggð, and Mellembyggð (the latter not so thoroughly researched), the Eastern, Western, and Middle Settlements respectively. These settlements were not townscapes, though some assembly sites have been identified, but isolated farmsteads existing along fjords and at the tips of skerries, situated to take advantage of the forests and fields of the highlands, rich in grass, and the seal populations in the bays.

Wider unsettled areas were called 'Obyggðir', a saga-term also used to describe the vast areas of tundra around the White Sea inhabited by *finnas*. Greenland was not inhabited by *finnas*, but the natives were of a culture with many convergent traits; the Dorset Palaeo-Eskimo nomads had started to emigrate beyond Greenland into North America by the ninth century. All we really hear about them from the European

---

* It is possible these patterns of disappearing and reappearing shielings and pit-houses are down to discovery bias. There has been minimal effort to identify pit-houses in Greenland, and likewise for shielings in Iceland.

perspective are vague mentions of abandoned structures upon the initial sighting of Greenland's shores in *The Saga of Erik the Red*, from *Hauksbók*.[132] The Dorset Culture lived in longhouses woven with reeds and animal fur. They carved the likenesses of animals like polar bears and seals out of walrus ivory and seem to have been linguistically and culturally distinct from the incoming Thule Inuit Culture, who migrated to Greenland from Siberia from the tenth or eleventh centuries. The Thule referred to the Dorset as the *tuniit*, and in later vernacular recordings of earlier folk stories, these *tuniit* are said to have been taller than the Thule but easily frightened and beaten in battle. There appears to have been minimal cross-cultural contact between the Dorset and Thule; the former seems to have disappeared in Greenland by 1500.[133]

Sandwiched between these two great migrations was the arrival of Scandinavians in Greenland. The way these Greenlanders built their farmsteads was already significantly adapted from Norwegian methods. We have already seen that on the Faroe Islands the addition of irrigation ditches and steep run-offs to help with animal waste and soil fertilisation was a priority. This would be repeated in Greenland at sites like Garðar and appears in the Icelandic sagas.[134] In the fifteenth-century *Saga of Ref the Sly*, the titular character retreats into a Greenland fjord to escape vengeful attackers. To prevent them from burning down his hall, he uses a complex system of wooden sluices connected to an inland lake to extinguish every flame before it can take hold. Palaeoecological analyses of the fields around Garðar indicate a wet lowland environment, artificially enhanced by manure and water from the surrounding highlands.[135] Clearly, the soils of Greenland needed constant supplements, which would have made subsistence quite a struggle. These agropastoral farmers may have been forced to abandon their farmsteads due to the short but intense growing season of Greenland and the long winters. Greenland's summers are excruciatingly short, but the days are very long. As a result, crops would grow at twice their normal rate but for half the amount of time they would elsewhere across the diaspora (save for northernmost Norway and Sweden). Therefore, while crops

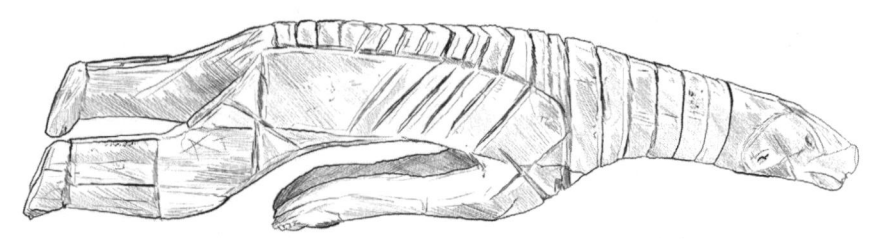

A 'floating bear' carving found near Igoolik, Northern Canada, dated between 1-500, the 'Middle Dorset Culture'.

would still grow, they would have to be stored for much longer than they would elsewhere. Evidence from numerous coastal farms and their pollen records reveals that farmers were leaving their homes for regular periods each winter, perhaps using the plentiful shielings spread across the hinterlands.

These shielings, in their hundreds, were small seasonal lodgings linking larger farmsteads together across the three areas of identified settlement. Eystribyggð was by far the largest and most fertile, with the easternmost settlement of Herjolfsnes being as far away from Eystribyggð as Mellembyggð was. Late Medieval artefacts from Herjolfsnes and other sites include *vaðmál*, a type of very thick winter clothing made of spun wool.[136] Even here, in the warmest part of Greenland, times were tough, and it is likely that Herjolfsnes enjoyed the most international trade out of all the settlements.[137, 138] In the comparatively isolated Mellembyggð, the mountains and fjords would have led to more snow drifts.[139] This would have have reduced the agricultural yield from the already hard-pressed farmland, a white sheet blanketing the crops. Worse still was Vestribyggð, facing the straits between Greenland and North America, which saw the coldest temperatures and the most dispersed farmsteads. Travel between the three sites would have been a long process on foot and by boat – Greenland is the largest island in the world and the European settlements stretched across an area as vast as Norway. The movement of information, goods, and people from Vestribyggð to Eystribyggð would have been arthritic.

But goods did move; walrus tusks harvested from *Norðrsetr* ('the northern seat', the hunting grounds by Disko Bay) by 'Norðrsetrmen' made it all the way down to the Arabic world, so too did polar bears to Norwegian courts in the eleventh century, and English castles in the thirteenth.[140] Such rarities brought a lot of wealth to Greenland, at least initially. Garðar and Brattahlíð on the southerly tip of Greenland probably gained most of this wealth, both being assembly sites and relatively highly populated.[141] These sites probably had the most cattle, everyone else made do with sheep, goats, and an increasing supply of seal and whale meat. Garðar and Brattahlíð had small churches first identified by Paul Nørlund in the 1920s. These churches, some surrounded by a small, curved wall akin to the earlier enclosures of Icelandic pit-houses, may very well have filled the role once performed by pagan ritual sites.

The settlement of Greenland was not on quite the same scale as Iceland but consisted of a few enterprising family groups which over time were joined by others who then spread up and down the fjords. It is plausible that the addition of churches to Greenland's archaeological record at the dawn of North Atlantic Christendom is a reason for the reduction of pit-houses; an adaptation not to environmental challenges but to a change in belief.

Thanks to sand drifts, we even know exactly how a lot of the turf-built farmsteads in Greenland were constructed, layer upon layer of sod brick laid in a herringbone pattern.[142] The absence of wood and available stone is reflected in the buildings. This saw some parallels in twelfth-century Iceland, at the site of Stöng, but the links do not end there.[143] The pit churches of Greenland are remarkably like those on the Faroe Islands that began to appear in the early twelfth century, and so too are the irrigation ditches. it is therefore possible that some of the settlers who came to Greenland came from the Faroe Islands and brought with them their own architectural styles and worldview.

Navigation between the two locations and across the wider North Atlantic probably involved some degree of knowledge about animal migratory patterns. A few stray mentions in the eleventh-century *Ælfric's Colloquy*[144] from England indicate that whale hunting involved driving a whale towards shallows to then beach and kill it, reminiscent of the sixth-century death of Porphyrios. Excavations at Flixborough in Lincolnshire uncovered a vast amount of cetacean remains, evidence of whaling along the River Humber and hunting of bottlenose dolphins, some minke whales, and even a stray orca.[145] Before the Viking Age, people off the coast of Norway were targeting Northern Right whales to harvest oil and blubber, creating by-products from their bones like gaming pieces.[146]

The farmstead model in Greenland was, by now, quite far removed from the original back in Norway. To recap, we have gone from a longhouse, outhouse, and pit house, all located in the infield, and then shielings and boat sheds in the outfield. In Greenland, the average rural settlement was now a small turf longhouse with subsidiary extensions as outhouses (farmers lived with livestock, as on pre-Viking Age farms). There would be a small church, and an array of shielings dwarfing the quantity seen elsewhere. The layout of farms would change even more in one final westward migration, to Newfoundland, but Scandinavians were also sailing (and perhaps skiing) beyond Greenland to other areas of North America.

In 2014, Patricia Sutherland[147] oversaw a fascinating excavation of a Norse-Thule trading outpost far to the north on Baffin Island, which may well be the *Helluland* described in *The Saga of the Greenlanders* account of Leif Erikson's voyage. If Greenland was cold and harsh, then Baffin Island was beyond even that; a deeper layer of *Niflheim*, home to darker things, darker beings. There is evidence of metalworking in a small crucible fragment found at the site, which is possibly not from the resident Inuit but from Scandinavians, along with the carved likeness of

Journeys

This unassuming figure has been widely argued to be an Inuit carving of a European settler or trader. It was found buried in an Inuit dwelling on Baffin Island dated to 1350.

a European settler done by a native artist. More research into this Thule-Norse heritage awaits in the land of the midnight sun.

Further north on Ellesmere Island[148] a set of scales was found, presumably used in trading activities with the Thule people. There are also runic inscriptions written in the extinct language 'Greenlandic Norse', from the Kingittorsuaq region, which mention a small family unit 'riding' somewhere and travelling together; much of the thirteenth- or fourteenth-century text has been eroded.[149] As the Greenland settlements progressed, walrus hunting became more and more of a major industry, the populations over-hunted. Disko Bay, *Norðrsetr*, likely became one of many hunting arenas as Scandinavians were forced further and further north into the white void of blizzards and shipwrecks, all in the name of trade and profit.

The Arctic islands around Greenland hosted a hubbub of activity between the Scandinavians and the Thule; icebergs and slurry would have slowed their crafts on their northerly voyages, and relations between the two migrant groups were tense, but nevertheless, they continued. This was the farthest north Viking Age people would ever reach, but by this point, they were so far removed from being vikingar that we may as well call them tusk-hunters. Here, in *Niflheim*, were the most isolated pockets of activity, people eking out a living in the black winter. Ultimately, however, Greenland would be the stage for the Viking Age's quiet denouement.

Vanaheimr

Two families made up the gods of the Old Norse cosmology, the Æsir and the Vanir, initially at war but later allied through marriage. While the giants and other beings represented the whims of nature, these gods represented order and civilisation. The Æsir included Óðinn and Þórr. The Vanir may have been predominantly fertility gods like Freyr and his sister Freyja, who appear to have also been invoked in battle rituals. Largely, we can assume that the Vanir were for the most part associated with crop cultivation and sex. The island of Frösön in Jämtland was dedicated to Freyr, and excavations there have revealed the stump of a birch tree surrounded by animal and human remains.[150] In an agriculturally based society like Viking Age Scandinavia, where warfare was important but also relied on successful rural subsistence, the Vanir and Æsir surely received an equal share of the people's reverence. These deities were important, yet their home is mentioned only once in the *Poetic Edda*, in the poem known as *Vafþrúðnismál*. The description given of *Vanaheimr* is vague; all we know is that it was the birthplace of one of the Vanir, home to 'wise powers'.

Fertile agricultural lands would of course be prime targets not just for settlement but also for raiding. Heading further south and east along the *Austrvegr* would have taken Scandinavian, Baltic, and Slavic vikingar past the hillforts, flash-weirs, and taxation barriers of Estonia, Latvia, and Lithuania, and onwards through grassy meadows and forests rich with the smell of pine. This Eastern Way, made up of several rivers, involved a certain amount of overland travel in which crews of slavers and traders would have to take their ship out of the water and fell trees to create a conveyor belt of logs to haul the ship to the next river. Either that, or they would utilise smaller rafts. These portages were necessary to avoid rapids

The branches of the world tree? The northern lights above Telegrafbukta, Tromsø, Norway. (Reproduced with permission from George Hieron, www.georgehieron.com)

A reindeer stands alone atop Kvaløya, an island off the coast of Tromsø, Norway. In modern Saami, this island is called 'Sállir' or 'Whale Island'. Both land and marine fauna were vital to the subsistence of sub-arctic peoples. (Reproduced with permission from George Hieron, www.georgehieron.com)

Left: Lying just north of modern Oslo, the small lake of Sognsvann, Norway, was one of many to dot the forested regions of Scandinavia, 'thin places' where the veil between worlds was faint. (Reproduced with permission from George Hieron, www.georgehieron.com)

Below: A view from Lemvig, Denmark, nestled in the Limfjord of the Jutland Peninsula. Lemvig originated in the thirteenth century, first recorded in charters as Læmwich, but the swampy terrain it sat upon had not changed since the early days of the raiders in the Kattegat. (Carolin/Adobe Stock 585021552)

Right: Now part of Sweden, Ljungbyhed in Skåne was once part of the Kingdom of the Danes during the Viking Age. Impassable forests like these likely served as 'frontier zones'; nebulous marches where all manner of threats – both real and imagined – lurked. It is no wonder maritime travel dominated in Early Medieval Scandinavia. (Megan McGowan)

Below: Likewise, in the Medieval Period, what is now Abisko National Park, northern Sweden, was considered terra nullius or 'nobody's land', because it was criss-crossed by Kvens, Saami, Finns, and other sub-arctic peoples. (Melanie/Adobe Stock 599162371)

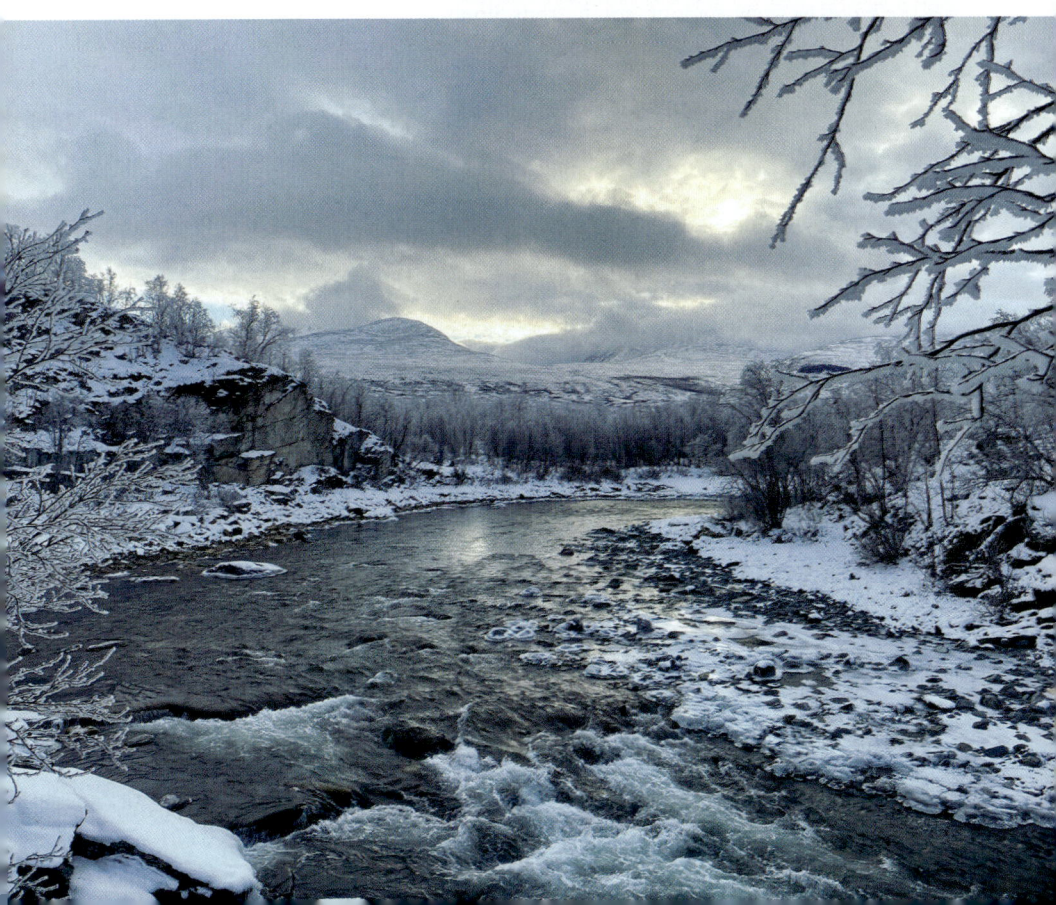

Above: An unnamed cairn near the site of Valhager, on the island of Gotland. A settlement between the fifth and sixth centuries, Valhager was abandoned amidst the climatic downturns of the 'Dust Veil'. (Viktor Lindbäck)

Below: The view looking south from Sumburgh Head, Shetland. A short sail along the whale road would take you past Fair Isle and onwards to Orkney. (Adam Collyer)

Above: The tidal flats near Blije, Friesland. Blije originated as a terpen settlement several centuries before the Viking Age but was first mentioned in the thirteenth century. These shores (and the marshes, at times of high tide) would have been home to an array of traders, travellers, and raiders from across the North Sea. (Hilbert Vinkenoog, History with Hilbert)

Below: The Giant's Causeway, Northern Ireland. In the Early Medieval Period, this basalt platform was part of the thalassocracy known as Dál Riata, a loose confederation of naval tribal groups extending between Irish and Scottish shores. As does the Giant's Causeway itself, linking with similar basalt structures in Atlantic Scotland. (Author's collection)

Above: The Neolithic Stones of Stenness, Orkney, might be the oldest monuments in the British Isles. One of them has been associated with 'Odin'. Our enduring fascination with Viking Age mysticism in the north may be the origin of this specific myth. In the Viking Age these pillars would have tantalised the minds of travellers, much as they do today. (Terry Wilden)

Below: A sun-kissed lake near Tampere, southern Finland. Near to Karjaa and Hiittinen, the site of Tampere has been inhabited since the seventh century, though it was likely out of reach of the vikingar until the twelfth and thirteenth centuries. (Paul Stein)

Above: The bounty of the Faroe Islands; a view from Streymoy. The peaks trap clouds, and the slopes are grazed by the indomitable Faroese sheep, a source of subsistence and wealth. This archipelago was named the 'Sheep Islands' for a reason. (Pedro/Adobe Stock 299172152)

Right: Down the rainbow bridge we flee, away from Ásgarðr? The view from Skógafoss, Iceland, has changed dramatically since the Viking Age, and the clue is in the name, Skógar, from Old Icelandic for 'forests'. This waterfall now sits amongst moss and rocks. Once sheltered by trees, it may have been a redoubt for the Skógarmaður or 'exiles' mentioned in thirteenth-century Icelandic law codes. (Adam Collyer)

A volcanic geyser in Iceland, one of many that have become mythologised as 'hellmouths' both pre- and post-conversion. (Neil Martin)

Agafay Desert, north of the Sahara, Morocco. Camel rides across this frontier were highly organised affairs. Recent isotopic analyses of camel bones indicate that they fed at arranged checkpoints, making long desert journeys tolerable for both mount and rider. It is unknown if vikingar travelled beyond the Sahara; would a view like this have tempted or frightened them? (Christian Jones)

Above: Layers of volcanic sediment in the extreme east end of Madeira, at São Lourenço. Sometime in the ninth century, at least one Scandinavian boat ended up here, and docked close enough to shore to allow mice to wander onto land. (Paul and Corinne Harvey)

Below: View from the Palatine Hill, where Romulus and Remus were found by the she-wolf. Rome and more importantly ideas of Rome survived into the Viking Age. (Caiden Tate)

Above: 'Langbarðaland' (Old East Norse for 'land of the Lombards') is mentioned on the Sö 65 runestone, Djulefors, Sweden; three others also reference military service in this location. The term most likely refers to the Byzantine province of Longobardia, in southern Italy, rather than Lombardy. (Pavel Rezac/Adobe Stock 278082801)

Below: Remnants of the 'Talaiot culture' of the Balearic Islands: the Necrópolis de Son Real, Santa Margarita, Majorca. Ancient megaliths and tombs like this may have looked familiar to roaming vikingar, considering their broad similarities with prehistoric sites across Orkney and Atlantic Scotland. (Author's collection)

Above: Pico Island, the Azores. In the ninth century, shepherds tended their flocks with this mountain in the background, though it was not named until the fourteenth century. If the Azores were visited in the Viking Age, even if just by one or two sailors, we might wonder what they called this distant mid-Atlantic archipelago. (Henner Damke/Adobe Stock 286048760)

Below: Somewhere between Igaliku and Narsarsuaq, Greenland. Here in the south, the first Scandinavian settlers established their farms near fjords and glacial lakes like this. (Emma Harty)

A dimly captured snapshot of the Labrador Coast, the blurry vestige of a half-remembered journey to the North American continent. The type of journey sagas would be written about. (Shaun Holdridge)

In England, as elsewhere across the Viking Age world, territorial borders were redefined. Sometimes these are recorded in land charters, or indicated by notable landmarks. It is thought that the name of The Bridestones, in Dalby Forest, Yorkshire, derives from Old West Norse for 'the brink stones' or 'the edge stones'. These prominent sandstone outcrops dominate the Staindale skyline; it would be no surprise if they acted as the border between farmland in the fledgling Danelaw. (Author's collection)

Above: Viking activity in Wales and south-west England was connected to wider events in the Irish Sea area. Here, in the Brecon Beacons, there were still ongoing frontier conflicts connected to Scandinavian incursions, however. In the early tenth century, a Mercian raiding party subjugated a small Brythonic kingdom here. The vikingar were not the sole military opponent of their day. (Author's collection)

Below: The Aegean Sea from Ana Koufinisi, near Athens. There was once a time where vistas like this would have been punctuated by the masts of Greek and Arab vessels, manned by mercenaries of Scandinavian and Baltic origin. (Jonah Walker)

Above: Born six years before the Battle of Hastings, King Eric 'the Good' of Denmark fell ill and died in Paphos, Cyprus, on pilgrimage to the Holy Land in 1103. Pilgrim's islands like Geronisos would have been home to small animal shelters and artificial reservoirs in his day, several decades after the Viking Age proper, but still a time of intrepid exploration. (Author's collection)

Below: The view from Snaefell, on the Isle of Man. The name comes from Old Norse for 'snow peak' – the old saying that 'six kingdoms' can be seen from atop this precipice indicates that Man might be the most central yet liminal spot on a Viking Age map. In the eleventh to thirteenth centuries, this lone island dominated the Irish Sea. (Shaun Holdridge)

The Iceland remembered in the sagas is a different world entirely to the one encountered in the eighth and ninth centuries. In them, it is the arena for tall tales and larger-than-life characters, superimposed onto a windswept, ash-covered isle. (Reproduced with permission from George Hieron, www.georgehieron.com)

There was candlelight, mead, and jubilation beneath the tumbled walls of Hvalsey Church one evening in 1408, at the last recorded wedding (and event) of the Greenland colonies. In the years following, this ultimate frontier of the Viking Age slowly succumbed to the same fate we are all destined to meet. Six hundred years later, its walls still stand, but there is no hint of what once transpired here at the end of the world. For the Greenlanders, their doom – their ragnarök – was a long-drawn-out affair with plenty of warning, but even in the settlements' twilight there was still time, and cause, for celebration. (Emma Harty)

across the River Dnieper. Some of the names of these rapids come down to us in various languages through runestones and sagas. In Old Norse each one appears to have embodied a different feeling, perhaps reflecting the minds of the weary travellers as they either steered through them or took the hard decision to haul their boat out of the water and lug it for miles.[151]

Sof Eigi was the first rapid, meaning 'Don't sleep' – the helm of the longship had to stay awake and aware, watching for the boulders beneath and those observing from the shore. *Holmfors* was the second, an 'island waterfall' – some of these rapids dropped over fifty metres. The third was *Gellandi*, the fourth *Eyforr*, and the fifth *Bárufors*: 'Roaring', 'Ever-Violent', and 'Wave-Waterfall'. Following them were *Hlæjandi* and *Strukum*, the latter meaning 'at the rapids'. *Hlæjandi* translates to 'Laughing'. Who was laughing? The natives waiting for a moment to strike from the shoreline? The sailors who had, by this point, successfully made it out of the most dangerous section of their route and were set to reach Constantinople?

For that was the ultimate destination of these river voyages. Constantinople was visited by Scandinavians probably as early as the middle of the seventh century. Clearly, it was worth it, for sailors repeatedly to undertake such arduous voyages. A journey down the *Austrvegr* would have taken months, through places safe or deadly. The tenth-century *De Administrando Imperio*, 'On the Governance of the Empire', written by Emperor Constantine VII, references St George Island as a haven for *Rus* sailors. Located after the Dnieper rapids, this was a redoubt where crews reattached their sails ready to head into the Black Sea towards the great city.

Travelling from the Baltic trading post at Truso, sailors would pass Kititten, Kaliningrad, and Wisihauten, all with evidence of intense trading activity from out of the Baltic Sea.[152] Graves and single finds across the wider regions of Sevastapol, Chernigov, and the rivers of the Desna and Dnieper reveal a landscape of movement and contact. Brooches, rings, pendants, Þórr's hammers, buckles, bridles, pins, and people were all shifted from Staraja Ladoga down the rivers to sites like Rjurikovo Gorodische, a pre-Viking Age hillfort later refortified and reinhabited by Slavic and Scandinavians. Sarskoe Gorodische is another such example, by Lake Nero, which likely functioned as an entrepôt given the presence of Arabic coins.[153] Across the edges of modern Russia, *Garðaríki*, 'the land of cities', was an area of variable Scandinavian presence. The Lower Volga basin appears to have been quite sparsely visited, but there is some activity in the lands of the Bulgar bordering the Mediterranean. Shestovitsa and Chernigov are both dotted with hillforts, each with evidence of international links. Aside from being well-defended military centres, these probably functioned as 'tax offices'. Travellers wishing to go down the *Austrvegr* must pay their dues to the local prince, armed and surrounded by his loyal men, the *druzhina*. These militarised zones may have become battlefields when travellers were not willing to pay. Three large barrow mounds near the Desna River, one of which containing a sword likely forged in Denmark, and another with a Þórr's hammer pendant, tell us this much. The chief 'cities' of *Garðaríki* were Kyiv, Novgorod, and Gnezdovo, owing to their position on the vital Dvina leg of the Dnieper trade route. These were proto-urban hotspots, with armed central citadels built of timber and exquisitely carved with local deities and customs. Weapon sacrifices and votive deposits were found nearby.

This vast open country, punctuated by timber cities like Kyiv, created insular and very powerful warlords from multi-ethnic backgrounds leading multi-ethnic armies. The spread of goods along the *Austrvegr* was matched by the spread of ideas; an entirely separate branch of Christianity – Greek Orthodox – would spread from Constantinople into the land of the *Rus* from the ninth century onward, distinct from the Roman branch spreading from western Europe.[154] This would have helped shape the unique identity of the *Rus*, caught somewhere between Scandinavian, Baltic, and Slavic, with Byzantine interests. There was a certain overlap with pre-Christian deities, too. Þórr is matched by Perkūnas and Perun, with some evidence of cult activity attached to one of these gods, or perhaps all three, at Chernihiv. There were other people in these lands who would not be included in the two-way assimilation as seen with the *Rus*.

Beyond the economically regulated lands of Garðaríki were seas of grass which eventually gave way to mountains; the steppes, home to people who spent much of their lives on horseback, Nomads. Many of the tribes were allied with Constantinople to thwart threats they deemed even greater; the *Rus* among them, but many were threats themselves.[155] It was these roaming horsemen who presented the greatest danger during times of portage, overlooking the river rapids, waiting.

The Khazar Qağanate were another society encountered by the *Rus*, whose fortunes would dip as the latter's rose.[156] Also allied every now and then as a proxy or buffer state of Constantinople, the Khazars were a polyethnic melting pot of various cultural, linguistic, and religious groups, Hungarians, Turks, others Slavic in origin. Some were Jewish, some Muslim, and others Tengrists. In fact, the entirety of *Garðaríki* and its surroundings, connected via the *Austrvegr*, was a polyethnic landscape, with blurred borders

Journeys

and ever-changing power dynamics, so most if not all these ethnic descriptors are in part misnomers. This was a land of opportunity. It is no wonder that so many vikingar would seek their fortune and stake their claim in the East.

The West offered different opportunities. Newfoundland was first visited by Scandinavians at the dawn of the eleventh century and settled at least seasonally by 1021.[157] Newfoundland may very well be the mythical *Vínland hið góða* ('Vinland the Good') mentioned in Icelandic sagas, an island where berries and barley grew all year round. The only problem was the resident *skrælingjar* (possibly 'weakling', 'yeller', 'dried skin', or something equally insulting), who posed a significant challenge for the unprepared and over-stretched farmers, not the battle-hardened vikingar of the eastern world. The only identified settlement of Scandinavian origin so far located on Newfoundland is L'Anse Aux Meadows, thanks to the work of Helge and Anne Ingstad in 1960.[158] The site is not a farm, nor really a home, at least not for any length of time. This final adaptation of the Norse farmstead model saw the grand longhalls and farmsteads transform into turf-built waystations for the repair of boats. There was a small smithy on site, smelting bog iron into clench nails to repair small vessels, but nothing in the way of permanent settlement, just booths made of sailcloth and sod.

Near to L'Anse Aux Meadows across the wider Hop's Bay region there is evidence of caribou drives. These are difficult to date but it is possible they are the work of these Scandinavians attempting to gather resources on the edge of the world.[159] Newfoundland really was the last stop for Scandinavians in the Viking Age. They had no conception that the island was the tip of an entire continent. Although resource expeditions were launched further west, into the Gulf of St Meadows region and probably beyond. A silver coin from the reign of Olaf *Kyrre* turned up in Maine, and black bear fur is found in both the L'Anse Aux Meadows and Greenland archaeological record.[160,161]

The farthest west Scandinavians travelled in this period is likely somewhere in the Cape Tanfield locality, near Hudson Strait. This was *Skrælingeland* – Canada and North America – the wider untamed wilderness home of nomadic hunter-gatherers. This was a terrifying place to the minds of Greenland farmers. Within a hundred years of the establishment of the L'Anse Aux Meadows settlement, it had been abandoned. Never again would inroads be made to settle this island, to take advantage of the fertile natural landscape.

The ultimate destination lay east, beyond the *Austrvegr* was the city of cities, *Mikligarðr*, the capital of the world and the surviving centre of

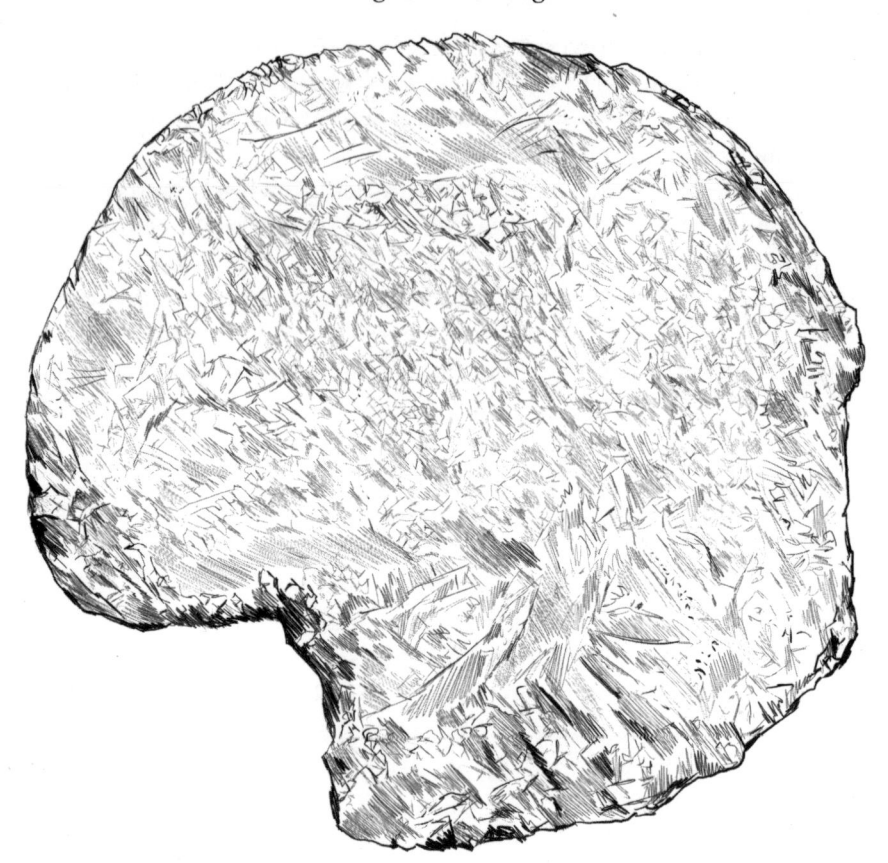

The 'Maine Penny' (or 'Goddard Coin'), minted somewhere in Norway between 1070-1080. There is evidence of perforation on the coin, indicating that it was worn as a pendant, along with spectroscopic traces of horizontal erosion that could have only been the result of centuries buried in damp soil. To this day, debate continues as to the veracity of the find. The location was an archaeological site at a Native American settlement in Brooklin, Maine. It remains a possibility that the 1957 discovery was a hoax, but current academic opinion holds that the Maine Penny is legitimate evidence of Native American and European contact.

the Roman Empire, first mentioned in Old Norse in the Icelandic Sagas. Constantinople was no city filled with ghosts, split between the past and the present, but the still beating heart of Rome.

Ásgarðr

The gods look down on us. *Ásgarðr* is mentioned three times in the *Poetic Edda*, and later traditions render it as 'above' the earthly realm of men. Did Early Medieval Scandinavians believe that far above the clouds, beyond the stars, was the home of the Æsir and Vanir? According to Snorri, Ásgarðr was connected to *Miðgarðr* by a bridge. *Ásgarðr* had many regions. It was not just made up of the royal halls of Óðinn and his brood, but an enlarged and enlightened version of our own world. *Ásgarðr* was, essentially, *Miðgarðr* but bigger and better. The halls in the rolling hills of *Ásgarðr* were the homes of a variety of gods, some who dwelt in the realm eternally and others who lingered there every now and then on vacation. The Vanir, for instance, may have hailed from *Vanaheimr*, but Freyja and Freyr lived in *Ásgarðr*.

Like the architecture of the realm, the behaviour of the Æsir and Vanir can be best seen as a heightened version of the behaviours we have been considering. While in the earthly realm the vikingar strove to ascend social strata through conquest and word-fame, so, too, was reputation and 'saving face' important in the realm above. In *Ásgarðr*, we hear many tales of Þórr's drunken escapades or the vengeful punishments of other gods against Loki. Snorri made euhemeristic attempts to ground the Æsir and Vanir, placing them in real history for Christian sensibilities. He claimed they were refugees from Troy, battle-leaders with long-lasting legacies, erroneously worshipped as deities by pagans.[162] Really, we can never know the origins of these figures, but they were clearly real to the people of the Viking Age. So too was their realm.

It has also been argued that Constantinople was the inspiration for *Ásgarðr*, but this is probably not the case. Really, *Ásgarðr* was an idealised vision of everyday life on a grand scale, inspired by real places and real cultures. For the average European traveller, Constantinople would be the greatest sight they would ever see, its marble towers glistening with gold, the multiple impervious walls manned by the infantry of the Byzantine army. Such forces, the Akrites units, had already tackled vikingar in Anatolia in 818. Constantinople itself would be attacked several times in later years, demonstrating the power and perhaps the arrogance of Scandinavian warlords who thought that they could scramble over the mighty walls as they could in Paris, Canterbury, and Seville. Constantinople was defended not just by a highly organised military separated into distinct units but also by ships armed with the infamous 'Greek fire'. These were real dragons, the bane of wood-built fleets of longships.

For a martial society, the city of cities represented not just an opportunity but arguably *the* opportunity of the Viking Age. The thirteenth-century *Gulaþing* laws from Norway state that 'if (a man) goes to Greece, then he who is next in line to inherit shall hold his property.'[163] Various runestones and sagas commemorate voyages to *Grikkland* and Constantinople, and the exploits travellers got up to in the south.[164] Chief among these travelling warlords was Harald Sigurdsson, better known as Harald *harðráði*, but he was one of many Scandinavians who sought fame and fortune in the Varangian Guard of the Byzantine emperors. Both awaited on the frontlines, facing armies of Arabs, Bulgars, Cypriots, and later Normans.

After *Ragnarǫk*, it is prophesied that the last surviving spit of hospitable land will rise to meet the rubble of *Ásgarðr* out of the earth. There, at *Iðavellir*, the fields will one day be inhabited by new people. We will never know whether *Ásgarðr* was viewed as accessible by mortals, within walking distance, or as an entirely separate dimension separated by an impassable barrier. But it did exist, somewhere.

Hel

The last of these nine worlds is one whose very existence is disputed. Snorri Sturluson, our source for much of this, was a Christian, and he was codifying earlier beliefs transmitted to him via oral traditions and now-lost writings with a mindset that he shared with other Christians. Snorri's *Valhöll* was essentially Heaven; warriors went there after they died, but Early Medieval Scandinavian burials suggest that this was not the whole story. Many human remains are buried in such a way as to appear trapped in their graves. And what of the people who did not perish in battle? Where did they go? Would they go to either Óðinn or Freyja's halls in *Ásgarðr*? There is no cut-and-dry split between *Valhöll* and *Hel*. Snorri, however, did have preconceived concepts of Heaven and Hell. Pre-Christian Scandinavia had no such idea of 'good' and 'evil'. Some behaviours were clearly better than others: being generous, being honourable in battle, generating wealth for yourself and others, and being remembered well. In contrast, *níþ* described effeminate men, cowardly behaviour, general weakness, untrustworthiness (but not guile, for this was celebrated), and other such abhorrent qualities.

The second legendary Viking Age voyage on a par with Bjorn *járnsíða*'s would be the journey of Yngvar the Far-Travelled, who led the farthest flung raid ever, against the Arabs of *Serkland* near Azerbaijan, across the Caspian Sea.[165] How Yngvar and his fleet reached this destination from Sweden (where runestones commemorate the event) was via a lot of the locations covered thus far. It likely took over half a year to sail a fleet of longships from the Baltic Sea, down the rivers Dnieper and Volga, overland via portage past the guardians at Constantinople, and then along further rivers between the Black and Caspian Seas. Yngvar's efforts, from 1040-1042, were likely the talk of halls across Scandinavia for years afterwards. It really was a dramatic attempt at plunder across what was most of the known world at the time, and while there may have been other raids on the same scale, they were not recorded. At the end of Yngvar's voyage was death. Yngvar and most of his men ended their impressive journey six feet under.

Hel's location within the Old Norse cosmos is unclear. For Snorri, it was the place of 'evil men' and, later in the *Gylfaginning*, a being with the same name is sent there by Óðinn to rule over 'nine worlds'. Are these 'nine worlds' a reference to the Nine Realms or are they nine further realms within a wider one? This aspect of *Hel* is probably one of Snorri's own creations, mirroring the tribulations that awaited Christian sinners; the nine layers seen in later works like Dante's *Inferno*. But cold icy wastelands have long been associated with 'Hell'. *Hel* was said to be guarded by horrible beings, and beyond the gates were worse things still. Baldr, the most beautiful and innocent of the Æsir, was sent to *Hel* after being murdered, the event that would lead to *Ragnarǫk*. The handsome Baldr, however, is a character only ever depicted in a good light:

The second son of Odin is Baldr, and good things are to be said of him. He is best, and all praise him; he is so fair of feature, and so bright, that light shines from him.
Gylfaggining XXII

Why would he be sent to *Hel*? In the earlier *Poetic Edda*, *Hel* has no such connotations, it is simply a place filled with the dead, and it is only later manuscripts which add the story about Baldr.

There are observable similarities with the Classical idea of the afterlife, such as a hound-like guardian (*a la* Cerberus), and the twelfth-century *Deeds of the Danes* refers to a specific route to *Hel* known as the *Helvegr*.[166] The *Poetic Edda* references this same road, along which the character Brynhild converses with a dead giant about her life. Lives of well-travelled folk in the Viking Age would have been worthy of conversation. How far did the furthest roads lead?

Beyond Constantinople and south of the Caspian Sea was Baghdad. Created atop a Persian village of the same name by the Abbasid Caliphate in the late eighth century, Baghdad was a purpose-built city. In the circular walls were gates leading in all cardinal directions, main streets connecting those, side streets connecting the main streets, back alleys connecting the side streets – and over a million and a half people.[167] There is some evidence Scandinavians reached Baghdad, but those engaged in trade along the Silk Road would have encountered individuals *from* Baghdad (such as the famous Ibn Fadlan) in other markets in other realms. We can reasonably postulate that vikingar operating in the east would be aware of Baghdad, an unparalleled metropolis dwarfing even Constantinople, and some may well have visited it.

Fuelling Baghdad was the flow of silver from the Abbasid-owned mines in Tajikistan and Tabaristan, silver veins that ran for leagues underground beneath the snow-capped peaks,[168] heavily contested, very productive.[169] Raw silver was processed at locations up and down the Islamic world. In Baghdad silver was melted into moulds and coinage. From Baghdad, Abbasid silver dirhams flowed up the westward routes, starting from the base of the world.

Beyond The Nine Realms

Ásgarðr is unique in the wider collection of cosmic realms as having temples within it dedicated to other beings; the Æsir and Vanir are recounted making sacrificial offerings. But to what? Themselves? Others? Further mirroring *Miðgarðr*, the realm of the gods was home to exaggerated versions of the very temples Scandinavians were already using to venerate *their* gods. Who were the gods that the Æsir and Vanir venerated? Was there another layer above even *Ásgarðr*? The endless levels of cosmic society may have kept on rising, again demonstrating that the world of the gods was in many ways a heightened version of the mortal plane. In later chapters, we will see how Scandinavians evolved not just to the level of kings but, by the eleventh century, emperors. Above an emperor was a god, and above the gods...?

Beyond Baghdad were the wider Silk Roads, extending in all directions. Trade via the Silk Roads had reached Scandinavia long before the Viking Age, facilitated by the economic growth of the Roman Empire and various Chinese dynasties, goods like the Helgö Buddha. It wouldn't be until the eighth century that Scandinavians would begin exporting rather than just receiving goods, as far as we know. Later in the Viking Age, Tang Dynasty jade found its way onto the necks of wealthy women, as revealed through the work of Megan Hickey.[170] Other research has indicated silk from either Constantinople or Persia was reaching Scandinavia between 800 and 1050.[171] People travelled down the Silk Roads of course, but were they travelling from Scandinavia? We will never know, but from Constantinople, the journey along the Great Royal Road would take an individual straight to the Bay of Bengal, in northern India, home of the carnelian bead found near Repton. By the even longer Imperial Highway, one could visit the realm of the Song, Liao, Jin, and Xia dynasties. At the very end of the Silk Roads was the South China Sea and the port at Shanghai, and beyond even that was Nara Japan and the Pacific Ocean. We cannot assume Scandinavians were making such journeys, but they were engaged with the Silk Roads and all the peoples along them via middlemen. These realms were connected, from Japan in the east to *Vínland* in the west.

Before 1960, the only 'evidence' we had for Viking Age Scandinavians visiting *Vínland*, North America, were two Icelandic sagas. Decades of research have flown by correlating the geographic descriptors and language used and the real physical landscape of Newfoundland, and still debates persist. The settlement at L'Anse Aux Meadows doesn't seem like the semi-legendary *Vínland*. It is not sheltered, nor is it in a particularly resource-rich area fit for farming. *Vínland* has been placed at various spots up and down the wider Gulf of St Meadows and the Great Lakes of Canada. Icelandic author Þorunn Valdirmarsdottir[172] is among the most diligent to apply the same '*Vínland* Saga' logic elsewhere across the American continent, correlating an account in the lesser-known *Eyrbyggja Saga*[173] with a place further south. While fragments of *Eyrbyggja Saga* survive from the thirteenth century, most renditions of it are from fourteenth-century compilations.

The saga tells us an Icelander named Bjorn *Breiðvíkingakappi* was madly in love with the wife of his friend, so much so that he felt he could no longer even dwell on the same island. Bjorn sailed westward. Thirty years later a ship of Icelanders led by Gudleif washed up on a far-away shore while sailing out in the Atlantic. Stepping off their boat onto an unknown beach, Gudleif and his men were greeted by men who spoke alien tongues, who captured them and took them to their chief. Their chief was an Icelander, and his name was Bjorn. Bjorn revealed that he had been in the land for thirty years since leaving Iceland, and he had been heralded as a ruler ever since arriving. The locals remembered that Bjorn had come from the ship adorned with a dragon prow. Gudleif and his men later decided to leave the foreign land and return to Iceland, while Bjorn stayed in his new home.

The individuals that Gudleif had encountered were thought to be Irish due to the unfamiliarity of their dialect. Even before the Viking Age, there were rumours of individuals from the island like St Brendan[174] travelling all the way across the Atlantic Ocean and back again. The idea of 'Greater Ireland' or *Hvítramannaland* formed from such tales.

Bjorn's fiefdom is described as thick with reeds and reefs, with treacherous waters, and some argue the natives are described as 'painted'. Valdismarsdottir has equated Bjorn with a figure from Toltec history, and that *Eyrbyggja Saga* is describing two voyages to the Yucatán Peninsula, Mexico. Fragmentary Toltec codices mention a leader known as Ce Acatl Topiltzin from the ninth and tenth centuries, whose moniker was borrowed from earlier Olmec beliefs about Quetzalcoatl, the 'winged serpent'.[175] Allegedly, this figure introduced fundamental ideas of civilisation, abhorring human sacrifice, creating supporting pillars inside buildings, as well as law and basic rights.

There are a peculiar amount of coincidences here but coincidences are all they are; the primary sources on Ce Acatl Topiltzin divorced from Hernando Cortez and his conquistadors are very slim and they, unlike later Spanish accounts, do not mention that Quetzalcoatl was a 'white bearded god who came from the East'.[176, 177] The thirteenth-century *Landnámabók* also mentions the Icelander Ari Mársson, who similarly

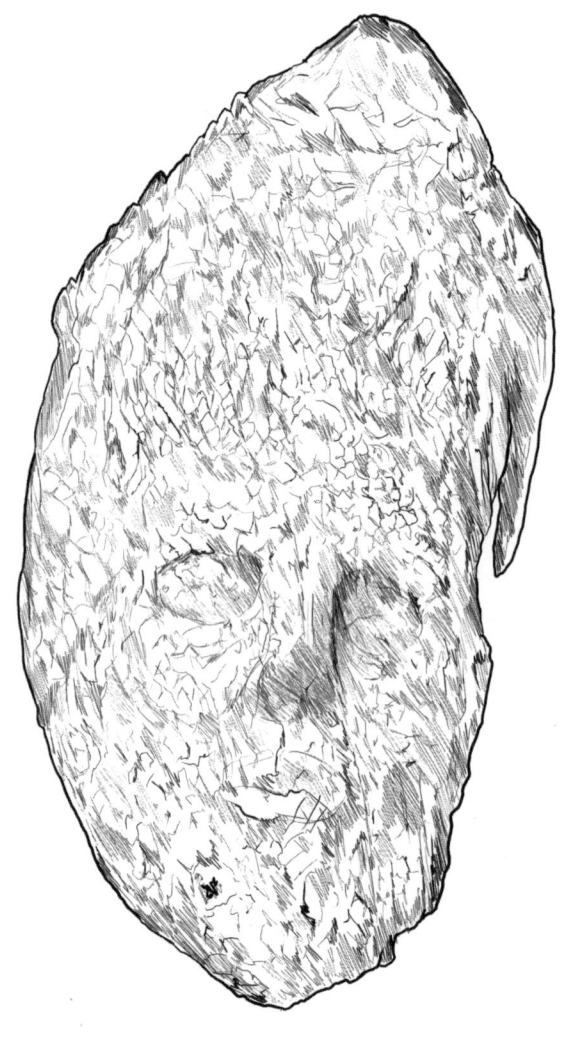

The 'Tecaxic-Calixtlahuaca Head', discovered in the eponymous pre-Hispanic burial site in 1933. The origin of what has been described as a 'clear depiction of a Severian emperor (193-235)' awaits clarification. It is possible that the head, made from terracotta, was placed as a hoax, but thermoluminescence testing reveals it as having a likely origin between 100 BCE-500 CE. What is most likely is that it is an example of Mesoamerican artisanship, and not a foreign import.

travelled far away to *Hvítramannaland* where he was baptised against his will. *Hvítramannaland* (or 'White Man's Land') hails from a long line of fictitious otherworlds that predate the Viking Age and so, like the *Brettland* of *Jómsvíkinga saga*, must only be considered evidence of the idea of 'elsewhere'. Pure fiction.

The idea of Early Medieval Scandinavians in Toltec Mexico is entertaining but it is close to impossible that *Eyrbyggja Saga* is recounting a real place. We must keep it as it is, a story, though that was true of the *Vínland* sagas for centuries. Physical evidence for pre-Columbian transatlantic contact is minimal, with claims like the Tecaxic-Calixtlahuaca Head being attributed to Roman artisans ignoring unique local craftsmanship.[178] There is also the genomic and skeletal similarities between *Cannis Ingae pecuaris* (the 'Inca dog') and Danish breeds that some have seen as proof of transatlantic contact, though this could be from middlemen breeding dogs from Newfoundland all the way down to South America.[179] There is an even more outrageous idea that Scandinavian *vikingar* were in Paraguay and Brazil, based on toponymic similarities and folk myths, but this 'research' was conducted by a member of the SS in the 1940s.[180] The Kensington Runestone is now recognised as a modern forgery, part of our enduring obsession with imagined transatlantic travels of the Viking Age.[181]

While some sagas clearly do describe real locations, they are interspersed with an equal number of fictional landscapes. Perhaps it is worth analysing oral accounts and saga-analogues from other societies across history, like Polynesian tales that seemingly describe the first Antarctic voyages sometime in the twelfth or thirteenth century, to better assess to what extent we can truly rely on mythical descriptions of once-real locations.

Power

> In the centre of the field were the whitening bones of men, as they had fled, or stood their ground, strewn everywhere or piled in heaps. Near lay fragments of weapons and limbs of horses, and also human heads, prominently nailed to trunks of trees.
>
> Section 1.61 of Tacitus's Annals, first century CE.

In 9 CE, three Roman legions led by Publius Quinctilius Varus comprising around eighteen thousand armoured men on horseback and foot, complete with a retinue of camp followers, were defeated at a place called *saltus Teutoburgiensis* ('the forest of Teutoburg'). This battle was one of the Roman Empire's first major defeats. Rome and its generals would retaliate in the years following, and the result was a geopolitical stalemate across the Elbe. Rome either had no desire to or could not advance further north into and beyond Germania, and so for the next three centuries, imperial policy would dictate proxy wars, buffer states, and forced alliances rather than invasions.

Impact on the modern German foundation myth aside, the Battle of Teutoberger Wald was a significant international event. Identifying the site of the battlefield has been a recurring issue, but the most likely location is Kalkriese Hill in Saxony.[1,2] Contemporary coinage from the reign of Emperor Augustus, Roman military equipment and sling pellets have been found in abundance, along with a 24-kilometre stretch of raised embankment surrounded on one side by miscellaneous battle debris; the failed Roman advance. This 'battle corridor' has reshaped our understanding of how the Battle of Teutoberger Wald was fought. Instead of one massive, single confrontation, the battle appears to have been waged over a much wider area of the country, perhaps not all at once: with multiple small skirmishes, individual cohorts of the three legions attempting time after time to scale the small earthwork of the federation led by Arminius, to no avail. They were routed, and ultimately lost, the legions never re-established.

And the enemy? The Suebi, the Cherusci, the Frisii, the Catti, Tencteri, Sigambri, Usipeti, Mattiacti, Batavi, and Cauci? And what of all the other names the Romans called the 'barbarians at their gates' and the names that these 'barbarians' gave themselves? The outcome of Teutoberger Wald for the victorious commanders was a degree of limited tribal centralisation and a later consolidation of power. The physical aftermath was described by Tacitus based on the accounts of soldiers sent to recover the remains years later: a landscape filled with bleached bone and faded gore. The equipment that these eighteen thousand legionaries, centurions, and auxiliaries had been carrying was stripped from their corpses and recirculated around and beyond the Roman frontier.

Here there was never a 'fall' of the Roman Empire. Unlike other provinces such as Gaul, Germania would only see sparse Roman activity. Only one conclusively identified piece of Roman armour has been recovered from the Kalkriese site so far; a cuirass[3] removed from a fallen legionary and boiled in water to the point where the metal had started to burst and crack. The leading theory is that the individual wearing the armour had been sacrificed, in line with Tacitus's remarks on the brutality of Rome's enemies. The Roman legions and mercenaries advancing into new territory now faced hordes of barbarians wearing *segmentata* armour and wielding *gladius* swords, charging into battle behind shields. After Teutoberger Wald, where did all this equipment go once stripped from the battlefield? And how did this affect Scandinavia?

Pieces of the Past

At Stenungsund, in Gothenburg, Sweden, ceramic goods from the Roman Empire were found dated between 1-300, along with the charred remains of human bones. At Tjoerring in Jutland, a farmstead has been found laid out in a similar plan to a Roman villa, as if to emulate marble in timber.[4] On the Danish island of Falster, a collection of silver cutlery and tableware inscribed with the name 'SILIUS' were found in 1920.[5] Near Horsens, a *pugio* (dagger) was discovered,[6] so too a *gladius* near Odense, and several coin hoards on the island of Funen.[7,8] A number of very rich grave deposits from this pre-Viking Age show that there were wealthy individuals or client kings ruling beyond Roman authority. In Scandinavia, Danes were enjoying the benefits of established trade with Rome. The idea of Rome in Late Iron Age Denmark was as a powerful

Forgotten Vikings

empire far to the south, capable of bestowing upon magnates means to consolidate their power in their own lands.

Roman geographer Claudius Ptolemy would describe the southernmost regions of Scandinavia on a vague map of wider Germania,[9] based on earlier sources which mentioned the ritual bog sacrifices to a goddess called Nerthus[10] across the Jutland Peninsula. Ptolemy's greater Germania consisted of the Cimbrians, Teutons, Sviones, Saxons, Anglons, Sudeten, Marovingi, Langobardi, Goths, and Danduti, Latinised names for the groups that would in turn become known to us as Angles, Saxons, Danes, Svears, and Geats. Beyond Denmark, Roman goods become scarcer, but in Hellvi on the island of Gotland in 1980 researchers discovered something extraordinary: a late first-century cavalry mask in the likeness of Alexander the Great.[11] This mask had had its eyes removed, and one of them had been replaced and fixed with a new silver orb. Years later, the site of the discovery was re-excavated to find a second silver eye and the remains of a residence dating to the seventh century.[12] This mask, rusting and oxidised, had been mounted on a post in a chieftain's hall in the middle of the Baltic Sea. We do not know how long it had been there, but it was already over five hundred years old by the time the hall had been abandoned. Discovered alongside were drinking horns from the seventh century.

The 'Hellvi Mask', a Roman cavalry helmet mutilated to resemble the visage of Óðinn, perhaps.

An eyebrow from a seventh-century helmet, like the Sutton Hoo example, was also discovered in the same area. There are certain parallels between Roman parade helmets and later Vendel and Viking Age designs; they all feature crests and are gilded to invoke a powerful presence. Helmets were symbols of status and dominion for both. The very absence of helmets in the Early Medieval Period from the archaeological record in many places has been seen as pointing to their significance – these were items to be passed down through the generations, rather than buried alongside spears and swords.[13, 14, 15] The fact so many pre-Viking and Viking Age helmets feature face designs, and across Britain, Frisia, and Scandinavia were adorned with foil fragments depicting legendary scenes and motifs, leads some to believe that these were inherently ceremonial pieces, not necessarily for battle. Warlords of the time would have likely scoffed at our distinction.

For Scandinavians in the Late Iron Age, power came from seamanship and warriorhood. The Nydam Mose boat (200 CE) is contemporary with Roman goods and ideas influencing the magnates of Denmark and beyond. The individuals ritually submerged in the peat were warriors, trained from a young age to kill and plunder, but they were not raiding beyond Scandinavia. The most raided place during the Viking Age was not England, Ireland, France, or the Baltic states, but Scandinavia itself. A runestone from Bro, Sweden, mentions individuals who kept a 'viking watch', for piratical attacks. These quasi-mythical 'sea kings' had evolved into their role over the course of several centuries of contact with other militarised societies. Chief among them was Rome.

David Castriota has been a leading proponent of the idea of 'Romans without Rome' how the concept of power was shaped by interactions with the Empire and with its decline. For people in Germania and Scandza, the Roman Empire never really declined, for it had only ever had a minimal sporadic impact there. But these people were the inheritors of that same idea of power. They were the *new* Romans.

Such is one way of thinking. Guy Halsall[16] has also written on the spread of violence in the post-Roman world, across both Britain and elsewhere. Rome's impact would eventually prove detrimental to itself. Technologically, there is an evolution of helmet typology from the third to the ninth centuries. The Coppergate Helmet, as one example, a mix between a 'Northern ridged helmet' and a *spangenhelm*, borrows design motifs from fourth-century Roman examples. In The Netherlands, in Duerne, a Roman helmet was found inscribed with the rank of *equites stablesiani*; a cavalry warrior, and it is the same design of both the contemporary Berkasova Helmet from Serbia and the later Coppergate example.[17] Through either material or metaphysics, the idea of Rome –

the idea of power – was shaping Early Medieval society. For Scandinavia, these fragments of Roman imperialism were valued as treasures by the elites on Gotland, the island that would become the single richest landmass in all of Scandinavia. In Denmark and Norway, and wider Sweden, Rome lives on through helmets like the one found at Sutton Hoo, or the Valsgarde example. At the site of Västra Vång, in Blekinge, two Roman busts were discovered dated to before the Viking Age. The residents of these coastal sites, pirates, 'sea kings', were the inheritors of that power; a new military elite[18] rising out of the ashes of the Dust Veil to take advantage of the North Sea economy. Theirs was a society untouched by Rome, but aware of its power, in a world inhabited by supra-natural beings, watched over by the Æsir and Vanir, who even from their halls of gold could not prevent the ultimate doom; *Ragnarǫk*.

Our narrative so far has taken us into the first half of the tenth century. The Great Heathen Army and its continental counterparts had settled in various areas of Christendom and had started to integrate. Iceland had been settled and Greenland had probably been sighted. Ireland's insular rulers were confronted by the Hiberno-Norse who spread across their sea kingdoms. What would become the duchy of Normandy had just been given to Ganger-Hrolf and his men, and the children of King Ælfred had reshaped warfare – *and power* – to better protect the future of their country. They were becoming *bretwaldas*; imperial-styled rulers over all England.

The Early Medieval western world was flooded with ideas and fragments of Empire. Polities were fighting over land, territory, wealth, agriculture, trade routes, religion, and status. They were fighting over fragments of power. Fragments of Rome.

Rivers of Slaves & Silver

By the tenth century, the West and East of the Viking diaspora were more or less integrated. Travellers along the *Austrvegr* were carrying slaves from the rich *longphuirt* of Ireland, who may have made up a significant percentage of the first waves of settlement to Iceland further north. Fuelling it all was the flow of silver from the Abbasid world in Baghdad, and beneath those shimmering rivers of coin and bullion were millions of slaves.

Kidnapped from the *túatha* of Ireland or the emirate of Nekor, purchased as property from the Eurasian steppe or the markets of Hedeby, slaves were passed between burgeoning kingdoms and nation states on a grand scale during the Viking Age. After the Scandinavian conquest of Strathclyde in 870, Irish sources relate how 'a great prey of English, and Britons and Picts' were sold into slavery. The slave trade had

Power

already existed in Antiquity, but the superior maritime technology of the Scandinavians allowed it to expand hugely. For them, slaves were not people, as even Arabic sources relate. A Viking Age warlord dreamed of the day when he would acquire masses of slaves. Contemporary accounts like the encounter between Ibn Fadlan and other Arabic travellers along the waterways of the *Rus* mention how individuals could use slaves for their own pleasure before selling them on. This was a dark world for anyone not at the top of society, and for those at the bottom, slaves, thralls, or *þrælar*, it was darkest.[19, 20]

At the centre of this massive intercontinental slave trade in Scandinavia was Gotland, home to the single largest dirham hoard ever found (the Spillings Hoard)[21] and the greatest frequency of coin hoards altogether. The entire shoreline of Gotland appears to have been one long series of jetties belonging to various wealthy farmsteads; this was an island paradise of the *nouveau riche* of the Viking Age.[22, 23, 24] It is possible silver was even buried ritually on the island, along with with standing picture stones.[25] Gotland was the gateway to the *Austrvegr*, to Constantinople.

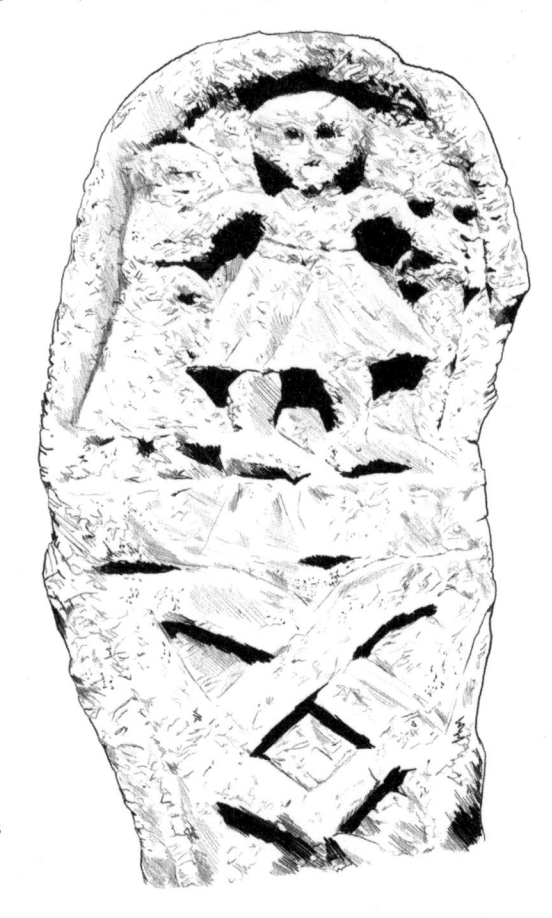

One of the few depictions of slavery across the Early Medieval world is a cross fragment from Weston, Yorkshire. One side appears to depict a woman being kidnapped by a man armed with a sword. The tenth-century date of the cross shaft indicates that this man was likely a vikingr.

While nearly invisible in the archaeological record, save for a few depictions like the 'hostage stone' from Inchmarnock, Scotland, or the odd iron manacle or chain discovered in Dublin or Hedeby, the sheer quantity of slaves that were travelling across the known world in the tenth century must have been enormous. Just think of the work required to make a single longship, From the tree to the nails, to the sail, all the way to the animal figurehead, elaborately carved and sometimes gilded. (These figureheads had to be removed from the prow in times of peace to avoid enraging spirits of the land.)[26]

And contemporary annals record fleets numbering in the hundreds. How much of this work would have been done by slaves on farms, rural estates, and in magnate's halls is unknown, but the most menial and time-consuming tasks that required the most labour surely were. Certain elements of the process, such as selecting the right tree, creating the keel and prow, and designing the sail, may have been the sole work of artisans, or at least overseen by them.

This was not just men's work. Women's role in the home was vital to successful raiding.[27,28] But women held power, too.[29] Of course the Viking Age was not an egalitarian utopia. But women, like their husbands, sons, and brothers, still travelled far; some of the earliest Icelandic settlements were likely established by family matriarchs, and many Viking Age graves across modern Russia are of women from Scandinavia.

A modern reconstruction of a larger Viking Age warship classified either as a *skeid* or *drakkar*. This model is now known as the Sea Stallion, or Skuldelev 2, based on a sunken vessel recovered near Roskilde, Denmark. The timbers to make the vessel were traced to Dublin and have been dated to no earlier than 1042.

The backbone of ship construction, and probably also building construction, farm labour, and all sorts of other pivotal and forgotten parts of the Viking Age, were the slaves. Without slaves, the scale of viking incursions across Europe and beyond would have been far smaller. Without slaves, the Viking Age may have never have changed the fates of various countries forever. Without slaves, the first truly identifiable kings of the Viking Age would not have emerged.

Kings Across Land and Sea

Much has been published on the concept of pre-Viking Age 'sea kings', mentioned in *Heimskringla* and legendary sagas as *sækonungr*.[30] Archaeologically, evidence is minimal and the principal *sækonungr* mentioned are all fictitious composites described in sagas and poems. Nevertheless, across southwestern Norway, a few elite residences[31] have been identified across the petty kingdoms that existed prior to centralisation in the late ninth century, and they do appear to have been the homes of powerful magnates. Avaldsnes, for example, was an agrarian residence but not a rural farmstead. It doesn't appear to have created its own resources, but was plundering them and subsisting on the work of others, a piratical headquarters for a militant warband. Far to the north at Borg, the same appears to be happening, except directed towards the Saami. In the tenth century, conflicts emerged between the powerful jarls of Lade (or *Hlaðir*) in central Norway and the kings of the southwestern provinces, sea kings looking to expand their dominions.

The migration of warriors and people from Norway over to Orkney and the Hebrides, and possibly also Shetland, were the first instances of *landnám* in the Viking Age, and by the tenth century powerful kingdoms had developed there. Not kingdoms of land, but kingdoms of water. And they were ruled over not by the *sækonungr* of legendary fame, but by real sea kings.

And we even know how naval power was demonstrated in the Viking Age. Off the coast of Stavanger, in Norway, longships have been tentatively located at the bottom of the deep fjords. The theory is that these boats were involved in the Battle of Hafrsfjord fought in 871. Some of these ships were tied together via chains, creating mobile flotillas that men could walk across during battle, others had rocks placed within them to allow them to sit lower in the water and retain their rigidity. Near Hedeby, five longships were discovered having been purposefully scuttled to damage the underside of invading boats.[32] These longships were not just boats but in times of naval warfare, mobile battle platforms. At the Siege of Paris in 845 and the second in 885-886 the vikingar fought across the deep waters of the Seine and the many islands between the banks. Abbo the Crooked wrote of the siege in his poetic *Wars of the City of Paris* thirty years later, describing river rafts and land constructions created on-site by the vikingar.[33] Their camps were home to women, livestock, and family groups. These sites were unremarkable but plentiful, a natural evolution of earlier Scandinavian camps established across the Carolingian realms throughout the early ninth century. These were not just 'winter camps', but autonomous communities defended by earthworks used as either temporary or permanent bases for months or years on end.[34] In 843, the *Annals of St Bertin* mention 'households brought over' by vikingar into their military strongholds.

Writing in the 890s, the word 'mangonel' is used by Abbo, roughly translating as 'siege engine':

> Into the city they hurled a thousand pots of molten lead, and the turrets on the bridges were knocked down by the catapults... They advanced behind painted shields held up above to form a life-preserving vault. Not one of them dared lift his head out from under it. And yet underneath they felt constant blows.

This probably refers to some kind of battering ram. Later in the siege, the viking army resorted to setting their own ships alight and sending them down the Seine to take out valuable bridges into the city to isolate the surrounding guard towers.

By the tenth century, these demonstrations of naval superiority, either on rivers or on the open ocean, were at the core of violent regimes in Scandinavia and across the North and Irish seas. Whether raiders became chieftains and chieftains became jarls and jarls became kings is up for debate in terms of both chronology and terminology; were the 'kings' referenced by the *ASC* as leading the Great Heathen Army really 'kings' in the same way Godfrid was in 810? Would the 'kings' of the Irish Sea in the tenth century be recognised by King Æthelstan as an equal or under-king?

The Irish Sea had long been a thoroughfare between kingdoms. From the late fifth century, the polity known as Dál Riata covered parts of Ireland, the Hebrides, and Galloway. This was a partially naval-based kingdom, its reach extending across disparate archipelagoes and island chains. Colm Cille was a famous Dál Riatan whose prowess on the water helped to found Iona. Vikingar had raided Iona multiple times to the point of desolation by the middle of the ninth century, or so chronicles say. The buildings sat empty. Dál Riata by this time had shrunken to a few nominal regions of Ireland and the Scottish isles, its frontiers in Atlantic Scotland contested by the kingdoms of Fortriu and Strathclyde.

Early Medieval Scandinavian raiders would take advantage of such conflicts, and powerful leaders like the pagan Thorgest would see their opportunities increase as Dál Riatan fortunes fell. Mael Sechnaill and other Irish Rí would use Danish and Norwegian warriors in their retinues to further their own ambitions. In 854, *The Annals of Ulster* record 'A great war between the *gennti* and Máel Sechnaill together with the *Gall-Goídil*'.

The *gennti* are the heathens, essentially a viking army. The *Gall-Goídil*, on the other hand, are a linguistic mystery, but their appearance here has led some to belive this is the first written reference to a hybridised Scandinavian-native population: the Hiberno-Norse, or Norse-Gaels. By the tenth century, *Gall-Goidil* would be a term used in reference to the western coast of Atlantic Scotland inhabited by Scandinavian migrants.[35] They were the last of the kingdom of Dál Riata, which by now had fallen into obscurity, disrupted by viking activity, as was most of 'Pictland' by 900 CE, enveloped by the emergent polity of Alba in Scotland and the dominion of what has been termed the 'Kingdom of the Isles', a Norse-Gaelic territory that covered parts of Ireland, the Isle of Man, Wales, the Hebrides, Orkney, and Atlantic Scotland. While Alba was a land-based polity taking advantage of the divisions caused by Scandinavian incursions into the previous kingdoms of Scotland, the coastal belt and its archipelagoes were the place to be for *sea* kings.

It is unknown when such a Kingdom of the Isles emerged, or if it was even recognised as a distinct area by contemporaries. Kjetill Flatnose is attested in the thirteenth-century *Landnámabók* and *Orkneyinga saga*[36] as the man responsible for the conquest of Celtic-speaking Scotland (sometimes referred to as 'Pictland') and Dál Riata, and the original founder of the Kingdom of the Isles. He may be a derived version of a real historical figure named Caitill Find,[37] a ruler of the *Gall-Goidill* who fought in Ireland in 857, however, the most obvious comparison is, once again, Harald Fairhair. Both Fairhair and Flatnose are powerful rulers who are said to be the single founders of their respective kingdoms; they are, in effect, propagandist fiction written to legitimise later rule, though no doubt they both preserve traces of reality.

In 870, contingents of the Great Heathen Army led by 'kings' Amlaibh and Ivarr harried the stronghold of Strathclyde at Dumbarton Rock before returning overseas to their bases in Dublin. Amlaibh is described in the *Fragmentary Annals* as being a 'king' from *Lochlainn*, which some have argued to be the Hebrides, though in other mentions it could simply just be 'Northlands' or 'Northlanders'.[38] Later in the same decade it appears there had been infighting between Ivarr in Dublin and Halfdan, another 'king' of the Great Heathen Army, who then returned to Northumbria to reign over York. The fortunes of Dublin and York would affect the territories between them. Subsequent dynasts Ragnall Ivarsson and Olaf Guthfrithsson would in the early tenth century shift their powerbases between Dublin, the Hebrides, the Isle of Man, and York, depending on where resistance was weakest. Ivarr, once a leader of the army, had created a dynasty in Northern Ireland that would become a recurring problem for kings of the English in the following decades. Ragnall was one such member of the dynasty and a relative of his, Sigtryggr, would succeed in York upon his death. Olav *Cuarán* (meaning 'crooked sandal', an Old Irish epithet still unexplained)[39] would be the first Scandinavian ruler of these territories to be recognised as such by contemporary sources, as *Rex plurimarum insularum*, 'King of the Isles'. What Olav's kingdom looked like is difficult to say. It was not linked by roads but coastal highways, and so the time taken to travel between his various power centres would have been shortened. Settlements on Orkney and the Hebrides dating from this period further demonstrate the display of power through the construction of larger and larger estates. The farmstead identified at Bornhais on South Uist[40] would have been visible from both land and sea. Like Jarlshof, on Shetland, this was a wealthy magnate's estate, perhaps at some point a stop-over for Olav *Cuarán* on his travels across his watery realm.

The Bay of Skaill[41] on Orkney, home to the Neolithic site of Skara Brae, was another such site. Deerness, nearby, situated atop a massive sea stack, looks to have been the base of a military force using the Irish and North Seas as their hunting grounds.[42] We know that Picts and Dál Riatans had maritime technology – naval battles are recorded in the seventh century – and it is likely such skirmishes were happening here in the tenth.

A fascinating theory has been put forward by David Fletcher that the recurring dragon motif found on fifth- to tenth-century helmets, along with other jewelled accessories, refers back through time not just invoking ancestral, but prehistoric, veneration. From Yorkshire's coastline at Whitby down to Lyme Regis and across the North Sea to the southern coastlines of Norway and Sweden there is a subterranean stratum dated to the Late Jurassic and Early Cretaceous Periods. This is the layer where Mary Anning found her famous plesiosaur fossils, long-necked marine reptiles. Specimens of these 'serpents' have been found on the Swedish coastline. Is it possible that fossilized plesiosaur and pliosaur skeletons, so similar to dragon motifs, were specifically used by artisans in the Early Medieval Period as inspirations in their iconography? This idea of power extended beyond humanity, into the supra-natural world.

Guardians

Vikingar were not just a force to be reckoned with on water. In England, the final few years of army activity up and down the country saw the creation of several archaeologically identifiable militarised zones around York. Yapham, Pocklington, and Aldwark all seem to have become the bases of contingents of the Great Heathen Army, the bulk of the forces remaining in the city itself. At the contemporaneous Torksey site, we find what resembles a gigantic migratory community more equivalent to a mobile polity than an armada. Across the Yorkshire villages and their hoards and single finds, however, the evidence points towards these areas being occupied by only the warriors, not their families and followers. Where were the non-combatants? Perhaps they were in York, transforming the city from an 'Anglo-Saxon' *wic* to an Anglo-Scandinavian *portus*; from *Eoferwic* to *Jórvík*.

Within one or two generations of settlement, the Scandinavians who were now farming and trading in the old kingdoms of Northumbria, Lindsey, and parts of Mercia had carved out for themselves a large tranche of eastern England, with more territories to follow. By the first decade of the tenth century, Cumbria and parts of Lancashire would join these land divisions, segmented into ridings from the Old Norse *þriðjungr*, meaning 'a third part'. We nowadays refer to this territory as 'the Danelaw', but the term only originated in the eleventh century. It was still in use in the reign of King Henry I (1100-1135) to distinguish areas north of Watling Street.

The greatest threat to the north of England at this time was not Danes or other vikingar, but the *Ænglisċ*, the forces of Eadward the Elder and Lady Æthelflæd, hellbent on their conquest of the remaining kingdoms of England. Their successor, Eadward's son Æthelstan, would follow suit. The vikingar who had once been members of invading armies, owners of violently acquired treasure like the Bedale Hoard, were now veterans sitting in their farmsteads watching their sons go off to fight in a new kind of battle, a defensive one.

The construction of *burhs* started by King Ælfred changed warfare in England. Gone were the undefended waterways flowing into the hearts of kingdoms. Now, the river routes were guarded. The opportunities for raiding in the south of England became fewer and fewer, though in Danish-owned territories, the Rivers Ribble, Ouse, and Humber remained open to the wider 'Viking' world, at least for now.

At a certain point, these new Anglo-Scandinavians must have felt a closer connection to the native men of Lindsey or Deira than the Norwegians sighted in the Humber Wash. The Yarm Helmet, found in Yorkshire, is the only Anglo-Scandinavian helmet currently discovered.[43] This was the gear of a soldier but not a raider, a guardian.

Forgotten Vikings

The Yarm Helmet from the eponymous Yorkshire village; metallurgical analysis currently places it in the tenth century, though there are arguments for an earlier, pre-Viking Age date.

By the middle of the 910s, Lady Æthelflæd had refortified Chester and the route between Dublin and York had become monitored and more than likely taxed. Upon her death in 918, her brother Eadward the Elder would assume her territory and begin styling himself as King of the

West Saxons *and* Mercians. There were a few victories over Deira and a peace treaty with Sigtryggr in 926. Eadward would die a year later, and after a brief succession crisis, his eldest son Æthelstan would succeed to the throne and continue the multi-generational Ælfred dream. This dream was not altruistically to unite England, but to achieve West Saxon supremacy. Ælfred's chief objective was to rid his kingdom of the viking threat, not to unite the country. That came later, and because of viking activity. In his treaty with Guthrum, Ælfred's 'share' of Wessex, East Anglia, and Mercia is referred to as belonging to the '*Angelcynn*' – the English. It was viking activity that had created at least some sense of 'Englishness' and 'Danishness' in late ninth- and tenth-century England. The constant cycle of viking raids on England had created the *burhs*, state centralisation, and peaceful settlement in the Danelaw. England was now no longer as easy a target as it once was, owing to the power of Ælfred's progeny.

It was still a target all the same. In 919, the *burh* at Bedford was burned by Ragnall and his forces, and following Sigtryggr's death in 926, his kinsmen would attempt to recapture York repeatedly over the following three decades. East Anglia, southern Mercia, and Lindsey were all captured by Wessex, followed by Deira and finally Bernicia in the north, which had remained a holdout against Scandinavianisation the whole time. But such a process of reconquest would threaten the other kings of the British Isles. Hywel Dda, the king of *Wealas* (Wales), Owain of Strathclyde, Constantin of Alba, and Olaf Guthfrithsson of the Isles, among others. As the world of the English was expanding, theirs was shrinking. Thus, vikingar could cannily play the role of mercenaries, taking advantage of political tensions, as will be seen at Brunanburh.

State centralisation was playing a key role in the reshaping of the Viking Age world, not just in England, but also in Scandinavia. Archaeological excavations at Birka have revealed a sizeable tenth-century cemetery in the shadow of the hillfort, a military garrison whose dead were buried just outside the walls. A graveyard filled with hundreds of weapons. The Bj.581 grave[44] is one such burial, arguably the most famous burial from the entire Viking Age. For many decades, the Bj.581 grave, with its weaponry, horses, hounds, armour, and military regalia, was viewed as the archetypal Viking Age elite's tomb. This was a powerful man who had taken his glory into the afterlife. Except it wasn't. In fact, this was no man. Modern skeletal analyses determined that the individual designated 'Bj.581' was a woman. Also of note is the burial of a possibly intersex individual found at Suontaka, in Finland. Clearly holding positions of authority, these individuals may have been the leaders of *hirðs*, a military term originally used to describe small retinues of loyal warriors but which by the tenth or eleventh centuries may have evolved into a descriptor of household guards. Osteological analysis of Bj.581's forearm have not revealed the telltale evidence of a lifetime spent pulling back the drawstring of a bow, so it is possible she may have been the brains behind operations and not the brawn. The same must be said for the Suontaka individual, found near the hillforts of Häme. They, like Bj.581, were buried with grave goods belonging to contradictory identities: a sword with no sign of use, feather bedding, and furs from inner Finland. Like many Viking Age chieftains, the commanders of the Birka and Häme *hirðs* were fearsome strategists and charismatic leaders, no doubt.[45] But they were not *vikingar*, at least not as far as we can tell from the location of their graves and the treasures within. Situated within Scandinavia itself, outside of a hillfort created to *defend* towns from viking raids, if Bj.581 and the Suontaka individual are to be labelled as 'warriors', then they were guardians, not aggressors.

Bj.581 was not a shieldmaiden. Outside of Wagner's nineteenth-century depictions of shieldmaidens as beautiful fighting women destined for tragic deaths, most of the evidence we have for warrior women in the Viking Age and its preceding period comes from the *Saga of the Volsungs* (from the *Poetic Edda*) and the Valkyrie figure from Hårby, Denmark, which depicts an eerie armed female.[46] These sagas refer to shieldmaidens in the same manner others referred to the earlier 'sea kings', fictitious amalgamations forged into an idealised military template. The shieldmaidens could be described as the perfect Viking Age warriors.[47] They were fierce in battle, said to be undefeated, and yet beautiful and cunning, and they used their many talents to ascend the social hierarchy.

Sweden by this time was still a collection of petty kingdoms in viable terrain and separated by 'wastelands'; while we cannot identify any of these places, we can work out how they were structured by looking at post-Roman England. Here, the 'river and wold' model determined the creation and continuity of small kingdoms – their 'core' territory would be based around river basins, with wolds and upland areas functioning as 'marginal' territory, the borders.

Across Viking Age Scandinavia, peer-polity competition was at work. Adam of Bremen, writing in the late eleventh century, claimed that the last King of the Danes, Helgi, was defeated in battle and his lands conquered by Olof the Brash from Sweden. Indeed, Denmark disappears from the historical record for a brief period following the death of Danish 'kings' Gudefrid and Sigfrid who died at the Battle of Leuven in 891. This was also the end of viking incursions on the continent for a time. Tenth-century Francia was going through some degree of political re-consolidation. Adam's comments are unreliable, but the absence of

Power

A small silver figurine depicting a valkyrie from the village of Hårby on the Danish island of Funen. The eyes of the figure show traces of niello, implying that they were painted black. In the earliest writings, the valkyries were 'choosers of the slain', said to stalk battlefields. Some accounts even describe the valkyries as pre-selecting people for death during the battles.

evidence is itself evidence. After the deaths of Gudefrid and Sigfrid, who may not have even been kings in the same sense that Godfrid was in 810, the Kingdom of the Danes fell into turmoil. This is contemporary with Wulfstan of Hedeby's voyage. He says that such a kingdom, *Denemearc*, still existed, but he never mentions a ruler. Helgi slots into the gap but he may as well have been called by any name, the same goes for Olof the Brash whose epithet comes from an even later source, Saxo Grammaticus writing in the thirteenth century. Evidence for who was actually running things in Denmark at this time is murky, but a burned ship and jetties in Hedeby[48] dated to the dawn of the tenth century point to some kind of military oversight.

Sometime later, the Sædinge Runestone[49] was carved commemorating some struggle between 'Sunder-Swedes' and 'Southern Danes', perhaps an annexation of territory, but the runes are mostly illegible and worn. Two further stones, however, named the Sigtrygg Runestones, found near where Hedeby once stood in modern Germany, are better preserved, and the longer of the two reads: 'Ásfriðr made the memorial, the daughter of Odinkar, after King Sigtrygg, her son together with Gnupa. Gorm made the runes.'

So in the first three decades of the tenth century there were individuals like Sigtrygg and Gnupa ruling over parts of Denmark. Some have argued that these characters hailed from a rival Swedish dynasty, separate from Godfrid and Horik's lineage from the ninth century. Manuscript recensions of the tenth-century chronicler Widukind of Corvey's *Deeds of the Saxons, or the Three Books of Annals*[50] describe a Swedish king called Chnuba who was forced to convert to Christianity in 934. Whatever the case, Sigtrygg Gnupasson was succeeded by another relatively unknown figure sometimes rendered in later sources as Harthaknut but elsewhere as Hardegon.

A hoard discovered at Silverdale in Lancashire in 2011[51] featured coins minted in the reign of a tenth-century king named Airdeconut, perhaps an anglicised version of 'Hardegon', who Adam of Bremen says hailed from 'Normannia', which could either be Normandy or Northumbria.[52] Airdeconut is the latest king from the Viking Age to be identified as a real figure at the time of publication; we do not know the extent of his territory, or for how long he ruled, but a safe guess would be areas of Cumbria and Lancashire around the year 900 prior to the oncoming wave of migration by the Hiberno-Norse.

Like his contemporary coin-kings from York's numismatic record, Airdeconut is hidden from us. We can infer a little more about Knútr and Sigfrøðr, however: their predecessor Guthred was buried beneath a minster in York, having seemingly brought about a rapprochement between Northumbrian Danes and the Bernician cult of St Cuthbert. Knútr's coins, inscribed with *CNVT*, as described by Thomas Williams, form the shape of the cross with the letters at the four cardinal points. This Christian symbolism signals a change in power dynamics, something Harald Bluetooth would later follow: to secure territorial dominion was no longer to loot Christianity but join it.

Like Airdeconut, Sweden and Denmark are obscured at this time, at least until the middle of the tenth century, when a figure named Gorm the Old appears to have recaptured the Jutland peninsula from a rival dynasty and ruled there for around fifteen years. Norway throughout all this turmoil was ruled over by several kings; one in the southwest, but more in the central region around Trondheimsfjord, these were the Earls of Lade, *ladejarler*. Central Norway and the lands to the north remained a politically autonomous region well into the eleventh century, independent not only in rulership but beliefs. It was these frozen provinces that clung onto old beliefs the longest.

A figure called Haakon the Good may have ruled over both the south and north of Norway, but as a tenth-century Scandinavian king, his sources are also dubious. By the late twelfth century, sources and sagas were claiming he was fostered at King Æthelstan's court in Wessex, which, if true, is possibly the first state-to-state king-to-king recognition between England and Norway. Archaeologically all we can really ascertain from sites across Scandinavia is that many were abandoned. Kaupang seems to have faded following the dwindling popularity of pagan ritual practices at the site, while at Vorbasse in Denmark, pre-existing farms had been torn down and replaced by larger field systems given over to wealthier landowners.[53] Gorm the Old is referenced on a near-contemporary source now called the Jelling Stone,[54] and he was mentioned by his son Harald – better known as Harald Bluetooth.

Fire and Ice – Words and Wisdom

While kings were unifying the Scandinavian homelands, power was being dispersed more democratically in Iceland, a new commonwealth divorced from dynastic troubles. One may have hoped so, anyway. Following the period of settlement from 871-930, most of the earliest farms around the coasts of Iceland had been abandoned to be replaced by larger and sturdier constructions further inland. These newer farms were likely made by the same families or their offspring. This is aside from the Skagafjörður region in the north, where the settlers appear to have nailed it the first time, or perhaps the fact that their farms were not abandoned tells us that Iceland was not as 'democratic' as later sources made it out to be.[55,56]

Sagas describe the Goðorð system, in which local chieftains and family elites would represent themselves and their interests as speakers at regional assemblies to amicably discuss issues.[57,58] The chief assembly was at Þingvellir, next to an exposed ridge of cooled lava and the roaring water of the Axe-river, a dramatic location for such lofty conversations.[59] One can imagine the ruckus at such an event, days of drinking and feasting following a long overland trek across the geyser fields and ice plains. There were probably some arguments that got out of hand. Any violence would likely be solved in ritual combat along the Axe-river, or through the actions of a lawspeaker or *lǫgsǫgumaðr*. The *Lǫgsǫgumaðr* not only had to speak the law, but they also had to know it inside and out, none of it written down. The law had to be remembered and then passed on from generation to generation.[60] Assembly sites like this existed on regional and local levels all over the Scandinavian diaspora; from Lincolnshire to Craven, Greenland to Sweden.

A Goðorð was nominally overseen by a Goði, a family leader, who would represent the interests of those who complained about issues to him, and then either attend assemblies himself or send a 'Thingmann' to speak in his place. Unlike kings, chieftains, jarls, or raid leaders, a Goði did not have defined limits to his power. His constituents could choose to be represented by another Goði if they so pleased.

Iceland was not some kind of democratic utopia, however. It was still characterised by blood feuds and kin-killing, which is one of the main reasons why this early commonwealth was established at the 'All-Thing'. The thirteenth-century *Landnámabók* traces its information from several earlier law codes from Iceland, which describe the behaviour of its residents, the financial consequences of certain crimes, and the punishment of lawbreakers.

Judicially, according to *Landnámabók*, Iceland appears to have been broken up into four administrative districts, each with nine Goðar, a total of thirty-six across the island. These Goðar oversaw the appointment of judges for each Goðorð, along with the men required to reinforce the rules. These militarized peasants were the *leiðangr*, conscripted into service through levy, a system which had originated in Norway and was in use in the ensuing conflicts of the eleventh century.[61]

Throughout this period of alleged democratic rule, many small fortifications constructed of turf and stone were built across Iceland, setting the scene for the later 'Sturlung Age', which would see these Goðar rise to the status of kings, and fall in and out of favour with monarchs overseas.

Riki

Rorik of Dorestad disappears from the historical record of the Carolingian Empire for a brief period in the 860s and 870s, only to return much later as an old man shortly before his death. Meanwhile, a character named Rurik, one of three brothers mentioned in the semi-fictitious twelfth-century *Primary Chronicle*,[62, 63] appears as one of the first-named Scandinavian rulers over the *Austrvegr*, the first *Rus* kings.

It goes without saying that Rurik can be placed alongside shadowy figures like Harald Fairhair, Erik Bloodaxe, and Kjetill Flatnose. The similarity with Rorik's name is just a coincidence. The *Rus* are first mentioned in Carolingian sources. A delegation of '*Rhos*' appeared in the court of Louis the Pious as early as 834 when they were falsely imprisoned through being associated with the vikingar raiding up and down the Seine and Loire. This shows that to the Carolingians, the distinction between these new *Rus* ambassadors and their Danish adversaries was minimal.

Ibn Fadlan, the Arabic traveller along the Volga and Dnieper routes, encountered a crew of *Rusiyah* in the early tenth century and described them as being similar to men from Scandinavia.[64] It is unclear if the customs Ibn Fadlan described in relation to these men, their funeral practices, can be then applied to the rest of the Scandinavian world. The *Rus* burned their dead, according to Ibn Fadlan, on a mighty ship pyre later encased in a mound of earth, following the ritual rape and sacrifice of a slave girl who was then stabbed by a local Slavic or Scandinavian woman called 'the Angel of Death'. We do not have any further description of this 'Angel', aside from the fact she was elderly and had her 'daughters' with her. Perhaps she had come down the river routes with the vikingar (almost like a spiritual guide just in case someone died en route) or maybe she was a local Slav representing local customs who had been asked (or forced) to help with the chieftain's burial.[65]

By the tenth century, then, much like in parts of England, the identities of these travelling Scandinavians had started to merge with their new neighbours, in this case, the various Eurasian peoples along the steppes and riverways. Whether we can call 'the land of the *Rus*' a distinct polity is moot. The *Primary Chronicle*, compiled by a few anonymous authors, opens with the following: 'These are the narratives of bygone years regarding the origin of the land of Rus, the first princes of Kiev, and from what source the land of Rus had its beginning.'

According to the *Chronicle*, in 859 raiders from Sweden imposed their will and taxation upon the local peoples, only to be repelled. Later, they were invited back following internal tribal disputes, and so the three brothers Rurik, Sineus, and Truvor came, while other raiders (referred to as *Vaerangoi* here, from the Greek term for vikingar) by the name of Askold and Dir captured Kyiv. Dynastic disputes followed, as is the norm, and by the 880s Rurik had been succeeded by Oleg the Wise, who became the first ruler of the polity later known as the Kyivan-Rus.

It is clear, though, from the archaeological material referenced in the previous chapter and from the 818 attacks on Anatolia perpetrated by *Rus* raiders, that there were already raid leaders up and down *Austrvegr* exercising their power. The natives who interacted with Scandinavians along the waterways did so through a mixture of trade and violence, and probably marriage. Yaroslav the Wise is a famous figure from the eleventh century, a relative of Harald Sigurdsson and thus, at least to some extent Scandinavian, but he ruled over Novgorod and his name is of Slavic origin. Something happened that separated the earlier raiding groups of the first half of the ninth century from the genuinely politically distinct 'kings' of the tenth. The best explanation is that the economy changed from a small-scale fur and amber trade to a large-scale slave trade made possible by Arabic silver. This was serious money[66] and attracted powerful competitors, venture capitalists who built up bases along the trade route to better secure funds. Oleg's early reign, described in the *Primary Chronicle*, features a log of people he invaded and imposed tribute upon: the Drevlians, the Poliane, the Severiane, the Vyatichi, and the Radimichs. All this was done in tandem with another powerful inter-regional and poly-ethnic polity on a par with *Rusland*, the Khazar Qağanate, who were sometimes allies and other times nemeses.

The seminal work on viking activity in the east has been done by Marika Mägi[67] of the University of Tallinn, and it reflects the evolution of power and territory grab seen in the west. Raiding as we have seen evolved into settlement and eventually saw the rise of multi-ethnic kings. Oleg was one such, but only the first historically identifiable figure in a long line of ruthless subjugators and wealthy warlords of *Rusland*. Distinct in the east, though, was the early formation of city-states. While cities no doubt existed by the tenth century; true urbanisation was not to be found in Scandinavia proper. It was beginning to take hold in the markets of *Jórvík* and Dublin, but a travelling merchant from those lands would have been shocked by the scale of Novgorod, Kyiv, and Gnezdovo Gorodische. These were the timber fortresses of *Garðaríki*, named in fifteenth century (and later) manuscripts of the legendary *Göngu-Hrólfs Saga*. It was the Kingdom of Cities, and it was ruled over by kings.

A New Age

One thing consistent across this diaspora so far, and its many rulers of various shapes and sizes, was the idea that even at the greatest extent of their power, the moment a ruler died, their former kingdom was thrown into chaos. The first years of Oleg's reign saw him impose heavy tribute and taxation on territories just on the periphery of his own, as if to reimpose the order his unknown predecessors had already enjoyed before their deaths. Across the Kingdom of the Isles, Dublin and York were repeatedly claimed by different parties, and even with some degree of assimilation into the wider English sphere there was little consistency. In 954 the final Scandinavian ruler of York was defeated and expelled, but what Eirikr of York was actually ruling over is unknown. His 'Kingdom of *Jórvík*' probably did not extend too far beyond the city, considering he is said to have been betrayed and killed by a confidant on Stainmore on the edge of the Yorkshire Dales.[68] The power of these Northumbrian vikingar was dwindling as the idea of *Anglalond* grew stronger, but in Scandinavia, a new nation-state was forming, out of the ashes of an earlier kingdom. This was Denmark, and its apparent creator was Harald Bluetooth.

Perhaps not. So much stress is placed on Bluetooth's actions that we forget that his father Gorm the Old had probably already made significant headway in recapturing the Jutland peninsula from whichever dynasty had ruled it beforehand. Whether he was pagan or Christian, Gorm was a key player in the tenth-century evolution of Scandinavian kings. Now, these kings were no longer simply the most powerful military elite of their day, ruling over hydrarchies and raiding armies, they were attempting to be national figureheads, too. Part of this came through the creation and maintenance of large state projects, like the earlier Danevirke but achieved through more centralised means. Bluetooth echoed the activities of other continental and British kings. He minted the first coins of Scandinavia, he kept some degree of military order via the refortification of parts of the Danevirke and the creation of Trelleborg forts, and he built and repaired bridges to aid movement of goods across his lands. The Ravning Bridge, over seven hundred metres long, must have used an entire forest in its construction.[69] Our earlier analogy of the time, effort, and resources taken to create a single longship is dwarfed by the construction process of the Ravning Bridge, designed to bypass bog meadows, but more importantly to show off.

Bluetooth had fleets. Like many kings, his state fluctuated according to military activities beyond his borders. Later sagas all paint Bluetooth in a negative light, claiming he repeatedly lost battles against the mythical Jomsvikingar, but it is clear at least that this king of Denmark had armies and armadas, and was not afraid to use them. It is plausible Bluetooth exercised some control over the Vestfold region of Norway, too, and parts of the wider southwest region, locked in combat with Haakon the Good and the first historically identifiable Swedish king, Erik the Victorious. Unlike Denmark, however, neither Norway nor Sweden's earliest monarchs can claim to have ruled over an area fairly coterminous with the modern country. Bluetooth is alone in this, even if he did not have dominion over all the 'Danish' islands, matched by the wealthy magnates of Gotland to his east and the unique material culture of Bornholm closer to home.

Bluetooth marks a change in the process of Viking Age figures obtaining and then maintaining their power within Scandinavia. The 950s-970s see a transition from the earlier viking activity of roaming polities like the Great Heathen Army to war waged by state-sponsored armies designed to extract wealth from rival countries

Vorbasse and Trabjerg, which had previously been relatively small farming communities, were completely reorganised to make way for purpose-built sheep farms, home to many more animals.[70] This same process occurred all over Denmark in 'the golden age of the sheep farmer'. Behind the production of the many sails of viking longships were millions and millions of sheep, sheared after months spent eating grass on the verdant highlands. The act of raiding had gone from being a technological, economic, and psychological response to the lack of opportunities within Scandinavia, to becoming the entire raison-d'etre of the state. Denmark, Norway, and Sweden, to variable extents, had become polities which existed to facilitate raiding. Viking activity would generate obscene wealth from slaves, which would then be circulated back into Scandinavia to be used in the construction of halls, farms, and longships, which would be sent back out over the waters to repeat the process. This was a vicious and profitable cycle, and it redefined power in the Viking Age.

'Never before this, were more men slain ... by the sword's edge'

As Scandinavian rulers became more and more powerful, so did their enemies. These emerging nation states like France, England, and Denmark, were butting heads repeatedly as their borders became more rigidly defined. Amidst all of this were viking armies taking advantage of these disputes, but now their leaders had become involved in the very same political game. The emergence of Denmark as the first nation-state of Scandinavia marks the slow death of the Viking Age, and one of the last hurrahs of this age was one of the most well-known Early Medieval battles; Brunanburh.

Like Teutoberger Wald, Brunanburh's battle site remains a mystery, though as with Kalkriese Hill, Bromborough on the Wirral has been suggested as the most likely location.[71, 72] The significance of the event comes not from the location but from the kingdoms involved. Facing the English was a coalition of governments: Constantin's Alba, made up of earlier Pictish, Brythonic, and Scottic elements; Owain's Strathclyde, made up of Norse-Gaels and Britons; Hywel Dda's *Wealas*, itself comprised of various smaller kingdoms he had united through warfare and clever negotiation; Olaf Guthfrithsson's Hiberno-Norse from Dublin to York, likely joined by Northumbrians and Anglo-Scandinavians from the north, too; and probably many unmentioned commanders. We also hear of vikingar joining the armies of King Æthelstan, contingents of Anglo-Scandinavians who lived in Mercia and East Anglia, for instance, but also the saga-character Egil Skallagrimmrson, who in his eponymous tale is mentioned alongside his own warband and others from Orkney who helped win the day for the English.

Brunanburh, as bloody as it was, and as triumphant as its eponymous poem in the [A] *Anglo-Saxon Chronicle* is, would not create a united England. Within two years, King Æthelstan died, and his united kingdoms fell apart in the north. They would be recaptured and lost repeatedly until 954, when Eirikr of York was killed at Stainmore.

Before Brunanburh, vikingar were engaged as mercenaries all over the globe, and carved out their own pagan niches, remaining an ever-present threat. In the run-up to Brunanburh, their targets of England, France, Germany, and elsewhere started to consolidate and respond to the danger, becoming harder and harder to weave in and out of. After Brunanburh, vikingar would have to counter these responses to their viking activity, and become nation-states themselves, complete with their own armies and monarchs. Granted, Denmark, Norway, and Sweden would suffer a lot of growing pains, and it wouldn't be until the middle of the eleventh century that the Viking Age could be said to end within Scandinavia. It is at this halfway point in the tenth century when things started to change.

Not just the countries themselves, but also the people. On an individual level, belief systems were being reshaped by exposure to the wider world; economies were becoming larger and larger, international trade was now commonplace and with it, the movement of multi-ethnic peoples into and out of Scandinavia. The cosmological Old Norse worlds were becoming more and more *normal*, for lack of a better word. This grandiose universe made of wild elements and home to fantastical beings was now becoming a web of countries, nations, and city-states, with interlocking trading webs and expeditionary forces. The world was being tamed by the very people who had once looked upon it with wonder and awe.

The idea of power was changing. It was no longer about stealing fragments of pre-existing power structures, it was about *becoming* a power structure, becoming a nation. Early Medieval Scandinavians, nation creators or vikingar, were coming to the same crucial realisation that the first kings of France and Britain in the sixth and seventh centuries had: to be a true king, to obtain *true* power, power which would not immediately dissipate upon one's death, required converting to the faith of the White Christ, to God, to Christianity. Ironically, by rejecting the Æsir and Vanir, beings who were powerful but did not rule over the world of man, and by accepting a deity who *did* indeed rule over all, and thus acknowledging that there would always be a greater power, Scandinavian kings were achieving more status, glory, and word-fame than they could ever have achieved beforehand.

But there was still a long searoad to follow, one fraught with dangers.

Nemeses

Tóla had this stone raised in memory of her son Haraldr, Ingvarr's brother. They travelled valiantly far for gold, and in the east gave [food] to the eagle. [They] died in the south in Serkland.
From Runestone Sö 179 in Södermanland, Sweden, about the 1040-1042 campaign of Yngvar the Far-Travelled.

The world which vikingar had previously been able to take advantage of (political infighting, border disputes, the painful formation of nation-states) had been changed by their intrusions, making traditional viking activity so much harder. In terms of the later tenth century and onwards, the 'classic' viking raids (meaning those that were perpetrated by coalitions of raiding parties and not overt state-funded attempts at conquest or tribute) stretch further and further afield. The age of 'going viking' was in its twilight years. Standing in the way of these raiders was a variety of obstacles: monarchs of impressive states, tribal confederations that acted as their buffers, alliances of enemies seeking revenge, even simple farmers and fishermen on the other side of the world, unimpressed with their new European neighbours.

The Idea of Nations

By 960, Harald Bluetooth, King of Denmark, had converted to Christianity. Legend has it that he was convinced when the missionary Poppo held a hot iron bar in his hands and revealed them a week later to be completely unblemished, protected by his God.[1] Like Guthrum before him, Bluetooth's conversion was probably out of political expediency rather than devotion, though it is always possible spirituality played a greater role than we allow for. Harald's conversion must be set against the

The Jelling Stone, or Jelling II, Rundata DR 42, the largest of the two runestones found at Jelling, Denmark, was erected during Harald Bluetooth's reign. It reads in Old East Norse: 'King Haraldr ordered this monument made in memory of Gormr, his father, and in memory of Thyrvé, his mother; that Haraldr who won for himself all of Denmark and Norway and made the Danes Christian.' When it was carved sometime in the 980s, the Jelling Stone would have been brightly painted.

backdrop of the late tenth century, when the kingdom of Denmark came up against its most powerful rival: the Ottonian dynasty of Germany.

Following Charlemagne's annexation of Saxony, a few native elites were installed as vassal rulers. We have already seen one such count, Egbert, responsible for manning the fort of Itzehoe against Danish invasions in the early ninth century. A century or so later, the Saxons had become one with the wider Carolingian territories. King Arnulf of East Francia, the same ruler who had defeated Gudefrid and Sigefrid in 891 at the Battle of Leuven, was supported on his campaigns into Italy by members of this Saxon elite. By the tenth century, the Carolingian Empire had all but disintegrated. Arnulf still ruled in the east, in modern Germany, while King Odo held sway over the lands surrounding Paris. Charlemagne's dream was dead, but each territory still held considerable power. So much so that in 919, Henry the Fowler, later successor to

Arnulf and nominal ruler over East Francia, was offered the title of *Rex Francorum*, to restore all of Charlemagne's empire. He refused – such a task would be near impossible given the turmoil of the time – and instead set about uniting the various confederations along the borders of Saxony under one crown. Henry had obtained considerable power and territory through his annexations, enough for his title of *Dux* to be passed onto his son Otto as *Rex*. Otto, now King of East Francia, oversaw the successful defeat of the Magyar threat in 955 and was later crowned as Holy Roman Emperor, like Charlemagne before him. Otto II, 'the Red' and Otto III followed. Between them, the Ottonian Dynasty was seen as saving Christendom from eastern threats, and their state would outlast them a further few generations.[2] The silver mines of Ottonian Saxony in the Upper Harz[3] would fill the void left by the drying up of the flow of Abbasid silver; theirs was a rich nation, and it bordered Bluetooth's Denmark.

With such powerful neighbours, Bluetooth ran the risk of not only being excluded from the wealth of the European sphere but also of being at the mercy of a church-sponsored Christian invasion. Had he not converted, Bluetooth may have been next on the list of targets immediately following the quelling of the Magyars in 955. In this regard, the conversion of Scandinavian kings in the Viking Age may be seen as an allegiance not to God but to the church itself. The church was an abundantly wealthy institution which could install and uninstall rulers in Early Medieval Europe. The first kings of Britain had acquiesced to its authority in order to secure their dynasties beyond their own deaths. It was responsible for funding Charlemagne's bloody conquests of Frisia and Saxony. Bluetooth, like York's Guthred and Knútr before him, saw that sharing in the wealth from religious institutions could now no longer be done through raiding, but by alliance. This had the added benefit of excluding Denmark from any such Ottonian invasion.

But conflict would still arise. As Bluetooth's Denmark became more and more consolidated through state projects like the Ravning Bridge, so too did Otto's East Francia. Dendrochronological dating of the Danevirke along the southern border of the Jutland Peninsula reveals that between 950-970, Harald Bluetooth had overseen mass extensions, timber palisades dwarfing those of his predecessor Godfrid, accommodating the whole of Hedeby. Where it had previously been an emporium in the hinterlands beyond the Danevirke, now it functioned as part of the Danevirke itself, protected as a fortified market centre. This would have unintended consequences, however. In 975, Otto II captured both at once.

The eleventh-century Fécamp manuscript of Dudo's *Deeds of the Norman Dukes*[4] describes communication between Bluetooth and Richard I of Normandy before this. In 961 a request for military aid was sent to Denmark, to aid the Normans against one Count Thiebault. This unspecified conflict indicates a general sense of unease between the nominally Scandinavian settlers around Rouen and the 'true' Franks of Chartres and Ermenonville,[5] thus the request for Danish support. Chartres was allegedly burned by this Norman-Danish coalition the year after. Whatever the case, Bluetooth's involvement in this conflict between Richard and Lothair of West Francia was over by 966. A year earlier, churches in the Danish markets of Aarhus, Ribe, and Hedeby were excluded from Ottonian taxation, included as they were under the vague episcopal see of Hamburg-Bremen by this point.

The first churches in Scandinavia were small wooden affairs and had been present in the country since the early ninth century. By the tenth, Christian communities were firmly rooted. It would take a while longer for the conversion to take hold across the rural hinterlands. Upon Otto I's death, Bluetooth may have believed that Ottonian fortunes had waned – perhaps the expectation was that, as with Louis the Pious' death, it would facilitate opportunistic raiding. He was wrong.

Otto's successor responded by raiding Denmark and capturing Hedeby and large swathes of the Danevirke, though ultimately, within a few years, Bluetooth had clawed back the lost territory and secured the town.[6] Bluetooth's Denmark had enemies at its southern border, but what of the north?

Like many before him, this Danish ruler had his eyes on the rich trade of the Northern Way, much to the ire of the *ladejarler*. Raids on either side of the Kattegat had occurred throughout his predecessors' reigns and it is likely they continued throughout Bluetooth's. Sagas talk of an ongoing dispute between the *ladejarler* and exiled sons of the character Erik Bloodaxe, in which Bluetooth occasionally intervened. Norway's historicity for this period is still questionable but the archaeological record does reveal wealthy estates around Trondsheimfjorden and the abandonment of Kaupang. In Kaupang's hinterlands were pagan ritual sites, however, which remained in usage, much like the cult site identified at Borre.[7, 8] Trondsheimfjorden would later become the location of Niðarós, the first capital of the Christian kings of Norway, built within the wealthy agropastoral fjords of the *ladejarler*. Sweden saw similar development, though would not crystallize into anything resembling a nation-state until much later. Under Erik the Victorious and his successor Olof Tax-King, mainland Sweden remained a confederation of smaller polities based around earlier tribal divisions like the Svear and Götar.

Bluetooth's greatest threat would not be from these outsiders, but his own bloodline. His son Sweyn Forkbeard revolted against him in the 980s and by 986 had taken over. His reign was a bloody one, though much of the carnage was in England. Denmark persevered. This was no longer a fractured realm vulnerable to power vacuums and territorial fragmentation as seen with Godfrid's defeat in 810, it had evolved, although the transmission of power from Bluetooth to his son was not a peaceful affair.

Land Sharks

Between the last few years of Bluetooth's reign and his defeat at the hands of his son, several forts had been constructed across his territory, which included parts of southern Sweden. Today we call them 'Trelleborgs' named after the most famous example. These Trelleborg forts were circular, containing a grid-like pattern of houses and roads, with a few gates.[9] The longhouses, rectilinear and wooden supported by external posts, were large even by earlier magnate standards, and each Trelleborg fort had at least four of them. The largest of the examples, found at Aggersborg, has been dated between 975-980 and was inhabited for no more than twenty years, in common with all the forts.[10] Some seem to have been abandoned, fading into the surrounding landscape, showing minimal signs of repair akin to the Ravning Bridge, which has led some to argue that these were not functional fortresses but short-lived demonstrations of state power. Others, like Nonnebakken, became enveloped by or acted as foundations for later towns.[11]

The reasons for these fortresses, in use between the two reigns of Bluetooth and Forkbeard, have long been debated. Initially, they were believed to have acted as training camps like the mythical Jomsvikingar base at Jomsborg[12] used ahead of Sweyn's invasion of England, or as barracks, however, it is likely that they acted as manifestations of a greater top-down power structure than these earlier Scandinavian kingdoms were used to. Bluetooth's reign was beset by conflict from both north and south, and later by internal rebellions. Fortresses like these, similar in concept to English *burhs*, allowed for a standing army to be based along important roads and crossings, capable of rallying quickly to any nearby flashpoint much more quickly than in earlier days, thereby preventing raiding. This Viking Age king had created 'anti-viking' outposts. Trelleborgs functioned as physical manifestations of the power of Bluetooth, making his mark on the landscape in a much more practical way than the barrow mounds of pre-Christian rulers. Bluetooth and Forkbeard's power was not rooted in ancestral veneration but in the here and now.

Forgotten Vikings

The pre-Viking Age hillforts and ringforts of Scandinavia have already been mentioned. There are similarities between the layouts of the Trelleborgs and their antecedents, though their usages were very different. Ringforts are a convergent design found across many societies; in Belgium,[13] The Netherlands, and Germany similar shaped forts to the Trelleborgs have been identified through aerial photography, such as at Domburg and Middleburg on the island of Walcheren.

During Henry the Fowler's rule over Saxony, the fortification of towns along the eastern borders had already begun. This strategy was the *Burgenordnung* or 'castle order',[14] referenced in Widukind of Corvey's *Deeds of the Saxons*.[15] These were not just castles for defence but also homes for refugees fleeing areas already ravaged. The castle regulations stated that *burgs* were to be used as bases for cavalry troops, capable of defending against Slavic raiders from over the Elbe and, later, the Magyars. In this way, the Ottonian *burgs* mirrored the Ælfredan *burhs* – a reminder that, while Ælfred was indeed Great, he was not a genius in thinking up ways to deal with raiders.[16] Even in Spain, the immediate response to the Sacking of Seville is recorded in the near-contemporary *Ta'rikh*, which states how one Abdullāh Ibn Sinān was hired to create large walls to defend against further viking raids.

The defences in Saxony were principally created in response to the growing threat posed by a different raiding entity, the Magyars, a collection of cultural and linguistic groups from modern Hungary, who had recently acquired territory in the region known as *Etelköz* between the Dnieper and Carpathian basin, and were launching land-borne attacks across multiple borders.[17] The Magyars are the forgotten middle child between Attila's Huns and Genghis Khan's Golden Horde; nomadic cavalry warriors skilled with the recurve bow who decimated vast armies across Europe on their rampages through Germany, France, and Spain. The Magyars had initially been checked by the Khazar Qağanate, however the rise of the Kyivan-Rus state and the shifting allegiances of the Abbasid Caliphate and Byzantine Empire had weakened them by the late ninth century. The Khazar Qağanate would remain in some form until the thirteenth, but their status as the sole federation in the Volga-Bulgar area had passed onto the Kyivan-Rus, a state and later an amalgam of principalities in Eastern and Northern Europe from the late 9th to the mid-13th century, and the threat of the Magyars moved ever westward. The Magyars and *Rus* likely came into contact and conflict repeatedly over the ninth and tenth centuries. The sheer frequency of Magyar raids overland into western Europe must indicate at least some form of relationship with the Kyivan-Rus; either leaders like Oleg the Wise were letting Magyar invasion forces pass through their territory, or they were themselves being defeated and thought it best to leave the Magyars to it.

Regardless of how they reached western Europe, the Magyars were to fill the brief void between bouts of viking activity. There are some indications that in a few unlucky years Francia faced assaults from *both* invaders; the 862 entry for the *Annals of St Bertin* notes that 'The Danes plundered and laid waste a great part of his kingdom with fire and sword. Also enemies called Hungarians, hitherto unknown to those peoples, ravaged [Louis the German's] realm.' The Magyars and *vikingar* were similar; both were nomadic raiding armies made up of individual clans with war leaders who exacted tribute from captured cities and were confronted by the creation and consolidation of fortified centres along their lines of attack. If the tenth-century *vikingar* dominated the waterways, then the Magyars menaced the land. Twenty years before, that same annal lamented incursions from not just *vikingar* but also Greek, Berber, and Arab pirates across southern France. This 842 entry reminds us that, while devastating, *vikingar* were not the sole arbiters of destruction.

While there is no evidence Magyar incursions ever spilled into Denmark, Bluetooth's Trelleborgs were borrowing design principles from Henry the Fowler and Otto I's defensive *burgs*.[18] While visually distinct, the purpose of the Trelleborgs was to subdue raiding attempts much like the anti-Magyar fortifications in Germany, and thus represented a similar degree of state consolidation by Bluetooth, mimicking his more powerful neighbour.

Against *Ásgarðr*

By the tenth century, the Kyivan-Rus had become a relatively centralised federation of fortified towns along the river routes, acting as a buffer zone between the nomadic peoples of the steppes and the raiders of the southern Baltic. Despite its links to Scandinavia, the Kyivan-Rus was becoming more and more Slavicised over time, its dominion extending over new territories and its language evolving over the years. As the Kyivan-Rus grew, so did the proportion of local peoples making up its warriors and officials. Over time, the Scandinavian element of the Kyivan-Rus elite faded. Byzantine treaties between *Rus* elites show a gradual Slavicisation of names.[19]

The purpose of many of these treaties was to prevent further military action between Constantinople and its northern neighbours. At first, *Rusland* could barely be described as a Qağanate in the ninth century, though by the 870s state formation was taking place. Constantinople already had threats to deal with from the Abbasid world, it did not need another foe, and so deals and trades were made with the new Kyivan-Rus. First appearing in Roman records in 838, the tenth-century *Life of St. George of Amastris*[20] states that *Rus* had sailed up the Bosporus straits surveying the city of Constantinople for weak points. In 860, the first real attempt at a siege would occur. Photios, a patriarch writing behind the city walls, possibly responsible for adding the *Rus* incident to the *Life of St George*, described them as a 'swarm of wasps'. Their fleets battered the mighty stone walls, unable to break through but still proving a problem on the water.[21, 22] This siege was well timed, again demonstrating that knack of making the best of political strife, for the Empire was already struggling with the Abbasid advance into Asia Minor during this year and the main army was away from the city. Even a swarm of wasps can eventually kill.

And they did. Monasteries and towns along the Sea of Marmara were pillaged, and according to Photios, the entire countryside was 'ravaged by flame'. This was the first and perhaps only attack against Constantinople performed by the *Rus*. In 907 another invasion was allegedly attempted by Oleg the Wise, though Roman sources do not mention it.[23]

During the tenth century, the *Rus* were active as part of Byzantine forces in Crete and Italy, and it seems scheming patriarchs like Nicholas Mysticus[24] were using the *Rus* against their enemies, manipulating and bribing, as politicians do best. Constantinople was too powerful a target for viking armies, however, and so attention in eastern Europe tended to be directed at the Khazar Qağanate. In the 960s, after many generations of warring and trading with the Khazars, the leader of the Kyivan-Rus, Sviatozslav, was said to have decimated 'Biela Viezha', the white towers of Khazaria's capital on the northern shores of the Caspian Sea. This capital was also known as Itil. In 913 and 943, *Rus* armies had paid tribute to the Qağanate based at Itil before travelling through their lands onto more profitable targets on the southern and eastern Caspian shores, such as Azerbaijan and Iran. Now, the target was not the Volga Bulgars, but the Qağanate itself. The fortresses of Šarkel and Tmutarakan were captured first, in a sweeping campaign led by Sviatoszlav that is best compared with the Danish and Norwegian invasions of England in the eleventh century. This was a state leader exercising state power. Both Šarkel and Tmutarakan were stone compounds, heavily defended by the multi-ethnic troops of Khazaria, and so must have been a serious challenge for the joint naval and land-based armies of the Kyivan-Rus.[25, 26] It is possible Šarkel was built by Byzantine engineers for the Qağanate in the early ninth century, according to *On the Governance of the Empire*, perhaps to defend against the growing power of the *Rus* or other nomadic threats.[27, 28] Tmutarakan had begun as a maritime colony established by the Cretans as *Hermonassa* sometime in the sixth century BCE. By the 960s, it had been refortified by Roman client states and the Bosporans, and finally the Khazars. It would then fall into ruin thanks to the *Rus*.[29, 30]

The prize was Itil, the capital of Khazaria, home to beautiful orchards and vineyards and enriched by trade with various nations. The city was home to many several judicial systems, Pagan, Muslim, Jewish, and Orthodox Christian judges oversaw petty crimes. There were at least seven places of worship to cater for all. Itil's fall would spell doom for the Khazar Qaǧanate, never again would it pose a threat to the Kyivan-Rus. Sviatozslav's rule was total, and his successors would make good use of the victory. The Samosdelskoye site in the Volga Delta[31, 32] has so far proved to be the best option for the historical Itil, much of the city having been engulfed by the Caspian Sea. In the eleventh century, Muslim visitors to the site described Itil as desolate.[33]

It is wrong to view the *Rus vikingar* as a geographically distinct force. One of the symbols of the Kyivan-Rus following the late ninth century was the diving falcon, seen on personal adornments from across the Scandinavian diaspora.[34] It appears in the military holdouts on Brittany, for instance, and was possibly influenced by the 'dove' seen on Byzantine numismatics, prolific across the Kyivan-Rus. These armies, sometimes Scandinavian, more often polyethnic, had wide territories to roam. A warrior might one year fight in Al-Andalus and in the next go to war against *Serkland*. It was wherever there was opportunity, and in the late tenth century, opportunities had started to increase in the west.

Armies Across Europe

The activities of the Great Heathen Army in England, as we have already seen, were not unique. The armies repelled by Ælfred and his progeny were similar to the armies defeated at Leuven in 891. By the tenth century, raiding armies like this still existed, but whereas the Great Heathen Army was effectively a cluster of roaming polities with a significant non-military component trailing behind, the Scandinavian armies which launched campaigns against England in the late tenth century were not intent on staying, though of course land would be conquered. These new viking armies were much more regimented.

Since Brunanburh, England had faced a few internal dynastic threats, though largely the Scandinavian incursions had been limited to Wales and areas around the Kingdom of the Isles. In France, the situation was the same; an area of land had been settled by Scandinavians and raiding was focused elsewhere. For England, this was the 'Danelaw'. For France, this was the Duchy of Normandy. Elsewhere, however, armies would begin to ramp up activity from the 960s to the 1000s. The sweeping campaigns of the Kyivan-Rus are the best comparison; state-sponsored armies with defined leadership. It is likely that contingents of Sviatozslav's campaign against the Khazar Qağanate then headed westwards with their falcon jewellery to raid, say, Spain.

Following the Sacking of Seville and the 859-861 raids, viking activity in Spain had been curbed by the increasing Umayyad defence. Now, the only areas of the Iberian Peninsula not protected by shore forts and watchtowers were those not under the umbrella of Al-Andalus: the Christian kingdoms of northern Spain.

Galicia was first on the list, pillaged by one Gundered and his fleet of one hundred ships according to the twelfth-century *History of the Legion* and *Chronicle of Naierense*, along with thirteenth-century manuscripts of Pelagius's *Book of Chronicles*, all written in Spain and Portugal.[35,36,37] From 968 to 971, this force occupied a so-far unidentified area around Santiago, in Galicia. An expert on the topic, Ann Christys,[38] has raised doubt as to the historicity of these events, given the current lack of corroborating archaeological evidence. None of the individuals mentioned in these sources for the 968-971 campaigns, apart from Sisnando Menéndez (who perished defending Santiago de Compostela), can be identified as real figures.

Viking activity across the Iberian Peninsula has seen less modern research, despite being such a core part of the European sphere. Charters record land around Santiago in 996 and the Río Ulla as featuring old fortresses from *dies Lordemanorum* ('the day of the Northmen'). Irene Garcia Losquiño's work has already revealed various possible sites for viking army camps around Spain and Portugal. It is reasonable to suggest the Great Heathen Army's rampages in England can be compared to the later activities of Scandinavian armies on the Iberian Peninsula, but it is also plausible that tenth-century viking activity on the Peninsula largely took the form of sporadic lightning raids, and nothing long-term or on a larger scale.

According to the fourteenth-century *Al-Bayan al-Mughrib* ('Book of the Amazing Story'), Lisbon was also raided in 966, but by a much smaller fleet than Gundered's.[39] This same source, along with twelfth-century Castilian annals[40] and their continuation in the three texts of the *Annals of* Toledo,[41] mention continued raiding in Córdoba between 971 and 972. Evidence of Viking activity in Spain is unfortunately textual rather than material. We know that raiding in Galicia plays a large part in certain sagas, so Iberian raids were not viewed as particularly unusual. The best evidence for these later campaigns comes from the eleventh century. Olafr Haraldsson, who would later become the king of Norway, may very well have started his career pillaging León and

Al-Andalus. Both *Heimskringla* and the *Chronicle of the Portugese*[42] highlight Norwegian and Danish raids between 1008 and 1016: 'The Northmen came to the Castle of Vermudo, which is in the province of Braga.' Castropol, Betanzos, Ribas de Sil, and Tui in Pontevedra are also mentioned, all sites of important religious and secular communities on the periphery of Arabic influence. The Kingdom of León was significantly weaker than Al-Andalus, having been created following the division of the previous larger territory of Asturias in the late ninth century. León borders the Atlantic Ocean and features estuaries and inlets which would have been very familiar to *drakkar* crews seeking fjords to hide in; Rías Bajas is attested as one of these hideouts following the Battle of Fornelos in 968.

Weak compared to Umayyad Spain, León was at least the strongest of the three Christian kingdoms of the Iberian Peninsula, annexing Castille in the late eleventh century amidst more viking raids, and existing alongside the Kingdom of Navarre on the Pyrenees border. Often, these rivalries between the Christian kingdoms spilt over into the Caliphate's territory, with León becoming nominally allied with Córdoba at least for a while. Spain was teeming with warriors from far and wide, Danes, Norwegians, Swedes, Frisians, and English making up the raiding groups, fighting against Christians of Hispanic, Frankish, and Basque descent, who were, in turn, fighting the Arabs and Berbers, and mercenaries from even further south.

Local official Amarelo Mestáliz sold land in Portugal to raise funds to ransom his daughters from the *Leodemanes* in a 1015 charter, while one from nine years later states that the land of Tui, recently annexed by King Alfonso V of León, was still showing signs of damage by the *gens Leodemanorum*. Other charters and accounts from 1028, 1032, 1055, and 1068 indicate a spread of viking activity, including the refortification of castles against their depredations, along with their temporary allegiances with the Basque. The Phoenician lighthouses of Torres de Oeste, Torre de Lanzada, and Torre San Sadurniño were refortified by Alfonso V against further raids from the north; small but imposing fortresses all, which provided a network of bonfires alerting towns of impending danger, mimicking the earlier Umayyad response in central and southern Spain. The abundance of coastal fortifications and naval forces of the Iberian Peninsula between the ninth and eleventh centuries can be attributed to responses to viking incursions, but it is likely that *vikingar* were only one problem the Christians and Muslims of Spain had to deal with.

The Council of Coyanza in 1055 decided to allow the exemption of the day of rest on Sunday in the event of viking activity, and a generation later at the Council of Husillos, an official from Santiago was pardoned for his collaboration with 'northmen' in 1088. Contemporaneous documents feature frequent off-hand mentions of viking activity. The threat posed by Scandinavians was often given as a reason for the funding of defensive measures, standing armies, and military promotions, even if these claims were bogus. The 'Northmen' were clearly a problem, though the scale appears inflated and obscure in Arabic sources. Many pages are dedicated to exaggerating the feats of individuals responsible for thwarting viking incursions, but the incursions themselves are repeatedly mentioned alongside piratical attacks by other groups, and so were not seen as particularly important in isolation. Whatever the case, vikingar *were* in Spain fairly frequently across the tenth and eleventh centuries, doing what they did best.

And, as always, these vikingar were in England. A more sombre poem than the *Battle of Brunanburh*, the eleventh-century *Battle of Maldon*,[43] recounts an attack by Danes against Ealdorman Byrhtnoth and his loyal warriors in 991. Unlike the previous poem, which celebrates the formation of *Anglalond*, the *Maldon* poem laments the devastation caused by the 'wolves' who had 'been given too much land'. The *Battle of Maldon* was written with the hindsight that the fight was the precursor of darker times.[44] England lacked an Ælfred in the 990s, and would soon fall to the Danes, but not perhaps in a way expected in the Viking Age.

England did have Æthelred the Ill-Counselled, the latest in a short but powerful line of monarchs over all of England. These revived viking raids were going to war against an entire country. There was no gap between viking activity following Brunanburh, however. Wales, Ireland, and Man continued to suffer their fair share of either raids or general occupation. By the mid-tenth century, Dublin was highly sought after by both the Irish and Hiberno-Norse. England, however, remained unscathed throughout this time. In 980, near Gwynedd, in Wales, *two* joint Welsh and Danish armies went head-to-head over ownership of Anglesey. The Church of St David's in Menetia suffered repeated raids through to the eleventh century.[45] Over the next twenty years, however, England was back into the crosshairs: Southampton, Cheshire, Padstow, Portland, London. It was Sweyn Forkbeard who had sent the raiding party to Maldon, and it was Sweyn (and thus Denmark) who had benefitted from the 10,000lb of silver extracted as tribute.

Around the same time, the flow of Abbasid silver moving from Baghdad through the Kyivan-Rus state slowed to a trickle and then ceased altogether. Birka started to see less and less footfall before being abandoned in the eleventh century, its *hirð* left behind in their graves. The reason is multi-faceted; the dissolution of the Khazar Qağanate in the 960s, along with its consistent trade routes and oversight, can't have helped. But in fact, the spread of dirhams across the Scandinavian diaspora is in itself inconsistent. From 850 onwards, the quantity along *Austrvegr* started slowly to decline, while in Scandinavia the heyday of the dirham appears to have been 900 CE in terms of regular flow, though the actual number of dirhams would reach a peak in 950. In Danish-occupied parts of England, the hybrid coinage (minted both locally and abroad) mixed with Arabic bullion provided a choice of currency. Many dirhams from across England and The Netherlands show evidence of being 'cut' to test their silver content, as well as being worn as pendants. The vast majority were melted down to form the bulk of the bullion economy. These dirhams were coming not just from Abbasid lands but further afield, from the Samanid Dynasty, which coincidentally started to decline from 962 onwards.[46]

An imitation dirham from Het Hogeland, The Netherlands. The 'kufic script' on the coin reveals this dirham as a fake; it is gibberish, so too does the fibula on the obverse. This false dirham was likely made by a Scandinavian or Frisian in the ninth century to imitate the illustrious coinage coming from the east, and then worn as a brooch.

In England, the vast bulk of these dirhams have been found at Torksey and across Lincolnshire.[47] Over one-hundred-and-fifty single finds in Lincolnshire alone, dwarfing the count from all other counties of England. This mirrors the *sceatta* finds. The role of marshlands and islands (like Torksey) in these exchange networks cannot be overstated.

But by the late tenth century, Byzantine *milliarenses* start to crop up all over the *Austrvegr*, taking the place of earlier dirhams as Scandinavian mercenaries sent home their payments for services in the Varangian Guard.[48] These coins, importantly, did not flow west like earlier Arabic issues. Not only had the flow of dirhams slowed, the Abbasid Caliphate was feeling the heat. Like Rome before it, the sheer size of the polity that had once been governed solely from Baghdad had been fragmenting ever since the late eighth century.[49] The Umayyads were a law unto themselves in Spain, the Idrisids and Aghlabids held North Africa, and the Samanid and Saffarid Dynasties contested Iran and the eastern caliphate. North Africa would later be subsumed by the splinter faction of the Fatimid Caliphate while Egypt became an autonomous domain ruled over by the Isma'iilism Fatimid sect. These divisions were sometimes secular in nature, borne out of political struggles both internally and against Constantinople, but other times they were religious.

The impact of divisions within the mighty Islamic Caliphate would be felt across the world; the burgeoning Scandinavian nations that had grown fat on the sale of slaves for Arabic silver needed a new source of income. As fortunes dipped in the east, the economy of England, owing to years of peace uninterrupted by viking raids, had grown rather appetising.

The sheer quantity of wealth extracted year after year from King Æthelred's England demonstrates that, even after substantial economic losses, the country could still function and muster consistent armies. The key trade of England was wool; the population of sheep dwarfed that of humanity, and all across the shires, Englishman and 'Dane' alike became rich from the its exportation.[50, 51] In 994, 16,000lb of silver was paid to viking armies, 24,000lb in 1001, 36,000lb in 1007, 3,000lb from Canterbury alone in 1009, 48,000lb in 1011, 17,900lb the next year, and an ultimate extortion of 82,500lb in 1016 upon Cnut the Great's conquest.

Overseeing all this tribute and taxation was a crumbling government barely held together by Æthelred and his ill-counsel, politicking and bickering ealdormen, contrasting with a *growing* economy in Scandinavia. Sweyn Forkbeard and his son Cnut were leading Denmark, while Olaf Trygvasson and later Olafr Haraldsson were leading Norway. Infighting would of course occur later and armies of Denmark and

Norway began to clash, but as of 1016 the various shifting allegiances of these Scandinavian warriors and their retinues had resulted in total victory over England. Sweyn died in 1014 after being hailed as king of the English, and despite being one of the first rulers to hold any real sway over a politically united Denmark, his armies disbanded immediately upon his death. His son, Cnut, would finish the job of conquering England two years later, but he had not been offered the throne of Denmark simply by being paternally related.

Feeding The Eagle

While Norwegian and Danish armies predominantly raided England, Swedish forces led by Olof Tax-King or other unknown rulers led their forces eastward. Again, this division is a little too neat. Runestones record the activities of Swedes alongside Sweyn Forkbeard in the west,[52] but we can safely say from the activities of individuals like Yngvar in 1040 that the bulk of Sweden's warriors were looking towards the Kyivan-Rus for their wealth, and beyond. Yngvar the Far-Travelled occupies an interesting position. By 1040, both Norway and Denmark were almost consolidated states, with Sweden lagging slightly behind. Yngvar, amassing a massive fleet to travel hundreds of miles east to raid, despite not being a king, is a throwback to the early days of the Viking Age, when the distinction between a 'king' and a 'raid leader' was blurred. While Harald Sigurdsson is often considered 'the last Viking', his attempted conquest of England in 1066 and actions in the Byzantine world were more of an echo of an already fading way of life within Norway and Denmark, whereas Yngvar really *was* the 'last hurrah' in his campaign to *Serkland*.

The expanding Kyivan-Rus had already made aggressive inroads into the southeastern world beyond the Khazar Qağanate in the early tenth century, but following its dissolution the path was clear to raid the Caspian Sea. At the foot of the Caucasus Mountains, the local Emir Maymun of *Bab al-Abwab* (modern Derbent) requested military aid from the Kyivan-Rus in 987.[53] Two years later, he was on the receiving end of their spears. *Bab al-Abwab*, the 'gate of gates', was a Persian stronghold initially created in the sixth century BCE but conquered by Arabs in the seventh century CE. By Maymun's day, *Bab al-Abwab* was an administrative centre, hotly contested by the Khazar and Arab worlds. The Great Wall of Gorgan, a massive brick-built work extending from the city to the Caspian Sea, still stood as a formidable defence against any would-be invaders. The *Hudud al-'Alam* ('Boundaries of the World')[54] indicates that by 982, the previously vassal Shirvanshah Dynasty had taken a more active role in the city, leading it as a new capital of an independent Persian state.

Falcon-adorned warriors of the Kyivan-Rus would play an active role in Shirvan's fortunes.[55] In 1030, they were paid to suppress a revolt in Beylagan, a town on the western foothills of the Caspian Sea, by the magnates of the city of *Arran* (modern Ganja) even further west into the mountains. In 1032-1033 the Kyivan-Rus was bolstered by the Iranian nomadic mercenaries known as the Alans in their own support of the Christian state of Sarir's invasion of Shirvan.[56] Sarir, a Christian kingdom surrounded by paganism, had flourished between modern Georgian, Armenian, and Avarian borders from the sixth century CE onwards.[57] Following the disintegration not just of the Khazar Qağanate but also of the Abbasid Caliphate, Sarir carved out a territory for itself, constantly at odds with Shirvan. This multi-national 1033 campaign ended in defeat, forcing the armies of the Kyivan-Rus to focus their attentions elsewhere, assisting the Oghuz Turks in the Terek estuary and, later, around Khwarazm in Central Asia near the Aral Sea, as put forward by historian Omeljan Pritsak.[58]

Evidence of Viking activity in the Far East is, as expected, very scant. Across the Dukhan Heights and the sand flats of the Qatar Peninsula, past Twar al Huraithi and the rocky outcrops of the Persian Gulf, there are a series of rock carvings that might just be depictions of viking crews aboard their longships, like the petroglyphs back home in far-away Scandinavia.[59, 60] Beyond the southern Mediterranean down towards the Red Sea via portage, Guy Isitt has argued that certain depictions of sailboats are distinct from previously known vessel types in the area. Of Jabal Jusasiyah Group 1's petroglyphs, over twelve individual sites and their associated carvings display striking similarities to the typical Scandinavian *drakkar* plan, with six to eight oars and that familiar arched keel. The thirteenth-century saga about Harald Sigurdsson even states he went 'westward with many men, which the Vaeringer call Saracen's Land'. This has long been interpreted as Africa, but the term *Serkland* is a vague descriptor used by saga writers to refer to the general area of Saracen occupation between East Africa and around the Persian Gulf. A fifteenth-century saga about Yngvar, possibly based on an earlier Latin manuscript, makes repeated reference to the Red Sea and a land 'called Siggeum'. Most of the nearby petroglyphs from Huwar Island resemble local ship types, like the Arabian dhow or *sambuk*, making the Group 1 sites stand out even more. In fact, even an Arabic source, written by Ibn Khurradādhbih, describes viking activity as far east as *al Sin*.[61] China.

Over the Ural Mountains and near the Aral Sea, *Serkland* did not necessarily mean 'Saracen's Land' but perhaps 'land of silk' derived from the Latin *sericum*.[62] A Kyivan-Rus presence in Khwarazm is attested, on the very edge of the great melting pot that was the Samanid Dynasty's

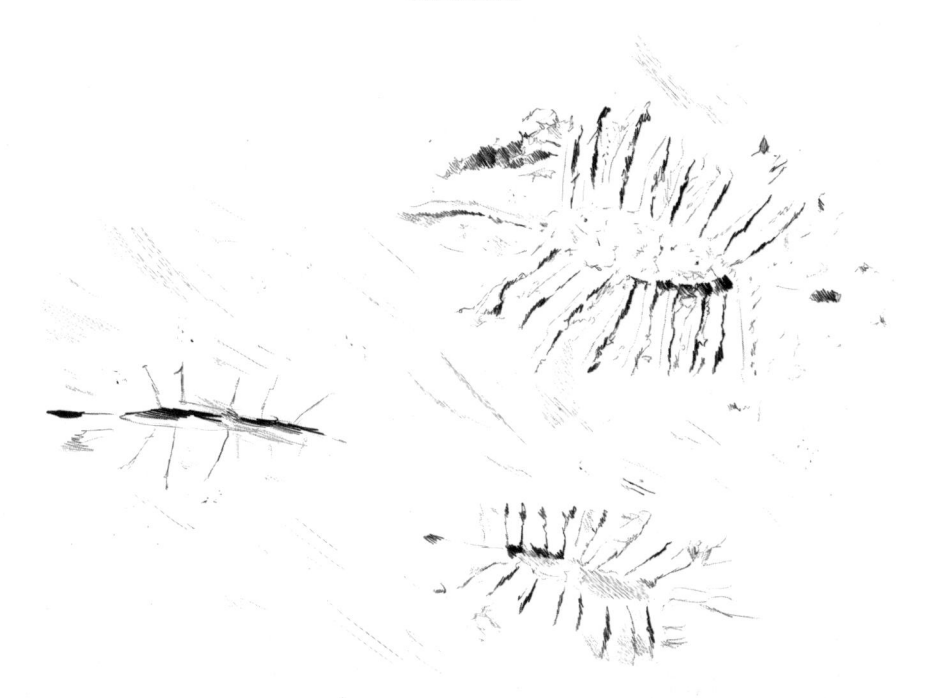

Some examples of the Jabal Jusasiyah Group 1 petroglyphs, possibly depicting Scandinavian longships. These illustrations are based on examples across sites 320 and 321.

realm, home to the highest footfall along all the Silk Roads through the fortress cities and markets of Merv, Samarkand, Wasit, and Bukhara. The Helgö Buddha has been traced to the Swat Valley, near Afghanistan, and there is another example of an exotic find in Sweden, in Hamrånge, Gästrikland, an incense burner from Iran dated to the tenth century.[63] Both the Gotland and Öland islands feature burials with jugs from Central Asia, and so does a site in Aska, in Östergötland. As urbanisation increased in the Late Viking Age, histopathological analyses of skeletons in Sigtuna have revealed the spread of leprosy from China.[64] Not only this, but Indian coins minted at Ohind, in Pakistan, have been found in Poland, Estonia, and on Öland. It is worth keeping in mind that while we view *Austrvegr* as a route heading east, for some it was a route heading west, *Vestrvegr*, and while travel to Scandinavia may have been far rarer, it still occurred.[65]

The final recorded expedition of the Kyivan-Rus into *Serkland* is the most famous but cannot definitively be classified as a Kyivan-Rus offensive, being launched by a Swedish dynast called Yngvar. Somewhere on the emerald uplands of Shida Kartli, near the ruins of the administrative town of Kaspi that had been ravaged by Arabs, a great battle was fought between King Bagrat IV of Georgia and Duke Liparit IV of Kldekari.

Previously allies but now bitter enemies, the two royals clashed over the proliferation of tenured serfdom within the new Bagratic Kingdom of Georgia, which had recently won its independence from Arab rule. Bagrat IV had been merciful to emir Ali ibn-Jafar, based in the Georgian city of Tbilisi, prompting an uprising by his vengeful subordinates. With Byzantine support, the rebellious Duke Liparit attempted to place a pretender, Bagrat's half-brother Demetre, on the throne of Georgia. Liparit was a force to be reckoned with. Having defeated the Shaddadid Dynasty in modern Iran in 1034, the duke had almost seized victory in 1038 when besieging Tbilisi.

At least a thousand *varangoi* fought with Liparit, routing Bagrat's army at the Battle of Sasireti.[66,67,68] From there, Liparit's campaign led them to the cities of Kutaisi and Ardanuç, the former by the eleventh century the grandest city in Georgia.[69,70] Ardanuç was a mountain fastness in what is now Türkiye.[71] Barely any of these warriors made it there and back, succumbing to disease along the way according to *The Georgian Chronicles*. Siege warfare drained such armies, and their bodies fed the eagle far away in *Serkland*. It is highly likely that the *varangoi* mentioned in the chronicle are Yngvar's forces.

Yngvar himself would not make it back to Sweden, but the voyage is another example of vikingar finding opportunities for mercenary work wherever they could.[72,73,74] So far we've seen this in the Basque Country in the eighth century, Ireland and Frisia in the ninth, England in the tenth, and now Georgia in the eleventh. Yngvar's voyage is the last great viking raid. There have been recent debates regarding the actual date, some placing it earlier in the 1020s.[75] Regardless, this was an expedition in search of plunder and word-fame, in search of glory that would outlast the raiders' mortal lives. It worked.

But the *Scandinavian* element of these armies was being diluted through cultural assimilation and integration, and soon the many lands of the Viking Age were picking new fights with new villains.

The Kindred of Ireland

This new reality is exemplified in Ireland at the Battle of Clontarf in 1014, in which the Hiberno-Norse of Dublin fought an alliance of Irish warlords led by the famous figure Brian Bóramha. The battle, however, had vikingar on both sides. As in England, the resident vikingar had taken advantage of the political schisms between the many *túatha*, but this had paradoxically created a united front, so that it became very difficult for them to continue raiding as they once had.

Ireland was last mentioned alongside the 'Kingdom of the Isles' which included Man, the Hebrides, and Orkney, controlling a large part of the trade route between Dublin and York. Set against this thalassocracy were the land-based politics of Ireland proper. As the Scandinavian threat in Ireland became embedded from the 830s onward, powerful local Rí rallied their own forces against the common enemy. Ruling over most of the north was the dynasty of the Uí Néill, based at Tara.[76] They had dominion over many *túatha*, territories which could be parcelled up and annexed by greater neighbours quite easily. The Uí Néill claimed rightful kingship over the other Irelanders (which also included the Irish based across the Hebrides and Atlantic Scotland) due to their ownership of the Hill of Tara, an ancestral king's seat with ritual importance dating back to the Neolithic Period. But Tara had never been *their* ancestral territory, it became so upon conquest. Throughout the ninth and tenth centuries, the various warring dynasties of Ireland occasionally set aside their differences to rally against the Scandinavian menace. Though quite often Scandinavian *vikingar* would find employment with Irish armies going up against other Irelanders.

Fairly often, Rí would have to set aside their own ambitions to serve under a Ruiri, or 'overking', who held dominion over several *túatha* at once. Even a Ruiri, however, would be subservient to a Rí Ruirech (a 'king of overkings'), of which two ruled the northern and southern halves of Ireland (Leth Cuinn and Leth Moga, if you were to split the island across County Meath).[77] Rarely, the title of Ard Rí is seen in sources like the *Chronicle of the Scots*,[78] which essentially translates as 'High King of all Ireland'. This hierarchy was complicated, with many regional powers all vying for dominion over one another. The Scandinavians had inserted themselves right into the middle of this complex game of thrones and founded their own dynasty, the Uí Ímair, in the late ninth century. Far to the south of Ireland, in the comparatively tiny polity of Tuadmumu, there was a branch known as the Dál gCais[79] who, like the Uí Néill, claimed lineage from a legendary ancestor or ancestral site. In the tenth century, the Dál gCais appear in records seeing minor successes through the marriage alliances and politicking of their ruler, Cennétig. This was Brian Bóramha's father.[80]

Brian Bóramha, better known in his anglicised form as Brian Boru, was a member of the Dál gCais who would use the political fragmentation caused by Scandinavians in Ireland for his own gain. As the powerful dynasties in the north of Ireland like the Cenél nEógain started to weaken under foreign threat, the fortunes of the Dál gCais would rise.[81, 82] Claiming origins from the legendary figure Cormac Cas, Brian's genealogy was a fiction. Indeed, the Cenél nEógain of the Uí Néill dynasty weren't even kin of *their* legendary ancestor, Eógan, the son of Niall of the Nine Hostages (who was associated with Tara, which is why the Uí Néill annexed the land).[83] Early Medieval Ireland was a hodgepodge of very powerful but small warbands all claiming ancestral links to their forebears, and thus kingship. Many of the prefixes of these various dynasties simply mean 'family' or 'children of'. For instance, the Cenél nEógain are the 'Kindred of Eógan', not a geographically defined territory like, say, Lindsey in England, but also not nomadic like the Magyars.

The Irish were also fighting over cattle. Brian's epithet – Bóramha – may mean 'Brian of the Cattle Raid'.[84] His father Cennétig and some of his older brothers were all Rí before he got a chance, and their reigns were all characterised by attempts to strengthen the Dál gCais' power. Brian would be the most successful, piggybacking on their earlier victories and land grabs, and in the latter half of the tenth century he would become the Ruiri of Munster. This brought him into conflict with a rival warlord, Máel Sechnaill II of the Clann Cholmáin (whose power base was Clonmacnoise, raided by Thorgest in the ninth century). Máel was also a powerful Ruiri *and* a member of the Uí Néill dynasty, frequently launching military campaigns from his territory of Mide against the Scandinavians of Dublin. By 980, his forces had captured Dublin and defeated Olav *Cuarán*, who ended his days as a monk on Iona, a monastery that had a century earlier been all but destroyed by pagans. This victory only made Máel a greater target in the eyes of Brian. In the final decade of the tenth century, the two men had signed the Bleanphuttoge Accord according to the *Annals of Inisfallen*, each ruling over the two halves of Ireland; Brian held the southern half of Leth Moga, and Máel held Leth Cuinn. Supposedly, they were at peace.

Conflict continued. Brian, now the Rí Ruirech of Leth Moga, started to raid his *own* lands, which now included the Scandinavian kingdom based around Dublin. In 999, Dublin was sacked by Brian, before an even greater battle in the following century. According to the fourteenth-century recension of the *Annals of Tigernach*,[85] the residents of Dublin were all enslaved. While probably an exaggeration, later sources a decade on describe the 'foreigners yoked to the plough' – a bitter irony, perhaps, that now the Irish were enslaving the Scandinavians.

Dublin by this time was a substantial trade and production centre, no longer merely a *longphort* but a *dún*: a fortified residence, home to kings, merchants, slaves, servants, livestock, warriors, women, children, families, Irish, Scandinavian, English, and many more. The Uí Ímair had been expelled first in 902, going on to cause problems in England for Eadward and Æthelflæd. By 917, they had returned to Dublin, though the town they had once known had grown into a joint Irish-Scandinavian venture. By Brian's raid in 999, both his armies and the armies he was fighting against were a combination of natives and foreigners. The Scandinavians of Ireland were changing. Their kingdom, called *Dyflinarski* in the Icelandic *Landnámabók*, was a Hiberno-Norse territory, a polity of rich traders and elite militia, and it was highly valued. Many Irish armies, including Brian's, employed the services of *súaitrech* or Norse mercenaries.[86] Commercial and military longships crowded the dark waters of the Liffey, ready for international travel. One of the five Skuldelev ships recovered from the waters near Roskilde in Denmark was dendrochronologically traced to Glendalough, Ireland.[87] This was a city of ships and only one of many. All the *longphuirt* established along the south and east coasts of Ireland were high-value targets. Brian had already captured some earlier in his career, such as Leinster, adding their longships and vikingar to his own forces. Excavations in the Wood Quay area of Dublin have revealed that the waterfront was an impressive sight in Dublin's heyday; tall earthen banks were lined with walkways in some cases made from old ship timbers. *Knarrs* docked from far and wide to unload their barrels and strongboxes of foreign goods as *drakkar* left the harbour, ready for war.

Brian quickly ascended through all the ranks of Irish kingship. Not content to be overlord of one half of the island, Brian went straight for the jugular. By assaulting the spiritual core of the Uí Néill dynasty, at Tara, and by forcing his will upon the ecclesiastical hub of Ireland, Armagh, Brian was able to sever Máel Sechnaill II's ancestral claim to kingship and reaffirm his own. Added between 1005-1012, a single page of the ninth-century *Book of Armagh*[88] refers to Brian not just as an Ard Rí but as *Imperator Scotorum* – an emperor over all Gaels. One can imagine Brian watching over the scribe's shoulder as this was written. Near contemporary with Brian's supreme dominion was Otto III's succession to the rank of *Imperator Romanorum*,[89] and King Eadgar of England's symbolic coronation on the River Dee,[90] where all other kings of the British Isles submitted to him. Powerful rulers previously unseen in the post-Roman world emerged. Soon, a Scandinavian would join this field, as discussed in the next chapter.

The Battle of Clontarf was the dramatic end to Brian's long career. In 1014, he would fall leading his forces to victory against Sitriuc Silkbeard of Dublin. The importance of Clontarf was overstated by earlier historians as the definitive end of the Viking Age in Ireland, but its depiction in various texts (such as the sixteenth-century *Annals of Loch Cé*)[91] has changed modern perceptions. Seán Duffy[92] reaffirmed Clontarf's importance, but more so as a demonstration of the mixed Irish and Scandinavian armies on both sides. Sitriuc Silkbeard's mother, Gormflaith, was married to Brian, and Silkbeard himself continued to reign until 1036 even after his defeat at Clontarf. He was minting his own coins as a Christian.[93] The Battle of Clontarf is essentially the final act in the propaganda piece that is the *War of the Irish against the Foreigners*, mentioned earlier, and while certainly important, would not be the dramatic blow that expelled all the vikingar from Ireland. In fact, by 1014, the Scandinavians and the Irish had started to integrate. There were still divisions, but vikingar from Leinster and Limerick were fighting alongside Brian's armies, just as vikingar from Orkney and the Hebrides were fighting alongside Sitriuc. The Skuldelev ship traced to Glendalough was built thirty years *after* Clontarf and it is a classic Viking Age *drakkar*. Clearly, Scandinavian military operations were still being undertaken in Ireland, but they were being launched, for the most part, from the island, not towards it. The heyday of viking activity in Ireland was over, and even though Imperator Brian had fallen in battle, he had managed to turn the tide.

Conflict continued across the Scandinavian diaspora on a smaller scale. The world of the Viking Age was not all set piece after set piece. What of the farmers and fishermen, living on the edge of the world? What nemeses did they face?

First Contact

Without realising it at the time, the first Scandinavians to set foot on the shores of *Markland*, today the Porcupine Strand of the Labrador coastline of Canada, were the first Europeans to visit North America. This was not unsettled land. Far away from the noise and clamour of Clontarf, far from the campaigns of the Kyivan-Rus and Swedish expeditions, far from London and Cnut's new grip on England, there were Greenlanders eking out a living in the seasonal settlement we now know as L'Anse Aux Meadows, on the northernmost tip of Newfoundland. They had already explored to some extent the islands near the North Pole; Baffin Island and the archipelagoes between, and possibly the Groswater Bay region of Labrador, given the description of 'ice mountains' in the sagas. Newfoundland, however, is so far the only identified area of settlement.

This was a temporary camp for resource gathering. The Greenlanders resident here for six months of every year likely sailed in either *knarr* or rowing boats around Newfoundland and into the Gulf of St. Meadows region of Canada. The ever-unreliable sagas describe wide-ranging expeditions in this new realm lasting weeks on end in search of local produce. Eventually, amidst the sun-dappled forests and endless white sands, these first Greenlanders would encounter the Native Americans.

Described nowadays as the Point Revenge Culture, the *skrælingjar* encountered by the Greenlanders were likely ancestors of pre-colonial Algonquian speakers. The Dorset Culture had also migrated out of Greenland to North America prior to Scandinavian settlement, further complicating this array of identities and languages. There would be close to zero intelligibility between Old Norse speakers and the natives, so it is no surprise that relations depicted in the sagas are often a tense and violent affair.[94] But still, trade did occur. The Maine Penny found at the Goddard Site was minted in Norway between 1070-1080, and yet was found amongst a trade site on the other side of the Atlantic Ocean. The penny probably found its way there through lots of deals up and down the coast; a Beothuk chieftain takes a fancy to the silver penny offered to him by a Greenlander, he then trades it to a buffalo herder, who then sells it to a Naskapi fisherman, and so on until it reaches the Goddard Site. There is minimal archaeological evidence of the activities described in the *Vínland* episodes of the sagas, but some material from North America did make its way over to the Greenland colonies; traces of black bear and buffalo fur, along with at least one Native American arrowhead found amongst skeletal remains. Perhaps evidence of a trade deal gone wrong? Many *tristur* boats found in Greenland contexts can also be traced to Canada, created from native larch, which does not grow in the Arctic.[95]

The Greenlanders were also dealing with *skrælingjar* on their own island.[96] First described to Norman king Roger II in the twelfth century by the geographer al-Idrisi in his *Nuzhat al-Mushtaq* (known in the west as 'The Book of Roger'),[97] information about the Thule Inuit Culture was carried south from Greenland along with their exports of walrus ivory and polar bear fur, to be listened to by interested parties in the markets of Hedeby, Dublin, London, and further afield. He writes:

> There are also sea animals of such enormous size that the inhabitants of the inner islands use their bones and vertebrae in place of wood in constructing houses. They also use them for making darts, clubs, lances, knives, seats, ladders, and, in general, all things which are elsewhere made of wood.

The sixteenth-century manuscript of the *History of Norway*[98] describes the Thule, based on accounts from the thirteenth century:

> On the other side of Greenland, toward the North, hunters found some little people whom they call 'Skraelings'; their situation is that when they are hurt by weapons their sores become white without bleeding,

but when they are mortally wounded their blood will hardly stop running. They have no iron at all; they use missiles made of walrus tusks and sharp stones for knives.

The term *skraeling* here described the Native Americans but also the Thule Inuit, carrying derogatory connotations. These two populations were entirely different ethnically, linguistically, and culturally. While interactions between the Greenlanders and Native Americans were sporadic and fraught with danger, in Greenland itself the Thule Culture migrated southwards from *Norðsetur* towards the settlements. By the fourteenth century, archaeological deposits show that the headlands of the southern fjords were occupied by Thule people, while the inner fjords and harbours were settled by Scandinavian farmers. This was a landscape of constant activity and interaction. Though the Thule are depicted as villains almost all the time; the thirteenth-century *Flóamanna saga*[99] describes 'witches hunting seals' and they were even blamed for the later abandonment of Vestribyggð in a papal letter from 1348.[100] These accounts are biased, of course, though there is some archaeological evidence for the Thule recycling old pieces of Scandinavian equipment from Ellesmere Island down to southern Greenland.

Inuit tales, a parallel to saga traditions, first recorded down by Henry Rink in 1875,[101] describe the Thule's repeated aggressive interactions with the *Qavdlunait* – the 'foreigners'. Of the oral traditions passed down, at least five feature definite depictions of Thule-Norse reactions and all of them are negative. In *Ungortok, The Chief of Kakortok*, a stray killing of a Greenlander leads to an inordinately violent response; the *Qavdlunait* allegedly burn and slaughter an entire 'town' of the Thule. It is telling that the least fraught tale is one of a Greenlander taking two Thule children into his own custody as farmhand slaves.

In contrast to the situations in Ireland, England, and the Kyivan-Rus, the Scandinavians of Greenland did not attempt any assimilation. The Greenlanders continued to hunt seals by waiting for them to beach, never copying the harpooning or ice-hole boring of their Thule neighbours; nor did they substitute their *vaðmál* clothing for the superior seal skin, nor borrow the whalebone building techniques of the Thule. It is possible that the Greenlanders were attempting to keep up with European trends and cling to their own values, but their decision to not assimilate or at least borrow elements of the Thule way of life would ultimately prove to be their undoing.

Out here on the edge of the world, across the *Furðustrandir* (wonder strands)[102] of the Labrador Coastline and the ice sheets of Greenland,

Scandinavians were proud of their heritage and refused to change while their cousins elsewhere assimilated and intermarried. But were these people even what we would consider to be vikingar? The Greenlanders were farmers, fishermen, tusk-hunters; the only violence they saw was likely a skirmish every now and then with a polar bear, or across the sea with the Beothuk. The world of the Viking Age was changing and so too were Scandinavians themselves. By the first half of the eleventh century, it is difficult to see how the Viking Age and its characteristics could continue.

Flux

I have called myself Grim,
I have called myself Wanderer,
Warrior and Helm-Wearer,
Famed One and Third,
Thunder and Wave,
Hel-blind and One-eye...
Extract from *Grímnismál* ('The Sayings of The Masked One')
translated by Jackson Crawford (2015).

Cnut, son of Sweyn Forkbeard, succeeded to the English throne in 1016 after a military campaign that had started before he was born.[1] Initially ruling only half of the country, with the south ruled over by incumbent King Edmund Ironside, son of Æthelred the Ill-Counselled, within a few short months Cnut had taken total control. In his first five years as king of England, this Danish overlord reshaped the political sphere and installed his own vassals as earls across the provinces of Northumbria and Mercia. Within ten, he was politicking across the North Sea to Denmark, and vying for territorial control over Norway.[2] By the end of his reign, in 1035, Cnut – now 'The Great' – had made a pilgrimage to Rome, secured an alliance with Holy Roman Emperor Conrad II, conquered Norway and, if we are to believe his state propaganda, also parts of Sweden. Deserving of his epithet, Cnut is the most successful Scandinavian figure from the Viking Age.[3] But can he really be considered a 'Viking?'

The characteristics most associated with Scandinavians in the Viking Age only loosely apply to Cnut and his armies. The forces of Denmark were not a disparate roaming polity of individually led warbands like the earlier Great Heathen Army. After Sweyn's death, it is true that the

Danish army did temporarily break up and return to Denmark, but Cnut rallied them the following year. Danish soldiers were still raiding like their ninth and tenth-century counterparts, but their motives were slightly different; Cnut's aim was to join the wider European network (and the institute of the church), and not to pillage it. Since Bluetooth's time, Denmark had become just another country of Europe. Norway was soon to follow, and then so would Sweden.

Cnut's 'North Sea Empire' of England, Denmark, and Norway should perhaps be considered the very end of the Viking Age, at least within central Europe. The idea of a hereditary monarch making a Christian pilgrimage to Rome and securing trade alliances with the Holy Roman Emperor would have been unheard of in tenth-century Denmark.

Hamr

Was this change only superficial? Within Old Norse cosmology, through Snorri's writings and the *Poetic Edda*, along with relevant archaeological material, researchers have theorised that the idea of 'the self' within the minds of Viking Age Scandinavians was codified differently to today.[4,5] The concept of multiple layers of identity has been raised regarding kin groups and the renegotiation of power structures in the post-Roman period. Eahlswith, Ælfred's wife, was a member of the tribe called the *Gaini*, but also a Mercian, and more broadly an 'Anglo-Saxon'. How did she view herself?

The concept of multiple layers of personhood emerges through such works as *Eyrbyggja saga*, *The Waking of Angantyr*,[6] *Hrólfs saga kraka*, and *Víga-Glúms saga*;[7,8] tall tales full of supernatural elements. The physical bequeathing of one's luck sprite to another, individuals projecting their mental essence in the form of an animal, and barrow mounds filled with the vengeful *draugr*, whose minds have left their bodies behind as vacant shells. The outermost layer of personhood was a shell, the *hamr*, the shape of a person; how a person *wants* to be seen outwardly. Beneath that is how that person saw *themselves* – thought, mind, memory, the *hugr* of a person.[9] The *hamr* and *hugr* of a person are intertwined; a person's's *hugr* could leave their body as a projection, and one could also reshape one's *hamr*. The ability to do this – 'shapeshifting' – had its own term. An individual skilled at remodelling themselves was *hamrammr*; 'shape-strong', capable of changing their outwards appearance at will, perhaps to a bear, or to a wolf, or to a European monarch. The *hugr* is distinct from the Christian idea of a 'soul'. The Old Norse word *sál* is only a translation of the pre-existing word, such a concept did not exist in pre-Christian Scandinavia.

Beneath the *hamr* and *hugr* were two separate beings, the *hamingja* and *fylgja*, companion-like entities that could leave a person and be passed between others.[10, 11] The *hamingja* represented one's luck in battle and life. An individual with particularly good luck had a particularly potent *hamingja*, while someone with terrible luck would find themselves without a *hamingja* altogether, it having 'run out' so to speak. Bettina Sommer[12] views the *hamingja* of a person as a gift belonging to a family, their inherited skill and fortune, perhaps. The *fylgja* is a little more complex, essentially an 'ancestor spirit' (always depicted as female), passed down through kin groups and bloodlines,[13] prescient about what is to pass and knowing what has already passed. At the very core of a person's identity was a link back down the generations and a guide to take the link to their offspring. We would call such a concept fate.

'The Viking way' – ancestor veneration, an emphasis on battle victory and ring-giving, exploration, and wealth, on word-fame and supranatural beings – these aspects of personhood crystallise all those elements into four distinct layers. But like with the 'nine realms', there was no rigid determination that personhood was limited to four.

The *hamr* of a person could change. The fifteenth-century *Vatnsdæla saga* mentions the *Úlfhéðnar* or 'wolf-skins', people who could take on the outward appearance of wolves to better defeat their enemies. An *Úlfhéðnar* didn't physically turn into a wolf, but the 'shape-strong' individual may have become so enraged and embroiled in their own battle-frenzy that they became a snarling and ravenous beast resembling the behaviour of a wolf: the 'berserker walk' – a man pacing forward oblivious to arrows and spears whizzing past his head.[14] Shape-changing in a broader sense is a very common motif in the *Poetic Edda*. Óðinn, to use the most famous example, frequently dons disguises. Sometimes he is an old crone, or he has warped his *hamr* into the shape of an animal. Loki turns into a fish and a horse.

'I am called Mask, I am called Wanderer,' says Óðinn in *Grímnismál*,[15] revealing himself to his foe, as he peels back layers and layers of false identity, false *hamr*, before announcing his true self. Earlier in the pre-Viking period, gold bracteates and jewellery from across northern Europe depict abstract forms like the Weapon Dancer transitioning into birds and horses. The concept of shape-changing was not new to the Viking Age, it certainly played a role within the cosmological milieu that preceded it.

In 1948, a belt buckle was found in York dating to the Viking Age. It was shiny, green, and looked like it was made of copper. It was made of bone and had been dyed using melted trace elements to resemble a fully metal adornment, the outward appearance of the buckle had been reshaped to resemble something of greater value. The owner of the belt buckle, perhaps unable to drum up the funds to purchase a metal one, had taken a shortcut. Marketgoers in Coppergate may have walked past him and thought 'He has a nice belt,' not knowing he had changed his *hamr* to give them that impression. Similar to our modern obsession with brands and designer clothing, such tricks would be a new but common phenomenon in the Viking Age world, as urbanisation slowly increased.

Following Brian Bóramha's posthumous victory at Clontarf, the strength of the Scandinavian elite resident in Dublin had started to crumble, already weakened in the thirty years since Olaf *Cuarán*'s defeat in 980. By 1052, Dublin had followed the way of York and ceased to function as an independent polity. These two strongholds were now part of territories owned by others, no longer powers unto their own. Physically, these changes manifest themselves through earthworks and archaeological remains. Around Dublin, between 1000 and 1100 a third layer of turf wall was added to the pre-existing Scandinavian *longphort* defences, crested with a wooden palisade and, later, a stone revetment. This was a fully functioning maritime town by the time Brian conquered it, a fine prize for any ruler. Finds from Fishamble and Winetavern Streets, Wood Quay, and Temple Bar are all consistent in this respect; either gaming pieces carved in the likeness of longships, model boats used for teaching techniques, or timber from ships reused as walkways.[16,] [17] Clench nails for ship repair and tools for scraping off barnacles and

The belt buckle from Coppergate, York. Its depiction here hides its true form; is it really made of bone?

re-caulking the clinker planks have been found; the air was thick with the smell of tar.[18] York was much the same: layers of crushed cobble placed atop earlier wooden gangways dated to the eleventh century, brushwood rafts and timber groynes constructed to manage flooding at Hungate, and small warehouses used for the storage of fine cargo, like Baltic amber or Tang Dynasty silk. Along Skeldergate, there is the possibility that future excavations will reveal an array of waterfront structures from the Viking Age river-port.[19] York was flourishing by the eleventh century.[20] These were multi-ethnic cosmopolitan centres, and they were not alone.

London, Limerick, and Wexford were all briefly under Scandinavian control in the tenth and eleventh centuries. During Cnut the Great and his son Harthacnut's reigns, London saw busy trade from *knarr* capable of carrying over thirty tonnes of cargo, alongside massive Frisian trading vessels.[21] Over the Irish Sea, the fortified *longphuirt* of Limerick and Wexford had outgrown their timber palisades and become almost as prosperous as Dublin. Excavations at the former have revealed a Hiberno-Norse turf wall over ten metres long beneath King John's Castle,[22] the Normans having repurposed it for the base of their fortress. A similar structure likely existed at Wexford, too, having been described as a *murum* by Gerald of Wales, the same word used to describe the fortresses of Dublin and Limerick. Waterford is home to one of the earliest multi-storey Viking Age buildings, a street-level shop with a waterfront-level cellar carved from stone, and also impressive earth banks clearly modelled after Dublin's own, perhaps in response to the conquests of Brian Bóramha. The pre-existing waterfronts at Lincoln and Hedeby were improved in Cnut's time. Large jetties and tall timber fences to accommodate the growing size and scale of mercantile ships along the River Witham have been found at Brayford Pool, Lincoln, along with longship parts in eleventh-century layers from Doncaster.[23] Meanwhile, in Denmark, Hedeby itself seems to have been re-founded in a smaller northern area referred to contemporaneously as *Sliaswich*,[24] with some of its functions shared with the burgeoning site of Roskilde, where so many boats have been recovered. In 1995 and 1996, jetties dwarfing the size of ninth- and tenth-century constructions were unearthed at Hedeby, suggesting that like its British and Irish counterparts, the town was fit to burst.

There would also be new towns. Kaupang had long fallen out of use, replaced by an ecclesiastical centre at Niðarós in central Norway, and similar changes were occurring in Sweden and Denmark, where established trading settlements were eclipsed by purpose-built royal ventures. This was yet another manifestation of power. Where before there had been Kaupang, occupied by petty lords and only overseen by a king, now there was Niðarós, the royal residence. Where before there had been Birka, sprawling across the Lake Mälaren region and home to several local elites, there was now Sigtuna, thirty kilometres to the north, built in 980 along the important overland routes to Gamla Uppsala. Sigtuna's position here made sense in a tactical and religious sense. Gamla Uppsala was a pagan hotspot, steeped in hundreds of years of tradition, and Sigtuna was not just a royal base but a Christian one. As coins were minted and ships were built and repaired ready for Baltic trade,[25] Christianity changed the *hugr* of the urban Swedes.

The rural and urban spheres of the Viking Age would change at different rates in different countries. On both the large and small scale, Viking Age Scandinavians were emulating their neighbours and reforging their identities into new and exciting forms, but were these changes only superficial? And at what point can we say an individual like Cnut changed from a 'Viking' like his antecedents to something closer to a High Medieval monarch? Was the change simply a mimicry of more prosperous neighbours, the geopolitical equivalent of the York bone buckle? Or did it go deeper than that?

Scandinavians evolved tremendously throughout this period, and while in many ways we can say that their outward appearance certainly changed, did their *core* change? Did their *hugr*?

Hugr

The Christianisation of Scandinavia is seen as one of the nails in the coffin of the Viking Age. But the Old Norse cosmology was always fluid. It had already changed considerably between pre- and post-Dust Veil times, and so the transition from paganism to Christianity was only the latest and most dramatic example of the *constantly* fluctuating nature of these belief systems.

Such a story can be best told through pictures. On the island of Gotland, a unique artistic expression developed from around 400 CE and would flourish in the following centuries. On this island, wealthy and fat from the slave and silk trades, merchants and craftsmen would carve their own dioramas: picture stones. From the fifth century, some of the earliest stones, designated 'Type A', display rotating sun discs and spiral-like celestial formations. These appear at the centre of all these Type A stones, as the main element; something worthy of reverence. Sune Lindqvist worked through the bulk of these picture stone classifications, observing repeated motifs and developing art styles over the years. An encircling serpent often appears alongside these pre-Viking Age solar orbs, perhaps Jǫrmungandr, the serpent that surrounds the world. A lot of the picture stones depict images very similar to those found on fifth-century bracteates, like abstract horses and the aforementioned sun discs, but interestingly, the latter motif disappears completely after the mid-sixth century – after the 536 climate disaster. Are we seeing a shift from a sun-worshipping belief system to something else? This would concur with our arguments put forward so far, of a total restructuring not just of agriculture and leadership, but also of religious hierarchy and psychology. Later Gotland picture stones, like the 'Type D' examples dated to the tenth century, display scenes of famous characters like Völundr the Smith, Óðinn (in his bird form), and Loki, but no sun discs. One example depicts a dark, multi-legged beast, probably Fenrir, whose kin swallow the sun during *Ragnarǫk*. The Weapon Dancer motif emerges on tenth-century picture stones, mainly found near Visby, along with the motif of two worlds, one atop the other, sometimes accompanied by etchings of longships. It has been argued that these ships are the bridge between worlds, a bridge between life and death.

Recently, Sigmund Oerhl[26] has re-analysed many of these picture stones with digital software to reveal details invisible to the naked eye. One such is a depiction of Loki, bound by snakes to a rock, dripping with poison. While still a depiction of Loki, digital analyses revealed that many

Two Gotland picture stones displaying the transition in belief systems. On the left is a 'Type A' example, Hablingo Havor I, and to the right is a 'Type C/D' variant, Klinte Hunninge I.

of the brush strokes used to paint the figure were made considerably later than the surrounding scene, and that the male-presenting god may have been repainted as a woman. Loki, like the belt-wearer in Coppergate, had changed his or her *hamr*.

The Gotland picture stones were visible across the landscape of Gotland and beyond. Edward Moore[27] of the University of Lancaster has digitally mapped the 'viewsheds' of landmarks such as Northumbrian standing crosses, determining how visible they would be from specific distances, and how that then affected the landscape around them. Such an approach would be fascinating to apply to the Gotlandic picture stones. It is likely that they formed a matrix of storytelling. One farmer may have had the first act of Völundr the Smith's tale on his land, but over yonder, there might be a grassy knoll with the sequel engraved upon another stone. The Gotland picture stone tradition reveals an ever-changing pantheon of characters and of motifs and religious beliefs. Like their *hamr*, the *hugr* of the Early Medieval Scandinavian world was being reshaped. In some cases, these adaptations were strengthening and adding to an already sophisticated belief system, but in others, they would replace it entirely. The situation in Rouen in 911 heralded such an evolution.

Following the *Treaty of Saint-Claire-sur-Epte*, King Charles the Simple of West Francia granted land in Rouen to a contingent of *Nortmanni* as a fiefdom. They were to swear allegiance to him, and to Francia, to prevent further viking raids and attempts by other groups. This contingent, likely including hangers-on from the Battle of Tettenhall in 910 and veterans from the Ælfred campaigns of the late ninth century, was seemingly led by one Ganger-Hrolf, who would later be known as Rollo. Two centuries later, the Benedictine monk Goffredo Malaterra wrote one of several histories on the Normans. In his monumental Sicily-oriented piece charting the chronology of Robert Guiscard and Roger I, *The Deeds of Count Roger*,[28] he wrote the following on the first 'Normans':

> Specially marked by cunning, despising their own inheritance in the hope of winning a greater, eager after both gain and dominion, given to imitation of all kinds, holding a certain mean between lavishness and greediness, that is, perhaps uniting, as they certainly did, these two seemingly opposite qualities. Their chief men were specially lavish through their desire of good report. They were, moreover, a race skilful in flattery, given to the study of eloquence, so that the very boys were orators, a race altogether unbridled unless held firmly down by the yoke of justice. They were enduring of toil, hunger, and cold whenever fortune laid it on them, given to hunting and hawking, delighting in the pleasure of horses, and of all the weapons and garb of war.

Rollo would be the first of these enterprising Scandinavian warlords to be given land in Neustria, the westernmost portion of the Frankish kingdom overlooking the English Channel. This was a prime spot for raiding not Francia but elsewhere; we have already seen the damage the Scandinavian army wrought in Brittany, for example, but it is likely they remained a danger in England, too. Interestingly, though, the areas around Rouen granted as a fief to Rollo were already largely under Scandinavian control, as evidenced by material and toponymic evidence found across the Roumois and Pays de Caux colonies.[29, 30] Rollo's gift and the treaty itself were merely *official* grants of territory already given over to vikingar. Talou, Caux, and Evrecin were added to the Scandinavians' Frankish territories. This first grant was not equally spread. While Rollo led the new wave of settlement in Caux and Roumois, quickly adapting to Frankish hierarchies and political rules (it appears Rollo split his own land between his trusted men, but importantly did not rule as a vassal to King Charles), in North-Contentin the situation was different. Here, there is toponymic evidence for a *thing*-style governmental structure and even by 1027 land charters reveal very Scandinavian-sounding names for the territories: *Haga* and *Helganes* are two examples.

Two more land grants would be given to the Scandinavians of Rouen. In 924, reaffirming an earlier 918 agreement, Rollo's lands were restated as *anneure*, expressing the fact that these territories were not simply a vassal state but an entirely independent territory given as a permanent gift. The generosity of King Charles the Simple may well have factored into Rollo's alleged rapid conversion to Christianity, something his progeny would follow. By 933, the 'Count of Rouen' would have ruled over an area roughly coterminous with modern Normandy, bringing him into conflict with the other vikingar settled in Brittany. Rollo died sometime before the final land grant, succeeded by his son William, a French-sounding name. However, considering William is attested to having been born outside of Rouen in *more danico* (meaning 'in the Danish way', through a partnership rather than a Christian marriage), it is likely that he had another name before his baptism. The contemporary chronicler Flodoard of Reims[31] would describe Rollo and his first son as 'Counts of Rouen', the title of 'Duke of Normandy' not appearing until later. William quelled a rebellion against his rule led by his own Scandinavian settlers. This was only the first instance of conflict in his life. Soon, Count William had become embroiled in the petty squabbles of local lords and their land grants across West Francia and beyond, and by 942 had been reinstalled as Count following a dispute with King Louis IV. He would be assassinated that year.

William's successor, Richard, would be even further away from his antecedents in terms of language and custom, though would maintain relations with Harald Bluetooth of Denmark. Normandy was from then on a fiercely independent polity surrounded by feuding Frankish neighbours, constantly attempting to assert dominance. While we can be sure that the *lingua franca* of these Scandinavians had, by the eleventh century, been almost completely 'Frenchified', certain loan words from Old Norse still exist in Modern French, such as *quille* for 'keel', from the Old Norse *kjóll*. Local law also reflected a Scandinavian past; a charter from 1030 refers to the legal ownership of *fiskigardha* (fisheries) and *valseta* (whaling stations) by the ruling elite, along with all shipwrecks, like later laws in Denmark.

Despite constantly suffering from border disputes and assassination attempts, the Duchy of Normandy would persevere, shedding its pagan Scandinavian skin for something continental, thoroughly Christian, and mostly French, but unique. Rollo's vikingar and their progeny had integrated, but even in 1066 they would retain their more fearsome skills.

In the east, a similar process of acculturation was occurring. By the reign of Sviatozslav I (943-972), the golden age of the *Rus* had begun.[32] Following the fall of Itil and Khazaria, the *Rus* had achieved a monopoly on eastern European trade and all the riches that would come with it. They had mastered the waterways, the shorelines, the weirs, and rapids: patriarchs *and* matriarchs of the ruling elite exerted their power from the fortress at Kyiv. Sviatozslav's mother, Olga, had resisted the spread of Orthodox Christianity initially, but by the time of her grandson Yaropolk, she was heralded as a saint due to her later baptism. Yaropolk was succeeded in 978 by Vladimir the Great, whose Old Slavic name denotes a faint Old Norse origin; *Volodiměr*, from '*Valdamarr*'. By the end of the tenth century, the customs and language of the *Rus* had, like the growing Norman state, become more and more 'native'. This process of Slavicisation would play a key role in the later formation of Russia as a nation-state, taking the Kyivan-Rus further and further away from their Scandinavian roots but retaining that heritage and raiding behaviour.

Vladimir the Great was, according to the *Primary Chronicle*, a devout pagan, founding a temple dedicated to local Slavic gods like Perun and Mokosh and others at Kyiv, but within a few years of his accession would convert to Christianity. A bold military leader, Vladimir annexed more and more territory, encroaching on Byzantine lands until he would finally be offered marriage to Anna Porphyrogenita, sister of Roman Emperor Basil II. Following such a dynastic coup, Vladimir turned his pagan centres to ash, founding church after church across the timber towns of Garðaríki. Granted, all this could be a fiction whipped up to highlight the benefits of both a Christian and Byzantine union, but it did reflect real changes across the Kyivan-Rus. Innumerable client polities submitted to Vladimir's reign shortly after, as he established a council made up of his twelve sons to manage his various principalities. Like Rome and the Abbasid Caliphate before him, Vladimir's dominion was becoming too large to control. A child of Vladimir's first marriage, Sviatopolk, would rebel against him and, following his father's death, succeed to the throne. Sviatopolk, later given the epithet 'the Accursed', reigned for only four years, dying somewhere in Poland after seeking refuge following a military defeat at the hands of his brother Yaroslav. In 2004, skeletal remains from a cemetery dated between the tenth and twelfth centuries in Bodzia, Poland – richly provided with grave goods – was found to contain haplotypes similar to those recovered from other princely *Rus* elites. It is possible this is Sviatopolk.[33]

Sviatopolk's opponent and successor, Yaroslav, later given the epithet of 'the Wise', would engage in international politicking on a scale hitherto unseen from a Grand Prince of Kyiv. Allied with *Anund* Jakob of Sweden, Yaroslav would engage his brother Mstislav from 1024 onwards with mixed success, conquering Tartu in Estonia in 1030, lands in Poland from 1031, and finally assuming his brother's territory in 1036 following his death. Yaroslav dominated the *Austrvegr* from his base at Novgorod, fostering relations with dynasts from Sweden (like Yngvar the Far-Travelled) and Norway (like Harald Sigurdsson), and even attempting in 1043 a siege of Constantinople. Principally, though, Yaroslav's main opponents were the roaming nomadic steppe tribes, and in an ironic twist of fate, *his* fortified lands were subject to sporadic raiding. While the Kyivan-Rus would continue to grow and develop following Yaroslav's reign, by this point the journey to the formation of a Russian state and surrounding principalities was well on its way. Yaroslav was a powerful royal leader protecting his lands using wooden castles and economic treaties. Where his antecedents – the *Rus* – had ruled the waterways through cruelty and guile, Yaroslav did so through official means, occupying the hillforts that had once been obstacles to his ancestors.

At what point did the *Rus* change from 'Scandinavian' to 'Slavic'? It is likely they were always mixed, with the Slavic element becoming more and more pronounced over time. Vikingar were, after all, masters of cultural assimilation and integration. Even in the tenth century, when Ibn Fadlan wrote his famous description of a local burial, it is likely that the internment had native influences. Shortly after Scandinavians started to make inroads along *Austrvegr*, they created a new and unique power base, and by the dawn of the twelfth century, were an important economic polity.

Hamingja

While the minds of Scandinavians were being reshaped by their neighbours and environments, so too would their battle strategies. The *Rus* first came to Constantinople as traders and raiders, then sent as delegates in the 830s and as an army in the 860s. Towards the end of the tenth century, however, the *Rus*, and Scandinavians from further afield, were serving as mercenaries for Constantinople's protection and outreach. The city had always offered opportunities for a canny vikingr, but now such fortune and battle-luck could be increased tenfold through service in the Varangian Guard. From the late ninth century, contingents of the *Rus* were fighting alongside Byzantine forces, though it would not be until 988 that the Varangian Guard was formally established as an elite and *Christian* fighting unit in service of the Emperor.[34, 35] In earlier years, warriors from the Kyivan-Rus had acted as mercenaries for Rome: in Crete in 902 and 949, in Syria in 955, and elsewhere across Constantinople's peripheries such as Bulgaria and around the Volga basin. During this time, *Rus* warriors were classed as part of the wider 'Great Companions', or *Hetaireia*,[36] groups of foreign bodyguards from a variety of locales. In 988, however, after years of unofficial and wider service from Slavic and Scandinavian vikingar, Emperor Basil II, 'The Bulgar Slayer', requested aid from Vladimir's Kyivan-Rus. The response was a delegation of around six thousand *Rus* soldiers to Constantinople, a follow-up on an earlier treaty from 971 when the Kyivan-Rus had been defeated by Byzantine forces in Bulgar lands. The grand-scale politicking of Vladimir the Great in the Roman theatre had resulted in a profitable arrangement for future *Rus* entrepreneurs. Now, they could choose to serve the richest figure in all of Christendom and be well rewarded for it.

From 989, the Varangian Guard would see active service across the Byzantine world; in Italy, Sardinia, Bulgaria, Sicily, Athens, and elsewhere.[37] A marble statue of a Piraeus lion currently sits outside The Arsenale in Venice, and has done since the late 1600s when it was plundered during wars against the Ottoman Empire. The Lion of Piraeus originated from the harbour of Athens, and carved into its flank is a handful of runes.[38] While we cannot be certain if these runes were carved by traditional vikingar or those serving in the Varangian Guard, the number of other Scandinavian runestones that mention 'service in *Grikkland*' would point to the latter.[39] The runes read:

> Haakon with Ulf and Asmund and Örn conquered this port. These men and Harold Hafi imposed a heavy fine on account of the revolt of the Greek people. Dalk is detained captive in far lands. Egil is gone on an expedition with Ragnar into Romania and Armenia.

There is another inscription which mentions one 'Harold the Tall', which some have argued to be Harald Sigurdsson himself, better known as Harald *harðráði*, arguably the most famous of all the Varangian Guard.[40] What did Egil and Ragnar encounter in Romania and Armenia, and who had captured Dalk in the 'far lands'? We can only wonder. Harold *harðráði*'s journey is much better documented.

Upon leaving the court of Yaroslav the Wise in the early eleventh century after fleeing defeat at the Battle of Stiklestad in Norway, Harald would head down the *Austrvegr* and seek his fortune in Constantinople. Over the better part of two decades, he served under three emperors, fighting the Arabs, Normans, and Bulgars across the Adriatic and Aegean Seas. He also served as a guard during Empress Zoe's pilgrimage to Jerusalem. Harald's distinguished career with the Varangian Guard would end with his dramatic escape from the city amidst a series of revolts. Many legends later became attributed to Harald's adventures in the Guard, such as his imperial love affairs and his blinding of Emperor Michael V. Several official Greek documents mention one 'Araltes', a leading Scandinavian figure.[41, 42, 43] 'Araltes' is mentioned in the *Strategikon of Kekaumenos* (written between 1075 and 1078)[44] as ascending to the rank of *spatharokanditos*, a middling official Byzantine post. Very impressive for a foreigner in imperial service, but nothing compared to true Greco-Romans, like the general George Maniakes, whom Harald would come to blows with on several occasions. The array of colourful characters Harald would encounter in the Varangian Guard must have been paralleled by other Scandinavians serving in this same regiment. It was an attractive position in terms of wealth and opportunity. The world Harald and other Varangians would have encountered out there beyond Constantinople would have been breathtaking: the crumbling ruins of Mycenaean cities, the faded grandeur of Jerusalem, and perhaps even the birthplace of Christ himself may have been visited on a tour of duty.

From the late tenth century, all Scandinavians serving the Roman Empire would have been Christian, yet they retained their uniqueness. *Vaerangoi* and 'Varangian Guard' comes from an Old Norse word '*væringi*' broadly meaning 'sworn companion', and accounts from as late as the twelfth century would describe the unit as distinctly different to all other imperial forces. In 1080, Princess Anna Komnene in her *Alexiad*[45] mentions the 'axe-bearing barbarians from Thule' – visually, the Varangian Guard was distinct in and out of their armour. Their signature weapon was a broad-bladed axe, slung over the shoulder while on guard. The excitement of active battle was rarer than the sheer boredom of the average Varangian's day, guarding the Emperor as he went to sermon after sermon. The runes carved across the Ayasofya in Istanbul, once a Byzantine cathedral, were probably etched during such a slow day. 'Halfdan wuz 'ere' is a fair translation of one.[46, 47]

The very best Varangian Guard would be awarded lamellar plate of the highest quality; shimmering gold mail coats that hung down to their knees. The bulk of military equipment was likely brought from Scandinavia or the Kyivan-Rus: the signature Viking Age sword, for instance. These warriors were likely tall and weathered men, with complexions distinct from their Byzantine comrades. Even here, in the city of cities, Scandinavians retained their identity, and it wouldn't be

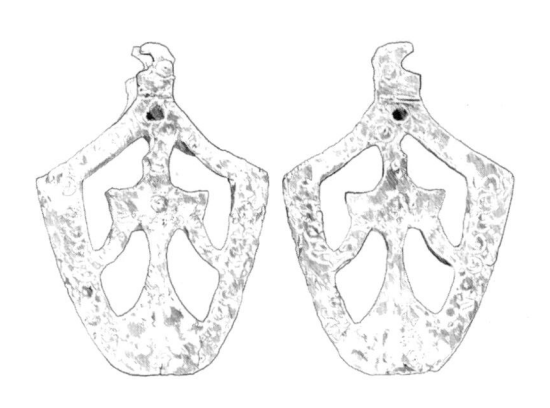

Two common accoutrements of the Varangian Guard, one decorative and the other utilitarian. A Varangian's takeaway from Constantinople might have been the symbol of the falcon. Whilst lacking the importance of ravens and crows, falcons still appear in the Icelandic corpus (see page 205) and were seen as symbols of aristocracy in the Early Medieval Period. Their appearance on sword-chapes found between Constantinople and the Austrvegr (like these examples from Birka, above) indicate high status and Greco-Roman influence.

Right: A reconstructed example of a 'Dane Axe' or long-shafted broad-bladed axe (Type M), based on a find from Langeid in Sedestalen, Norway, dated to the eleventh century.

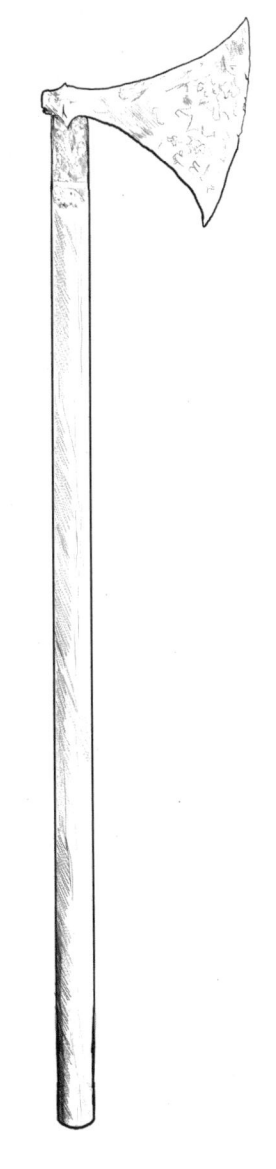

until after the Norman Conquest of England that the Scandinavian character of the Varangian Guard started to change, by this point replaced by Anglo-Scandinavians fleeing William the Bastard's rule over England.

The last time we mentioned England it had also just been occupied by a foreign interloper, in 1016. This was not a Norman, but a Dane, and his name was Cnut the Great. In the last few decades of the Viking Age Scandinavian monarchs (no longer simply just 'warlords') were competing over entire nation-states, and in Cnut's case, he would rise to be the most powerful of them all. England was the first piece of the jigsaw, next came Denmark. In 1019, Cnut's brother Harald Sweynsson died, leaving the throne of Denmark empty. It was claimed almost immediately, with local rebellions squashed and international responses from *Anund* Jakob of Sweden repelled. Border conflicts continued between the two countries throughout the 1020s, as Cnut's grip over the Jutland peninsula and surrounding islands and provinces remained firm. *Anund* Jakob continued the rule of his father Olof Tax-King, who was the first monarch to mint coins within Sweden.[48] Olof, like Olaf Trygvasson of Norway and Sweyn Forkbeard of Denmark, was part of a new generation of Scandinavian monarch, slowly breaking into the wider European network. Jakob (given the Norse name *Anund* later in life) had been forced to quell his fair share of rebellions too, but his grip on Sweden as a modern polity was still incomplete; the deep-rooted pagan holdouts represented the last gasp of the old ways.

Norway had been annexed to some extent by Sweyn Forkbeard upon the defeat of Olaf Trygvasson in 1000, but following his death, the lands had not come to Cnut but to another, Olafr Haraldsson, who had previously been raiding England alongside Sweyn and his son. Haraldsson, having been baptised in England at the court of Æthelred the Ill-Counselled, would go on to become an extremely devout ruler across the Northern Way, establishing churches along the fjords and forcibly converting all those who did not wish it. It had taken a long while for Christianity to establish a foothold in the disparate communities of Norway, but now it was here in a state-authorised and aggressive capacity, and it was here to stay. While Cnut and Jakob were both at least nominally Christian, they were not engaged in anywhere near the same level of religious enforcement. Haraldsson would become the focus of the first Scandinavian saint's cult after his death, with churches and communities in his name emerging all over Europe within a decade or two.[49, 50] Haraldsson's Norway was in Cnut's firing line, though he was occupied throughout the 1020s with securing not only England

and Denmark but also the future of his descendants by maintaining international links.

One of our best sources for this period's complex politics is the *Encomium Emmae Reginae*,[51] written in 1042 in praise of King Cnut's second wife, Lady Emma of Normandy, the previous wife of King Æthelred. Emma is one of the more intriguing and powerful figures of the eleventh century; a canny politician, ruthless and relentless in securing her own aims and the future of her children. Even following Cnut's death in 1035, Emma continued to act as unofficial ruler over her sons until her own death. Her heritage also had Scandinavian roots; she was the daughter of Richard of Normandy. While we cannot be certain, it is possible that Cnut's 'North Sea Empire' was also Emma's; this 'power couple' had a strong working partnership that allowed each of them to further their own ambitions.

By 1028, Cnut had ousted Olafr Haraldsson from Norway and secured his dominion over the kingdom. By this point, Cnut was styling himself as King of England, Denmark, Norway, and parts of Sweden, too. He exacted tribute from the territories of the Wends and the immediate borders of Scandinavia. His dominion over Sweden is however doubtful.[52, 53] While there are coins minted in this decade that say 'Cnut, King of the Swedes', the *Anglo-Saxon Chronicle* only mentions Jakob as ruler of the country, following his victory over Cnut in 1026 at the Battle of Helgeå. Like Danish rulers before him, it is likely that Cnut's 'Swedish' territories only included a few areas on the southern coast. Regardless, Cnut achieved his imperial ambitions, though our modern label for his territories, the North Sea Empire, emerged over five hundred years later in John Speed's 1623 *Histoire of Great Britaine*.[54] At the time, it was most likely referred to as a union of kingdoms ruled by one overlord.

Cnut was the single most powerful figure from the entire Viking Age, but can we really consider him a *vikingr* in the same sense that his antecedents were? While his career had started through raids on England, in which he slaughtered prisoners and extracted tribute, he had maintained his grip on power through politicking and international alliances. His rule over Norway was partially achieved through the regency of his first wife, Ælfgifu of Northampton,[55] where she was installed in 1029.[56] Cnut was a Christian monarch fighting other Christian monarchs across Scandinavia and beyond, with each ruler having their own national armies composed of individual warbands. By the eleventh century, all the elements that had once characterised the onset of the Viking Age had started to shrink. In 1030, Cnut would resecure his hold on Norway at the Battle of Stiklestad, in which a bankrupt Olafr Haraldsson would return from his exile in Sweden to recapture his throne. His army, made up of loyalists and including his brother Harald Sigurdsson, was dwarfed by Cnut's international fleet. He wasn't even in Norway to lead it but at home in England, dealing with more important matters. Where once there were warrior leaders at the forefront of the shield wall, there was now a new form of power. Haraldsson, in contrast, was very much in the thick of the fighting, and he would die with his arms raised in prayer to the Christian God.

Following this ultimate victory, Cnut's union of kingdoms would not last. His family's luck ran out. After his death in 1035, the countries of England, Denmark, and Norway would all revert to their own rulers, and we cannot really consider these characters as vikingar either. Magnus the Good, son of Olafr Haraldsson, took the throne in Norway, and Cnut's own two sons Harold Harefoot and Harthacnut would both have short-lived reigns in England and Denmark before they were replaced. Harthacnut's successor, Edward the Confessor, was the last king of the West Saxon bloodline, and engaged in international relations with Svein Estridsson's Denmark. Between 1045 and 1047, Edward refused to send help in the ongoing wars between Norway and Denmark, fearing an invasion himself from Magnus the Good. This turmoil within England was somewhat pacified by the stabilising force of Earl Siward of Northumbria, who had been installed in the 1020s by Cnut. Only a second-generation Danish immigrant, Siward (or Sigurðr *Digri*) lived through four successive English monarchs and knitted Northumbria into the greater tapestry of England for the first time in history. While it had officially been part of 'England' since the tenth century, it was Siward who married the courts of Wessex with the blood of Northumbria, ensuring a lack of rebellions during his period as earl. His son Waltheof would lead the rebellion against William in 1069, going against his father's own peaceful legacy.

While Cnut's empire did not outlast him, the changes he had wrought upon the 'Viking' world very much did. After 1035, international raiding and a few holdouts of paganism did continue, but even the invasion of Harald *harðráði* in 1066 looks almost nostalgic. The luck, the *hamingja* previously enjoyed by Scandinavian vikingar, had changed for the worse. Nations were larger and more united, and imperialism was back. Men like *Imperator* Brian, King Eadgar of England, or perhaps Ottos one-through-three were stronger and emulating Rome. The game was different now, with larger stakes and more power to be taken in one concerted effort, consequently the opportunities for traditional viking activity had diminished. But the baton of 'going a-viking' would not be dropped, it was passed to a new form of vikingar, with new targets to raid.

Fylgja

The *fylgjur* exist within all of us; they are our past, present, and future, our ancestry, and our progeny, all informed by one ethereal female or animal figure. At the very core of a standard vikingr was not a brutish male but a lone woman holding the threads of fate. It is the women of the Viking Age who carried and bore these rulers, who secured the future of bloodlines, and while they may remain in the background for many histories, they were undoubtedly at the forefront of contemporary minds.

Or perhaps that is a romantic view of the situation. Some *fylgjur* may have been represented by animal spirits. Whatever the case, how people in the Viking Age perceived their own identity was surely changing. In England, second and third-generation migrants who were once the children of raiders were now tied to their ancestrally acquired land.[57,58] When new Hiberno-Norse raiders came a-viking in the 910s or when Sweyn Forkbeard's Danes ravaged the land eighty years later, many of these Anglo-Scandinavians may have felt a closer connection to the idea of *Anglalond* than to their raiding cousins. The law code designated 'IV Eadgar',[59,60] from the late tenth century states: 'This measure is to be common to all the nation, whether Englishmen, Danes, or Britons, in every province of my dominion ... this addition is to be common to all of us who inhabit these islands.' In law codes from Leicester we find one Earl Orm consistently supporting Eadgar's rise to the throne throughout the mid-tenth century; a Scandinavian with chips bet on the English crown. In 973, traditions describe King Eadgar being rowed along the River Dee by eight lesser kings including a Scandinavian, Maccus, the 'arch-pirate' king of the Isles.[61] While probably propaganda, it does display the idea that all were one under the English crown.[62]

While formally part of England, the Danelaw and Old Norse-speaking lands likely maintained a unique regional identity, which strengthened their connections not with the House of Wessex down south but their ancestors over the sea. There is a reason why Sweyn and Cnut would rally at *Gegnesburh* (Gainsborough) in Anglo-Scandinavian territory ahead of taking the throne of England. There is a reason why Sweyn waited until he had crossed the traditional boundary of Watling Street before beginning his violent rampage across the countryside. These Anglo-Scandinavians were kinsmen.

On the 13th of November 1002 the infamous St Brice's Day Massacre took place on the orders of King Æthelred. Two years later, a charter from Oxford stated that 'All the Danes who had sprung up in this island, sprouting like cockle amongst the wheat, were to be destroyed by a most just extermination.' However the rest of the account only really speaks of 'the afore-mentioned town', Oxford, and not of a nationwide genocide. Archaeological evidence from St John's College, Oxford, and near Ridgeway Hill in Dorset point to the systematic beheading and burning of around one hundred individuals of Danish descent, dated between 960-1038, though whether these can be related to the massacre is another question. The event, regardless of its scale, was nevertheless evidence of the political fragmentation and ethnic divisions that had sprung up across England during this second wave of viking activity. It was not the threat of the Danes, who had likely assimilated to a significant degree into English society, but the need for a 'common enemy', that had prompted Æthelred's command.

In 1066, Harald did not go for the economic and governmental trophies of the south, but straight for York. At the Battle of Fulford, he claimed ownership of the town and thus, in theory, dominion over the entire north of England and the trade routes over the Irish Sea. Perhaps, then, Harald and his Norwegian kinsmen saw a certain pre-existing bond between their countries and northern England. While formally recognised as one country, lands north of Watling Street may have been viewed as closer to Scandinavia, culturally and linguistically.

But the eleventh-century Danelaw was not homogenous, nor did it have a capital centre. Scandinavian migrants in East Anglia had a different culture to those on the Yorkshire Wolds. The Cuerdale Hoard, a silver hoard buried in Lancashire between 905 and 910, contained some extremely rare coins minted in honour of King Edmund, by then a saint. King Edmund had been ruler of East Anglia in the 860s when he was allegedly martyred in a brutal fashion by the leaders of the Great Heathen Army. A cult rapidly sprang up around his death like blood from a wound, and later folk stories originate from earlier oral traditions.[63, 64]

The most famous tale, first written down in the thirteenth century, describes how Edmund's head was recovered when loyalists followed a wolf which had been urging them to follow it for weeks; 'Here, here!' it barked. The wolf had been guarding the head and saw to it that the late king was made whole again. Roger of Wendover's rendition of this tale relates the wolf to Ragnar *Loðbrók* of all people, that legendary Danish character who was the father of the Great Army's leaders and, thanks to the TV show, the archetypal 'Viking' for many people.[65] Roger was merging two folk tales into one, an English Christian tradition about a saintly king martyred by vikingar, and a Scandinavian pagan story. Ragnar – the wolf – was apologising for the murder of King Edmund by returning his head years later. John of Worcester, writing earlier than Roger and with less of a mind to bridge the chasm between English and Danes, relates how Edmund came back from the dead to kill Sweyn Forkbeard in 1014.

Flux

The Cuerdale Hoard was likely buried by a Scandinavian raider only about three decades after the death of King Edmund. Following the Battle of Edington in 878, Guthrum was baptised and made ruler of East Anglia. Perhaps he was responsible for the minting of these coins. The cult of Saint Edmund emerged following Guthrum's death, and it is likely that it was started to some degree by East Anglian Scandinavians, perhaps a method of uniting with their new Christian neighbours. Elsewhere in England, coins from tenth-century York feature the iconography of both St Peter and Þórr, keeping both Christians and pagans on side, or rather attempting subtly to merge the two. It was the activities of Scandinavian *vikingar* which had prompted such newfound religious devotion in England.

In the aftermath of widespread monastic devastation across the continent and the British Isles, religious communities were on the back foot by the end of the ninth century, without their accustomed funds, security, and status. New monastic institutions were created to fill the vacuum left behind by such ruins, taking a new and important role in education and artistry. Ælfred the Great was a proponent of this change over in England, but the origin of what is now referred to as the tenth-century Benedictine reform truly began in 909 in Cluny Abbey, Burgundy, and spread from there.[66] As viking activity in the west temporarily decreased in the tenth century, Benedictine monasteries flourished, sponsored and maintained by wealthy English nobles.[67, 68, 69] By the time of Sweyn Forkbeard's raids on England, his Danish and Norwegian soldiers were going up against a devout nation, and Cnut would conquer and then assimilate with it. Cnut would eventually be interred in the Old Minster of Winchester, along with his son Harthacnut, the cathedral of the kings of Wessex. Cnut's posthumous position here associated him with the native *and Christian* kings in England, rather than his own pagan and Scandinavian heritage. This desire for religious reform and unity was a bond connecting all European nations by the end of the tenth century, and Scandinavia was slowly joining. From sea wolves to guardians of Christian saints, from church-burners to church founders.

Already mentioned is the fact that many Old English genealogies began with or at least featured Wōden, the equivalent or possible precursor to the Old Norse Óðinn.[70] By the ninth century, some featured Bældæg, possible equivalent to the god Baldr, the unwilling precipitator of *Ragnarǫk*. Wōden was evidently once a deity. By the time we see his and Bældæg's names mentioned in regnal lists, it is as mortals, euhemerised from god to man. West Saxon genealogies place Wōden in the real world: he had never been a god at all but was instead a powerful chieftain mistakenly believed to be a god.[71] Later, through a desire to not be seen as descendant from a pagan house, West Saxon leaders amended this yet again. Wōden became a devout Christian (and a relative of Noah) who had relapsed into paganism before returning to the rightful faith, according to Syriac sources.[72] This affirmed Christianity as having *always* been the correct faith, and it mirrors Snorri Sturluson's later rationalisation of the Old Norse gods. The Æsir and Vanir were not deities, but remarkable mortals from a time long ago in a land far away, who had become erroneously deified in folk memory. Christians were disenfranchising and changing paganism just as paganism was creating the conditions which would strengthen Christianity. The ancestry – the *fylgja* – of the West Saxon courts had been indirectly amended by viking activity, and as Scandinavians themselves converted to Christianity, their world was being uprooted and tampered with, watered down into something mundane and mortal, in exchange for the White Christ.

There were moments when the old ways were remembered. In 1006, amidst the wars between Sweyn and Æthelred, the *ASC* relates how the English forces rallied at an ancient Bronze Age burial mound 'because it had often been said that if they sought out Cwichelm's Barrow [the enemy] would never get to the sea'; a belief that forces from their own pagan past might save their skin from the ravages of Forkbeard. Evidently, Cwichelm still abided in his wormy tomb.

The Viking Ages

We read and hear of a Viking Age that lasted between 793-1066. In this book the idea of a much longer Viking Age has been addressed, having already been established by previous scholars.[73] In reality, considering the scale of the Scandinavian diaspora in the Early Medieval Period, this 'Viking Age' is a collection of Viking Ages. For England, the Viking Age is considered to be 793-1066, from the first recorded viking raid to the Battle of Hastings, which not only extinguished the dynasty that had been fighting Scandinavians for so long but also cemented a new Norman regime that had been established *by* Scandinavians a century earlier. We might replace the Battle of Hastings with the Battle of Stamford Bridge, where Harald *harðráði* fell against the King of England in the same year, but there would still be glimpses of viking activity *after* 1066 across the British Isles.

For the Scandinavian heartlands, the Viking Age clearly started much earlier than 793 but would end near enough the same time, when the last embers of Swedish and Norwegian paganism were extinguished. Viking activity would recur until the thirteenth century across the Isle of Man, the Hebrides, and Orkney, while in Iceland the 'Sturlung Age' would perpetuate a lot of the petty power struggles established centuries earlier. Even further north, in Greenland, it would take until the late fifteenth century for the Viking Age to finally end. We could further periodise the Viking Age into several subdivisions; the Early Viking Age from 536-878, the 'High' Viking Age from 878-937, and the Late Viking Age from 937-1066, but we'd still be missing some things and could be accused of putting up unnecessary dividing walls. The Viking Age would also be revivified in the Baltic Sea. It had many ends, just as it had many beginnings. Underpinning some of these 'Viking Ages' was a belief system that had originated long before them, and the idea of a cyclical cataclysm that would end all things, but also birth and new life: *Ragnarǫk*. 'the doom of the Gods'.

The old gods had many names. We know them in this book as the Æsir and Vanir, but they were not immortal. Like the inevitable doom described in the lines of *The Battle of Maldon*, their end, and the end of the Viking Age, was approaching.

Faith

> All in the remotest islands or among the barbarian tribes had heard the call of Christ. The time had come for the Welshman to give up hunting in his forests, the Scotsman forsook his familiar fleas, the Dane broke off his long-drawn-out potations, the Norwegian left his diet of raw fish.
>
> Mention of the First Crusade in William of Malmesbury's twelfth-century *Deeds of the Kings of the English*.

There is evidence as far back as 200 CE of powerful Iron Age elites in Scandinavia ruling over pockets of land and dominating neighbouring territories. Even prior to the 536 climate disaster, depictions very similar to later visualisations of Óðinn emerge in the form of the Weapon Dancer motif. The Old Norse belief system was not a static faith, it was merely the latest development of a north European pagan cosmology that had been evolving over thousands of years. Nowadays, we know the 'Old Norse religion' through the *Poetic Edda* and Snorri Sturluson; he condensed all that he had gathered from earlier traditions and transformed chosen elements into a popular format. But Snorri Sturluson didn't really *know* about the Old Norse belief systems, he was working on the evidence he had at the time almost two hundred years after the beliefs had mostly died out. And how can we be sure that the pagan beliefs practised by Swedes in the eleventh century were the same as the ones practised by those in the eighth? How can we be sure that a magnate in the Lofoten Islands would be worshipping the same gods in the same way as a warlord near Hedeby, or a farmer on Gotland?

There was no top-down structure for Old Norse paganism, it splintered into various guises throughout the Viking Age. World events such as the

Dust Veil would have undoubtedly added to and reshaped these belief systems, and the spread of Christianity may have had some initial effects *prior* to conversion. In the very twilight of Viking Age Scandinavia, as Christians continued to raid one another across the North Sea, there were still holdouts of *forn siðr* – the old ways.

Worlds within Worlds

The concept of *forn siðr* or *heiðinn siðr*[1] ('heathen ways') only really came into existence as a necessary identifier of the enemy of Christianity. Early Medieval Scandinavians had no single catch-all name for their belief system until they encountered a religion that did. Christianity, despite its various strands, was relatively monolithic and overseen, there was no such authority ensuring all Old Norse believers did things in a specific way, and as a result, these old ways were varied. The mythology we have today is the most accessible rendition of what was a complex and regional affair. We think of the Old Norse pantheon as regimented, but archaeology tells us it was anything but.

While Snorri Sturluson's writings are undoubtedly our single most valuable textual source for *forn siðr*, we cannot rely upon them in isolation. What we know about *forn siðr* beyond Snorri is largely through interpretation of material evidence; amulets, pendants, grave goods, sacrificial sites, ritual deposits, votive offerings, temple structures.[2]

We can ascertain something of how believers viewed the world through art styles. A variety existed across the Viking Age, stylistic phases which changed over the centuries and were influenced by external artistic influences.[3] The first identifiable true Viking Age style would be what we call either the Berdal or Oseberg style, named after their respective sites. Gripping beasts dominate the art of the Oseberg style, carved creatures whose claws act as frames for internal motifs. These first two styles had evolved through the preceding centuries before the Viking Age and would set a precedent for those to come, the Broa, Borre, and Jellinge styles, where the characteristic gripping beasts become more and more ribbon-like, with interlaced swirls, ring-chains, and filigree motifs. As the artwork became more complex, the depictions become more abstract.[4] The Jellinge style would eventually give way in the late tenth century to the Mammen style, characterised by even more prominent interlacing motifs – the same can be said for the later Ringerike and Urnes styles, the latter being the high point of animal depictions intermixed with spirals and crisscrossing tendrils. An art style that reflects the notion that all is connected, perhaps. There would be regional variations. The Urnes style, for instance, was quite different in England than in Scandinavia.[5] Much like the idea of *forn siðr*, these art styles exist in such a way that we can segment them into distinct periods as we do with music genres. Would an artisan making something in the early eleventh century know if the result was closer to Ringerike or Urnes style? These terms would have meant nothing to them, but the distinctions between the art styles were real. Carpenters in a cosmopolitan centre may have been renowned for their ability to carve sinewy ribbon work, while blacksmiths who had recently visited England would have brought their own new outlook to their creations.

Unlike Christianity, a pagan ritual did not require a specific, reserved location like a church, however, place names with elements like *-ve/vi* or *hof-* indicate spiritual connections.[6] Hofstaðir, in Iceland, with its array of sacrificially buried cattle skulls, was clearly both a farm *and* a temple, and the many landscape features ending in *-vi* across Scandinavia such as Torsvi and Ullevi may have been sacred places. The outdoor veneration of deities also separated *forn siðr* from Christianity; Torsvi and Ullevi may have been glades dedicated to Þórr and Ullr respectively. Ullr is an obscure Old Norse deity scarcely mentioned by Snorri, but the location of Ull- place names indicate the figure may have had some connection to forests and hunting.[7,8] The *Poetic Edda* references his domain as *Ýdalir* ('yew-dales'). Njǫrðr, a sea deity, is another important Old Norse god whose absence from Snorri's work belies his significance. Any seafaring culture would surely have venerated such a figure.[9] Again, the toponymic evidence tells us as much. Njarlunda, 'Njǫrðr's sacred grove', for instance, and at another such site (Lunda,

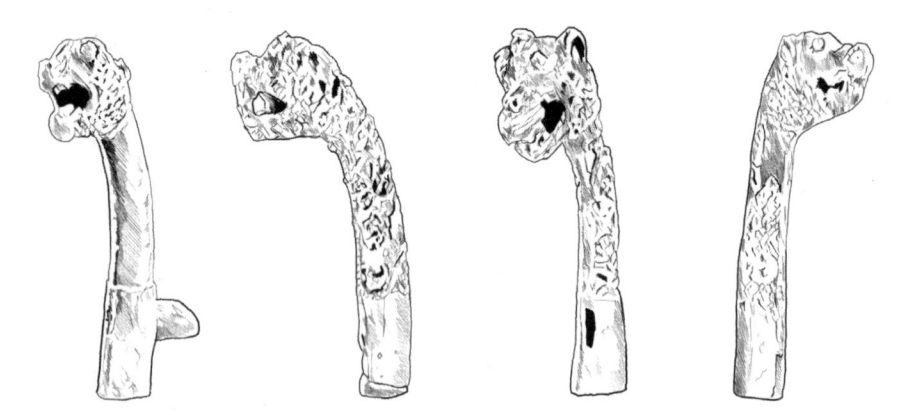

Four of the five exquisitely carved animal headposts found alongside the Oseberg ship when it was excavated in the early twentieth century. These 'beast heads' remind one of the Gripping Beasts of the Oseberg and Berdal styles. What started as a bulky monster became, by the eleventh century, a sinewy, serpentine creature. It is likely they are the work of artisans from across the Vestfold region and beyond. Maybe they were hired to pay respects to the matriarch entombed upon the ship, or perhaps the headposts are all family heirlooms of the deceased, gifts for the next world.

in Södermanland), there is evidence of ritually deposited beads, animal bones, burnt clay, arrowheads, and stones.[10] Käringsjön and Älvasjö in Sweden are 'hag-lake' and 'elf-lake'.[11] Whether these bodies of water were used for sacrificial rites we do not know, but their names had otherworldly connotations.

At Skedemosse Lake, on Öland, there is evidence of ritually butchered animals and broken weapons dated between 200-900; nearly forty young and old people of both sexes, one hundred horses, eighty cattle, sixty caprines, fifteen pigs, and seven dogs.[12, 13] For what reasons all of these people and livestock were killed will forever be a mystery, but the broken weapons are similar to earlier pre-Viking Age votive deposits such as the Hjortspring burial and the thousands of weapons found in Illerup Ådal.[14] The suffix of *-hoj/hog* might also have spiritual connections, normally associated with burial mounds, supernatural places in later Icelandic sagas.

Rituals did not always take place outside. Purpose-built structures for cultic activities appear between 200 and 500, before the Dust Veil. These were large wooden buildings supported by internal pillars richly carved like the Oseberg headposts. Adam of Bremen's contemporary description of a temple in Sweden[15] which he had heard about from second-hand sources mentions totem-like posts depicting deities, showered with offerings of blood and tiny gold foils.[16] The archaeological evidence for these cultic buildings is normally limited to post-holes and the outlines of walls, we are missing the decorated reality. The interiors were likely adorned with tapestries depicting scenes from the pagan corpus, not dissimilar to the Gotlandic picture stones, and the smoke billowing from the internal hearth would have no doubt created an other-wordly atmosphere. The Hellvi mask from Gotland sat in the centre of one such *hof*, its bronze metalwork reflecting the sparks from the fire beneath.

Other toponymic elements which indicate cultic sites include *-salr* and *-hörgr*, meaning 'hall' and 'cairn' respectively. We do not know how often pagan rituals were performed or if there was any set pattern to follow, but later Christian calendar dates have precedent for replacing pre-existing celebrations. The high number of depictions of Völundr and other legendary blacksmiths may suggest that even the act of forging weapons had ritual connotations. The art of transforming ugly bog iron into a shining blade may have been perceived as magic; the sheer number of kennings used to describe swords in skaldic verses hints at this. Swords were the 'glittering fish of the shield', they were 'the fires of wolf-wine', 'shaft-fires', 'battle-flames'; they were 'sword-belt stabbers', 'gilded tongues', 'world flames', 'the oars of the wound', and 'the kindred of the stabber'. A creative web of smithing, kinship, and sword-skill, the warrior's way.

Völundr is a character mentioned by Snorri and later works we can reasonably identify from archaeological material, but are there any others? At Snaptun, in Denmark, is a large stone made of steatite carved with the likeness of a beguiling figure with its mouth sewn shut.[17] Many have argued that this is Loki. But was Loki even a god? Later mentions of him and the complete absence of any identifiable Loki-worshipping location or adornment may suggest that he was not viewed as an equivalent to the other Æsir and Vanir but as something entirely

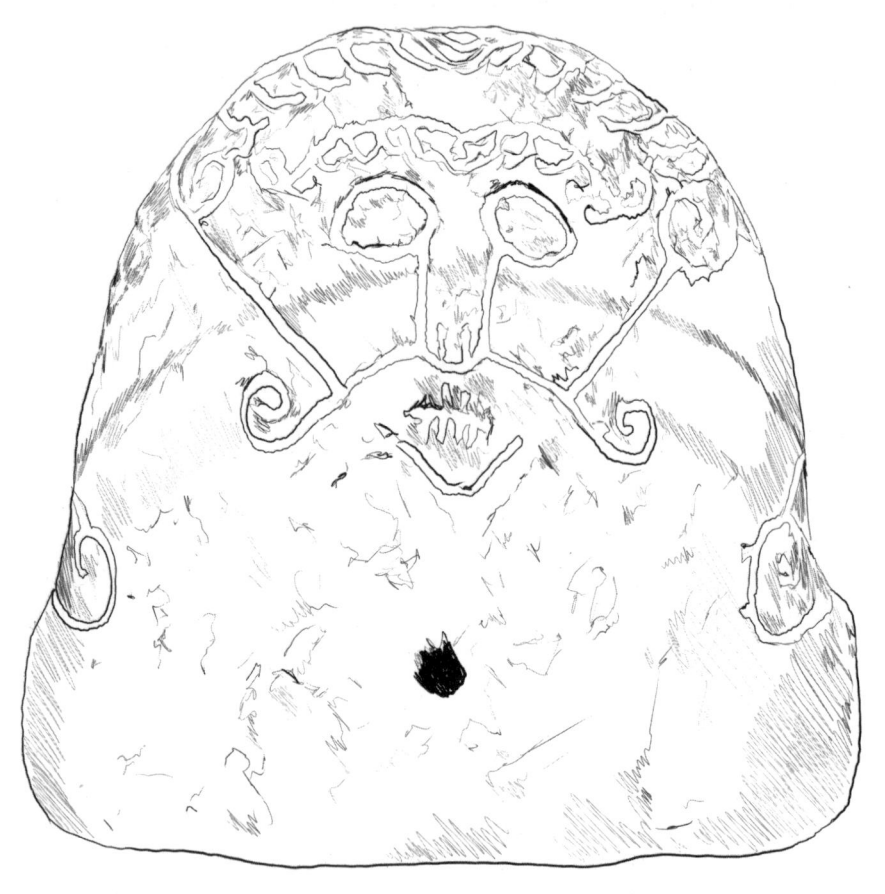

The Snaptun Stone was part of a Viking Age forge; the hole beneath the face would have bellowed out hissing steam and smoke while a blacksmith wove threads of iron and fire together. The face has been identified with Loki owing to the sewn lips. In the second part of Snorri's *Prose Edda*, Loki was punished for cutting the hair of Sif, the wife of Þórr, and was forced to pay dwarves to create a replacement wig made of spun gold. The dwarves, unhappy with how Loki had behaved, vowed to 'take his head', but were only given permission to sew his mouth shut instead.

different.[18, 19] The Old Norse version of a demi-god, perhaps, or maybe just an alternate manifestation of another deity?

One would surely meet these characters in the afterlife, but where would the *hugr* of a person end up? Popular depictions have it that all those who died in battle were to go to 'Valhalla', Valhöll, but this hall of the slain was possibly only one of several destinations for the valiant dead. In Valhöll, warriors who had fallen in battle would rise again every day for an endless cyclical celebration of meat, mead, and violence, ahead of the final showdown against evil at *Ragnarǫk*. This might have been unique to Valhöll, or practised in others, like Freyja's hall of Folkvangr

Rán, a deity mentioned by Snorri and the *Poetic Edda*, resided under the water with 'sea beasts'. Skaldic verses describe her hall as a residence for all those who drown at sea. There was also *Hel*. Further realms and their regions are hinted at in thirteenth- and fifteenth-century sagas like *Údáinsakr*[20, 21] and *Glæsisvellir*[22] – 'the undying plane' and the 'glittering fields'. The Elysian Fields of Greek mythology come to mind. All the deities had halls, some more than one. Frigg, Óðinn's wife, dwelled in *Fensalir*, the 'fen hall'.

Better not to die at all. The avoidance of such a fate may have required keeping figures and elements of the Old Norse world 'on your side'. In Stentoften, Sweden, a runestone dated to 600 mentions one 'Hathuwulf' having been given 'good growth' after the sacrifice of nine bucks and nine stallions.[23] This recurring motif of nine is also mentioned by Thietmar of Merseburg and Adam of Bremen's writings on Lejre[24, 25] and Gamla Uppsala. There, for the most grandiose of all pagan temples, they both write that nine of every species were sacrificed and hung from trees. There was clearly *something* to the number nine. Before his death, Þórr is said to have taken nine steps before succumbing to the poison of Jǫrmungandr, and Wōden – Óðinn's Old English counterpart – is mentioned in a tenth-century manuscript as striking a serpent with 'nine glory-twigs' in a medicinal ritual.[26]

Place names can reveal certain lost elements of the Old Norse belief systems. Can the same be said of personal names? Many colourful characters from the historical record like Bjorn *járnsíða* were given later epithets. Visaeti means 'he who sits in the sanctuary' The prefixes of Thorgest, Thorkell, Thorir, and Thorgils derive from the god Þórr.[27] We have already discussed Baltic and Slavic counterparts to Þórr, but there was also a Saami one, a hammer-wielding god called in some regional dialects Thoragalles.[28] It is unknown which deity came first.[29, 30] The Þórr/Thoragalles similarity is obvious but there is also the aforementioned crossover between the tales of King Harald Fairhair and one of his wives, Snæfríð, the daughter of a Saami ruler.[31] There was clearly a degree of tolerance between the Viking Age Scandinavians and the Saami, though this would start to change upon the advent of Christianity.[32] By the thirteenth century, tales from Hålogaland demonising the Saami and their *magus* rituals were a Norwegian attempt to redefine their own pagan past in response to the pagan present of the Saami; 'We are now reformed Christians, but look at these other wretches, worse than even our own pagan ancestors!'

The Saami would become viewed as part of the land, like a forest or a hill, rather than as people, and were synonymous with the Old Norse heritage of Scandinavia, not their own beliefs. The prominence of animal shamanism within Saami culture and the shape-shifting motifs in Scandinavian customs do indicate, however, that there was a crossover between the belief systems. Perhaps worshippers in Norway borrowed customs from their Saami neighbours, whereas the Danes were instead influenced by Christians on their southern borders.

Here Be *Hvítakristr*

The process of conversion to Christianity occurred at different societal levels at different rates. The phrase '*dauðr i hvitavaðum*' ('dead in white clothes')[33] appears across a few Swedish runestones from the ninth century onwards, probably in reference to baptismal gowns. Was it good to have '*dauðr i hvitavaðum*' applied to one's grave? Or was it for insurance reasons? Pre-conversion Danish laws[34] stated that the baptised could not inherit land from their families, so stating a relative died 'in white clothes' was a means to thwart later claims. Maybe it was not a mark of salvation but of shame created by other families: 'Your son died a Christian, how sickening!'

The spread of these runestones in northern Sweden and similar examples across Västergötland indicate that contrary to accounts from the time, Sweden was almost certainly not an undifferentiated pagan holdout. The runestones imply a knowledge of Christian theology independent of Christian missions. In fact, one of the main sources for the claim that Sweden was a pagan country as late as the eleventh century is Adam of Bremen, who aspired for the nation to join his archbishopric of Hamburg-Bremen.

It is possible that Sweden, home of many Varangian guardsmen, was more influenced by Greek Orthodox Christianity from Constantinople than western sects, thus arousing the ire of clergymen like Adam.[35] The act of commissioning theologically inspired runestones was the same line of reasoning that inspired earlier carvers to write their runes in the bodies of writhing serpents and scenes from pagan myth. These runestones

Faith

were created by artistic patrons, many of whom were learned women,[*] demonstrating their knowledge of all things otherworldly.

But a large part of this analysis must be guesswork. While all writing systems are inherently memory-based, there is something particularly obscure about the act of casting runes.[36] Many letters have multiple meanings, and when combined with other marks, take on new forms. Younger Futhark runic inscriptions are dated between the tenth and twelfth centuries, during the period in which Scandinavia began to be converted, a literary response to the erasure of pagan customs. The Old Icelandic phrase '*skiðaskipti*' ('change of customs') captures this; not a total domination of one religion over an another, but a slow transition.

Many runestones mention those who funded the runestone, the person who carved it, the person whose land the runestone is on, and events and other elements with no further context. Like the Gotlandic picture stones, the art of writing and then *reading* a runestone was drawing upon a long-standing folk memory which travelled back through time for over a thousand years. The Younger Futhark runic language used in the Viking Age had evolved from the Elder Futhark, which, in turn, had likely originated through interactions with epigraphic Latin from the Roman frontier.[37, 38] The motifs and characters mentioned were likely even older than that. Runes played an important part in the cosmological corpus, sometimes as a form of secret magic and wisdom.[39] It was not a 'magic alphabet', though, no more than any other language was.

Runes weren't just carved in stone. Coins, brooches, jewellery, weapons, perishable materials like wooden sticks, poles, and shields were all carved with charms, curses, declarations of ownership: 'Rannveig owns this casket.' Runes were placed strategically in the landscape, on well-trodden pathways and on the borders between petty kingdoms, especially in Sweden.

Imagine a speaker stood on a *hog* (burial mound) reading the inscriptions of a runestone. This required knowledge of an obscure written language and the ability to enunciate such shorthand. The Rök Stone in Sweden bears the longest runic inscription of them all.[40] Most others are short and to the point. The Rök Stone, on the other hand, is very different, containing among other things mentions of valkyries,

---

[*] The dedication at the start of this book I have shamelessly adapted from a real inscription, the Hassmyra runestone from Sweden, which reads something like: 'The good husbandman Holmgautr had this [stone] raised in memory of Óðindísa, his wife. There will come to Hassmyra no better housewife, who manages the estate. Red-Balli carved these runes. Óðindísa was a good sister to Sigmundr.'

sea-warriors, war booty from the time of *Beowulf*, and semi-legendary figures like Theodoric the Goth.[41] It includes the word *minni*, which many have translated into modern tongues as 'memory'. It appears in Snorri's *Ynglinga saga* as 'memorial toast'; perhaps, then, *minni* carried specifically oral connotations, not simply the act of memorialising something or someone, but doing it vocally. Reading the Rök Stone, like many runestones, was an act of bringing memories to life, creating

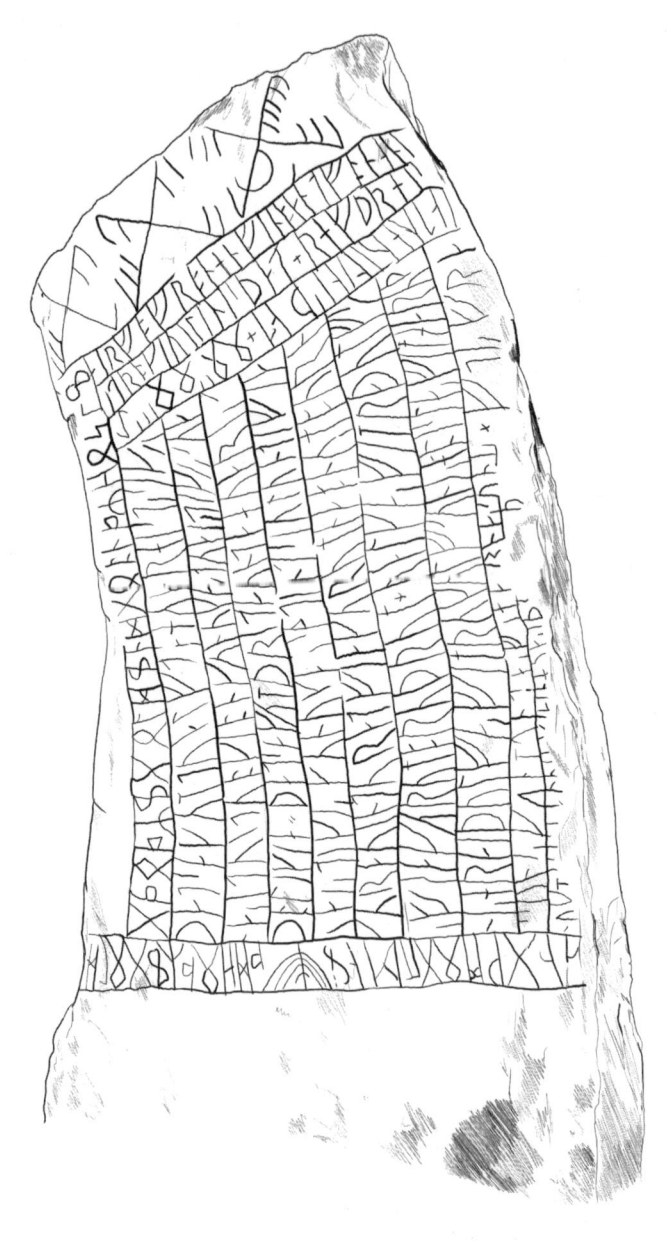

One face of the Rök Stone or 'Runestone Ög 136'. It is the longest runic inscription so far discovered from the Viking Ages. It requires awkward head-tilts to read.

Faith

a portal into the past.[42, 43, 44] And in the Late Viking Age, we can broadly understand that the 'past' represented paganism.

At the most human level was a process of cultural and ideological osmosis; people in markets hearing about 'the White Christ', *Hvítakristr*, which might have meant either Jesus or God or both; traders and raiders seeing the Christian cross on the necks of fellow merchants and visitors. 'What does that mean?' Christ is associated with the colour of baptismal gowns, the pale colour of the dead.[45] The common pagan motif of the Þórr's hammer pendant starts to appear in the archaeological record at this time, almost as a direct response to Christianity.[46] In this regard, the pendants did not necessarily represent Þórr or his hammer but rather the broader idea of *forn siðr* – 'If they have their own pendant, then why can't we have one?' Think of the diamond 'S' from Superman's logo, a symbol that many people around the globe would recognise – the hammer pendants were similar. This mention of a superhero does connect tangentially with Old Norse deities. These were not necessarily figures to be worshipped, but simply recognisable elements of an Early Medieval 'popular culture'. His favourite 'character' might be Þórr, but hers might be Freyr.

But just because those Þórr's hammer pendants are relatively young does not mean that the story itself and the character cannot be much older. Christianity was already spreading into Scandinavia naturally prior to Charlemagne's aggressive crusades in the late eighth century. It is possible such religious zealotry had a *negative* effect on the conversion of Scandinavians. Where beforehand Christianity was just another religion from afar, now it was the arbiter of death and destruction. This style of Christianity was an aggressive expansion, though later in the Viking Age, through the work of monks like Ansgar, official endeavours would be on a much smaller scale via the 'top-down conversion model'. If the natural spread of Christianity in markets was a 'bottom-up' and very slow effort, then converting a local elite like Herigar at Birka or Olaf Trygvasson, the king of Norway, was a quick way to ensure that (almost) all beneath their ruler soon followed suit. Obviously, this would not always be successful.

Across the North Atlantic diaspora, on the Faroe Islands, Iceland, and Greenland, the issue of emergent tribal powers was largely solved through the adoption of Christianity as the legal religion in 1000. The Goðar decided that to stop potential conflicts the people of Iceland must, democratically and in unity, choose *one* faith. And this may not have had so much pushback. Archaeological evidence across Iceland has revealed that the smallest farmsteads appear to have been the only ones with overt pagan displays, the largest manors lack such motifs and were probably Christian households. The proportion of migrants to these locations who

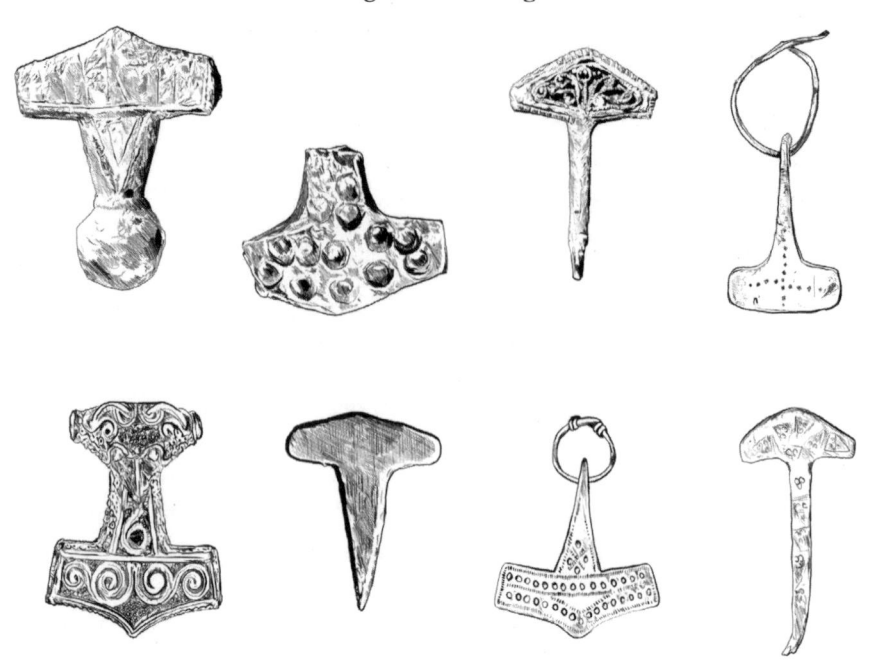

A selection of silver Þórr's hammer pendants from across the diaspora. Many have been recovered from female burials, perhaps worn as protective symbols. Examples have also been found alongside the moulds used to create them. Interestingly, some of these moulds were also used to create crucifixes, demonstrating the cultural and economic pragmatism so typical of North Sea merchants, who no doubt forged and sold both.

were slaves and captives from Christian communities may have also contributed.

Conversion was a practical choice. Ibn Khurradādhbih, writing in the 840s, mentioned a contingent of *al-Rus* who avoided paying taxation in the markets around the Caspian Sea by claiming that they were Christian.[47] Joining Christendom was not just about securing a place in the afterlife but also securing a better place in the mortal realm.

It is possible that pagans were being influenced by Christianity without being aware of it. In the Viking Age one of the most prominent exports from Christendom (particularly the Carolingian Empire) were swords.[48] Forged by Frankish smiths, the Ulfberht swords, the *+VLFBERHT+* group, were shipped abroad and heralded as mighty weapons, later copied.[49, 50] While not an overtly Christian item, it is possible that there was some vague association between the prominence of swords in the Early Viking Age and the expanding Christian world. Many of these swords bear cross motifs. Christianity was broadly understood as the future, The *new way*.

Faith

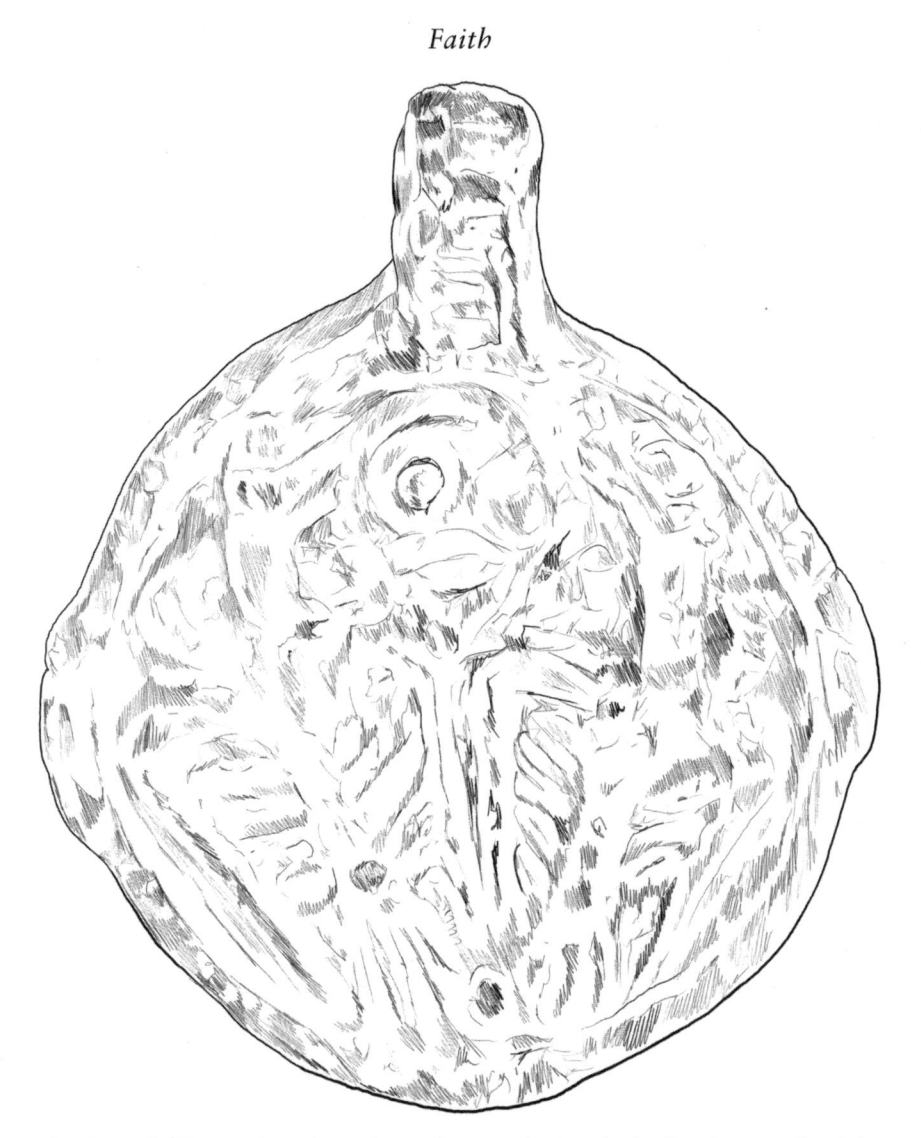

The face of Óðinn? This silver-gilt pendant marked with the familiar motifs of the Weapon Dancer was discovered in Winteringham, North Lincolnshire, in England. Kevin Leahy has convincingly argued that this tenth-century adornment is an example of 'militant paganism'; Scandinavian settlers in Lindsey becoming overtly and aggressively 'heathen' in the face of Christianity.

As Christianity became stronger on the borders of Scandinavia, insular pagan traditions became more codified and 'fixed', which ironically would create an easier means of conversion – soft, malleable materials can withstand greater pressure than hard yet brittle substances. In the late tenth century, there is an increase in overtly pagan skaldic verses like *Þórsdrápa* (later retold by both Snorri and Saxo), which may have been commissioned by Norwegian elites explicitly to combat the growth of

Christianity. This would also explain the proliferation of Þórr's hammer pendants.

The moment a paradigm or faith becomes calcified is the moment it can be replaced by another. To some extent this same happened with Old Norse paganism in the Viking Age. While Sweden did convert near enough at the same time as Norway and Denmark, it had the most enduring pagan holdouts, though these were small.[51] Just north of Sigtuna, as late as the second half of the eleventh century, burials with pagan elements were still being performed in Valsta.[52] Elsewhere, where ties to the land and thus *forn siðr* were weaker, like in the North Atlantic colonies, Christianisation was a much smoother process. There were fewer weeds to uproot. However, the geographic isolation of Iceland and Greenland likely created a spiritual environment of significant diversity, an admixture of pagan and Christian elements may have coexisted.

While Adam of Bremen's mentions of sacrificial poles and gold foils are supported by archaeological evidence, his belief that the temple on Gamla Uppsala was still in use as late as the 1080s is not. Encircling Gamla Uppsala and dated to that same century are an abundance of runestones bearing Christian inscriptions. While it is possible both belief systems coexisted, as they may well have done in eleventh- and twelfth-century Greenland, all evidence would point to Adam having written his 'contemporary' description based on earlier ones by visitors from the past.

The converted kings of Scandinavia, later described as noble and devout, must also be viewed as canny politicians. Being anointed by a bishop meant the number of competitors was reduced. Whereas in pre-Christian times the throne was basically up for grabs by anyone with an army, by disallowing individualised beliefs and local customs a king was securing his power, minimising the risk of resistance. With Christian scripture came increased literacy, also tremendously important for increasingly centralised kingdoms.

The pagan temple at Lejre[53] was destroyed towards the end of the tenth century, replaced by a church at Roskilde ten kilometres away from the new and state-overseen version of the previous site.[54,55] Sometimes these pagan temples were not replaced. In Slöinge[56,57] and Uppåkra,[58,59] in Sweden, contemporaneous great halls were torn down and left to rot. Spiritual leaders were being disenfranchised by new Christian kings, and their power waned as the new way became more popular. By 1085, Danish law codes indicate a new rank in society – the *stabularius* – loyal 'king's men' to oversee taxation and treasuries.[60] The institutions of the crown and the church were dominating society on every level. Very slowly, Scandinavia was becoming a collection of European nations, with the same systems, customs, laws, and kings. By the Christian capital of Sigtuna, near the old ruins of Gamla Uppsala, the barrow mounds of ancient pagan kings remained. They may have been long dead, but their presence in the landscape endured.

The Entangled (Un)Dead

When one of our loved ones dies, we may still feel a connection to their memory, but most people will be aware that they are forever gone from our mortal plane. For those in the Early Medieval Period in pre-Christian societies, archaeological and literary evidence points to a very different understanding of not just the passing of life but also the passing of time. We have already seen how space and distance were perceived differently in the Viking Age, but what about temporal connections and memory? Already mentioned are runestones and the mnemonic language of the Younger Futhark script; memorising and repeating verses carved on rocks is very different to reading a book. The same goes for Old English poetry. The texts we have today, such as the manuscript of *Beowulf*, are later vernacular transcriptions of stories which were meant to be told before the hearth in the mead hall, with appropriate intonation and pronunciation. Skaldic verses preserved in Icelandic Sagas give us a decent understanding of how stories were told, and how memories were brought to life.

While not a saga, to continue with the example of *Beowulf*, there is a moment towards the end of the piece where Wiglaf picks up an ancestral sword to help slay a fire-breathing dragon. Between the moment when Wiglaf picks up the sword *and before* it is used, there are several lines dedicated to the blade's history. We learn about the sword being passed to Wiglaf by his father Weohstan, who had used it in an ongoing dynastic conflict between the Geats and Swedes; before that, its original owner Eanmund and unnamed earlier owners are described, along with the future usage of Wiglaf's sword in struggles yet to come. All this information is mentioned between action beats; these past and future elements are temporally distinct from the 'present' action of the text but nevertheless thematically relevant. To modern readers, this can come across as poorly paced and unnecessary exposition; why do we need to know the provenance of the sword?[*]

---

[*] I first read J. R. R. Tolkien's *The Lord of The Rings* when I was 12. At the time, I felt the descriptions of elven ruins and what-not distracted from the plot. Tolkien was a scholar of Old English poetry, employing world-building and lore in much the same way skalds and scops once did.

Cătălin Țăranu has applied theories of 'quantum' entanglement to *Beowulf*, describing Wiglaf's sword as an item with several simultaneous entangled temporalities.[61, 62, 63] *Beowulf* was not written for modern readers of course, in fact in its original form it was not written at all. It was spoken, out loud in the mead hall, to audiences who lived and breathed the same world which existed within the poem. To these audiences, the story of Wiglaf's sword and how it came to be was just as relevant as the usage of the sword in the ensuing dragon fight. The past was just as present as the present.

So far, Cătălin's work has only been applied to literature and a few artefacts, but such a train of thought could reasonably see application elsewhere across the historical corpus. The idea of things in the past and future being just as relevant as things in the present is hard to wrap one's head around. The film *Arrival* (2016), visualises this idea very well in the final act, where the main character is simultaneously experiencing and influencing the past, present, and future at the same time, making each temporality equally valid. We can apply such an idea to the Viking Age.

We've already mentioned the various burial practices of the period, but none are as famous as Ibn Fadlan's account of a tenth-century *Rus* funeral along one of the rivers of *Austrvegr*. Read any history book on the Viking Age and you'll come to it. But there are two very interesting elements of the text normally left out. The first is that upon the final burning of the dead *Rus* chieftain atop his longship and earthen mound, the naked torchbearer walking towards the pyre covers all his orifices until *after* the body has been set alight. Why is this? We don't know, but it is possible this section of the account is describing a local or widespread custom preventing wayward spirits of the dead from entering bodies. By sealing every entrance, the torchbearer was preventing his dead lord's *hugr* from entering his shell and inhabiting him. Before the chieftain had even been installed on the pyre, however, in the ten days between his death and the final erection of the burial mound, Fadlan writes that he was sealed in a 'temporary grave' lined with temporary grave goods. If not the final resting place of the man's corpse – the man's *hamr* – then why would such a temporary accommodation warrant decoration?

Many pre-Christian societies buried their dead with treasures, but doing so for a burial that was only meant to be temporary is unique. Reading Fadlan's account, one can infer that these *Rus* were attempting to entertain their lord in the interim between his final days on the mortal plane and his first days in the next. Before he was burned and his *hugr* set free, this chieftain was stuck in his *hamr* and so needed at least a few trappings of the good life before his ultimate departure. This is

Faith

interesting and has some links with the wider idea that the dead weren't truly 'dead' in the sense that we might believe today; people rotted and withered away, sure, but their essence may have persisted. It was less of a case of 'Look over yonder, those burial mounds are where my forefathers are buried,' but 'Those burial mounds are where my forefathers *are*' – perhaps not tombs, but simply new homes altogether. This might be a stretch, but we can extrapolate further.

Place names, as observed so far, often feature personal or spiritual names as elements, such as Ullevi or Ingelheim. In England, many of the earliest Old English place names (particularly in marshland areas) are simply 'the estate of the followers of X' or 'the grove of the people of Y'. These ancestral names became connected to the places, so whenever a traveller was to venture past any of these locations, they would perhaps hear from others that 'This is the place of X or Y', not necessarily a long-dead ancestral figure, but an ancestor who was *still present* in some capacity. As with barrow mounds and Wiglaf's sword, these names and thus the people were still relevant, despite being elements from their perceived past. Really, it all depends upon how societies in the past viewed their own history, short and long-term. In the most intimate form, this was ancestral veneration, but more broadly it could be the shared motifs of long-dead or ancient legendary figures like Völundr the Smith or Sigurd the Dragon-Slayer. The idea and memory of a distant Empire influenced the post-Roman West. Ancestral veneration wasn't uniquely pagan. In the Christian world, hagiographies emerged from the eighth century. 'Saint's lives' can be subdivided into two forms: the *passio* (the conditions of their death/martyrdom) and *vita* (biographical) variants, tales of long-dead figures like St Winifrid, St Oswald, or St Guthlac.[64]

Post-conversion, there was no longer an array of different realms for the dead to travel to, nor multiple layers of personhood, there was simply the physical body, the soul, and either Heaven or Hell. The slow death of paganism meant that many practices and beliefs are now lost to us forever, those which weren't copied down on vellum. We will never know what Viking Age Scandinavians called their belief systems, or if such systems even had a name. We cannot ask which of the Æsir was the top dog, or if there was even a hierarchy. Such a thing may be a later Christian invention altogether.

The magic from the world slowly disappeared once Christianity took root. The many realms and peoples of the world had become nations and the wonders had been explained away by euhemerists and scripture. Would newly Christianised Scandinavians have believed that their pagan antecedents were idiotic heathens? Or did they think that they had lived in a different world from their own, one where pre-Christian powers were stronger? Were their ancestors no longer present, but elsewhere?

Dark Wings, Dark Words

Óðinn and his ravens Huginn and Muninn ('Thought' and 'Memory', note the similarity to *hugr* and *minni*) are a staple of the Old Norse cosmological corpus. Ravens and corvids would have still been present and just as smart as they were pre-conversion, so did opinions regarding them change? Were they seen as vestiges of the old ways?

Corvids, that most intriguing family of birds containing among others ravens, crows, rooks, chuffs, and magpies, are distributed across most of modern Europe, and despite the fluctuations in climate, we can postulate a similar distribution in the Early Medieval Period.[65] Importantly, carrion crows do not usually appear in Scandinavia outside of Denmark, nor do rooks, however hooded crows, ravens, and jackdaws all do, as far north as the Arctic. Crows appear repeatedly in Old English literature as the onomatopoeic *crawe*, but the word 'crow' was also used to describe other similar birds, much in the same way that the Old English word *hrafn* ('raven') was.[66] Starlings were interpreted by societies that predated the Viking Age as auspicious augurs of divine intervention, and they appear in a similar manner to Óðinn's ravens

Corvus corax, the common raven. But is this one 'Thought' or 'Memory'? The next time a crow cocks its head and looks at you, ponder on what it might be thinking, and to whom it then talks.

in Brythonic traditions. For Scandinavia, however, given the modern distribution maps of the corvid family, we can assume that Óðinn's ravens really *were* ravens, specifically, northern ravens, *Corvus corax*.

Scientific analyses of northern ravens have been undertaken in relation to memory and predatory response to visual stimuli. One study indicated that common ravens could recall a 'dangerous mask' (meaning a mask worn by researchers carrying dead ravens) for over four years, utilising a specific alarm call to alert others whenever they were in sight of said mask, even if the wearer was not holding a dead raven.[67] These ravens could differentiate between this mask and a similar one which had not been worn by researchers holding dead ravens.

This information was then communicated between the ravens who had seen both masks and ravens who hadn't, via a process of horizontal learning; this is the same process by which ravens and other birds learn tool usage. It isn't simply mimicry, meaning a raven sees another bird use a tool and then repeats the behaviour, but 'stimulus enhancement'.[68] One raven may attempt to snatch some food from behind a wooden hatch, and the next raven in line will attempt the same task but with a different tactic via trial and error. Corvids have been seen in both controlled experiments and out in the wild to be able to work and process different shaped tools to be used in different scenarios. They can also mimic human intonations and, as mentioned above, can identify people by facial recognition.

The Old English 'beasts of battle' include the carrion crow, and ravens appear as messengers of the Æsir in the Old Norse corpus.[69] A species of bird which displayed unparalleled levels of avian intelligence and could recognise both troublesome and friendly humans and pass on that information is impressive. It is no wonder that they were recognised as messengers of Óðinn.

Ulf from Vorbasse is having a rough day and a raven won't stop cawing outside his window, so he lobs a stone at it. For the next four years, every single other raven around Vorbasse loudly exclaims whenever he enters their vicinity, some even swooping down to attack him. Elsewhere, Freya from Ullevi, after a successful hunt, throws a scrap of meat out to her dogs but a raven snatches it before they can. Believing it was a gift, that raven then bestows upon Freya a stolen bead; something shiny, something that would usually be given to a mate. Such scenarios are played out today and would have happened back in the past. While we think of corvids as wonderfully intelligent birds thanks to millions of years of evolution, perhaps our ancestors thought of them as Thought and Memory, Huginn and Muninn. And perhaps these were not two separate birds, as depicted in art, but two traits shared between all crows.

Clever yes, but not cuddly. Carrion crows eat roadkill and even attack wounded animals. Later Christian traditions viewed crows as servants of the Devil, perhaps in some way a throwback to pagan days, when they were viewed as beings with more fluid allegiances.[70]

Different Ways

Like corvids, we too are a predatory species with fluid allegiances and (sometimes) reservoirs of intelligence. Viking Age Scandinavians were converting to Christianity from at least the start of the ninth century, and often these initial conversions were temporary *prim-signing* baptisms designed for immediate gain. While we can't be sure that all Christian converts in the Early Viking Age were political pragmatists, we can assume that those who were baptised under military and political pressure did so for motives beyond spiritual ones. But all those in Scandinavia who were slowly converting over multiple generations of seeing the cross in marketplaces or hearing preachers on the streets? No.

Some conversions, like Olaf Trygvasson and Olafr Haraldsson's in the 1000s, seem to have been a done deal after the initial baptism, as they went on to force Christianity upon their subjects thereafter. Earlier vikingar, however, like Guthrum and his Great Heathen Army, were baptised or offered Christian gifts multiple times before nominally converting.[71] One generation might have grown comfortable with the image of 'the Nailed God' on the cross in market towns over twenty or so years, without ever really coming round to the idea, but their offspring would have grown up with it, becoming more and more accepting of this new faith. If they converted, then their offspring would be born Christian. In England, the Sigurd gravestone found beneath York Minster[72] and the Gosforth Cross in Cumbria display hybrid artistry reflecting both Christian and pagan traditions, almost like a teaching tool for younger generations.[73, 74] Anglo-Scandinavian standing crosses such the Nunburnholme Cross,[75] Ashbourne Cross, and Crowle Stone[76, 77] are seen all across Danish Mercia and Northumbria, reflecting a period of religious assimilation. Even if there were those in the ninth and tenth centuries who reverted to paganism after converting to Christianity, theirs was a dying breed. Haakon the Good, who reigned over parts of Norway in the mid-tenth century, was Christian when fostered at King Æthelstan's court in England, but his rule over his homelands was tolerant of all faiths.[78] While not a reversal of conversion, Haakon's version of Christianity was certainly less dogmatic than later ruler Olafr Haraldsson's.

Faith

The Old Norse belief system was not a proselytising religion like Christianity, there are no accounts of Scandinavian or pagan missionaries attempting to enforce their beliefs on others. Thorgest, in ninth-century Ireland, with his alleged heathen takeover of Clonmacnoise, is an exception, though he and his wife's zealotry is almost certainly fiction. For examples of genuine apostasy, we must turn to the continent; the *Annals of St Bertin* brand Louis the Pious's nephew Pepin the Younger an 'apostate' who abandoned his post and 'lived like one of them [the Danish vikingar]'. How much of this is true and how much an attempt to tarnish the reputation of Pepin we cannot be sure. While we can be confident that Pepin joined the viking armies to secure power for himself, as Æthelwold did in 902, we cannot equate this necessarily to pagan belief. We do not even know, for instance, the extent of paganism within Viking Age England. While the kingdoms were all Christian, with Christian rulers, there may still have been quiet rituals practised behind hedgerows and in farmyards, in times of poor harvest when God had failed. In Frisia, we can be certain that paganism continued into the ninth century at least. There, in the marshes between the Danes and the Carolingian Empire, was a liminal zone of crisscrossing cultures trading ideas and material wealth and, quite possibly, belief systems. And the actions of Charlemagne in Frisia in the eighth century had no doubt provoked some pagan resistance.[79]

An edict from Ibn Habīb in his ninth-century *Great History*[80] states that 'It is not harmful to eat the cheese of the Rūm and so forth of the enemy among the Peoples of the Book. But one must not eat the cheese of the Majūs.' It did not matter from which branch of paganism these cheesemakers stemmed, just that they were not 'Peoples of the Book', one of the three Abrahamic religions; people like Scandinavian pagans.

Viking activity on the Iberian Peninsula and in the east would have brought Scandinavians into contact with not just Christianity but Islam, but there is only scant evidence that people were converting to the latter faith. Kufic script on textiles recovered from some of the Birka graves, along with a silver ring, were inscribed with 'Allah' or 'Ali' (The Prophet's cousin and son-in-law, worshipped by the Shia sect), but whether or not these writings were understood by the wearers is unknown.[81, 82, 83]

The same has to be said for many Birka burials containing crucifix brooches – were the wearers Christian? Did they see themselves as Christians like others did? Or was it just a nice brooch? One of the two individuals recovered from the Oseberg burial had strong indicators of Middle Eastern ancestry, so the likelihood of practising Muslims present in Viking Age Scandinavia cannot be ruled out.

Likewise, the evidence for Jewish vikingar is slim, based entirely around one character appearing in the thirteenth-century *Skáldskaparmál*[84] described as a 'clay giant with a mare's heart' argued by some to be a distorted reference to the Jewish myth of the Golem. Undoubtedly, people of the Jewish faith and pagan vikingar interacted on a large scale, likely before significant Christian-pagan contacts were made, as travel through Judaic lands along the *Austrvegr* was happening prior to western voyages.

Conversion to Christianity did not change the violence and ambitions of Early Medieval Scandinavians; vikingar still went viking, and kings still invaded, but by the eleventh century this was all done by 'just another European country' rather than a storm of heathen dragons emerging like 'a bolt from the blue'.

Even Older Ways

The recurrent motifs we think of when we hear the term 'Old Norse mythology' – the World Serpent, Fenrir the wolf, Loki, giants, *Ragnarǫk* – were all already old by the eighth century. Where did they come from?

Snorri's *Gylfaginning*, which broadly describes all the main players of the Old Norse cosmological world, describes the sun being pulled across the sky by the mystical horses Árvakr and Alsviðr. The Old Norse deity which represented the sun, the goddess Sól, likely harkens back to earlier Indo-European traditions much like the Gotlandic solar disc depictions. Many may have wondered, 'Where has Sól gone?' during the mid-sixth century. Such a belief might have led to the idea of Fenrir's wolf offspring chasing away the sun during *Ragnarǫk*, the world falling into darkness until Sól and her horses would be replaced by her own daughter, a new sun in the sky.

This contrasts with other Old Norse figures like Dagr and Nótt, who represented 'Day' and 'Night' respectively, themselves travelling across the sky on the backs of the horses Skinfaxi and Hrímfaxi. Mathias Nordvig has offered a climatological explanation for some of the recurring motifs of *Ragnarǫk*, building upon the Dust Veil theory. Nordvig postulates that lines from eddic stanzas referring to 'ashen eagles', 'barking wolves atop the mountain', 'the shaking of *Yggdrasil*', and 'dwarves howling in defeat from behind their doors' are all references to real volcanic eruptions across Iceland, such as the major one in 934.[85] The 'ashen eagle' was a pyroclastic flow, like the one that smothered the Icelandic farmstead of Stöng in the twelfth century. The 'rising waves' caused by Jǫrmungandr's thrashing were foreshocks of earthquakes, preludes to volcanic eruptions, first heard by dogs, who would then bark. Or perhaps the 'bark' was the initial eruption of a volcano. The 'howling

Faith

dwarves' is the hardest kenning to decipher; Nordvig suggests that, due to the recurrent belief that dwarves held up the sky, that the dwarves entering their 'stone doors' is the sky turning black with ash clouds and the sun disappearing. Primordial geological forces were in the minds of Early Medieval Scandinavians, things older than mankind.

In 1902, peat workers found a bronze represntation of a sun disc pulled by a chariot and two horses; one half of the sun representation was gilded, to represent daylight, the other was pure bronze, representing the dark.[86] The sun chariot had been submerged in Trundholm Bog, Denmark, but it was not submerged in the Viking Age or even in the immediately preceding period. The Trundholm Sun Chariot had been deposited around 1,400 BCE, in the Nordic Bronze Age. In contrast to Þórr's hammer, the image of the sun being pulled by horses was not a new tradition borne out of connection with Christianity, but an ancient one.

Sun worship is an observed and frequent phenomenon across many ancient societies, so the chariot is not unique, with similar depictions found in contemporaneous Ireland. But it does provide an antecedent to the later Old Norse cosmology.[87] This bronze model found in Trundholm Bog had been created a time when international motifs were being reproduced all around the Mediterranean and beyond, the result of cultural interaction and long-distance trade. The ancestor faiths of Old Norse paganism were a product of this intermingling of beliefs and customs. One can observe this with the World Tree motif, *Yggdrasil*, the tree that knits all the realms together. It might be incorrect to imagine *Yggdrasil* as a tree, but instead a metaphysical nexus linking alternate spaces in the way that a tree has branches. Though trees did have a significant pagan meaning; warriors are described as 'battle trees' in Old Norse literature, and in 772 Christian zealot Charlemagne ordered the destruction of something called an *Irminsul* in Saxony, understood to be some kind of wooden pillar or tree.

Tricorn motifs from as early as 200 CE depict a similar idea of 'links between worlds' and this is even present at archaeological sites. At Ismantorp, a ring fort on Öland island, nine gates to nine different chambers housing different kinds of animal remains have been identified dating back to the third century, possibly modelled on Roman fort designs.[88] While structurally based on Roman works, *spiritually* this structure and its impractical number of doorways surely had deeper connotations. At the centre of the excavated site was a posthole. If it was anything like other sites, then the post may very well have been adorned, or mounted with something like the Hellvi mask. A central pillar made of wood, surrounded by nine pathways to nine rooms.

There were clear borrowings from earlier Roman and Greek pantheons across Scandinavia. It would be wrong to consider Óðinn an exact analogue to Zeus and Jupiter, but there are some other echoes, animal sacrifice in both Mithraic worship from Roman Europe and later Viking Age cult sites, for instance; though this is perhaps too broad an equation. Nevertheless, there was a distinct split in pre-Dust Veil displays of Scandinavian paganism and post-Dust Veil ones. Where beforehand the sun was prioritised, now there was darkness – dark wings, dark words, dark gods, and a dark fate for all.[89]

No doubt the Old Norse cosmological world was influenced by the far travels of many Scandinavians. There is a peculiar mention from a lost Arabic source that states that in the interim when Bjorn and Haesten's famous viking voyage across the Mediterranean otherwise disappears from sources, they were in Alexandria, Egypt. Sometime in 861, Scandinavians allegedly sailed along the mouth of the Nile. There, they may have seen the carved likenesses of giant beasts: hippos, crocodiles, men with dog heads. They may have heard talk from the locals about their own ancient myths, of Osiris and Attis, deities who perpetually relived the same cycles. What must they have thought of such things, and how did that influence their minds?

From Raiders to Crusaders

If we want certain evidence that Scandinavians went that far east, then we must leave the Viking Age behind and look to a new era of pillage and wanton destruction, the crusades of the twelfth century. Barely forty years after 1066, Norwegian monarchs were sending vast armies overseas to plunder and ravage. These 'crusaders', despite being armed in a similar way to their antecedents and hailing from the same country, were no longer vikingar, but men of God, thus their rampages were righteous.[90,91]

In the aftermath of the Battle of Stamford Bridge and the death of his father Harald *harðráði*, Magnus II ascended from regent to become the king of Norway in 1066. Having already undertaken a failed overseas military expedition to claim Orkney and fight against the House of Wessex ten years prior, along with frequent engagements against Denmark and Sweden during his father's reign, Magnus was well positioned as a strong military leader to fill the gargantuan shoes of *harðráði*. Magnus ruled alone for less than a year before his brother returned from England – one of the few survivors of Stamford Bridge – to co-rule. This was Olaf *Kyrre* ('the Peaceful'), a stark contrast to his warmonger father. Upon Magnus II's death in 1069, King Olaf ushered in an unparalleled age of domestic calm for his country. Trade

Faith

blossomed, a coin bearing his face even reaching the Greenlanders in North America. According to *Heimskringla*, the modern town of Bergen (then called Bjørgvin) was founded by Olaf. His son, Magnus *berfœttr* ('Barelegs'), would focus his foreign policy on the Irish Sea, attempting and sometimes achieving suzerainty over the Kingdom of Man and The Isles for most of his reign until his death at Irish hands when the insular rulers, descended still from Olaf *Cuarán*, regained control. Magnus's son was Sigurd, better known by his epithet of 'the Crusader'. Sigurd the Crusader, the first crusader monarch from Europe, took Norway on a new form of raid; the rules of the game had changed, the scale had increased. Sigurd's crusade was arguably viking activity conducted under the guise of Christianity. A cruel twist of fate, and no doubt cruellest for the victims.

While Sigurd was away, his co-rulers and brothers Oystein and Olaf introduced taxation for his subjects to reinforce the status of the church within Norway, ensuring that the kingdom grew to unparalleled heights never seen in the Viking Age; this was now a prosperous and internationally active realm. From 1107, Sigurd's fleet of five thousand men aboard many *drakkar* sailed across the North Sea to England, where they wintered enjoying the hospitality of King Henry I. From there, they mirrored the behaviour of their forefathers and moved to secure territory in northern Spain.

After an unsuccessful winter, raiding began throughout Galicia. Later, the raiders took the castle of Colares, then Lisbon, and Alcácer do Sal before defeating an Arab fleet in the Straits of Gibraltar. In 1109, Sigurd's forces were pillaging the Balearic Islands which, two hundred years after Bjorn and Haesten's fleet had last visited, were now united as an independent principality ruled over by piratical emirs.[92,93] The account of the sacking of the Balearic Islands in *Heimskringla* is incredibly rich and detailed, relaying how Sigurd's forces fought Berber tribes on Formentera and Arab armies on Ibiza, securing some of the greatest treasures from their entire expedition. Mallorca was spared from such devastation and is absent from the primary sources, probably because it was the best fortified of the Balearics. Only a few decades separate Sigurd's activity across the Iberian Peninsula from his immediate antecedents in the Late Viking Age, and yet for their opponents, the impact would have been much the same; violent men pouring out of longships for gold and glory.

Were the times changing all that much? Perhaps not. In Sicily at the same time, the young Count Roger II was no doubt looking from his island territory at his approaching kinsmen of Christ. Sigurd and his forces lodged on Sicily for a short while. Perhaps the two rulers shared stories of their joint heritage; Roger II was only a few generations removed from the original Norman conquerors of the island, themselves once 'Northmen'.

By 1110, Sigurd had arrived at Jerusalem and had joined forces with King Baldwin I in a joint siege of Sidon, Syria. After an initial defeat at the hands of the formidable Fatimid navy,[94] Baldwin's army rejoiced at the sight of sixty longships on the horizon – perhaps the first time Christians would treat such a view as welcome. Going up against the slow but well-armoured *adrumūnun* and *shalandī* vessels, modelled on Roman designs but manned by hardened Arabic warriors, Sigurd's fleet faced a mighty challenge. Over nearly fifty days the Norwegian and Fatimid forces clashed on the turquoise Syrian waters, painting them red, the conflict only won by the arrival of a Venetian fleet sent to the aid of King Baldwin. The Fatimids were defeated, and Sidon was forced to surrender. Sidon joined Arsuf and Acre as the captured towns of Baldwin and Sigurd, the latter's reward being a splinter of the true cross. Sigurd proclaimed that he and his followers had come 'for the purpose of devoting [our]selves to the service of Christ'.

Christian treasures, no longer silver but made of wood, and given as reward, not taken as booty. How the times had changed from that raid on Lindisfarne.

A year after the Siege of Sidon, Sigurd's forces gave the bulk of their trophies to Constantinople before returning home, where the king would continue to rule for another nineteen years. Some of his men no doubt stayed behind to join the Varangian Guard, the aged Anglo-Scandinavian guards that fled Norman persecution forty years prior fast disappearing. Sigurd's crusade would be followed by a Venetian effort and then the Second Crusade, when a host of European nations would take part in pillage and slaughter, following in the footsteps of a post-Viking Age warlord.

Later, Denmark would also get involved along with Saxony and the old territory of the Obotrites in Wagria and Wendland, and Sweden would – according to biased sources – attempt 'righteously' to enforce Christendom in Finland for several decades in the thirteenth century, although there is minimal archaeological proof for such a claim.[95, 96] The crusades cannot really be considered as an extension of the Viking Age but they no doubt included a lot of occasions where traditional viking activity was employed; en route to Jerusalem the Iberian Peninsula was raided just as it had been in the 'true' Viking Age, and the military activity of Sigurd's forces is not so dissimilar to that of Yngvar the Far-Travelled operating in Georgia.[97] While the reasons for these new raids were very different, the effect on the ground would be much the same. Runic inscriptions from the Maeshowe mound on Orkney, carved by Scandinavians, reference the joy of exploring the 'south lands'. The carvers were likely armed pilgrims returning from Sigurd's crusade, or subsequent expeditions led by the Orkney jarls: 'Arnfithr Matr carved these runes with this axe owned by Gauk Trandilsson in the South land.'

All these expeditions would be characterised by death, destruction, and despair, but this time it was perpetrated not against Christendom but *for* Christendom. One Orkney Maeshowe inscription was found carved alongside a familiar symbol: 'Benedikt made this cross.'

Under a Black Sun: The Road to *Ragnarǫk*

After *Ragnarǫk*, Snorri writes that the world will be birthed anew. Baldr, the innocent god whose death started the cataclysm, among others, would survive the conflict and populate the new world, and he would be joined by mankind, no doubt, but also a whole host of wonderful unknown entities. There is very little written about the state of the cosmological world post-*Ragnarǫk*. A new pantheon of survivors will rule, and humanity will begin again from the seed of Lif and Lithrasir, and the realms and all their halls will seemingly become only three: *Gimli* for the righteous souls, *Sindri* for all those in between, and *Nastrond* for the damned. Evidently, this post-*Ragnarǫk* world was reflecting a potent Christian bias in Snorri's worldview. By hiding in Hoddmimir's Holt[98] in the belly of *Yggdrasil*, the survivors of *Ragnarǫk* were ensuring their future beyond what was supposedly the ultimate 'doom of the Gods'. If this final addition to Snorri's corpus is *not* a Christian conclusion, implying that after the death of paganism comes Adam and Eve and the righteous faith, then where would such a myth originate? Much like with the Dust Veil, *Ragnarǫk* did not end everything. The old status quo was unbalanced, with devastating effects, and for years there would be much carnage, but soon the world would heal and things would regrow, and a new status quo with new turmoils, triumphs, and trials would emerge.

There was no such end for the Viking Age, no great apocalyptic event that affected all of Scandinavia at once like the Dust Veil of 536. There was, however, a dramatic confrontation in 1030 between the forces of Olafr Haraldsson, once the king of Norway but by then a bankrupt leader of a small warband, and Cnut the Great's huge army at the Battle of Stiklestad. This was a Christian conflict between two Christian armies, fought over the territory of the Northern Way. Aside from being a very bloody battle and the start of Harald *harðráði*'s long career, it was also the location of the death of Scandinavia's first saint, and above all else, would signal a dramatic departure from the days of going viking.

The near-contemporary description of Olafr Haraldsson's death by Adam of Bremen says he was ambushed after the battle and killed. He was very quickly canonised by Bishop Grimketel at Niðarós (that local canonisation eventually confirmed by Pope Alexander III in 1164) and his cult grew to such widespread international acclaim that the Battle of Stiklestad took on a greater importance. One of the founding myths associated with the battle, where Olafr Haraldsson would die clutching a silver cross and praying to God, was the blood-red eclipse that occurred partway through. Via celestial dating, scientists are sure that an eclipse did indeed happen in Norway in 1030, not on the traditional date given for the battle but a month later, in August.[99, 100] Regardless, such an event came down to us through the sagas, becoming attached to Olafr Haraldsson's final moments within a few years. In a year when Norway was just on the edge of exiting paganism, the blotting out of the sun may have seemed like the wrath of God incarnate – or worse – the vengeful eye of Óðinn looking over his traitorous subjects, who had turned their back on *forn siðr*. Perhaps the black sun was representative of something older still; the bleeding maw left behind after Árvakr and Alsviðr towed the light away on their golden chariot, ahead of the end of times.

Olafr Haraldsson, after his death, would be later be known as *Rex Perpetuus Norvegiae*, the 'Eternal King of Norway'.[101] In an age of pragmatic warriors and canny traders who would travel the known world and experience so much, one of the greatest figures of the Viking Age was a Christian saint.

If one thing can be made clear about this enigmatic period, it's that the Viking Age was *already* the twilight of the Old Norse cosmology. This ever-evolving belief system had emerged out of numerous apocalypses, reworked to suit the people of different times. We will never know if *Ragnarǫk* really was inspired by the Dust Veil event – it could have been based on another historical cataclysm, for instance. The Finnish *Kalevala*[102] has some similarities with the *Ragnarǫk* tale, but even before the Iron Age, there was a Bronze Age climate disaster which resulted in decreased rainfall and a lack of agricultural yield across the Mediterranean, affecting Scandinavian trade and international relations. Perhaps this disaster was the one that inspired *Ragnarǫk*. Or perhaps that was only the previous *Ragnarǫk*.

From the literary and archaeological corpus, one gets the impression that through the prophecies heard by Óðinn, *Ragnarǫk* is not only an assured fate but also an event that has happened before. For the individual, this may have manifested itself in the idea that a raider might die at any point, so he may as well go exploring to seek word-fame while he could. In the minds of Viking Age people their cosmology was one of perpetual catastrophe. Things lived, then died, then lived again. Pantheons rose, then crumbled, and new ones took their place. Endlessly, this cycle of worlds and wars would repeat; there would always be a *Ragnarǫk* awaiting them in the future, but there would always be the hope of a new world beyond it. *Ragnarǫk* was, perhaps, always happening in the future, just as it was always happening in the past – an event forever entangled through numerous temporalities, ever present, ever-distant, and ever-approaching.

The Viking Age ended dramatically, some say, on the 25th of September 1066 at the Battle of Stamford Bridge.[103] Two kings met before the confrontation, shouting insults at one another before the battle lines clashed. King Harold Godwinson of England and his shimmering army of housecarls, having marched from as far away as the south coast, and King Harald *harðráði* of Norway, his forces caught unaware, barely able to put on their armour in time. Godwinson's brother Tostig, who had allied with the Norwegians, was offered a chance of peace, but Harald *harðráði* was offered only six feet of English soil, or 'however many more as he is tall'. He may well have been a tall man, as Scandinavian *vikingar* were often described. But Harald's men were Christian, and they were not simply raiding but attempting an invasion. It would not be Harald's conquest, however, that would spell the end. 1066 was a cataclysmic year for Anglo-Scandinavian England, with two major battles one after the other and the death of two powerful dynasts. Harald *harðráði* would fall, with his men barely escaping but going on to prosper as crusaders in the twelfth century, and Godwinson would meet his end soon after, against William the Bastard of Normandy.

Forgotten Vikings

Three roosters crow; one high above made of gold, one hidden in the forests of man, one soot-red in the halls of Hel. The blood-stained hound Garmr, the guardian of the Helvegr, breaks loose from his chains, and Heimdallr's long watch comes to an end. He blows Gjallarhorn for the first and last time, signalling his kinsmen to action; the swords and shields of the Slain march to form battle lines to defend Ásgarðr, joined by the screeching valkyrjur. Óðinn, aware of what is to come, seeks one last piece of wisdom from the decapitated head of his confidant, Mimir.

An English watchman stands guard, looking over the Channel at the distant mists of Normandy, its bluffs barely visible. The cold September sea laps against the shore. This is the last day of the watch. It is too late now to sail this year, perhaps war can wait for a few months. News comes from afar; the enemy has invaded, though these are different foes, and they have taken York. The troops march northwards.

Surtr's sons ride from Muspell, giants from Jötunheimar, the wolf Fenrir from the darkness, the corpse legions disembark from Naglfar, the encrusted ship of the Damned, and the world writhes; seas rise, cliffs sink, and the dwarves seal themselves shut behind stone doors. Óðinn, armed with his spear Gungnir, is swallowed whole by the threads of fate, dead.

The Norwegians fight valiantly, a lone axeman holds off an entire army of Englishmen with swing after swing of his broad blade. No advance is possible across Stamford Bridge after days of marching. Finally, the axeman is slain, killed from below, and the battle begins. Two shield walls meet; the clash of swords and spears is deafening.

Vengeance: Óðinn's son, Víðarr, breaks Fenrir's jaw asunder, as Þórr does battle with Jǫrmungandr, drowning in the poison left behind by the serpent's final gasp. Both fall and are joined by Freyr the fertility god, crushed by the blinding light of Surtr's flame. The world plunges into an inferno. After the battle, there is only silence.

Harald harðráði lay dead, allegedly struck by an arrow in his throat. Tostig Godwinson, brother of the English king, was also to fall. Despite their victory, no rejoicing would await England; the surviving Norwegians either chose a glorious death by rushing their enemy or were to flee elsewhere to live another day, while another far deadlier enemy was arriving on a different shore. There, at Hastings, the last shield wall of the Early Medieval Period was to crumble under Norman cavalry, and perhaps another arrow, this time through the eye of a different Harold.

But neither of these conflicts was the end. In the aftermath, Baldr and the survivors meet at Iðavellir, a virgin field unblemished by conflict, a new horizon on a new world. Hǿnir sends forth his divine eye to explore the virgin oceans beyond, as a new game begins. The corpse-eater Níþhǫggr flies across the horizon. What dire fates does this new future hold?

Faith

A later version of *Völuspá* describes an event following the world's rebirth: 'Then comes the mighty one to the judgement of the Powers, full of strength, from above, he who rules over all.'

Was this 'mighty one' Christ? Heralding the dawn of Christianity over the Old Norse world?

On the 25th of December 1066, William the Bastard of Normandy would be crowned king of England. This was done begrudgingly, and there were still pockets of resistance rallying against his rule. Something had ended that winter, but something had also begun; the age of castles, the High Medieval period, with knights and pageantry and jousting – the classic history that every English child reads about in school, born out of the death of the old world and the old ways. Something had ended, but something had also begun.

Fate

> Sweden then suffered serious harm,
> from the Karelians, causing great alarm.
> They sailed into Lake Mälar from the sea,
> whether calm or stormy it might be,
> secretly within the Svealand isles
> in stealthily advancing files.
> Once their minds to the idea did turn,
> that they the town of Sigtuna should burn,
> and so thoroughly they put it to the flame,
> that it since then has never been the same.
> There Archbishop Jon was killed,
> a deed that many a heathen thrilled.
>
> Extract from *Erikskrönikan* ('Eric Chronicle')
> written between 1250-1319.

After the raid on Lindisfarne, viking activity increased across the British Isles. The survivors of the raid moved across England sharing their stories with other monks and poor souls fearing the worst. Some, no doubt, would have stayed put in the monastery, rethatching whatever buildings may have been torched, clearing the dust and rubble.[1] The magnates of Bernicia in their royal palaces at Yeavering and Bamburgh may have redirected funds to assist Lindisfarne, restoring it to its former glory.

The bishop of the see, Higbald, passed away in 803. Later traditions claim that he issued a warning of the dire times to come before his final breath. The ageing monks at Lindisfarne and their apprentices would have received news of raid after raid against other sites. Perhaps they scanned the horizon for dragon ships every morning. The monastery may very well have been raided several more times since the initial attack, but the evidence is slim. We do know that amidst all this turmoil, beautiful Christian books like the *Durham Liber Vitae*, begun in the ninth century, were still produced. The Durham example would be outshone by the splendour of another confraternity book, the *New Minster Liber Vitae* produced in Winchester in 1031 by order of King Cnut and his wife Emma.

Following the conquest of *Eoferwic* and the fall of Northumbria in 867, the royal backing of the monastic community on Holy Island began to falter; while there remained an insular outpost of resistance in Bernicia, it was facing its own problems and could not support the struggles of Lindisfarne. Eight years later, the monastery was all but abandoned, its book-lands inhabited by wave after wave of Scandinavian migrants. The community who had once lived on the island took their treasures and the bones of St Cuthbert with them and roamed across the contested territory along Hadrian's Wall looking for a new home. This went on for many years, as vikingar became settlers and eventually 'English'. By the tenth century, the Lindisfarne community had all but vanished, survivors settling in Chester-le-Street and Durham, their lands divided and owned by new Hiberno-Norse warlords. In 918, the Hiberno-Norse Ragnall gave territories that had once belonged to Lindisfarne to his loyal followers Scula and Onlafbal. The *History of St Cuthbert* mentions Onlafbal by name – a cruel Scandinavian who, upon uttering the names of his pagan gods and profane blasphemies against St Cuthbert, was struck down by the spirit of the saint.[2] After the Battle of Brunanburh, the community of St Cuthbert could look upon England as a new and relatively stable Anglo-Scandinavian nation, give or take a few hiccups until the death of Eirikr of York in 954. It wouldn't be until the middle of the following century that Holy Island was reinhabited by a new monastic community, now even more devout than before. On the eve of the Norman Conquest, these monks were praying as usual, their world no longer one set upon by heathen raiders.

Then new conquerors came, and the abbey was rebuilt in stone; lime kilns were created to whitewash the masonry above the earlier structure.[3] The monks, with new continental ideas, were now in a new age with new forms of art, labour, and hierarchies. Lindisfarne, for better or for worse, had survived the devastation of the Viking Age and had emerged from the other side as a grand Norman abbey, and there it would stand for another half-millennium before meeting another grisly fate during the Dissolution.

These important historical events seem so definitive to us today, 'cut-off points' where one period ended and another began. But as has been argued throughout, nobody on 25 September 1066 would have woken up the following day aware that 'the Viking Age' was over. Their worldviews had not fundamentally changed. While it was a watershed year, slower processes were already changing Medieval society; an increase in labour and international trade was leading to an increase in serfdom and wealthy landowners. Times were changing, but not everywhere, and certainly not overnight.

Something Before, Something After

One of the more enduring motifs of Viking Age art is the serpent that encircles the world, Jǫrmungandr, sometimes rendered as *Miðgarðsormr*, 'the Earth worm'. Jǫrmungandr is the child of Loki and Angrboða, which grew so large that eventually its front end connected with its back, its fearsome teeth enclosed around its own tail, creating a perpetual loop. It is this loop that brought the initial balance to *Miðgarðr*, stabilising the world in perpetuity, and it is the *undoing* of that loop that allows the residents of *Útgarðar* (the 'out-yards') to pour into the inner world, beginning *Ragnarǫk*: earthquakes, tsunamis, the shifting of all things.

Depictions of Jǫrmungandr, like many other elements of cosmology, were the progeny of thousands of years of cultural and psychological evolution. There are similarities between Jǫrmungandr and the enduring Ouroboros motif seen all over the world; the snake that bites its tail, forever stuck in an infinite loop representing balance and order.[4] The name itself is from the Greek οὐροβόρος, meaning 'tail eating', and is thought to describe the relationship between the ending of one life (the shedding of skin) feeding back into the creation of another (the snake's next skin). Around the world, the Ouroboros symbol represents different things; fertility, death, and rebirth, and the overarching idea of repetition. The snake is always eating its tail because its tail has always been in its mouth, and so things should be. The Ouroboros represents a natural balance, a status quo that will always be met. After *Ragnarǫk*, balance will be restored to the world, and like the Ouroboros metaphor, *Ragnarǫk* will happen *again*, just as the snake will always be biting its tail. There is a flow and order to the cosmos. Balance will be undone, but then chaos will become order once more.

Jǫrmungandr's siblings Fenrir and Hel may also represent facets of time: the cycle of day and night, and the inevitability of death. Jǫrmungandr is also described as the 'All-Lands Girdler', holding space as well as time perpetually in balance.

Not only is fate written by the Norns, it is also doomed to repeat itself. Perhaps in the next cycle, *Ragnarǫk* will look slightly different, but the world crumbling to ash to make way for the next one is destined to happen. While there is no avoidance of *Ragnarǫk*, perhaps we should rest easy, because there will always be something after. The enduring myth of *Ragnarǫk* has certain similarities with *Hjaðningavíg*, a legendary event mentioned in a few written sources, including *Deeds of the Danes* and several skaldic verses. *Hjaðningavíg*, like *Ragnarǫk*, is a mythical battle that lasts eternally, with elite bands of warriors being raised from the dead every night by the sorceress Hildr. This cycle repeats endlessly, though in some versions it is written that the end of *Hjaðningavíg* will come once *Ragnarǫk* begins; one eternal battle is replaced by another.

After the Battle of Hastings, resistance to William the Bastard's conquest would soon emerge. At the start of the Viking Age, marshy enclaves impassable on foot but accessible by boat – like the Isle of Axholme – were prime territories for early *vikingar* on their enterprising raids. Here, at the very end of the period, it is to the Isle we once again sail. In 1069, three years after the dramatic events of the Norman Conquest, the south had fallen, but the north still had its hooks latched onto the old world in a last attempt at defiance. The Anglo-Scandinavians who had been living in the north for generations were joined by new Danish allies led by King Svein Estridsson.

Svein had for two decades feuded with Harald *harðráði* of Norway, each repeatedly raiding the other's emporia. Many of the longships recovered from excavations at Hedeby date to Svein's reign. His was a prosperous rule, bringing Denmark into the limelight of wider European politicking through enhanced royal gifts to the church and a restructuring of the roles slaves and freemen played within society. While he still conducted seaborne raids against his enemies, Svein Estridsson was following in the footsteps of predecessors like Cnut and adapting to the changing times. After his adversary's death at Stamford Bridge in 1066, Svein remained relatively unopposed in Scandinavia. It would take another few decades before Norway would be able to muster a military force on a par with that which Harald had led to England, and so, for a time, the greatest opportunities lay elsewhere. Three years into Norman rule, perhaps the view on the ground was that things could have gone either way.

There was one last hope for England, too. Edgar the Ætheling, grandson of Edmund Ironside who had been defeated back in 1016. If all of England could rally behind a respected dynast from the old bloodline, then perhaps resistance was possible.[5] Svein Estridsson and the forces of Denmark lent themselves to such a cause. Scandinavian interest in the fortunes of England in this period all stemmed from Cnut's time; complicated family allegiances and bloodlines meant that many Danish and Norwegian rulers held 'rightful' claims over the country,[6] and

Forgotten Vikings

William stood in their way. The case in 1069 had multiple angles; there was a homegrown rebellion in England rising against Norman tyranny, and invested foreigners could see opportunities for wealth and prestige. Attempting several assaults upon the south coast, Svein's fleet, led not by him but his sons, eventually rallied at Adlingfleet, just by the Isle of Axholme in the marshes of South Yorkshire. Mustering a larger force made up of local contingents, this immense army then captured York. 'All the peoples of the country' were allegedly on their side, according to the *ASC*. Earl Siward's son Waltheof would join them, a third-generation Scandinavian leading the charge against his oppressors. William's army, then in the Forest of Dean,[7] marched northwards to meet the insurgents and, like Harald *harðráði* three years prior, the Danes left York to establish a foothold elsewhere along river boundaries.

King Svein joined his army in 1070 as the conflict spread throughout the old kingdom of Lindsey. Once again, marshlands and their islands played an important role. York was recaptured by the Normans, and the genocidal campaign of destruction now known as the 'Harrying of the North' was begun by William. No devastation on that scale throughout the entire Viking Age had ever been perpetrated by Scandinavians. But in the south, King Svein and many local nobles mustered around the Isle of Ely to continue the resistance. Legends about Hereward the Wake would emerge from these fenlands, as would Norman bribes and peace treaties. By the end of the year, the Danish invasion attempt had been repelled. King Svein led his forces back to Denmark as his English allies faced death and devastation through the Harrying. But the rebellion was not dead.

Five years later, Svein's son Canute (later 'the Holy') gave his support to the 'Revolt of the Earls'. At least two hundred longships from Denmark harried the coastlines of England, again sacking York but not occupying it. The new wooden motte-and-bailey on either side of the River Ouse presented a significant challenge for the Danes, as Ælfred's *burhs* once had. Canute's involvement had come about when one of the three rebellious earls, Ralph de Guader, sailed over the North Sea to request military aid.[8,9] While successful in his demands, Canute's Danes would ultimately achieve very little, sailing southwards to rally at Flanders within one or two months. By 1076, this last serious attempt at resistance against the Normans had petered out.

There would be rumours of another. Following his father's death in 1076, Svein's eldest Harald *Hen* ('the Whetstone') would succeed to the throne of Denmark. Four years later it would pass to his brother Canute. As king, Canute remembered the military invasions of England he had led in his youth, and by 1085 had forged an alliance with Count Robert of Flanders and King Olaf *Kyrre* of Norway. Collectively, their combined naval force was said to be over one-and-a-half thousand longships, a truly Great Army, unlike anything seen in the Viking Age. Ultimately, however, on the eve of an invasion, Canute the Holy would die, killed by his own rebels, and all plans were abandoned. This invasion, the last such attempt any Scandinavian nation would make against England, was a genuine threat to King William. The *ASC* recounts how 'the king gave orders for the coastal districts to be laid waste, so that if his enemies landed they would find nothing which could be quickly seized.' This alleged devastation has been found nowhere in the archaeological record. Regardless, such an invasion would not come to pass.

A Tale of Two Conquerors

After 1066, two conquerors would emerge to stake their claim over the British Isles. The first was William, a tyrant who died in 1087 – 'God will punish him', wrote his chronicler. The second conqueror, far less known to history, was a Scandinavian named Godred *crúbach* (Gaelic for 'claw', though his epithet has various spellings, and its meaning is debated). Unlike William, Godred would not lay swathes of land to waste, though he would – in typical viking fashion – harry coastlines and pillage. Godred's origin is largely unknown, though he would emerge in the written records principally in the thirteenth-century *Chronicles of Mann*, in 1079, described as a mercenary who had survived the Battle of Stamford Bridge.[10] Due to his Gaelic epithet, it is probable that Godred's heritage was from the Hiberno-Norse Kingdom of the Isles or Dublin. After the Battle of Clontarf in 1014, Dublin remained a contested vassal town held in high regard by numerous Irish rulers until it was eventually conquered completely. Fifty years later, it became part of the larger dominion of *Rí Laighín* (Leinster), and any Scandinavian influence was only in the lower stratum of society, not the elite. Dublin remained an important political centre and its dominion extended over Man, which began minting coins around the same time.

It is unknown when Man fell under Scandinavian dominion, but it likely coincided with the exiling of the Gwynedd royal family to Wales in the mid-ninth century; the insular Manx people were of Brythonic origin and had retained a fierce independence in the preceding centuries. Between 1000 and 1035, at least a few sailors were regularly depositing coinage and bullion in what has been nicknamed a 'Viking Age piggy bank' hoard on Man, and there is a wealth of Norse-Manx stone sculpture across the island. By the time Godred appeared in the late eleventh century, this piratical enclave had a unique Christian culture and was likely under the dominion of the Scandinavian jarls of Orkney, but it was something of a peripheral zone. Godred's rule and his dynasty would change that.

Godred the Conqueror, after raiding the coasts of Man and subjugating the locals, would establish a small yet powerful thalassocracy that extended from the Hebrides down to Man, and a dynasty to rule it.[11] Godred would rule for almost twenty years, and during that time won dominion over Dublin, much to the distaste of Irish rulers. Caught between such powerful neighbours, Godred was a particularly resourceful chieftain operating beyond the usual end-date given for the Viking Age, though by 1094 his power was beginning to dwindle. His power base was on Man, that much is clear, though archaeological evidence for any halls or earthworks is slim until later reigns. In 1095, plague reached the British Isles, and one of the many victims was Godred. He was succeeded by his son, Lǫgmaðr. While it is unknown if Godred and his progeny styled themselves as 'Kings of Man and the Isles', that is the title attributed to them in later chronicles, and towards the end of the twelfth century we get the impression that these were not simply island-dwelling chieftains striving to harry their neighbours, but royalty in their own right, often becoming embroiled in international politics.[12] A far cry from the early days of the Viking Age.

Lǫgmaðr's reign would not start until 1103. The interim between his father's death and his succession saw the Norwegian king Magnus *berfœttr* occupy Man and the Hebrides until his own death.[13, 14] Like Frisia, these archipelagic communities of England, Scotland, and Ireland could be dismissed as peripheral zones, but their liminality only increased their importance. While earlier in the Viking Age vikingar had understood the importance of controlling the Irish Sea, it wouldn't be until *after* the Viking Age when this sea would become part of a formalised kingdom; not a peripheral zone but a central power occupying the trade routes, becoming wealthy by it.

Lǫgmaðr's chief antagonists would not be external opponents but rival dynasts: the sons of his father Godred, with claims to the sea kingdom. Lǫgmaðr's ambitions extended elsewhere, for the *Chronicles* recount how he was 'marked with the sign of the Lord's cross', likely revealing his status as a warrior of the First Crusade, or possibly the Norwegian crusade led by King Sigurd. In his absence (the textual evidence is murky) it is possible Irish influence extended over Man, for one Domnall mac Taidc of the fledgling Uí Briain dynasty (founded by the Brian who fell at Clontarf) is described as having ownership of the kingdom for a time. Whatever the case, by the early twelfth century, Man and the Isles were back in the hands of Godred's dynasty. Olafr Godredsson, who had been fostered in the English court of King Henry I, is attested to have brought

Fate

the thalassocracy into a new era of peace and prosperity. His reign was certainly a long one, ending in 1153. In his time, Olafr introduced reformed monasticism across his watery kingdom, influenced as he was by continental ideals in King Henry's court, along with a renewal of international trade. The famous Lewis Chessmen, carved from White Sea walrus ivory, date to Olafr's reign, likely intended for one of his powerful magnates on the Isle of Lewis where they were found.[15]

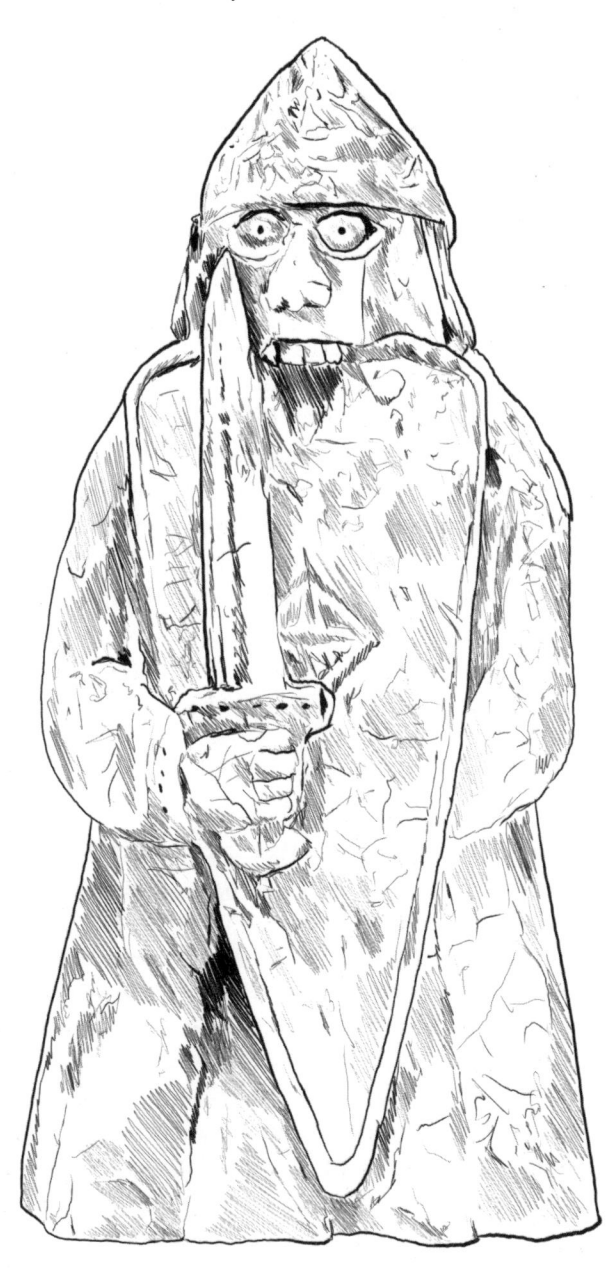

One of the Lewis Chessmen, depicting a 'berserk'. By the twelfth century, berserkers would find no home on the battlefield, but their status in contemporary poetic memory and courts endured. The creation of the chessmen predates the sagas where berserkers appear by a century.

Through both secular and ecclesiastical appointments, Olafr ensured that the Kingdom of Man and the Isles would not be left behind in the developing High Medieval world. The Hebridean lords remained just as powerful. Olafr's reign would end in his assassination, likely at their hands. In his successor Godred the Black's reign, the growing tensions between the Hebridean and Manx halves of the thalassocracy would erupt into civil war. Longships hurling projectiles from their decks across the Irish Sea; lords duelling and politicking over vast distances; contingents of lamellar-plated vikingar on both sides harrying the islands and their wealthy outposts. Ultimately, following the Battle of Epiphany in the winter of 1156, a clash of oars and sails, the sea kingdom would be split between Godred the Black's half of Man and the Outer Hebrides, and rival dynast Sumarliði's dominion over the Inner Hebrides.[16, 17] Further tensions would follow, but these two fiercely independent Scandinavian kingdoms retained their power.

The polities of Scotland and Ireland had yet to completely form and 'hangers-on' from the Early Medieval Period remained as petty kingdoms, as did Wales. The leading historian of this fascinating 'Late Norse' epoch, R. Andrew McDonald,[18] has described this thalassocracy as part of a 'long Viking Age' between traditional viking activity like Godred *crúbach*'s early raiding and the transition to High Medieval knighthood and statecraft by his successors. The kingdom was a prosperous one, attracting the attention of kings from as far away as Norway. Magnus *berfœttr*'s presence in the British Isles was more or less restricted to Man, shown in the form of the earthworks of his motte-and-bailey castles. Long gone were the D-shaped camps; the age of castles was upon the 'Viking world', just as it was across the rest of Europe. Excavated in 1912 on Fairy Hill at Cronk Howe Mooar was a sizeable motte very similar to another found in Wales constructed under the overlordship of King Magnus of Norway. It is highly likely that the Fairy Hill motte is a piece of physical evidence of the 1095-1103 Norwegian occupation of Man, found alongside arrowheads of Scandinavian origin. These castles would not be abandoned upon the death of Magnus *berfœttr*, the foreign interloper; they would remain key military centres in the centuries of Norse-Manx maritime rule. For most residents of Man, however, life would continue to be one of agricultural labour and pastoralism. Renowned as a fertile island, Man has seen extensive archaeological investigations regarding the Scandinavian farming strategies of the twelfth century and beyond. Such building types and practices may sound familiar: shielings for the upland areas, including a cluster of around thirty atop Snaefell, and an abundance of cattle bones dominating the archaeofaunal finds. Evidently,

Man became a resource-rich nation and a prime entrepôt, like Gotland and Mallorca before it.

Despite moving with the times, this final holdout of the Viking Age in the British Isles was, like *Ásgarðr*, doomed to fall.

The Last Kingdom(s)

Sumarliði's progeny eventually became one with the wider Scottish kingdom of Galloway, eventually forming several Norse-Gael clans known collectively as the Lords of the Isles, among them Clann Ruaidhrí and Clann MacDougall, ruled over by his two sons Ragnhald and Dubghall respectively. This rival dynasty's territories were, at times, subject to the influence of mainland rulers in Alba (coterminous with much of modern Scotland).

Godred the Black's death created another succession dispute on Man, between his eldest Raghnall and his chosen successor Olaf the Black; they would come to blows in a battle at the Tynwald in 1228, resulting in the death of Raghnall. The Tynwald, like Þingvellir in Iceland, has claims to being one of the oldest parliaments in the world, thanks to the prefix of *thing*, from the Old Norse system of regional governance. While archaeological evidence for such an early tenth-century system on Man is elusive, the name does reveal its existence, though a date for the establishment of the meeting place is unknown. Unlike Iceland, however, the Kingdom of Man and the Isles was not at this time a democratically ruled commonwealth, but a monarchy like England and the Scandinavian homelands. The elite of Man were aware of the status and prestige that could be achieved from being seen by others as an 'official' nation-state, rather than just a neighbouring petty kingdom. There are records of Manx Scandinavians being knighted in England, and extensive written accounts detailing political and economic relations between the English King John and King Raghnall.[19] A manuscript of letters and rolls from 1212 states that

> ... if any Wikini, or others, should offend in the territory of Reginald [Raghnall], king of Mann, you shall assist him in the destruction of his and our enemies; since he is bound to us by fealty and oath, to perform the same for us against those who offend in our territory.

The term 'Wikini' is interesting, a Middle English derivation of *wicingi* or *vikingar*, bringing this book almost full circle. Here, in the thirteenth century, we have a reference to Scandinavian coastal raiders pillaging the shores of the Irish Sea. It is known that King John also employed the services of Manx Scandinavians against his enemies, too. The Norse-Gael mercenaries known as the *gallóglach* (or 'Gallowglass')[20] formed a key element of infantry forces from the twelfth century until the sixteenth, first forged out of resistance to the Anglo-Norman invasion of Ireland and employed as elite warriors against all sorts of domestic threats. Scandinavians serving as elite foreign mercenaries was still happening two centuries after the Battle of Stamford Bridge.

By the mid-thirteenth century, the Kingdom of Man and the Isles was entering a new world of castle-building, chivalry, and statesmanship; insular rulers were crowned at the symbolically important Tynwald and maintained overseas relations with Ireland, England, and Scotland. Like their Viking Age antecedents, by becoming so embroiled in international politics they were forging a future but losing their individuality. The last sea kings who would ever rule in any shape or form were eventually defeated and their thalassocracy would be absorbed into greater Scotland by 1265, ending the 'long Viking Age' of the Irish Sea.

There were remnants. In Orkney, two fellow survivors of the Battle of Stamford Bridge were to continue as Scandinavian rulers, Paul and Erlend Thorfinsson. Like Godred *crúbach*'s progeny, they would also descend into infighting. Erlend's son, Magnús, Earl of Orkney, was martyred in 1117 when Paul Thorfinsson's own son Haakon double-crossed him at what was probably meant to be a parley. According to *Magnús saga skemmri*, an extract from the larger *Orkneyinga saga*, Magnús' grave later became a field of flowers, owing to his status as a virtuous saint.[21] Like Olafr Haraldsson before him, a Scandinavian warlord had become a posthumous symbol of Christian piety and harmony; the two literary traditions of saga and hagiography blending to create his lengthy obituary. If the compilers of the sagas felt it necessary to tell the full story so long after the arbitrary 1066 'end' of the Viking Age, then why shouldn't we?

The Earldom of Orkney was to operate semi-independently until the end of the fifteenth century, owing some allegiance to both Scotland and Norway throughout most of that time. Eventually, it would be ceded to Scotland as part of a wedding dowry between the two nations. Shetland would also be pawned off as part of a wider dispute that had originated in the very final years of the Kingdom of Man and the Isles.[22] By 1265, the conflict between King Alexander III of Scotland and King Håkon of Norway had reached boiling point; the disastrous Battle of Largs was fought in a thunderstorm, resulting in no victor but scores of dead kinsmen. King Håkon and his forces withdrew to Orkney in 1266 where death would strike them, increasing Scotland's power while diminishing Norway's. Shetland and Orkney were eventually annexed two centuries later, though Norwegian claims to Man would ever linger.

The Next World

While in the northwest sea kingdoms were holding out for hundreds of years after 1066, elsewhere the tradition of 'going viking' was being upheld by other people altogether. In the Baltic, the Viking Age was about to see a thematic resurgence in literature and chronicles, and this time it would be the Scandinavian nations at the receiving end of roaming heathens bearing axes, pouring out of beached longships.

It was across the Baltic where Scandinavian viking activity truly began: raiders and traders in eighth-century Grobiņa, Saaremaa, and Staraja Ladoga had already started interacting with the steady flow of Abbasid silver across *Austrvegr* long before a raid on Lindisfarne was even an idea. By the tenth century, the heyday of the Eastern Way oversaw native hillforts re-occupied and conquered by new Scandinavian overlords. By the eleventh century, this *Austrvegr* had evolved from a land of tightly knit trading communities and middlemen into the formidable Kyivan-Rus state based around Novgorod and Kyiv, a nation sandwiched between the Scandinavian homelands and the Roman Empire. All around the edges of the Kyivan-Rus, by the Baltic Sea, was a stateless buffer zone of wild chiefdoms.[23] Beyond the twelfth century, these Baltic lands were a final vestige of paganism and viking activity, between the consolidated nations of Scandinavia to the west and the emergent Grand Duchy of Lithuania and the Kyivan-Rus to the east.

Under Harald *harðráði*'s predecessor Magnus the Good, Norway had already started launching raiding expeditions into the Baltic. By the end of the Viking Age, these raids had evolved into what might be described as proto-crusades, and eventually true crusades; multinational Christian military expeditions into pagan territory with the express purpose of converting the locals while also amassing wealth. Contemporary writer Saxo Grammaticus described one of those monarchs, Canute the Holy, as a young, valiant fighter who 'annihilated the Couronians, Sembians, and Estonians' lands'. The unconverted Baltic lands and their lack of political centralisation made them the enemy of Christendom, and thus Scandinavia. They became the new bogeyman. Saxo also alludes to counter-raids from these lands against the Scandinavians, though archaeological evidence is minimal.

Sverris saga, composed for King Sverre Sigurdsson of Norway (1177-1202), includes earlier and later military expeditions into the Baltic lands led by King Valdemar and others, from coastal raiding to full-blown conquest.[24] Scandinavians were mirroring the raids of their ancestors in a new Christian context, much as they were in the crusades to the south and east. Peace charters describing Saaremaa express a need for increased security around the waters, implying that piratical *vikingar* from the Baltic lands were becoming a problem. Mighty stave churches now dominated the Scandinavian skyline, where before there had been pagan shrines and temples like Gamla Uppsala. Stave churches, like the rich eighth-century monasteries of Northumbria, made very tempting targets indeed.

Sometime in the 1120s, a man named Vidgaut was shipwrecked in the Baltic lands and was forced to fend off both spiritual and physical threats on his way back to his Danish lord, Canute the Holy. In 1170, *Knýtlinga saga*, a work of propaganda made for King Valdemar II of Denmark, references a huge battle between Danes and Baltic vikingar in Blekinge, Sweden. Saxo also mentions vikingar from the Baltic Sea arriving at Möre and Öland, burning and pillaging. None of the attackers are conclusively identified. In the saga, they are Oesellians (Estonians); in Saxo's work they are Couronians. This literary tradition must then be seen as general anti-Balt propaganda rather than anything describing real events, not too far removed from how English and Frankish annalists wrote of the *nordmanni* and *dene*, with no regard for geographic origin.[25, 26] While there was undeniably viking activity in the Baltic Sea as late as the thirteenth century, the scale is grossly exaggerated in the documentary record. In both 1203 and 1210, claims are made that Lister in Denmark was attacked by Oesellians from the island of Saaremaa, and so too was Gotland soon after. This would continue until at least 1226. Frequent off-hand mentions of Oesellian pirates in the *Livonian Chronicle of Henry* (c.1229) indicate that these raids were unremarkable and regular.

As Latvia began to feel the wrath of Christianity during the Northern Crusades, Latin authors started to compose biased accounts of its history. The *Livonian Chronicle of Henry*, written in Germany, describes how 'both Estonians and Couronians had the habit of plundering the Swedish and Danish coasts'.[27] The fifteenth-century *Visby Chronicle*,[28] from Gotland, describes a raid in 1187 against Sigtuna. This raid story may have originated from a section in the *Eric Chronicle*.[29] Vaguely identified heathens are the villains of the piece, blamed for the death of an archbishop. The *Eric Chronicle* was written during a Swedish war against the Karelian Slavs operating out of the White Sea and is very clearly propaganda.[30, 31] Both the *Eric* and *Visby Chronicle*s mentions of this attack are probably fictitious. A 1448 letter describes Karelian viking activity in Niðarós, Norway, with all the usual details of earlier Scandinavian viking raids:

> As regards our beloved sons, the natives and inhabitants of the island Greenland, which, as we are told, is situated at the utmost limit of the northern seas, north of the kingdom of Norway, in the Province

of Nidaros, so have their sad complaint come to our knowledge and shaken and disturbed our mind... From the neighbouring coasts of the heathens, the barbarians came thirty years ago with a fleet, attacked the people living there with a cruel assault... They carried the miserable inhabitants of both sexes as prisoners to their own country, especially those whom they regarded as strong and capable of bearing constant burdens of slavery, as was fitted for their tyranny.

Greenland has been mistakenly correlated with the overarching area of Arctic Norway and though the Niðarós episcopal see did at one time nominally include Greenland, historian Jack Douglas Forbes has argued convincingly that this piece of textual evidence instead refers to a genuine Karelian attack on Niðarós proper rather than one on Greenland.[32, 33] This reference does, however, indicate that by 1448 'Greenland' was synonymous with 'the unknown north'; the colonies having faded away into obscurity, and so were liable to become fictional victims of fictional attackers.

The Sigtuna raid has long been debated. Contemporary chronicles all but ignore it, instead discussing trading issues around the island of Gotland which could still be the work of vikingar. The *Livonian Chronicle of Henry* does, however, refer to a Scandinavian raid ten years later into the Baltic lands, where the Swedish jarl Birger Brosa ravaged 'Kurland' (Courland, Latvia) on behalf of the Danish crown. As in the earlier Viking Age, the differing principalities of Scandinavia had different targets to raid. While Sweden predominantly pushed for crusades into the thick taiga of Finland, Denmark harried the shores of the Baltic, though there was probably overlap. From the early thirteenth century onwards, these crusades increased in frequency and severity; hillforts across Finland, Estonia, and elsewhere such as Purtse Tarakalas, Tartu, and Soontaga, hint at military activity.[34] Masses of coin hoards containing pennies from Scandinavia and wider Europe were deposited for insurance purposes or as offerings.

While in the Viking Age there had been many hillforts up and down *Austrvegr*, by the thirteenth century these smaller sites had been absorbed by larger consolidated centres, ringing the death knell of rural communities and heralding the age of proto-urbanism. Towns would surely follow, distinct from previous centres like Truso yet also established by Scandinavians attempting to win Christian footholds in the Baltic lands. Scandinavian material culture dominates in the archaeological record, with Baltic and Slavic variations, and even into the 1200s pagans were being buried with typically 'Danish' brooches affixed to their chests. Daugmale and other hillforts would eventually be abandoned and fell into disrepair, as life across the Baltic moved slowly from piratical raiding to townships and commerce (Daugmale sits beneath what is now Riga, Latvia).[35] Later accounts refer to Saaremaa as a final holdout of viking activity even into the fifteenth century; a redoubt of slavery and backwater sea kings, raiders and ring-givers – seven hundred years earlier, the Viking Age had arguably begun on this offshore Estonian island.

This 'Second Viking Age' in the Baltic Sea would also come to an end. By 1169, the Kyivan-Rus started to crumble under Novgorodian independence. Sources from the city mention extensive raiding against Tartu especially. At the same time, the Arabic explorer al-Idrisi mentioned the first towns of the Baltic region: Qlury in Estonia, Anhu in Finland, and Flmus, Madsuna, and Sunu elsewhere.[36, 37]

Numerous factors contributed to the rise and fall of this second wave; an increase in raiding led to an increase in resistance, which brought with it military conquest, cultural assimilation, and urbanism. After *Ragnarǫk*, a new cycle had begun. Eventually, there would be no more spaces left on the map to 'go viking', no more unknowns.

Saga; to Speak

The time of the Icelandic sagas' composition coincides with the Baltic Viking Age and the Kingdom of Man and the Isles. It is no surprise, then, that both feature extensively alongside earlier semi-legendary figures and events from the 'true' Viking Age. *Orkneyinga saga*, for instance, brings the narrative to a close around the time of the last Manx kings, with twelfth-century raids on England perpetrated by King Eystein.

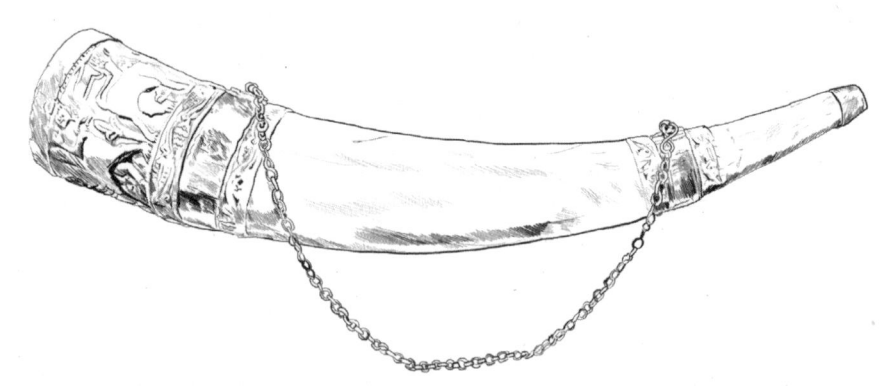

The Horn of Ulph, dated to 1030, given by an Anglo-Scandinavian as part of a 'deed of transfer' with his lands to the clergy of York. Carved from elephant ivory, possibly in Italy, this drinking vessel was allegedly filled with wine by Ulph, who proceeded to down the lot as further evidence of his solemn pledge. Scandinavians had knitted themselves into the ecclesiastical and political fabric of England, shedding their once 'alien' skin.

The Old Norse word *saga* means to speak, and *at setja saman* means 'to piece together'. Harald Fairhair, Bjorn *járnsíða*, Grimur Kamban and Yngvar the Far-Travelled were characters who deserved to be remembered long after their deaths as their word-fame demanded.[38, 39] Even Yngvar's voyage, which is certainly the most historical of the aforementioned, became a tale of dragons, giants, and Egyptian citadels by the time it reached the vernacular, populated with Roman and Greek monsters from the near-contemporary *Physiologus*. Disentangling history from fiction becomes a difficult task.

While lacking the illumination of their continental equivalents, the vernacular copies of the Old Norse sagas really are a thing of beauty. Crumpled manuscript folios reveal a web of complex colours and dyes, sometimes enhanced by complementary images and drawings, or personal additions by the scribe. Such scribes, like the skalds of old, brought the stories back to life and preserved them dutifully.

The Icelandic Commonwealth formally established early in the eleventh century had, as expected, splintered into a complex mosaic of petty rulers fighting over land and power.[40] These were kings in all but name, powerful chieftains from powerful families who, by the thirteenth century, were increasingly under the thumb of overlords from Norway. The Goðar who had once been tasked with keeping blood feuds from spiralling into chaos had by now amassed huge wealth from their dominion over local laws and politics.[41]

The assemblies at Þingvellir were increasingly no more than 'official' shouting matches between the principal landowners of Iceland, merely a screen to hide the shadowy goings-on behind the scenes, such as assassinations and blood feuds.[42] The most famous of all these Icelanders, Snorri Sturluson, the man responsible for *Heimskringla* and most of our literary sources for the Old Norse cosmology, was murdered in the cellar of his turf-built mansion in 1241.[43] Allegedly, his final words were 'Do not strike!' Snorri's opponents – and there were many – resented his power, rivalling that of a true monarch. Sandwiched between the ambitions of the Norwegian King Haakon IV and rival Icelandic chieftains, Snorri's days had been numbered for some time, but so, too, were those of 'democratic' Iceland. While a successful society for several centuries, eventually the democracy established as far back as the 930s had become warped by those in charge, a common outcome.

The sagas, with all their matter-of-fact musings, comedy and colourful characters, are such a fantastically entertaining read that they deserve wider recognition as one of the crowning achievements of humanity. Their origins were in Viking Age Scandinavia, a time and place of – if

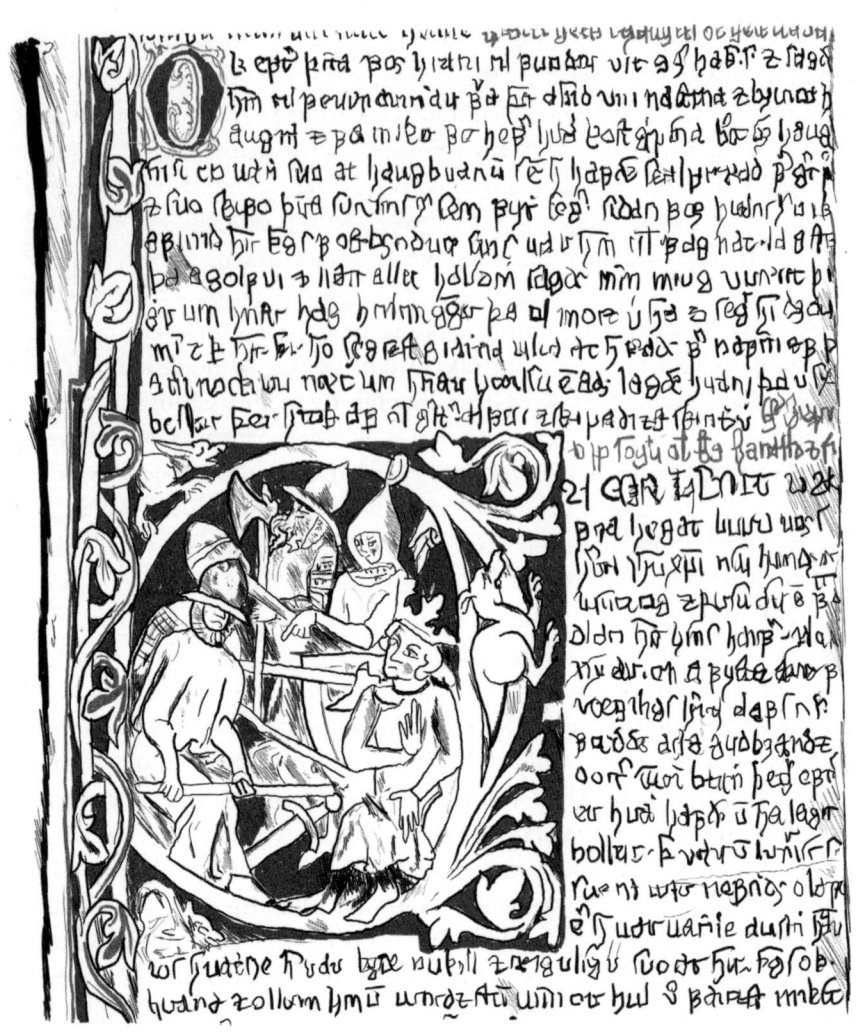

A page from the *Flateyjarbók*, commissioned in Iceland between 1387-1394, which tells among many others the tale of Erik the Red and the settlement of Greenland and Vínland. The vellum sheets – 225 folio-sized leaves or 450 pages – are richly illuminated with complex designs and artistic motifs. The Viking Age was long over, but its stories would never be forgotten.

other and usually later annalists are to be believed – nothing but pagan bloodshed and raiding. Hopefully, this book has proved otherwise. But bloodshed there was. In the tales, a cave in Iceland is frequently mentioned: Surtshellir, with two linked caves, Vigishellir and Beinahellir, the 'fire cave', housing the 'fortress' and 'bone caves'. In the earliest writings of *Landnámabók* Surtshellir is mentioned as an interesting natural feature – a gaping hole carved out of the rock by lava flows, and as late as the fifteenth century, *Harðar saga ok Hólmverja* references the place as a redoubt of bandits.[44, 45] In 2001, a seven-metre long turf-built house was uncovered within Vigishellir, a fortress for a subterranean criminal, reused and repurposed by bandits throughout the history of Iceland as a hiding place to escape local authorities.[46, 47] Over seven thousand skeletal remains were recovered from the nearby midden, some human, most animal, dating between 871-1800 CE. Dr Thomas H. McGovern analysed the bone fragments and concluded:

> The mix of domestic mammals present suggests that the cave's occupants had the ability to take a wide range of domestic stock from surrounding farms... Given the density of this midden and its composition, it would appear that the occupants of the cave must have had a heavy impact on the economies of the farms around them.

Was this the multi-generation abode of a criminal family, or a pit of dark elf worship? Whatever it was, Surtshellir reminds us of the long, long Viking Age.

Several skirmishes would be fought across Iceland in the final days of the commonwealth, between armed bands of men led by landowners. By the late 1240s, almost any and every ruler appointed as a regional leader was a vassal of Norway, and by the 1260s, any resistance to this change was all but quashed. After frequent failed attempts, the Norwegian crown finally achieved suzerainty over Iceland with the signing of the Old Covenant – *Gamli sáttmáli*, in 1264. It would be renewed in 1304 but for all intents and purposes, Iceland had been, for quite some time, subservient to the taxation and scruples of yet another European nation; the mythical allure of the place had faded, though the tales would not. This was the end result of a conflict that according to the sagas had been ongoing since the days of King Harald Fairhair and his flowing locks.

Branches of the World Tree

Because of the sheer amount of locations vikingar visited across the known world, it is tempting to see many different 'ends of the Viking Age' depending on where one looks. Consider the Scandinavian colonies around Rouen and Cotentin at the dawn of the Duchy of Normandy. Then, in the tenth century, Scandinavian vikingar were already becoming more and more like their French neighbours, though by the 990s their activities as mercenaries and pirates in Sicily and mainland Italy were not so far removed from traditional viking activity. There was still a prosperous slave market at Rouen exporting Irish and English wretches across *Austrvegr* and westwards to the Greenland colonies; Æthelred the Ill-Counselled repeatedly complained about such activities. His Danish enemies in the early eleventh century frequently wintered in Normandy, protected by their kinsmen and shielded from international law. Olafr Haraldsson, the saintly king of Norway, was to spend many a season in the court of Richard II, using Rouen as a base for raids in either direction. The slave market had long-lasting connections to Al-Andalus, Dublin, and the British Isles, and Frankish wine recovered from London can be dated to Cnut the Great's reign. Under the Norman sphere of influence the weaving markets of Flanders were hugely profitable centres in the international wool trade.

There would be conflict between Scandinavian settlers across the Cotentin Peninsula and Rouen, but also between them and their Breton and Frankish neighbours. Fierce wars of independence emerged out of the burgeoning state of Normandy. Starting under Rollo, a conscious Scandinavian-led state-building effort created an autocratic elite with no general assembly; distinct from the surrounding French lands, but also distinct from other contemporary Scandinavian colonies.[48] Eighty years later, Norman mercenaries were pillaging and harrying Italy,[49] but it is difficult to view their activities as an extension of the Viking Age, even if their paths routinely crossed with 'true' Scandinavian vikingar in the Varangian Guard. There was no clear-cut 'transition moment' separating the Viking and Norman periods; the character of the Duchy of Normandy changed over multiple generations, though it would remain coloured by its Scandinavian heritage.

Elsewhere across the diaspora, cultural assimilation, integration, and an increase in power and influence were separating the old from the new. Yaroslav the Wise during his reign over the Kyivan-Rus from Novgorod introduced legal codes like the *Russkaya Pravda* ('*Rus* Justice' or 'Truth'), and upon his death in 1054, the sun was starting to set on a regulated *Rusland*.[50, 51] Yaroslav's children competed for the throne of Kyiv and segmented the state into various principalities. Kin killing led to political fragmentation and an increase in the power of regional lords, some from the original ruling elite, others from local tribes.

The Kyivan-Rus would be reunified one last time under Yaroslav's descendant Mstiszlav the Great in the early twelfth century, though by this point a combination of the crusades and the opening of new trade routes to Africa and Asia led to a decrease in reliance on *Austrvegr*, and thus a fall in Kyivan-Rus fortunes. Mstiszlav's son Yaropolk II would rule over an unruly Kyivan-Rus, crushed under the weight of internal strife and external adversaries like the Turkic Cuman invaders. Something had to give, and Novgorod would emerge as the centre of a new republic. 'Lord Novgorod the Great' controlled old segments of the *Austrvegr* in eastern Europe and the various city-states, and it may have been on an upwards trajectory, if not for a notorious thirteenth-century villain.[52] Genghis Khan came from the east, and the Kyivan-Rus was no more.

Fragments of *Færeyinga saga* in *Flateyjarbók* recount how Sigmundur Brestisson brought Christianity to the Faroes in the late tenth century, and only a generation after, the Norwegian crown came with it. They were annexed, and by the fourteenth century were taxed from Bergen and subservient to the growing power of the Hanseatic League. The many merchants, craftspeople and traders of the Viking Age from Gotland, Saxony, the Baltic, Scandinavia, and the Kyivan-Rus had formed *hansas*, or guilds. Sometime in the twelfth century a confederacy of these *hansas* (later called the Hanseatic League) became fat-cat businessmen located in trading ports like Visby or Lübeck, exacting tax and tribute.[53] This collection of merchants dominated the trade routes that had begun in the Viking Age; these *hansas* became the new rulers of the oceans.

On land, while Norway and Denmark were effectively consolidated by the end of the eleventh century, Sweden descended into civil war in 1066 upon the death of King Stenkil. It is debated whether this conflict was over the diminishing of *forn siðr* and the strengthening of Christianity. It would not be until the semi-fictional king *Blot*-Sweyn died in 1088 that all vestiges of paganism in the upper layer of society were gone for good.[54,55] Sweyn is probably the same figure as Håkan the Red, an equally doubtful and possibly pagan Swedish monarch. Norway, Denmark, and Sweden continued into the succeeding centuries as Christian nations going about Christian work; crusading, and trading, but would eventually partially unite under the Kalmar Union in the fourteenth century to counter the Hanseatic League.[56] Meanwhile in Constantinople, the once great city, Scandinavian components of the Varangian Guard would trickle down to nothing after decades of crusading.

If the 'English Viking Age' ended in 1066, then perhaps elsewhere other branches of the Viking 'tree' ended at different times? The Baltic, Irish Sea, and Shetlandic branches have been described as ending at various intervals across the thirteenth and fifteenth centuries. Which, using this tree analogy, would be the longest of these branches? To find the final days of the 'Long Viking Age' one must set sail one last time for the edge of the world, to Greenland.

Dusk and Dawn

The fate of the colonies was dependent on various factors outside of the Greenlanders' immediate control. They could irrigate their soil using the dams and canals excavated at Garðar, they could shift their diet away from agropastoralism to one of marine subsistence and hunting, and they could routinely sail back and forth to the coasts of Labrador, or

Markland, for timber.⁵⁷ The name of *Markland* ('forest land') indicates just how isolated the Greenland colonies were. At the beginning of this book, the etymology of Den*mark* was considered; an identity shaped by borders and marches. Now, at the end of the long Viking Age, we have the vast untamed wilderness of *Markland*; an endless forest stretching beyond the white sands. To the Greenlanders, these forests were the marches at the end of the world, a buffer-zone between *inside* and *outside*. What horrors beyond comprehension might dwell in such murky green forests, what dark beasts? Here at the end of trade, travel, and exploration, was the border of all things.

The Greenlanders really were isolated. They could not sail through the sea ice to Norway at will, nor could they change the foul weather, become part of the economies of Europe, Africa, and Asia, or counter the power of the Hanseatic League. While the effect of the 'Little Ice Age' has perhaps been overblown in studies of the Greenland collapse, there is no doubt that there were increases in icebergs across the usual navigation routes, hampering contact.

Norðseturmen on their hunting trips would have to brave months of polar weather and sea storms before arriving at Disko Bay to hunt walruses, their population dwindling, before returning – and that was only *within* Greenland. Then, the tusks had to be processed, the hides had to be turned into ropes and skins for sea travel, and the goods had to be stored carefully in barrels for an even longer journey.

Greenlanders sailed for Iceland, offering the tusks to powerful Goðar alongside bulkier goods like polar bear cubs and salted delicacies. Some sales were made, but not enough. The Greenlanders then travelled onwards to the Faroes, bartering for new goods with the locals, then the Shetlanders, and the Irish and Norse at Dublin, Wexford, Limerick, and Waterford, the English too. Passing through the Kingdom of Man and the Isles, these Greenland sailors arrived at the flourishing markets of England and Normandy to sell their wares, picking up new goods along the way and hopefully some cash.

But still, not enough. From Normandy and Flanders to Frisia and Denmark, through the Kattegat into the waters of old, along the way the Greenlanders encounter similar salesmen, also selling walrus tusks, but these are harvested from the stock up in the White Sea. Arguments arise between the two crews. The *knarr* docks at the new markets in the Baltic lands, home to many people willing to spend. It has been many months now since the ship left Greenland; winter has come. Over a season, the crew stays put in the harbours of Gotland, sharing tales with travellers at Visby and Paviken. And then, a new year, time for new sales. Now, the *knarr* is not just selling walrus tusks (for the supply is dwindling), but all manner of wares picked up along the way. Along *Austrvegr* the crew travels, hoisting their boat out of the water when necessary, though the journey is less dangerous now than it had been in centuries past, the Novgorod Republic and smaller polities protecting the waterways from nomads. Still, the rivers ahead are dark.

More moons pass, and after resting at St George Island they finally sight the glistening towers of Constantinople. In the busy markets and packed alleys, opportunities become available the likes of which Greenlanders had never dreamed. But the effects of the crusades are showing; guards patrol the street. Perhaps one should travel on? To the Caspian Sea, to dry heat and buzzing flies. It is known that the merchants in Georgia and beyond will pay well for polar goods. By now, a full year into the journey, the battered *knarr* docks at Baghdad, and after a camel ride beyond, the traders sell their last walrus tusk. The return journey awaits.

Back in the Baltic Sea, as another winter draws near, longships appear on the horizon; but these are not traders, not even *hansa*. They are vikingar, and they have come to raid.

If even one shipful of Greenlanders died at any stage of that journey, then a significant portion of the colonies' manpower would vanish. These colonies were not bustling towns, not even market centres; they were farms composed of one or two families separated by miles. A hunting expedition to *Norðsetur* would have needed manpower from many families. The loss of an entire crew would have been a disaster; without hunters, without traders to bring money and building materials back to the colonies, times would have been tough. Now imagine this death by a thousand cuts worsened by all of the changes elsewhere in the world; the Hanseatic League dominating European trade and cutting corners to look for new, cheaper markets rather than relying on far-flung international exports; the opening up of Africa as a new source of richer and paler ivory; the dramatic rise and fall of various states and polities along the searoads resulting in redirected routes and new rules of taxation and trade. All this was happening thousands of miles away from the everyday lives of the farmers and fishermen of Greenland, but it was affecting them. Maybe they wouldn't notice it overnight, but over the years the rot would set in. A grandfather sitting at the back of the turf house at Herjolfsnes looks back upon his childhood as a time of prosperity – 'The goods flowed in those days!' – while his grandsons argue over who gets the finest cut of 'rabbit' meat for dinner. Their parents, starving, worry about what to serve tomorrow, and how long it will take the lads to notice that their dog Hati is missing.

In 1345, the Greenland colonies were excused from paying tithes to the Catholic Church on account of their poverty. This was four years after

Ivar Bardarsson, a Norwegian superintendent sent to oversee the clergy of Greenland, described Vestribygð as all but abandoned, with farmsteads in ruin, home only to wandering livestock and the roaming Thule Inuit.[58] Ivar blamed the fate of Vestribygð on the Thule but it is much more likely that Greenlanders were seeking a better life elsewhere. If seal populations dwindled then the Greenlanders, without the equipment to bore and hunt through ice sheets, would have had to rely on hare, ptarmigan, or the occasional caribou. A diet of solely rabbit meat – lean and lacking – would have been debilitating. They would, effectively, become trapped within their own skin and their own lands, unable to muster the energy to travel elsewhere. Cut marks on the bones of dogs located in Western Settlement farmsteads indicate desperate days. So, too, do insect analyses led by Eva Panagiotakopulu[59] and others: layers of filth in the rooms of farms, carrion flies, and maggots as indicator species of decay. While there is no evidence of cannibalism, perhaps the thought wasn't too far away.[60, 61, 62] Rumours would circulate regarding the apparent 'degeneration' of the inhabitants' bones, their skin warped, though this was more rooted in a demonisation of 'the other' than anything scientific.

The death of the Greenland colonies was slow, painful, and took place over multiple generations, and aside from a few drastic cases may not have even included death at all, but a migration back to Iceland and Scandinavia. In 1410, the last written reference to the Greenland colonies reached Iceland, recording a stranded vessel from elsewhere whose crew remained on the island for four years.[63] They witnessed the walrus hunting of the locals and may have seen one or two of the Thule, perhaps as solitary hunters. One of the stranded sailors, Torgrim Sölvesson, was to have a particularly trying sojourn. His wife Steinunn fell for a local named Kollgrimr. Accusing the man of witchcraft and of stealing not just his wife's *hamr* but her *hugr* too, Torgrim had the þing vote for his execution, and Kollgrimr was burned alive. Kollgrimr had been accused of using *galdr* on Steinunn, driving her insane through magical charms; here in the fifteenth century, a hundred years before the Reformation, was a man accused of practising *the old ways*, and for that he had paid a terrible price. It is worth mentioning that this was around the time the Black Death had started to ravage Iceland and Scandinavia, which no doubt also had a knock-on effect on the Greenland population. In times of stress and famine, accusations of witchcraft could gain a hold, especially in a backwater like Greenland. Its inhabitants were Christian, but they were not connected to any overseas church; perhaps their God took on an older guise.

Torgrim's sailing companion Thorstein fared much better during his stay. He fell in love with a local. On either the 14th or 16th of September

1408, Thorstein Olafsson and Sigrid Björnsdóttir were married at Hvalsey church, and together they left to live out the rest of their lives in Iceland. We can only hope that it was a happy union. A 1424 letter from Iceland written by Saemund Oddson, a relative of Sigrid, confirmed that the marriage was witnessed 'according to my advice and consent'.

That was the last record of the Greenland colonies. We can imagine many other Greenlanders followed Sigrid and migrated elsewhere, though many would have no doubt stayed, hoping for a change in fortune. The Danish cartographer Claudius Clavus[64] may have navigated near the island not long after, and it is possible sailors from Bergen visited in 1484, though if they had any sort of welcome is unknown, and eight years after that the Catholic Church demanded the monk Martin Knudsson travel there to investigate. No such expedition was undertaken. It was during this same period that the great saga traditions from Iceland began to change their literary approaches to Greenland; where it had previously featured as a lawless but very real land, as in *The Saga of Ref the Sly*, later tales characterise Greenland as a nebulous, unknowable frontier beyond the norm. It had become the new *Markland*, the new 'end of the earth'.

The Greenland of fourteenth- and fifteenth-century works like *Flóamanna saga*, *Bárðar saga Snæfellsáss*, and *Jökuls þáttur Búasonar* is one of troll-like women and undead sailors. It is simultaneously an unknown Arctic island and a timelocked frontier, still home to Erik the Red, almost as if the man (real or not) had become as temporally 'multiplied' as Wiglaf's sword in *Beowulf*. Through these works we get the impression of Greenland having already fallen 'off the map' even before the settlers finally abandoned it. This literary isolation would be challenged only by nearby *Helluland*, a semi-fictitious location probably inspired by Baffin Island to the west, often visited by Greenlanders. The *Helluland* of later sagas may as well be the realm of death, *Hel*, for it is certainly descibed as such. In the *Saga of Arrow-Odd*, the titular character's nemesis Ogmund is said to dwell in the bleak stone wasteland of *Helluland*, though it is moved to the far north above Greenland. If Greenland was now the edge of the map, then *Helluland* was beyond even that, somewhere in the void. A dark place for the dead. Ogmund has even been argued by modern scholars to be a personification of death; Arrow-Odd in this instance triumphing over death itself, rather than a mere mortal.

Following Columbus's news of the new world across the sea, Danish ambitions under naval officer Søren Norby in 1520 could have ushered in a second age of discovery both to and from Greenland, though such ambitions were never realised. By the end of the fifteenth century, it seems all life in the colonies had gone elsewhere, or gone entirely.

As mentioned in the first chapter, there is a codicil to the final testament. In a series of mid-sixteenth-century stories of travels to Greenland, one helmed by the fictional character Jon Grøenlander remarks how, in the year 1540, over a thousand years after this narrative of raiders and pagans began, a crew of sailors came upon something peculiar in the far north. Along the glacial coastline was an array of stone huts, mostly abandoned, along with sheds for drying fish and the remains of tools along the beach. Amongst the rubble lay a dead man, face-down in the snow. They saw his sealskins and spotted hood and thought that he must be an Inuit. But something wasn't right. The men turned him over: red hair, frieze-cloth clothes, a worn sheath knife nearby. He was like them, and he had died on the edge of the world.

This never happened, but the story reflects that sense of wonder, exploration, determination, and despair of the Viking Age. What had started with struggling farmers under a black sun in the Dust Veil of 536 CE had come to an end over a thousand years later in almost the same way, farmers eking out a living under dark skies and in biting bitter winds.

The sun that set on the late Scandinavian colonies of Greenland would rise again the day after, but there would be no children to greet that dawn, no dogs to howl at it, no farmers to hunt or till the fields. The Inuit would take over the ruins, sometimes living amongst the rubble but usually leaving the farmsteads to fall into disrepair, looting what they needed and heading off. The last echo of the Viking Age, ending not with a battle but an exodus of farmers, travelling southwards to seek better lands. We have heard this story before.

endir; Conclusion

The study of the Viking Age has already come so far from the days of antiquarian excavators and their literary antecedents. Since Sir Walter Scott first used the word 'Viking' in one of his poems we have been fighting a battle of definitions, but does it really matter? Even the word 'Viking' might not necessarily originate as a verb but as a noun all along. The 1874 *Icelandic English Dictionary* describes a 'Viking' as we would a 'voyage'; one cannot perhaps *go viking,* but one can go *on* a viking, defined there as a 'heathen raiding expedition'. In this regard, a 'Viking' is not a person, it is a journey. A Viking is a voyage, but specifically, one by Scandinavians operating between the eighth and eleventh centuries under pagan guises with the goal of raiding and ravaging wherever possible, to gain loot, slaves, prestige, and word-fame.

The concept of periodisation has come up much throughout this manuscript; that idea of arbitrarily signalling dates to demarcate the changes between one era and the next. Ever the bane of the academic, it is, nevertheless, a useful and accessible tool for discussing history, but as this book has hopefully demonstrated, such semantics can often leave us tied in knots, allowing too much history to fall on the cutting room floor, undiscussed. The Kingdom of Man and the Isles, for instance, even a mention of viking activity as late as 1212 in King John of England's courts.

Viking, Vikings, Vikingar. This most fascinating period of human history saw people sail to far-flung locations around the globe, to deal with unforeseeable challenges. Everyone has their favourite period of history, and the Viking Age has forever been mine, and forever will be.

Further Reading

Dawn

1. Scott, W. (1836). *The Bridal of Triermain, Harold the Dauntless, Field of Waterloo, and other poems.* Oxford University.
2. Brink, S. (2008). Who Were the Vikings? In: *The Viking World.* Routledge. pp.4–10.
3. Langer, J. (2002). The Origins of the Imaginary Viking. *Viking Heritage*, (4), pp.6–9.
4. Fransson, U. (2019). A farmstead from the late Viking Age and early medieval period. House constructions and social status at Vik, Ørland. In: *Environment & Settlement: Ørland 600 BC-AD 1250*: Archaeological Excavations at Vik, Ørland Main Air Base. Trondheim. pp.323–350.
5. Ellegård, A. (2008). Who Were the Heruli? *Scandia*, pp.1–34.
6. Heather, P. (2015). Heruli. In: *Oxford Research Encyclopedia of Classics.* Oxford University Press.
7. Ivanišević, V. and Kazanski, M. (2010). Justinian's Heruli in Northern Illyricum and their Archaeological Evidence. *Stratum Plus Journal*, 2010 (5), pp.147–157.
8. Russell, M. and Laycock, S. (2011). *UnRoman Britain: Exposing the Great Myth of Britannia.* Stroud: History Press.
9. Bollingberg, H. J. (1995). Copper-Alloyed Artefacts from Roman Imports in Scandinavia: Elemental Analysis. *MRS Proceedings*, 352, p.621.
10. Grane, T. (2013). Roman Imports in Scandinavia: their Purpose and Meaning? In: Wells, P. (Ed). *Rome Beyond Its Frontiers: Imports, Attitudes, & Practices.* Portsmouth, Rhode Island. pp.29–44.
11. Browning, R. (1962). Procopius: Secret History. Translated by Richard Atwater, pp. xvi, 150. Ann Arbor: University of Michigan Press, 1961. *The Classical Review*, 12 (3), pp.309–310.
12. Hindermann, J. (2022). *Sidonius Apollinaris' Letters, Book 2: Text, Translation and Commentary.* Edinburgh University Press.

Further Reading

13. Haggman, B. (1999). Eruli Influence in South Scandinavia – Migration and Remigration. Migracijske teme, 15 (1), pp.215–227.
14. Werner, J. (1949). Zu den auf Öland und Gotland gefundenen byzantinischen Goldmünzen, *Fornvännen*, Stockholm
15. Davis, C. R. (1992). Cultural Assimilation in the Anglo-Saxon Royal Genealogies. *Anglo-Saxon England*, 21, pp.23–36.
16. Tumėnas, V. (2016). The Common Attribute between the Baltic Thunder God Perkūnas and his Antique Equivalents Jupiter and Zeus. *Mediterranean Archaeology and Archaeometry*, 16 (4), pp.359–367.
17. Nijole, L. (1996). The Ancient Lithuanian God of Thunder: in Language, Folklore, Historical Sources. In: *Folklore Works*. 400.
18. Cusack, C. (2011). Pagan Saxon Resistance to Charlemagne's Mission: 'Indigenous' Religion and 'World' Religion in the Early Middle Ages. *The Pomegranate*, 13 (1), pp.33–51.
19. Frazer, J. G. (1983). The Worship of the Oak. In: *The Golden Bough*. London: Palgrave Macmillan UK. pp.209–213.
20. Adam of Bremen. Chapter 3. In: *Gesta Hammaburgensis ecclesiae pontificum Book IV (Descriptio insularum aquilonis)*.
21. Iversen, F. (2020). Law-territories in Scandinavia: Reflections of Tribal Coalitions. In: Ehlers, C. and Grewe, H. (Eds). *Rechtsräume. Klostermann*. pp.301–318.
22. Mellor, R. (2010). *Tacitus' Annals*. Oxford University Press.
23. Frank, R. (2000). The invention of the Viking horned helmet. *International Scandinavian and Medieval Studies in Memory of Gerd Wolfgang Weber*, pp.199–208.
24. Maddox, T. (2020). A storm of swords and spears: The weapon dancer as an enduring symbol in prehistoric Scandinavia. Fosl, P. S. (Ed). *Cogent Arts & Humanities*, 7:1, 1747804.
25. Coles, J. (1999). The Dancer on the Rock: record and analysis at Järrestad, Sweden. In: *Proceedings of the Prehistoric Society* (Vol. 65, pp. 167–187). Cambridge University Press.
26. Ling, J. (2014). *Elevated rock art. Towards a maritime understanding of Bronze Age rock art in northern Bohuslän, Sweden*. Oxbow Books.
27. Heaney, S. (Ed). (2000). *Beowulf*. London: Faber and Faber.
28. Schilling, H. (1887). The Finnsburg fragment and the Finn episode. *Modern Language Notes*, 2(6), pp.146–150.
29. Moulton, C. (1973). Theocritus and the Dioscuri. *Greek, Roman, and Byzantine Studies*, 14(1), pp.41–47.
30. Beck, H. (1965) *Das Ebersignum im Germanischen. Ein Beitrag zur germanischen TierSymbolik*. Berlin: W. de Gruyter.
31. Kovářová, L. (2011). *The Swine in Old Nordic Religion and Worldview*. PhD, Reykjavik: Félagsvísindasvið Háskóla Íslands.
32. Merkelbach, R. (2014). The Monster in Me: Social Corruption and the Perception of Monstrosity in the Sagas of Icelanders. *Quaestio Insularis*, 15, pp.22–37.

33. Taylor, T., 1992. The Gundestrup cauldron. *Scientific American*, 266(3), pp.84–89.
34. Dickinson, T. (2005). Symbols of protection: the significance of animal-ornamented shields in early Anglo-Saxon England. *Medieval Archaeology*, 49, pp.109–163.
35. Glosecki, S.O. (1986). Wolf dancers and whispering beasts: shamanic motifs from Sutton Hoo? *Mankind Quarterly*, 26(3), p.305.
36. Chadwick-Hawes, S. and Grainger, G. (2006). The Anglo-Saxon cemetery at Finglesham, Kent. *Archaeology Monogram*, 64.
37. Seebold, E. (1992). Römische Münzbilder und germanische Sym-bolwelt. In: Beck, H., Ellmers, D. and Schier, K. (Eds). *Germa-nische Religionsgeschichte. Quellen und Quellenprobleme*. RGA Ergbd. Berlin, New York. pp.270–310.
38. Seebold, E. (1994). Das erste Auftreten germanischer Bildelementeund Runen auf den Goldbrakteaten der Völkerwanderungs-zeit. In: Uecker, H. (Ed) *Studien zum Altgermanischen.Festschrift für Heinrich Beck*. RGA Ergbd. Berlin, New York: pp.600-618.
39. Ling, J., Chacon, R. and Chacon, Y., (2018). Rock art, secret societies, long-distance exchange, and warfare in Bronze Age Scandinavia. *Prehistoric Warfare and Violence: Quantitative and Qualitative approaches*, pp.149–174.
40. Bruce-Mitford, R. (1974). *Aspects of Anglo-Saxon Archaeology: Sutton Hoo and Other Discoveries*. London: Victor Gollancz.
41. Petersen, J. (1919). *De Norske Vikingesverd: En Typologisk-Kronologisk Studie Over Vikingetidens Vaaben*. Jacob Dybwad.
42. Finch, R. G. (1981). Atlakviða, Atlamál, and Vǫlsunga Saga: A Study in Combination and Integration. In Dronke, Ursula (ed.). *Specvlvm norroenvm: Norse Studies in Memory of Gabriel Turville-Petre*. Odense: Odense University Press. pp. 123–138.
43. Betageri, A. (2021). The Radiant River-Light of Love: Indo-European Heritage, 'Sati' in the Old Norse Epic Tradition and the Discourse on Love. MA, Delhi: University of Delhi.
44. The Prose Edda (Vol. 5). American-Scandinavian Foundation.
45. Gräslund, B. and Price, N. (2012). Twilight of the gods? The 'dust veil event' of AD 536 in critical perspective. *Antiquity*, 86 (332), pp.428–443.
46. Baillie, M.G. (1994). Dendrochronology raises questions about the nature of the AD 536 dust-veil event. *The Holocene*, 4(2), pp.212–217.
47. Larsen, L.B., Vinther, B.M., Briffa, K.R., Melvin, T.M., Clausen, H.B., Jones, P.D., Siggaard-Andersen, M.L., Hammer, C.U., Eronen, M., Grudd, H. and Gunnarson, B.E. (2008). New ice core evidence for a volcanic cause of the AD 536 dust veil. *Geophysical Research Letters*, 35(4).
48. Helama, S., Arppe, L., Uusitalo, J., Holopainen, J., Mäkelä, H.M., Mäkinen, H., Mielikäinen, K., Nöjd, P., Sutinen, R., Taavitsainen, J.P. and Timonen, M. (2018). Volcanic dust veils from sixth-century tree-ring isotopes linked to reduced irradiance, primary production and human health. *Scientific Reports*, 8(1), p.1339.
49. Eusabius' *Chronicle*. Trans. Robert Bedrosian.

Further Reading

50. O'Donnell, J. (1969). *Cassiodorus* University of California Press, Berkeley, CA.
51. Ochoa, G., Hoffman, J. and Tin, T. (2005). *Climate: the force that shapes our world and the future of life on earth.* London: Rodale Books International.
52. Helama, S., Saranpää, P., Pearson, C.L., Arppe, L., Holopainen, J., Mäkinen, H., Mielikäinen, K., Nöjd, P., Sutinen, R., Taavitsainen, J.P. and Timonen, M. (2019). Frost rings in 1627 BC and AD 536 in subfossil pinewood from Finnish Lapland. *Quaternary Science Reviews*, 204, pp.208–215.
53. Airt, S. & Noicaill, G. (1983) *The Annals of Ulster* (to A.D. 1131). Dublin.
54. Ab Ithel, J.W. ed., 2012. *Annales Cambriae.* Cambridge University Press.
55. Price, N. and Gräslund, B., 2015. Excavating the Fimbulwinter? Archaeology, geomythology and the climate event (s) of AD 536. In: *Past Vulnerability. Volcanic eruptions and human vulnerability in traditional societies past and present.* Aarhus: Aarhus Universitetsforlag.
56. Stamnes, A. (2016). Effect of temperature change on Iron Age cereal production and settlement patterns in mid-Norway. In: *The Agrarian Life of The North: Studies in Rural Settlement and Farming in Norway.* Portal. pp.27–39.
57. Iversen, F. (2016). Estate division: social cohesion in the aftermath of AD 536-7. In: *The Agrarian Life of The North.* Portal. pp.41–75.
58. Nordvig, M. and Riede, F., 2018. Are there echoes of the AD 536 event in the Viking Ragnarok myth? A critical appraisal. *Environment and History*, 24(3), pp.303–324.
59. Nichols, C. (2021). The Vendel Period: The Golden Age of the Norse. *Scandinavian Archaeology*, 23.
60. Wagner, D.M., Klunk, J., Harbeck, M., Devault, A., Waglechner, N., Sahl, J.W., Enk, J., Birdsell, D.N., Kuch, M., Lumibao, C. and Poinar, D. (2014). Yersinia pestis and the Plague of Justinian 541–543 AD: a Genomic Analysis. *The Lancet Infectious Diseases*, 14(4), pp.319–326.
61. Nicolay, J. (2017). Odin in Friesland: Scandinavian influences in the southern North Sea area during the Migration and Early Merovingian periods. In *Interaktion ohne Grenzen: Beispiele archäologischer Forschungen am Beginn des 21.* Jahrhunderts (pp. 499–514). Stiftung Schleswig-Holsteinische Landesmuseen.
62. Sawyer, P.H. ed. (2001). *The Oxford Illustrated History of the Vikings.* Oxford Illustrated History.
63. MacMullen, R., (1988). *Corruption and the Decline of Rome.* Yale University Press.
64. Graham-Campbell, J. (2018). Helgö Revisited: a new look at the excavated evidence for Helgö, central Sweden. *The Antiquaries Journal*, 98, pp.341–342.
65. Loveluck, C. (2007). *Rural Settlement, Lifestyles and Social Change in the Later First Millennium AD at Flixborough, Lincolnshire: Anglo-Saxon Flixborough in its wider Context.* Historic England.
66. Waller, J. (1982). Swedish contacts with the Eastern Baltic in the pre-Viking and early Viking Ages: The evidence from Helgö. *Journal of Baltic Studies*, 13(3), pp.256–266.

67. Uino, P., (1988). On the history of Staraja Ladoga. *Acta Archaeologica*, 59, pp.205–222.
68. Jarman, C. (2021). *River Kings: A New History of the Vikings from Scandinavia to the Silk Roads.* London: William Collins.
69. Pearson, A. (2006). Piracy in late Roman Britain: a perspective from the Viking Age. *Britannia*, 37, pp.337–353.
70. Cotterill, J. (1993). Saxon raiding and the role of the late Roman coastal forts of Britain. *Britannia*, 24, pp.227–239.
71. Andrén, A. (2014). Tracing old Norse cosmology: the world tree, middle earth, and the sun from archaeological perspectives, *Vägar till Midgård* 16. Lund: Nordic Academic Press.
72. Montgomery, J., Evans, J.A., Powlesland, D. and Roberts, C.A. (2005). Continuity or colonization in Anglo-Saxon England? Isotope evidence for mobility, subsistence practice, and status at West Heslerton. *American Journal of Physical Anthropology*: The Official Publication of the American Association of Physical Anthropologists, 126(2), pp.123–138.
73. Townend, M. (2002). *Language and History in Viking Age England: Linguistic Relations between Speakers of Old Norse and Old English,* Studies in the early Middle Ages v. 6. Turnhout, Belgium: Brepols.
74. *Alfred the Great: Asser's Life of King Alfred and Other Contemporary Sources.* Penguin UK, 2004.
75. *Widsith.* From the *Exeter Book.*
76. Hardison, B.C. (2022). Gildas' On the Ruin of Britain: A Scribal Edition Based on the Text Preserved in Cambridge, University Library Ff. I. 27 (Doctoral dissertation).
77. Ingram, T.J. (1912). *The Anglo-Saxon Chronicle.*
78. Reuter, T. (2013). The Annals of Fulda: Ninth-century histories, volume II. In: *The Annals of Fulda.* Manchester University Press.
79. Brown, D. (2000). The Fate of Greenland's Vikings. *Archaeology Archive.* Archaeological Institute of America.

Rise

1. *Historia Francorum* (History of the Franks)
2. *Liber Monstrorum* (Book of Monsters)
3. Tummuscheit, A. and Witte, F. (2019). The Danevirke: Preliminary results of new excavations (2010–2014) at the defensive system in the German-Danish borderland. *Offa's Dyke Journal*, 1, pp.114–136.
4. Dumville, D. N., Keynes, S. and Taylor, S. (Eds). (1983). *The Anglo-Saxon Chronicle: A Collaborative Edition.* Cambridge.
5. Beda, Ecbertus and Beda. (1990). *Ecclesiastical History of the English People.* Penguin Classics. Rev. ed. Latham, R. E. (Ed). Harmondsworth: Penguin
6. Dumville, D. N. (1976). The Anglian collection of royal genealogies and regnal lists. *Anglo-Saxon England,* 5, pp.23–50.
7. Mills, A. D. (1991). *A Dictionary of English Place Names.* Oxford; New York: Oxford University Press.

Further Reading

8. _____ Oxford paperback reference. 1st ed. rev. Oxford; New York: Oxford University Press.
9. Myres, J. N. L. (1986). The English Settlements. *The Oxford History of England* 1B. Oxford: New York: Clarendon Press; Oxford University Press.
10. Cooijmans, C.A. (2020). *Monarchs and Hydrarchs: The Conceptual Development Model of Viking Activity across the Frankish Realm (c. 750-940 CE)*. London: Routledge.
11. Cooijmans, C., (2021). Viking Dorestad: A Haven for Hydrarchy? *Dorestad and its Networks: Communities, Contact and Conflict in Early Medieval Europe*, pp.19–28.
12. Maryon, H. (1947). The Sutton Hoo Helmet. *Antiquity*, 21(83), pp.137–144.
13. Quinn, J. (1991). *The Saga of the Volsungs: The Norse epic of Sigurd the dragon slayer.* Parergon, 9(1), pp.153–154.
14. Stanhope, M. (2003). *The Stanhope Family Tree.*
15. Leahy, K. and Bland, R. (2009). *The Staffordshire Hoard.* London: British Museum Press.
16. Nebiolini, B. (2020). Silver hoards and the economic interrelationship of Viking York and Dublin (800-1000). *Journal of Irish Archaeology*, 29.
17. Adams, M. (2014). *The King in the north: the life and times of Oswald of Northumbria.* London: Head of Zeus.
18. Dumville, D.N. (1975). Nennius and the 'Historia Brittonum'. *Studia Celtica*, 10, p.78.
19. Echard, S. (2017). Historia Brittonum. *The Encyclopedia of Medieval Literature in Britain*, pp.1–3.
20. Forbes, H. (2018). Bretwalda. In: *The Oxford Dictionary of Late Antiquity.* Oxford University Press.
21. Fulton, H. (2017). Táin Bó Cuailnge, The Cattle Raid of Cooley. *The Encyclopedia of Medieval Literature in Britain*, pp.1–3.
22. Saxo Grammaticus (1894), *The first nine books of Danish history.* London: David Nutt.
23. Von Steinsdorff, K. and Grupe, G. (2006). Reconstruction of an aquatic food web: Viking Haithabu vs. Medieval Schleswig. *Anthropologischer Anzeiger*, pp.283–295.
24. Smiley, J. (2005). *The Sagas of the Icelanders.* Penguin UK.
25. Ling, J. and Cornell, P. (2017). *Violence, Warriors, and Rock Art in Bronze Age Scandinavia: Feast, Famine or Fighting? Multiple Pathways to Social Complexity*, pp.15–33.
26. Bengtsson, B. (2011). Sailing rock art boats. *Journal of Maritime Archaeology*, 6, pp.37–73.
27. Jensen, J. (1989). The Hjortspring boat reconstructed. *Antiquity*, 63(240), pp.531–535.
28. Giles, M. (2020). *Bog Bodies: Face to face with the Past.* Manchester University Press.
29. Wickler, S. (2019). Early boats in Scandinavia: New Evidence from Early Iron Age Bog Finds in Arctic Norway. *Journal of Maritime Archaeology*, 14(2), pp.183–204.

30. Arenhold, L. (1914). The Nydam Boat at Kiel. *The Mariner's Mirror*, 4(6), pp.182–185.
31. Phillips, C.W. (1940). The excavation of the Sutton Hoo ship burial. *The Antiquaries Journal*, 20(2), pp.149–202.
32. Nordeide, S.W., Bonde, N. and Thun, T. (2020). At the threshold of the Viking Age: New dendrochronological dates for the Kvalsund ship and boat bog offerings (Norway). *Journal of Archaeological Science: Reports*, 29, p.102192.
33. Peets, J., Allmäe, R. and Maldre, L. (2010). Archaeological investigations of Pre-Viking Age burial boat in Salme village at Saaremaa. *Archaeological fieldwork in Estonia*, 2010, pp.29–48.
34. Konsa, M., Allmäe, R., Maldre, L. and Vassiljev, J. (2008). Rescue excavations of a Vendel Era boat grave in Salme, Saaremaa. *Archaeological fieldwork in Estonia*, 2008, pp.213–222.
35. Price, T.D., Peets, J., Allmäe, R., Maldre, L. and Price, N. (2020). Human remains, context, and place of origin for the Salme, Estonia, boat burials. *Journal of Anthropological Archaeology*, 58, p.101149.
36. MacLeod, M.A. (1998). The moot question of urbanism: recent excavations at Birka. *Northern Studies*, 33, pp.11–24.
37. Kuz'mlV, S. (2000). Ladoga, le premier centre proto-urbain russe.
38. Davidan, O. (1982). Om hantverkets utveckling i Staraja Ladoga. *Fornvännen*, 77, pp.170–179.
39. Sindbæk, S. M. (2009). Open access, nodal points, and central places. *Eesti Arheoloogia Ajakiri*, 13 (2), pp.96–109.
40. Skre, D. (2014). Avaldsnes: A sea-kings seat by the Norðvegr. Lecture, University of York.
41. Leroy, I. (2024). Quentovic and after. Early medieval occupation on the banks of the Canche. Conference, Fourth Dorestad Congress.
42. Sindbæk, S. M. (2007). The Small World of the Vikings: Networks in Early Medieval Communication and Exchange. *Norwegian Archaeological Review*, 40 (1), pp.59–74.
43. LYH (1839). SCEATTAS. *The Numismatic Chronicle* (1838-1842), pp.152–160.
44. IJssennagger, N. (2017). *Central Because Liminal*. PhD, Groningen: University of Groningen.
45. Galestin, M.C. (2007). Frisii and Frisiavones. *Palaeohistoria*, pp.687–708.
46. Vinkenoog, H. (2023). *Pre-Christian Paganism in Early Medieval Frisia*. Conference, University of Oslo.
47. Siccama, S. (1730). *Lex Frisionum, sive, Antiquae Frisiorum leges*. Impensis Haered. Lanckisianorum.
48. Roxburgh, M., IJssennagger, N., Huisman, H. and Van Os, B. (2018). Where Worlds Collide. A Typological and Compositional Analysis of the Copper-Alloy Mounts from Viking-Age Walcheren. *The Medieval Low Countries*, 5, pp.1–33.
49. Vinkenoog, H. (2020). A Frisian Element in The Great Heathen Army. Undergraduate dissertation, Cambridge: University of Cambridge.

Further Reading

50. Hines, J. and IJssennagger, N. eds. (2017). *Frisians and Their North Sea Neighbours: From the Fifth Century to the Viking Age*. Boydell & Brewer.
51. Lyons, J.M. (1918). Frisian Place-Names in England. PMLA, 33(4), pp.644–655.
52. Harvey, A. (2023a). *Sceattas and Saltmarshes: The Role of Lindsey in 6th-Century Economies in England*. In: The Circulation of Commodities and Material Networks across Medieval Europe. 2023. University of Leeds.
53. Leahy, K. (2007). *The Anglo-Saxon Kingdom of Lindsey*. Stroud: Tempus.
54. Libby, K. (2022). Early Medieval Copper Alloy Dress Accessories in the Kingdom of Lindsey. PhD Thesis, Sheffield: University of Sheffield.
55. Jarvis, E. (1850). Account of the discovery of ornaments and remains, supposed to be of Danish origin, in the parish of Caenby, Lincolnshire. *Archaeological Journal*, 7(1), pp.36–44.
56. Hill, D. (2000). Offa's Dyke: pattern and purpose. *The Antiquaries Journal*, 80(1), pp.195–206.
57. Whitehead, A. (2018). *Mercia: the Rise and Fall of a Kingdom*. Amberley Publishing.
58. Becher, M. (2003). *Charlemagne*. Yale University Press.
59. Story, J. ed. (2005). *Charlemagne: Empire and Society*. Manchester University Press.
60. Mayr-Harting, H. (1996). Charlemagne, the Saxons, and the Imperial Coronation of 800. *The English Historical Review*, 111(444), pp.1113–1133.
61. (1954). *Alcuin's Life of St. Willibrord*. C. H. Talbot.
62. Hen, Y. (2006). Charlemagne's Jihad. *Viator*, 37, pp.33–51.
63. Flierman, R. (2016). Religious Saxons: paganism, infidelity and biblical punishment in the Capitulatio de partibus Saxoniae. In *Religious Franks* (pp. 181–201). Manchester University Press.
64. Nicolle, D. (2014). *The Conquest of Saxony AD 782-785: Charlemagne's Defeat of Widukind of Westphalia*. Bloomsbury Publishing.
65. Greeley, J.A. (2020). *After the Horror: Traumatic Loss and the Search for Meaning in Alcuin of York's Writings about Lindisfarne and Northumbria*. In: R. G. Sullivan & M. Pages (Eds.), *Art and violence in the Middle Ages and the Renaissance* (pp. 149–171). Cambridge Scholars Publishing.
66. Rozier, C.C. (2020). *Writing History in the Community of St Cuthbert, C. 700-1130: From Bede to Symeon of Durham* (Vol. 7). Boydell & Brewer.
67. Larrington, C. (2017). Weird, remote, monstrous: Our historical relationship with the Vikings. TLS. *Times Literary Supplement*, (5977), pp.28–29.
68. Nelson, J.L. (2013). *The Annals of St-Bertin: Ninth-Century Histories, Volume I*. Manchester University Press.
69. Ashby, S.P. and Leonard, A. (2018). *Pocket Museum: Vikings*. Thames and Hudson.
70. Sauvage, R. and Mokkelbost, M. (2016). Rural buildings from the Viking and early Medieval Period in central Norway. In: Iversen, F. and Petersson, H. (Eds). *The Agrarian Life of The North 2000 BC-AD 1000; Studies in Rural Settlement and farming in Norway*. Portal, pp.275–292.

71. Øye, I. (2009). Settlement patterns and field systems in medieval Norway. *Landscape History*, 30 (2), pp.37–54.
72. Myhre, B. (1973). Iron Age Farms in South-Western Norway. *Norwegian Archaeological Review*, 6 (1), pp.14–19.
73. Myhre, B. (1974). Iron age farms in Southwest Norway: the development of the agrarian landscape on Jæren. *Norwegian Archaeological Review*, 7 (1), pp.39–40.
74. Myhre, B. (1980). Gårdsanlegget på Ullandhaug: gårdshus i jernalder og tidlig middelalder i Sørvest-Norge = Die eisenzeitliche Siedlung auf dem Ullandhaug: die Häuser der eisenzeitlichen und frühmittelalterlichen Höfe in Südwestnorwegen, AmS-skrifter 4. Stavanger: Arkeologisk museum i Stavanger.
75. Myhre, B. (1982). Settlements of Southwest Norway during the Roman and Migration periods. *Offa*, 39, pp.197–215.
76. Myhre, B. (2000). The Early Viking Age in Norway. *Acta Archaeologica*, 71 (1), pp.35–47.
77. Stylegar, F. A. and Grimm, O. (2005) Boathouses in Northern Europe and the North Atlantic. *International Journal of Nautical Archaeology*, 34 (2) pg. 257
78. Eriksen, M. H. (Ed). (2015). *Viking Worlds: Things, Spaces and Movement*. Oxford: Oxbow Books.
79. Eriksen, M. (2019). *Architecture, Society, and Ritual in Viking Age Scandinavia. Doors, Dwellings, and Domestic Space*. Cambridge University Press.
80. Curle, Alex. O. (1935). The Excavations at Jarlshof, Sumburgh, Shetland. *The Antiquaries Journal*, 15 (1), pp.26–29.
81. Clark, J. G. D. (1958). Excavations at Jarlshof, Shetland. By J. R. C. Hamilton. Ministry of Works Archaeological Reports, No. 1, pp. 228, figs. 91, pl. XL, folding plan. H.M. Stationery Office, Edinburgh, 1956. Price £3 3 s. *Proceedings of the Prehistoric Society*, 23, pp.240–241.
82. Baxter, K. (2014). Jarlshof Lost and Found: Low-altitude aerial photography and computer-generated visualisation for the interpretation of the complex settlement remains found at Jarlshof, Shetland. *Internet Archaeology*, (36).
83. Dockrill, S. et al. (2019). The Pictish Village and Viking Settlement. Excavations at Old Scatness, *Shetland*, 1.
84. Small, A. (1964). Excavations at Underhoull, Unst, Shetland. *Proceedings of the Society of Antiquaries of Scotland*, pp.225–248.
85. Small, A. (1965). A Viking longhouse in Unst, Shetland. In: Niclasen, B. (Ed). 1965. Torshavn. pp.62–70.
86. Arge, S.V. (2008). The Faroe Islands. In: *The Viking World*. Routledge. pp.579-587.
87. Griffiths, D. (2019). Rethinking the Early Viking Age in the West. *Antiquity*, 93 (368), pp.468–477.
88. Graham-Campbell, J. (2019). *Vikings in Scotland: An Archaeological Survey*. Edinburgh University Press.
89. MacLean, D.W. (2017). *Portmahomack: Monastery of the Picts*. by Martin Carver.

Further Reading

90. Fraser, J.E. (2009). From Caledonia to Pictland: Scotland to 795, *New Edinburgh History of Scotland*, 1. Edinburgh: Edinburgh University Press
91. Mackenzie, H. (2019). *Essay on the Life and Institutions of Offa, King of Mercia, AD 755-794*. Good Press.
92. Harvey, A. An Isle Of Britons, Frisians, & Scandinavians In North Lincolnshire. In: *Early Medieval Britain: Continuity & Change*. 2023. University of Lancaster.
93. Petts, D. (2013). Expanding the Archaeology of Holy Island (Lindisfarne). *Medieval Archaeology*, 57, pp.302–307.
94. Casswell, C., Petts, D., Wilkins, B., Jago, I., Ungemach, J. and Hogue, J. (2018). Lindisfarne: The Holy Island Archaeology Project. Assessment Report and Updated Project Design, DigVentures.

Storm

1. Denninghaus, F.N. (2019). Arrangement of space inside Ölandic ringforts. A comparative study of the spatial division within the ringforts Eketorp, Sandby, and Ismantorp. (Master Thesis in Archaeology, Lund University.)
2. Ilves, K. (2022). Approaching the complexity of Late Iron Age hillforts through their landscape setting: The case of the Åland Islands. In: *Fortifications in their Natural and Cultural Landscape: From Organising Space to the Creation of Power* (pp. 213–230). Zentrums für Baltische und Skandinavische Archäologie: Schriften des Museums Für Arcäologie Schloss Gottorf.
3. Holck, P. (2006). The Oseberg ship burial, Norway: new thoughts on the skeletons from the grave mound. *European Journal of Archaeology*, 9(2-3), pp.185–210.
4. Bonde, N. and Christensen, A.E. (1993). Dendrochronological dating of the Viking Age ship burials at Oseberg, Gokstad and Tune, Norway. *Antiquity*, 67(256), pp.575–583.
5. Frei, K.M., Mannering, U., Price, T.D. and Iversen, R.B. (2015). Strontium isotope investigations of the Haraldskær Woman – a complex record of various tissues. *ArcheoSciences*, 39, pp.93–101.
6. Hjardar, K. and Vike, V. (2016). *Vikings at War*. Casemate.
7. Tweddle, D. (1983). The Coppergate Helmet. *Fornvännen*, 78, pp.105–112.
8. Wester, K. (2000). The mystery of the missing Viking helmets. *Neurosurgery*, 47(5), pp.1216–1229.
9. Williams, T. (2012) *Viking Warfare*. By IP Stephenson. Amberley. Stroud,
10. *Chronicon Namnetense*.
11. Montgomery, J.E. (2008). Arabic sources on the Vikings. In *The Viking World* (pp.574–585). Routledge.
12. Lewis, S.M. (2021). Vikings in Aquitaine and their connections, ninth to early eleventh centuries (Doctoral dissertation, Normandie Université.)
13. Supéry, J. (2021). First Mentions of the Vikings in the West. SL Critical Study, 1. University of Bordeaux.

14. Supéry, J. (2020). *The Vikings in Aquitaine, A Missing Piece of the Invasions.* Tuskaland editions.
15. *The Mozarabic Chronicle.*
16. Dance, R. (2008). Beowulf and Lejre, *Medieval and Renaissance Texts and Studies 323.*
17. Thurborg, M. (1988). Regional economic structures: An analysis of the Viking Age silver hoards from Öland, Sweden. *World Archaeology*, 20(2), pp.302–324.
18. Adamczyk, D. (2018). How and Why Did Dirhams Flow to Scandinavia during the 9th Century? *Quaestiones Medii Aevi Novae,* (23), pp.139–151.
19. Jeanneau, C. (2015). *Les moines de Saint-Philibert de Noirmoutier et les invasions scandinaves.*
20. Scholz, B.W. and Rogers, B. eds. (1970). *Carolingian Chronicles: Royal Frankish Annals and Nithard's Histories* (Vol. 186). University of Michigan Press.
21. *Royal Frankish Annals.*
22. Hill, D. (2020). Offa's and Wat's Dykes. *Offa's Dyke Journal*, 2, pp.141–159.
23. Reuter, T. (2013a). The text – The Annals of Fulda. In: *The Annals of Fulda* (pp. 15–142). Manchester University Press.
24. Reuter, T. (2013b). The Annals of Fulda: Ninth-century histories, volume II. In: *The Annals of Fulda.* Manchester University Press.
25. Halsall, P. (1996). The Annals of Xanten. Internet Sourcebook Project. New York: Fordham University.
26. *Annales Vedastini.*
27. *Codex Vigilanus.*
28. *Chronicom Sebastiani.*
29. Ibn Abd-el-Hakem: *The Islamic Conquest of Spain.*
30. *al-Muṭrib min Ash'ār Ahl al-Maghrib.*
31. Stefansson, J. (1908). The Vikings in Spain: From Arabic (Moorish) And Spanish Sources. *Saga-Book*, 6, 31–46.
32. Coupland, S. (1998). From poachers to gamekeepers: Scandinavian warlords and Carolingian kings. *Early Medieval Europe*, 7(1), pp.85–114.
33. Zaroff, R. (2003). Study into Socio-political History of the Obodrites. *Collegium Medievale*, 16, pp.5–36.
34. Bouchard, C.B. (2017). The divine king behind the funny stories of Notker the Stammerer. In *Emotions, Communities, and Difference in Medieval Europe* (pp. 194–204). Routledge.
35. Adams, M. (2018). *Aelfred's Britain: War and Peace in the Viking Age.* London: Head of Zeus.
36. Mitchell, J. (2021). Abul-Abbas and All That: Visual Dynamics between the Caliphate, Italy and the West in the Age of Charlemagne. In *Transmissions and Translations in Medieval Literary and Material Culture* (pp. 186–219). Brill.
37. Christie, E.J. (2014). The idea of an elephant: Ælfric of Eynsham, epistemology, and the absent animals of Anglo-Saxon England. *Neophilologus*, 98, pp.465–479.

Further Reading

38. McKinnell, J. (2005). Hávamál B. *Saga-Book*, 29, pp.83–114.
39. Yi, A.T. (2019). A Fresh Look at Codex Regius (L019) and Its Transcription in the IGNTP Edition of John. In: TC: *A Journal of Textual Criticism*, 24, pp.1–12.
40. Skre, D. ed. (2007). Kaupang in Skiringssal: Excavation and Surveys at Kaupang and Huseby, 1998-2003. Background and Results (Vol. 1). Aarhus Universitetsforlag.
41. Jensen, S., Madsen, P.K. and Schiørring, O. (1983). Excavations in Ribe 1979–82. *Journal of Danish Archaeology*, 2(1), pp.156–170.
42. Feveile, C. and Jensen, S. (2000). Ribe in the 8th and 9th century: A Contribution to the Archaeological Chronology of North Western Europe. *Acta Archaeologica*, 71(1), pp.9–24.
43. Kilger, C. (2008). Kaupang from afar: aspects of the interpretation of dirham finds in northern and eastern Europe between the late 8th and early 10th centuries. In: *Skre, Dagfinn (ed.) Means of Exchange. Dealing with Silver in the Viking Age*. Kaupang Excavation Project.
44. Von Holstein, I.C., Ashby, S.P., Van Doorn, N.L., Sachs, S.M., Buckley, M., Meiri, M., Barnes, I., Brundle, A. and Collins, M.J. (2014). Searching for Scandinavians in pre-Viking Scotland: Molecular Fingerprinting of Early Medieval Combs. *Journal of Archaeological Science*, 41, pp.1–6.
45. Ashby, S.P. (2014). *A Viking Way of life*. Amberley Publishing.
46. Hilberg, V. (2008). Hedeby: an outline of its research history. *The Viking World*, pp.101–111.
47. Hilberg, V. (2023) Hedeby: new perspectives. *On the Edge of The Viking World*. York Archaeological Trust Richard Hall Symposium.
48. Schwennicke, D., Isenburg, W.K. and von Loringhoven, F.B.F. (1998). *Europäische Stammtafeln: Die deutschen Staaten* (Vol. 1). J.A. Stargardt.
49. Nicolle, D. (1997). Arms of the Umayyad era: military technology in a time of change. In *War and Society in the Eastern Mediterranean, 7th-15th Centuries*, pp. 9–100. Brill.
50. Supéry, J. (2020). The Aquitanian miracle and the navy of Eleanor. *March*, 3, p.8.
51. Amory, F. (2001). The historical worth of Rígsþula. *Alvíssmál*, 10, pp.3–20.
52. Treadgold, W. (1988). Three Byzantine provinces and the first Byzantine contacts with the Rus. *Harvard Ukrainian Studies*, 12, pp.132–144.
53. MacAirt, S. (1988). *The Annals of Inisfallen*. (Ms. Rawlinson B 503).
54. Hilberg, V. and Kalmring, S. (2014). Viking Age Hedeby and its relations with Iceland and the North Atlantic: Communication, Long-distance Trade, and Production. In: *Viking Archaeology in Iceland: Mosfell Archaeological Project* (pp. 221–245).
55. Prichard, J.C. (1849). *The Life and Times of Hincmar, Archbishop of Rheims*.
56. Winroth, A. (2012). *The Conversion of Scandinavia*. Yale University Press.
57. Sawyer, B. (1993). *Medieval Scandinavia: From Conversion to Reformation, circa 800-1500*. U of Minnesota Press.
58. Feveile, C. (2012). Ribe: Emporia and Town in the 8th and 9th Century. *From one sea to another. Trading places in the European and Mediterranean*

Early Middle Ages: Proceedings of the International Conference, Comacchio 27th-29th March 2009 (pp. 111–122).
59. Oliver, N. (2018). *The Story of the British Isles in 100 Places*. Random House.
60. Barrett, J., Beukens, R., Simpson, I., Ashmore, P., Poaps, S. and Huntley, J. (2000). What was the Viking Age and when did it happen? A view from Orkney. *Norwegian archaeological review*, 33(1), p.1.
61. Goodacre, S., Helgason, A., Nicholson, J., Southam, L., Ferguson, L., Hickey, E., Vega, E., Stefánsson, K., Ward, R. and Sykes, B. (2005). Genetic evidence for a family-based Scandinavian settlement of Shetland and Orkney during the Viking periods. *Heredity*, 95(2), pp.129–135.
62. Macniven, A. (2021). *Vikings in Islay: The Place of Names in Hebridean Settlement History*. Birlinn Ltd.
63. Macniven, A. (2013). Modelling Viking Migration to the Inner Hebrides. *Journal of the North Atlantic*, 2013(sp4), pp.3–18.
64. Sharples, N., Ingrem, C., Marshall, P., Mulville, J., Powell, A. and Reed, K. (2015). The Viking occupation of the Hebrides: evidence from the excavations at Bornais, South Uist. In: *Maritime Societies of the Viking and Medieval World*, pp.237–258.
65. Ritchie, A., Noddle, B., Bramwell, D., Wheeler, A., Evans, J.G., Spencer, P., Smith, J.H., Jackson, K.H., Collins, G.H. and Fanning, T. (1979), Excavation of Pictish and Viking-age farmsteads at Buckquoy, Orkney. In: *Proceedings of the Society of Antiquaries of Scotland* (Vol. 108, pp. 174–227).

Shadow

1. Lund, N. (1989). Allies of God or man? The Viking expansion in a European perspective. *Viator*, 20, pp.45–60.
2. Renaud, J. (2008). The Duchy of Normandy. In: *The Viking World*, pp.453–457.
3. Gierszewska, M. (2010). Topography changes from the Middle Ages to the Present in the Area of the Palatium of Ingelheim (Doctoral dissertation, University of Salzburg).
4. Melnikova, E. 92011). How Christian Were Viking Christians? *Ruthenica*, Suppl, 4, pp.90–107.
5. Trinks, I., Neubauer, W. and Hinterleitner, A. (2014). First high-resolution GPR and magnetic archaeological prospection at the Viking Age settlement of Birka in Sweden. *Archaeological Prospection*, 21(3), pp.185–199.
6. Kalmring, S., (2012). The Birka proto-town GIS, a source for comprehensive studies of Björkö. *Fornvännen*, 107(4), pp.253–265.
7. Lambecius, P. (1652). Vita S. Anscharii primi archiepiscopi Hamburgensis conscripta a S. Remberto ejus successore, in *Origines Hamburgenses*, Hamburg, 167-240
8. Mhaonaigh, M. (1996). Cogad Gáedel re Gallaib and the annals: a comparison, *Ériu* 47.
9. Gerald of Wales. *The History and Topography of Ireland (Topographia Hiberniae)*. Penguin Classics 1982.

Further Reading

10. Connellan, O. (1846) *The Annals of Ireland, translated from the original Irish of the Four Masters* [Annals from 1171 to 1616]. Dublin.
11. O'Halloran, C. (2007). The Triumph of 'Virtuous Liberty': Representations of the Vikings and Brian Boru in Eighteenth-Century Histories. *Eighteenth-Century Ireland/Iris a dá chultúr*, pp.151–163.
12. Stewart, J. (1970). The Death of Turgesius. *Saga-Book*, 18, pp.47–58.
13. Hadley, D. and Richards, J.D. (2018). In search of the Viking Great Army: Beyond the winter camps. *Medieval Settlement Research*, pp.1–17.
14. Dawn, H. and Julian, R. (2021). *The Viking Great Army and the Making of England*. Thames & Hudson.
15. *Vita Sancti Liudgeri*.
16. Van Es, W.A. and Verwers, W.J.H. (1980). Excavations at Dorestad 1. *The Harbour: Hoogstraat*, 1.
17. Coupland, S. (2010). Boom and Bust at 9th-century Dorestad. In: *Dorestad in an International Framework*, pp. 95–103.
18. Coupland, S. (1988). Dorestad in the ninth century: the numismatic evidence. *Jaarboek voor munt-en penningkunde*, 75, pp.5–26.
19. Cooijmans, C. (2015). The Controlled Decline of Viking-Ruled Dorestad. *Northern Studies*, 47, pp.32–46.
20. Coupland, S. (2007). *Carolingian Coinage and the Vikings. Studies on Power and Trade in the 9th Century*. Ashgate: Variorum Collected Studies.
21. Besteman, J. (1997). *Vikings in North Holland?* North-Holland.
22. Besteman, J. (2004). *Land, Sea and Home: Settlement in the Viking Period*: proceedings of a conference on Viking-period settlement at Cardiff, July 2001. Leeds: W.S. Marley & Son Ltd.
23. Downham, C. (2008). Vikings in England. In: *The Viking World* (pp. 365–373). Routledge.
24. William of Jumièges. *Gesta Normannorum Ducum (Deeds of the Norman Dukes)*
25. Hadley, D.M. and Richards, J.D. (2016). The winter camp of the Viking Great Army, AD 872-3, Torksey, Lincolnshire. *The Antiquaries Journal*, 96, pp.23–67.
26. Richards, J.D. (2020). Gareth Williams (ed.), A Riverine Site Near York: A Possible Viking Camp? *Northern History*.
27. Lewis, S. (2016). Rodulf and Ubba. In Search of a Frisian–Danish Viking. *Saga-Book*, 40, pp.5–42.
28. Forester, T. ed. (1853). *The Chronicle of Henry of Huntingdon: Comprising the History of England, from the Invasion of Julius Cæsar to the Accession of Henry II. Also, The Acts of Stephen, King of England and Duke of Normandy*. H.G. Bohn.
29. Waggoner, B. (2009). *The Sagas of Ragnar Lodbrok*.
30. Murphy, L.J., Fuller, H.R., Willan, P.L. and Gates, M.A. (2022). An Anatomy of the Blood Eagle: The Practicalities of Viking Torture. *Speculum*, 97(1), pp.1–39.
31. Loveluck, C.P. (2001). Wealth, Waste and Conspicuous Consumption. In: *Image and Power in the Archaeology of Early Medieval Britain*, Oxford: Oxbow, pp.79–130.

32. Loveluck, C.P. (1998). A high-status Anglo-Saxon settlement at Flixborough, Lincolnshire. *Antiquity*, 72(275), pp.146–161.
33. Tipper, J., (2008). Secular and ecclesiastic dynamics at Anglo-Saxon Flixborough. In: *The early medieval settlement remains from Flixborough, Lincolnshire: the occupation sequence, c. AD 600-1000* (Excavations at Flixborough Volume 1).
34. Atkinson, D. (2007). *The early medieval settlement remains from Flixborough, Lincolnshire: the occupation sequence, c. AD 600-1000*. Historic England.
35. Walton, P. (1989). *Textiles, cordage and raw fibre from 16-22 Coppergate* (Vol. 17). York Archaeological Trust.
36. Ottaway, P. (1989). Anglo-Scandinavian Ironwork from 16-22 Coppergate, York: C. 850-1100 AD (Doctoral dissertation, University of York).
37. Spall, C.A. and Toop, N.J. (2008). Before Eoforwic: new light on York in the 6th–7th centuries. *Medieval Archaeology*, 52(1), pp.1–25.
38. Mainman, A. (2019). *Anglian York*. Blackthorn Press.
39. Kershaw, J., Jarman, C., Weber, H. and Horton, M. (2022) The Viking Great Army North of the Tyne: A Viking camp in Northumberland. In *Viking Camps* (pp.96–116). Routledge.
40. Lavelle, R. and Roffey, S. (2020) West Saxons and Danes: Negotiating Early Medieval Identities. In: *Danes in Wessex: The Scandinavian Impact on Southern England*, c. 800-1100, eds. Ryan Lavelle and Simon Roffey. Oxford: Oxbow Books. 7-34.
41. Liebermann, F. (2013) *The National Assembly in the Anglo-Saxon Period*. Tübingen: M. Niemeyer,
42. Coupland, S. (1999). The Frankish tribute payments to the Vikings and their consequences. *Francia*, 26(1), pp.57–76.
43. Coupland, S. (1991). The fortified bridges of Charles the Bald. *Journal of medieval history*, 17(1), pp.1–12.
44. Suzuki, S. (2013). *The meters of Old Norse eddic poetry: Common Germanic inheritance and North Germanic innovation* (Vol. 86). Walter de Gruyter.
45. Asser, J. (1983). *Alfred the Great: Asser's Life of King Alfred and other contemporary sources*. Penguin UK.
46. Bremmer, R.H. (2012). Grendel's Arm and the Law. In: *Studies in English Language and Literature* (pp.121–132). Routledge.
47. Higham, N.J. (2005). *King Arthur: Myth-making and History*. Routledge.
48. Sturlason, S. (2011). *Heimskringla, The Norse King Sagas*. Read Books Ltd.
49. Fulk, R.D. (2012a). Þorbjǫrn hornklofi, Haraldskvæði (Hrafnsmál). *Skaldic Poetry of the Scandinavian Middle Ages*, 1, pp.91–91.
50. Fulk, R.D. (2012b). Anonymous Poems, Eiríksmál. *Skaldic Poetry of the Scandinavian Middle Ages*, 1, pp.1003–1004.
51. Poole, R. (2012). Tindr Hallkelsson, Hákonardrápa. *Skaldic Poetry of the Scandinavian Middle Ages*, 1, pp.336–336.
52. Fulk, R.D. (2012c). Eyvindr skáldaspillir Finnsson, Hákonarmál. *Skaldic Poetry of the Scandinavian Middle Ages*, 1, pp.171–171.

Further Reading

53. Byock, JL (2004). Social Memory and the Sagas: The Case of 'Egils saga'. *Scandinavian Studies*, 76 (3), pp.299–316.
54. Winterbottom, M. (1995). The *Gesta Regum* of William of Malmesbury. *The Journal of Medieval Latin*, 5, pp.158–173.
55. Skånland, V. (1966). The year of King Harald Fairhair's access to the throne according to Theodoricus monachus. *Symbolae Osloenses*, 41(1), pp.125–128.
56. Lincoln, B. (2019). *Between History and Myth: Stories of Harald Fairhair and the Founding of the State*. University of Chicago Press.
57. Kjartansson, H.S. (2006). English Models for King Harald Fairhair? In: Thirteenth International Saga Conference.
58. Halsall, G. (2013). *Worlds of Arthur: Facts and Fictions of the Dark Ages*. OUP Oxford.
59. Hadley, D., Groothedde, M. and Fermin, B. (2020). *The Viking Great Army moves on: new evidence*. Newsletter of the Society for Medieval Archaeology, (63): 3.
60. Price, N. (2020). *The Children of Ash and Elm: A History of the Vikings*. Penguin UK.
61. Wormald, P. (2013). *On pa wæpnedhealfe: kingship and royal property from Æthelwulf to Edward the Elder*. In: Edward the Elder (pp.264–279). Routledge.
62. Beresford. G. (1999). *Goltho: the development of an early medieval manor c. 850–1150*. English Heritage.
63. Hill, D. (1969). The Burghal Hidage: the establishment of a text. *Medieval Archaeology*, 13(1), pp.84–92.
64. Wallace, P. (2017) *Viking Dublin: the Wood Quay excavations*.
65. De Paor, L. (1978). Viking Dublin. *Dublin Historical Record*, 31(4), pp.142–145.
66. Little, G. (1957). *Dublin Before the Vikings*. Dublin: M. H. Gill and Son.
67. Downham, C. (2010). Viking camps in ninth-century Ireland: sources, locations and interactions. *Medieval Dublin*, 10, pp.93–125.
68. Griffith, D., Hadley, D.M. and Harkel, L.T. (2013). *Everyday life in Viking-age towns. Social approaches to towns in England and Ireland c. 800-1100*. Oxbow Books.
69. Graham-Campbell, J. (2019). *Vikings in Scotland: An Archaeological Survey*. Edinburgh University Press.
70. Townend, M. (2014). *Viking Age Yorkshire*. Blackthorn Press.
71. Downham, C. (2008). *Viking kings of Britain and Ireland: the dynasty of Ívarr to AD 1014*. Dunedin Academic Press Ltd.
72. Redknap, M. (2020). Viking-age settlement in Wales and the evidence from Llanbedrgoch. In: *Land, sea and home* (pp.139–175). Routledge.
73. Graham-Campbell, J. (2012). *The Cuerdale hoard and related Viking-Age silver and gold from Britain and Ireland in the British Museum*. British Museum Press.
74. Downham, C. (2004). The Good, the Bad, and the Ugly: Portrayals of Vikings in 'The Fragmentary Annals of Ireland'. In *The Medieval Chronicle III* (pp.27–39). Brill.

75. Graham-Campbell, J., Hall, R., Jesch, J. and Parsons, D.N. (2016). *Vikings and the Danelaw*. Oxbow books.
76. Hadley, D.M. (2002). Viking and native: rethinking identity in the Danelaw. *Early Medieval Europe*, 11(1), pp.45–70.
77. Hadley, D.M. (2000). *The Northern Danelaw: its social structure, c. 800-1100*. A&C Black.
78. Doviak, A. (2021). Doorway to Devotion: Recovering the Christian Nature of the Gosforth Cross. *Religions*, 12(4), p.228.
79. Bailey, R.N. (2000). Scandinavian myth on Viking-period stone sculpture in England. *Old Norse myths, literature and society*, 2.
80. Caples, C.B. (1976). The Man in the Snakepit and the Iconography of the Sigurd Legend. Rice Institute Pamphlet, *Rice University Studies*, 62(2).
81. Gazzoli, L. (2022). Adam of Bremen and the early (pre-995) history of Norway 1. In *Adam of Bremen's Gesta Hammaburgensis Ecclesiae Pontificum* (pp.108–120). Routledge.
82. Downham, C.E. (2004). Eric Bloodaxe-axed? The Mystery of the Last Viking King of York. *Mediaeval Scandinavia*, 14.
83. Driscoll, M. J. (1995). *Ágrip af Nóregskonungasǫgum*. Viking Society for Northern Research Text Series 10.

Journeys

1. Byock, J., (2005). *The Prose Edda*. Penguin UK.
2. Larrington, C. ed. (2014). *The Poetic Edda*. Oxford University Press, US.
3. Abram, C. (2009). Gylfaginning and early medieval conversion theory. *Saga-Book*, 33, pp.5–24.
4. Valtonen, I. (2008). The North in the 'Old English Orosius'. A Geographical Narrative in Context. *Neuphilologische Mitteilungen*, 109(3), pp.380–384.
5. Bately, J.M. (2015). The Old English Orosius. In *A Companion to Alfred the Great* (pp. 297-343). Brill.
6. Orosius, P. (2010). *The seven books of history against the pagans* (Vol. 50). CUA Press.
7. Urbańczyk, P., (2009). On the reliability of Wulfstan's report. *Wulfstan's Voyage*, pp.43–7.
8. Jagodziński, M.F. (2009). The settlement of Truso. Wulfstan's Voyage: *The Baltic Sea Region in the Early Viking Age as Seen from Shipboard*, pp.182–98.
9. Gardeła, L., Eriksen, M.H., Pedersen, U., Rundberget, B., Axelsen, I. and Berg, H.L. (2014). Vikings in Poland. A critical overview. *Viking Worlds: Things, Spaces and Movement*, pp.213–34.
10. Valk, H. (2008). The Vikings and the eastern Baltic. In: *The Viking World* (pp.509–519). Routledge.
11. Bogucki, M. (2006). Grobiņa: a sign of an early future port of trade in the Balt Lands. In: *Transformatio mundi: the transition from the late migration period to the Early Viking Age in the East Baltic*, ed Mindaugas Bertašius (pp.93–106). Kaunas University of Technology Department of Philosophy and Cultural Science.

Further Reading

12. Gunnarsson, D. (2012). The Scandinavian settlement at Grobiņa, Latvia: the connections between the settlement, the local population and Gotland. Bachelor Thesis, Gotland University.
13. Hedenstierna-Jonson, C. (2020). Entering the Viking Age through the Baltic. In: *Relations and Runes: The Baltic Islands and Their Interactions During the Late Iron Age and Early Middle Ages*. Visby: Riksantikvarieämbetet.
14. Kriiska, A. and Sikk, K. (2014). Archaeological test excavations at the Mesolithic and Iron Age settlement site Jägala-Joa IV. *Archaeological field works in Estonia*, (2013), pp.45–54.
15. Mägi, M. (2015). Bound for the eastern Baltic. Trade and centres AD 800–1200. *Maritime Societies of the Viking and Medieval World*, pp.41–61.
16. Jarockis, R. (2008). Eketė Iron Age and Early Medieval hill-fort settlement complex. Aerial archaeology and remote sensing. *Archaeologia Baltica*, 9, pp.8–14.
17. Jones, M.C. (1998). Death of a language, birth of an identity: Brittany and the Bretons. *Language Problems and language planning*, 22(2), pp.129–142.
18. Price, N.S. (1986). The Vikings in Brittany. *Saga-Book*, 22, pp.319–440.
19. Price, N. (2008). The Viking Conquest of Brittany. *The Viking World*, p.458.
20. Short, W.R. (2017) Hurstwic: The Walking Dead in the Sagas: Zombies of the Viking Age. YouTube.
21. Jakobsson, Á. (1998). History of the Trolls? Bárðar saga as an Historical Narrative. *Saga-Book*, 25, pp.53–71.
22. Hughes, SF, (2016). The Evolution of Monster Fights: From Beowulf versus Grendel to Jón Guðmundsson lærði versus the Snæfjalladraugur and Beyond. *Telling Tales and Crafting Books: Essays in Honor of Thomas H. Ohlgren*, 24, p.49.
23. Finlay, A. (1990). Níþ, adultery and feud in Bjarnar saga hítdœlakappa. *Saga-Book*, 23, pp.158–178.
24. Thoma, S. (2021). A Friend in níþ: On the Narrative Display of Gender and níþ in Njáls saga. *Characters and Texts in Old Norse-Icelandic Saga Studies*, pp.57–86.
25. Stuart, J. (1865), Notice of excavations in the chambered mound of Maeshowe, in Orkney, and of the runic inscriptions on the walls of its central chamber. In *Proceedings of the Society of Antiquaries of Scotland* (Vol. 5, pp. 247–279).
26. Berman, M.A. (1985). The political sagas. *Scandinavian Studies*, 57(2), pp.113–129.
27. Schulte, M. (2016). Raising doubt about Norway's Origin. University of Agder.
28. Indrelid, S. (1975). Problems relating to the Early Mesolithic settlement of southern Norway. *Norwegian Archaeological Review*, 8(1), pp.1–18.
29. Jakobsson, M. (1997). Burial Layout, Society and Sacred Geography, A Viking Age Example from Jämtland. *Current Swedish Archaeology*, 5(1), pp.79–98.
30. Magnell, O. and Iregren, E. (2010). Veitstu hvé blóta skal? The old Norse blót in the light of osteological remains from Frösö church, Jämtland, Sweden. *Current Swedish Archaeology*, 18(1), pp.223–250.

31. Kallio, P. (2014). The Diversification of Proto-Finnic. *Fibula, Fabula, Fact: The Viking Age in Finland*. Finnish Literature Society, pp.155–168.
32. Mundal, E. (2000), July. Coexistence of Saami and Norse culture reflected in and interpreted by Old Norse myths. In *Old Norse Myths, Literature and Society*: Proceedings of the 11th International Saga Conference (pp.346–355). Centre for Medieval Studies, University of Sydney.
33. Raninen, S. and Wessman, A. (2014). Finland as a Part of the Viking World. *Fibula, Fabula, Fact: The Viking Age in Finland*, 11. Finnish Literature Society, p.327.
34. Edgren, T. (2008). The Viking Age in Finland. *The Viking World*, pp.470–484.
35. Wickholm, A. (2008). Reuse in Finnish cremation cemeteries under level ground examples of collective memory. BAR International Series, 1768, p.89.
36. Cook, R. ed. (2001). *Njal's saga* (Vol. 6). Penguin UK.
37. Heininen, L.K., Storå, J., Frog, F. and Ahola, J. (2015). Geopolitical perspectives on Åland in the Viking Age. In *The Viking Age in Åland: Insights into Identity and Remnants of Culture* (pp.323–348). Academia Scientiarum Fennica.
38. Holmqvist, E. and Ilves, K., (2022). A compositional study of a gold-plated Viking Age pendant from the Åland Islands. *Fornvännen*, 117(1), pp.63–67.
39. Carpelan, C. (1993). Comments on Sami Viking age pastoralism, or 'the fur trade paradigm' reconsidered. *Norwegian Archaeological Review*, 26(1).
40. Baranowski, S. and Karlén, W. (1976). Remnants of Viking age tundra in Spitsbergen and northern Scandinavia. Geografiska Annaler: Series A, *Physical Geography*, 58(1-2), pp.35–40.
41. Kuusela, J.M. (2014). From coast to inland. Activity zones in North Finland during the Iron Age. *Fibula, Fabula, Fact. The Viking Age in Finland*, pp.219–241.
42. Vilkuna, J. (1984). Ancient skis of central Finland. *Fennoscandia archaeologica*, (I).
43. Weinstock, J. (2005). The role of skis and skiing in the settlement of early Scandinavia. *Northern Review*, (25/26), pp.172–196.
44. Price, T.D., Arcini, C., Gustin, I., Drenzel, L. and Kalmring, S. (2018). Isotopes and human burials at Viking Age Birka and the Mälaren region, east-central Sweden. *Journal of Anthropological Archaeology*, 49, pp.19–38.
45. DeAngelo, J. (2010). The North and the Depiction of the 'Finnar' in the Icelandic Sagas. *Scandinavian Studies*, 82(3), pp.257–286.
46. Dugmore, A.J., Church, M.J., Mairs, K.A., McGovern, T.H., Perdikaris, S. and Vésteinsson, O., (2007). Abandoned farms, volcanic impacts, and woodland management: revisiting Þjórsárdalur, the 'Pompeii of Iceland'. *Arctic Anthropology*, 44(1), pp.1–11.
47. Jónsson, B. (2015). 4 Seljaland, Vestur-Eyjafjallahreppur, Iceland. *Into the Ocean: Vikings, Irish, and Environmental Change in Iceland and the North*, 8, p.75.
48. Sveinbjarnardóttir, G. (2012). The earliest settlement of Iceland. *Norwegian Archaeological Review*, 45(2), pp.225–227.

Further Reading

49. Eriksen, S.G. (2022). Readings in Times of Crisis: New Interpretations of Stories about the Settlement of Iceland. *Scandinavian Studies*, 94(2), pp.143–173.
50. Ćirić, J. (2020). Viking Age Excavation Could Rewrite the Story of Iceland's Settlement. *Icelandic Review*.
51. Ebenesersdóttir, S.S., Sandoval-Velasco, M., Gunnarsdóttir, E.D., Jagadeesan, A., Guðmundsdóttir, V.B., Thordardóttir, E.L., Einarsdóttir, M.S., Moore, K.H., Sigurðsson, Á., Magnúsdóttir, D.N. and Jónsson, H. (2018). Ancient genomes from Iceland reveal the making of a human population. *Science*, 360(6392), pp.1028–1032.
52. Arge, S. V. et al. (2005). Viking and Medieval Settlement in the Faroes: People, Place and Environment. *Human Ecology*, 33 (5), pp.597–620.
53. Orchard, A. (Ed). (2011). *The Elder Edda: a Book of Viking Lore*, Penguin Classics. London: Penguin.
54. Bending, J. et al. (2013). Toftanes. A Viking Age Farmstead in the Faroe Islands. *Acta Archaeologica*, 84 (1), pp.8–239.
55. Hansen, S. (1988). The Norse Landnam in The Faroe Islands in The Light of Recent Excavations at Toftanes, Leirvik. *Northern Studies*, 25, pp.58–84.
56. Merkyte, I. and Hansen, S. (2013). Toftanes, a Viking Age Farmstead in the Faroe Islands: Archaeology, Environment and Economy. *Acta Archaeologica*, 84(1), pp.5–239.
57. Dahl, S. (1970). The Norse settlement of the Faroe Islands. *Medieval Archaeology*, 14(1), pp.60–73.
58. Curtin, L., D'Andrea, W.J., Balascio, N.L., Shirazi, S., Shapiro, B., de Wet, G.A., Bradley, R.S. and Bakke, J., (2021). Sedimentary DNA and molecular evidence for early human occupation of the Faroe Islands. *Communications Earth & Environment*, 2(1), p.253.
59. Buckland, P.C. (1991). Insects, man and the earliest settlement of the Faroe Islands: a case not proven. *Fróðskaparrit-Faroese Scientific Journal*, pp.107–113.
60. Arge, S. V. (2014). Viking Faroes: Settlement, Paleoeconomy, and Chronology. *Journal of the North Atlantic*, 7 (sp7), pp.1–17.
61. Brewington, S. (2011). Fourth Interim Report on Analysis of Archaeofauna from Undir Junkarinsfløtti, Sandoy, Faroe Islands. No. 56. NORSEC Zooarchaeology Laboratory Report.
62. Brown, J. L. et al. (2012). Shieling Areas: Historical Grazing Pressures and Landscape Responses in Northern Iceland. *Human Ecology*, 40 (1), pp.81–99.
63. Sveinbjarnadottir, G. (1991). Shielings In Iceland. *Acta Archaeologica*, 61, pp.73–96.
64. Lucas, G. (2008). Pálstóftir: A Viking Age Shieling in Iceland. *Norwegian Archaeological Review*, 41 (1), pp.85–100.
65. Kupiec, P. (2016). Transhumance in the North Atlantic: an interdisciplinary approach to the identification and interpretation of Viking-Age and Medieval shieling sites. PhD, University of Aberdeen.
66. Nordal, G. (2008). The Sagas of Icelanders. *The Viking World*, pp.315-318.

67. Einarsson, B. F. (2008). Blót Houses in Viking Age Farmstead Cult Practices: New Findings from South-eastern Iceland. *Acta Archaeologica*, 79 (1), pp.145–184.
68. Lucas, G. and McGovern, T. (2007). Bloody Slaughter: Ritual Decapitation and Display at the Viking settlement of Hofstaðir, Iceland. *European Journal of Archaeology*, 10(1), pp.7–30.
69. Lucas, G., Batey, C., Gudmundsson, G., Lawson, I.T., McGovern, T.H. and Simpson, I.A. (2009). Hofstaðir: Excavations of a Viking Age Feasting Hall in North Eastern Iceland. Reykjavik: Institute of Archaeology.
70. Jakobsson, Á. (2009). the Fearless Vampire Killers: a note about the Icelandic Draugr and demonic contamination in Grettis Saga. *Folklore*, 120(3), pp.307–316.
71. Fregel, R., Ordóñez, A.C. and Serrano, J.G. (2021). The demography of the Canary Islands from a genetic perspective. *Human Molecular Genetics*, 30(R1), pp.R64-R71.
72. Atoche Peña, P. and Ramírez Rodríguez, M.Á. (2017). C14 references and cultural sequence in the Proto-history of Lanzarote. University of Las Palmas Research Group.
73. Healy, J.F. (1999). *Pliny the Elder on Science and Technology*. Clarendon Press.
74. Smith, G.M. (1914). Herrick's Hesperides. *The Modern Language Review*, 9, p.373.
75. de Galindo, J.D.A. and Glass, G. (1767). *The history of the discovery and conquest of the Canary Islands*. Facsimile Elibron Classics 2005.
76. Jones, E.P., Eager, H.M., Gabriel, S.I., Jóhannesdóttir, F. and Searle, J.B. (2013). Genetic tracking of mice and other bioproxies to infer human history. *Trends in Genetics*, 29(5), pp.298–308.
77. Rando, J.C., Pieper, H. and Alcover, J.A. (2014). Radiocarbon evidence for the presence of mice on Madeira Island (North Atlantic) one millennium ago. Proceedings of the Royal Society B: *Biological Sciences*, 281(1780), p.20133126.
78. Plutarch, B.Y. (2018). *Parallel lives*. Endymion Press.
79. Byock, J. (2017). *Viking Language 1: Learn Old Norse, Runes, and Icelandic Sagas*. Jules William Press.
80. Christie, J.B. (1969). Reflections on the Legend of Wayland the Smith. *Folklore*, 80(4), pp.286–294.
81. Jørgensen, L., Pestell, T. and Ulmschneider, K. (2003). Manor and Market at Lake Tissø in the Sixth to Eleventh Centuries: The Danish 'Productive Sites'. *Markets in Early Medieval Europe: Trading and Productive Sites*. Macclesfield: Windgather, pp.175–207.
82. Henriksen, P.S. and Holst, S. (2014). First evidence of lime burning in southern Scandinavia: lime kilns found at the royal residence on the west bank of Lake Tissø. *Danish Journal of Archaeology*, 3(2), pp.119–128.
83. Skre, D. (2014). Avaldsnes: a sea-kings' seat by the Norðvegr. Lecture, University of York.
84. Christensen, T. (1991). Lejre beyond legend, the archaeological evidence. *Journal of Danish Archaeology*, 10(1), pp.163–185.

Further Reading

85. Munch, G.S., Johansen, O.S. and Roesdahl, E. eds. (2003). *Borg in Lofoten: A Chieftain's Farm in North Norway* (Vol. 1). Trondheim: Tapir Academic Press.
86. Henriksson, G. (2003). The pagan Great Midwinter Sacrifice and the 'royal' mounds at Gamla Uppsala. Calendars, Symbols, and Orientations: Legacies of Astronomy in Culture. Uppsala: Uppsala Astronomical Observatory Report (59).
87. Ljungkvist, J. and Frölund, P. (2015). Gamla Uppsala: the emergence of a centre and a magnate complex. *Journal of Archaeology and Ancient History* (JAAH), (16), pp.1–29.
88. Coghill, E. (2020). How the West Was Won: Unearthing the Umayyad history of the conquest of the Maghrib. *The Umayyad World*. Ed Andrew Marsham. London and New York: Routledge, pp.539–70.
89. Cachia, P. (2017). *A History of Islamic Spain*. Routledge.
90. Peterson, D. (2020). Quintana place names as evidence of the Islamic conquest of Iberia. *Journal of Medieval Iberian Studies*, 12(2), pp.155–176.
91. Headworth, H.G. (2004). Early Arab water technology in southern Spain. *Water and Environment Journal*, 18(3), pp.161–165.
92. Shinakov, E.A. and Fedosov, A.V. (2022). The Geopolitical Context of the Rus' Raid on Seville. *Vestnik of Saint Petersburg University. History*, vol. 67, issue 1, pp.5–22.
93. Stefánsson, J. (1908). The Vikings in Spain from Arabic (Moorish) and Spanish Sources. *Saga-Book*. London: Viking Society for Northern Research. 6: 32–46.
94. Price, N. (2008) The Vikings in Spain, North Africa, and The Mediterranean. In: *The Viking World*. Routledge.
95. James, D. (1978). Two medieval Arabic accounts of Ireland. *The Journal of the Royal Society of Antiquaries of Ireland*, 108, pp.5–9.
96. Niebrzydowski, S. (2001). The Sultana and her sisters: Black women in the British Isles before 1530. *Women's History Review*, 10(2), pp.187–210.
97. Rowland, J. (1990). *Early Welsh Saga Poetry: A Study and Edition of the 'Englynion'*. Brewer, pp.457–61.
98. Redknap, M. (2007). St Davids and a new link with the Hiberno-Norse world. In: *St David of Wales: Cult, Church and Nation*, Wyn Evans, J. and Wooding, J.M. pp.84–9.
99. *Chronicon Iriense*.
100. *Chronicon Sampiri*.
101. Garcia Losquiño, I. (2022). Viking Mercenary Activity in Galicia. *Journal of Medieval Iberian Studies*, 14(3), pp.357–370.
102. _____ (2019). Camps and Early Settlement in the Viking Diaspora: England, Ireland and the Case of Galicia. *Revista de Cultures Medievals*, 13, pp.37–55.
103. _____ (2023). The Viking Camps of Medieval Iberia. In: *Viking Camps* (pp. 189–205). Routledge.
104. *Chronicle of Alfonso III*.
105. Alatas, S.F. (2013). *Ibn Khaldun*.

106. Montgomery Ramírez, P.E. (2021). Colonial representations of race in alternative museums: The 'African' of St Benet's, the 'Arab' of Jorvik, and the 'Black Viking'. *International Journal of Heritage Studies*, 27(9), pp.937–952.
107. Savage, E. (1992). Berbers and Blacks: Ibāḍī slave traffic in eighth-century North Africa. *The Journal of African History*, 33(3), pp.351–368.
108. Parker, P. (2015). *The Northmen's Fury: A History of the Viking World.* Random House.
109. Smith, C.D., Gadd, D., Mills, N. and Ward-Perkins, B. (1986). Luni and the Ager Lunensis: the rise and fall of a Roman town and its territory. *Papers of the British School at Rome*, 54, pp.81–146.
110. Ward-Perkins, B. (1981). Two Byzantine houses at Luni. *Papers of the British School at Rome*, 49, pp.91–98.
111. Coates-Stephens, R. (1996). Housing in early medieval Rome, 500–1000 AD. *Papers of the British School at Rome*, 64, pp.239–259.
112. Dey, H.W. (2008). Diaconiae, xenodochia, hospitalia and monasteries: 'social security' and the meaning of monasticism in early medieval Rome. *Early Medieval Europe*, 16(4), pp.398–422.
113. Romano, J.F. (2016). *Liturgy and Society in Early Medieval Rome.* Routledge.
114. Alberti, A. (2022). Pisa in the Early Medieval Period. In: *A Companion to Medieval Pisa* (pp.81–106). Brill.
115. Cannada, K.V. (2006). *Etruscan Fiesole.* Honors Thesis, University of Mississippi.
116. Mas Florit, C. and Cau, M.Á. (2013). Christians, peasants and shepherds: the transformation of the countryside in Late Antique Mallorca (Balearic islands). *Antiquité Tardive*, 21, pp.217–232.
117. Cau Ontiveros, M.A., Riera Rullan, M. and Salas i Burguera, M. (2012). The early Christian complex of Son Pereto (Mallorca, Balearic Islands): excavations in the West Sector (2005-2008). pp.231–243.
118. Harland, J. (2023). Between Toledo, Carthage, and Constantinople: The Balearics in the Later 6th Century. In: *Ecclesiastical Networks and Actors: Linking Late Antique and Early Medieval Lifeworlds.* 2023. Leeds.
119. Hoskin, M. (1985). The Talayotic culture of Menorca: A first reconnaissance. *Journal for the History of Astronomy*, 16(9), pp.S133–S151.
120. Herben, S.J. (1939). The Ruin. *Modern Language Notes*, 54(1), pp.37–39.
121. Gabriel, S.I., Mathias, M.L. and Searle, J.B. (2015). Of mice and the 'Age of Discovery': the complex history of colonization of the Azorean archipelago by the house mouse (Mus musculus) as revealed by mitochondrial DNA variation. *Journal of Evolutionary Biology*, 28(1), pp.130–145.
122. Price, M. (2021). Vikings in Paradise: Did the Norse settle the Azores? NCBI, US.
123. Szabo, V.E. (2008). *Monstrous Fishes and the Mead-dark sea: Whaling in the Medieval North Atlantic.* Brill.
124. Bill, J. and Klæsøe, I.S. (2010). Viking Age ships and seafaring in the West. *Viking Trade and Settlement in Continental Western Europe*, pp.19–42.

Further Reading

125. Christensen, A.E. (1982). Viking age ships and shipbuilding. *Norwegian Archaeological Review*, 15(1), pp.19–28.
126. Batchelor, C. L. et al. (2019). Submarine Moraines in Southeast Greenland Fjords Reveal Contrasting Outlet-Glacier Behavior since the Last Glacial Maximum. *Geophysical Research Letters*, 46 (6), pp.3279–3286.
127. Crowley, T.J. and Lowery, T.S. (2000). How warm was the medieval warm period? AMBIO: *A Journal of the Human Environment*, 29(1), pp.51–54.
128. Hines, J. (2014). *Hrafnagaldur Óðins (Forspjallsljóð)*. Medium Aevum, 83(2), p.365.
129. Johansen, O. (1982). Viking Age farms: Estimating the number and population size. A case study from Vestvågøy, North Norway. *Norwegian Archaeological Review*, 15 (1), pp.45–69.
130. Madsen, C. (2014). Pastoral Settlement, Farming, and Hierarchy in Norse Vatnahverfi, South Greenland. Unpublished PhD Thesis, Denmark: University of Copenhagen.
131. Madsen, C. K. (2019). Marine Shielings in Medieval Norse Greenland. *Arctic Anthropology*, 56 (1), pp.119–159.
132. Park, R.W. (2008). Contact between the Norse Vikings and the Dorset culture in Arctic Canada. *Antiquity*, 82(315), pp.189–198.
133. Park, R.W. (2005). Growing up North: Exploring the Archaeology of Childhood in the Thule and Dorset cultures of Arctic Canada. *Archaeological Papers of the American Anthropological Association*, 15(1), pp.53–64.
134. Nørlund, P. and Roussell, A. (1929). Norse Ruins at Gardar: The Episcopal Seat of Mediaeval Greenland. *Meddelelser om Grønland*, 76, pp.1–170.
135. Buckland, P. C. et al. (2009). Palaeoecological and historical evidence for manuring and irrigation at Garðar (Igaliku), Norse Eastern Settlement, Greenland. *The Holocene*, 19 (1), pp.105–116.
136. Hayeur-Smith, M., Arneborg, J. and Smith, K. P. (2015). The 'Burgundian' hat from Herjolfsnes, Greenland: new discoveries, new dates. *Danish Journal of Archaeology*, 4 (1), pp.21–32.
137. Arneborg, J. (2006). *Saga Trails: Brattahlið, Garðar, Hvalsey Fjord's Church and Herjolfsnes: four chieftain's farmsteads in the Norse settlements of Greenland.* The National Museum of Denmark.
138. Christensen C.S. (2020) *The Vikings and their importance for the North Atlantic (Iceland, Greenland, North America) from the beginning of the expansion in the 9th century until the extinction around 1400.* Studia Humanitatis.
139. Edwards, K. et al. (2016). Towards a First Chronology for the Middle Settlement of Norse Greenland: 14C and Related Studies of Animal Bone and Environmental Material. *Radiocarbon*, 55 (1), pp.13–29.
140. Dugmore, A.J., McGovern, T.H., Vésteinsson, O., Arneborg, J., Streeter, R. and Keller, C. (2012). Cultural adaptation, compounding vulnerabilities and conjunctures in Norse Greenland. *Proceedings of the National Academy of Sciences,* 109(10), pp.3658–3663.

141. Edwards, K.J. and Schofield, J.E. (2013). Investigation of proposed Norse irrigation channels and dams at Garðar/Igaliku, Greenland. *Water History*, 5 (1), pp.71–92.
142. Berglund, J. (2001). Omkring dagliglivet på Gården under Sandet. Tidsskr. *Grønl*, 7(267), p.e278.
143. Dugmore, A.J., Church, M.J., Mairs, K.A., McGovern, T.H., Perdikaris, S. and Vésteinsson, O. (2007). Abandoned farms, volcanic impacts, and woodland management: revisiting Þjórsárdalur, the 'Pompeii of Iceland'. *Arctic Anthropology*, 44(1), pp.1–11.
144. Watkins, A. (2014). *Aelfric's Colloquy.*
145. Loveluck, C.P. (2001). Wealth, waste and conspicuous consumption. Flixborough and its importance for Middle and Late Saxon rural settlement studies. In: *Image and Power in the Archaeology of Early Medieval Britain*, Oxford: Oxbow, pp.79–130.
146. Hennius, A., Ljungkvist, J., Ashby, S.P. et al. (2022) Late Iron Age Whaling in Scandinavia. *Journal of Maritime Archaeology*. 18, pp.1–22.
147. Sutherland, P. D., Thompson, P. H. and Hunt, P. A. (2014). Evidence of Early Metalworking in Arctic Canada. *Geoarchaeology*, 30 (1), pp.74–78.
148. Schledermann, P. (1979). Norse artefacts on Ellesmere Island. *Polar Record*, 19(122), pp.493–494.
149. Hansen, K. (2008). *Nuussuarmiut* (Vol. 345): Hunting families on the big headland (p. 239). Museum Tusculanum Press.
150. Sandberg, N. (2017). Offerträdet.: *Spår av offer, blot och kult under vikingatiden på Frösön, Jämtland.*
151. Uspenskij, F. (2015). Towards the Etymology of the Names of the Dnieper Rapids in Constantine Porphyrogenitus: Βράσμα Νεροῦ. *Viking and Medieval Scandinavia*, 11, pp.231–239.
152. Androshchuk, F. (2008). The Vikings in the East. In: *The Viking World* (pp.541–566). Routledge.
153. Sedykh, V. (2015). Jaroslavl Volga Area in The System. Scandinavia and the Balkans. *Cultural Interactions with Byzantium and Eastern Europe in the First Millennium AD*, p.174.
154. Real, W. (2010). Biblical Apologetics for a Russian Viking King. *Footprints in the Ash*, p.8.
155. Noonan, T.S. (1992). Rus', Pechenegs, and Polovtsy: economic interaction along the steppe frontier in the pre-Mongol Era. *Russian History*, 19(1/4), pp.301–326.
156. Noonan, T.S. (2007). Some observations on the economy of the Khazar Khaganate. In: *The World of the Khazars* (pp. 207–244). Brill.
157. Kultems, M. et al. (2021). Evidence for European presence in the Americas in AD1021. *Nature*, 598 (7881), pp.1–16.
158. Ingstad, H. and Ingstad, A.S. (2000). *The Viking discovery of America: the excavation of a Norse settlement in L'Anse aux Meadows, Newfoundland.* Breakwater Books.
159. Kristjansson, J. et al. (2012). Falling Into Vínland: Newfoundland hunting pitfalls at the edge of the Viking World. *Acta Archaeologica*, 83, pp.145–177.

Further Reading

160. McKusick, M. and Wahlgren, E. (1980). The Norse Penny Mystery. *Archaeology of Eastern North America*, 8, pp.1–10.
161. Poole, R. (2011). *The Vikings and their Outreach: From Buddhas to Butternuts.* Lecture at the University of Western Ontario.
162. Gross, M. (2023). Archaic ancestors. *Current Biology,* 33(10), pp.R377–R379.
163. Larson, L. (2011). *The earliest Norwegian laws: being the Gulathing law and the Frostathing law.* The Lawbook Exchange, Ltd.
164. Jakobsson, S. (2016). The Varangian legend: testimony from the Old Norse sources. In: *Byzantium and the Viking World,* pp.345–62.
165. Böhm, M. (2019). Ingvar the Far-Travelled: between the Byzantium and Caucasus. A Maritime Approach to Discussion. Studia Ceranea. *Journal of the Waldemar Ceran Research Centre for the History and Culture of the Mediterranean Area and South-East Europe,* (9), pp.143–155.
166. Mazzorin, J.D.G. and Minniti, C. (2006). Dog sacrifice in the ancient world: a ritual passage. *Dogs and People in Social, Working, Economic or Symbolic Interaction,* pp.62–66.
167. Micheau, F. (2008). Baghdad in the Abbasid era: a cosmopolitan and multi-confessional capital. In: *The City in the Islamic World* (2 vols.) (pp.219–245). Brill.
168. Ilisch, L. (2020). Jabal al-Fidda: The Silver Mine and the Mint. In: *Dinars and Dirhams* (pp. 151–166). Brill.
169. Abdullaev, K. (2018). *Historical Dictionary of Tajikistan.* Rowman & Littlefield.
170. Hickey, M. (2014) Perler fra vikingtiden (Beads of the Viking-Age): A study of the social and economic patterns in the appearance of beads from Viking-Age sites in Britain. MA Thesis, University of York.
171. Vedeler, M. (2014). *Silk for the Vikings,* Ancient textiles series Vol. 15. Oxford: Oxbow Books.
172. Valdimarsdóttir, Þ. (1999). Vikings In Mexico 998AD. https://thorvald.is/?page_id=392
173. Böldl, K. (1999) *The Saga of the people of Eyr.* (Eyrbyggja saga)
174. Daly, D. (1904). The Legend of St. Brendan. *The Celtic Review,* pp.135–147.
175. Anderson, A.J.O. and Dibble, C. (1982). *Florentine Codex: General History of the Things of New Spain.* Salt Lake City: University of Utah Press.
176. León-Portilla, M. (2003). *En torno a la historia de Mesoamérica.* UNAM.
177. Morgunblaðsins, L. (1998). Of the Mexican Culture Hero Quetzalcoatl and his Contemporary Björn the Champion from Breiduvík.
178. Hristov, R.H. (2001). The Little 'Roman' Head of Calixtlahuaja, Mexico: Some Reflections. https://neara.org/pdf/Little%20Roman%20head%20ed.pdf
179. Madeleine, F. (1955). *Du chien néolithique de Bundsö au chien des Vikings et au chien des Incas,* Zurich.
180. Gonzalez, J.N. (1948), *Proceso y formación de la cultura paraguaya,* Asunción.
181. Williams, H. (2012). The Kensington Runestone: Fact and Fiction. *Swedish-American Historical Quarterly,* 63(1), pp.3–22.

Power

1. Wilbers-Rost, S., Morillo, A., Hanel, N. and Martin, E. (2009). The site of the Varus Battle at Kalkriese. Recent results from archaeological research. *Limes XX, Roman Frontier Studies. Anejo de Gladius*, 13, pp.1347–1352.
2. Rost, A. and Wilbers-Rost, S. (2010). Weapons at the battlefield of Kalkriese. *Gladius*, 30, pp.117–136.
3. Rost, A. (2005). Conditions for the preservation of Roman military equipment on battlefields – the example of Kalkriese. *The Enemies of Rome*, p.219.
4. Povlsen, K. and Kristiansen, S.M. (2023). Relationship between Fields, Banks and Farmstead at an early Iron Age site in Northern Denmark. *Journal of Archaeological Science*: Reports, 49, p.104042.
5. Winters, R. (2017). Making Money Divine: Roman Imperial Coins had a Unique Value in Scandinavian Cultures.
6. Madsen, O. (1997). Hedegård: A rich village and cemetery complex of the Early Iron Age on the Skjern river: An interim report. *Journal of Danish archaeology*, 13(1), pp.57–93.
7. Henriksen, M.B. and Horsnaes, H.W. (2006). Boltinggård Skov: A Hoard of Constantinian solidi from Funen, Denmark. *Revue numismatique*, 6(162), pp.259–271.
8. Horsnæs, H.W. (2009). Late Roman and Byzantine coins found in Denmark. Acedemia.edu, pp.231–270.
9. Efthymiou, M. and Dohrn-van Rossum, G. (2021). Ptolemy: Mapping the Globe. World and Global History.
10. Motz, L. (1992). The Goddess Nerthus; a New Approach. *Amsterdamer Beiträge zur älteren Germanistik*, 36, p.1.
11. Price, N. and Mortimer, P, (2014). An eye for Odin? Divine role-playing in the age of Sutton Hoo. *European Journal of Archaeology*, 17(3), pp.517–538.
12. Nilsson, J. (2016). Gotlandic Villas: Implications of the distribution of high status finds in Gotlandic Iron Age houses known as 'kämpgravar'.
13. Parrott, D. (2021). I am called Mask: An alternative function of the Vendel Period helmets of Northern Europe? *Scandinavian Archaeology* 2021.
14. Pollock, D. (1995). Masks and the semiotics of identity. *The Journal of the Royal Anthropological Institute*, 1(3), pp.581–597.
15. Back Danielsson, I. (2010). Sense and Sensibility: Masking Practices in Late Iron Age Boat-Graves. In: F. Fahlander and A. Kjellström, ed., *Making Sense of Things: Archaeologies of Sensory Perception*. Stockholm: Stockholm University, pp.121–140.
16. Halsall, G. ed. (1998). *Violence and Society in the Early Medieval West*. Woodbridge: Boydell Press.
17. Evelein, M.A. (1911). Ein römischer Helm des Leidener Museums. *Praehistorische Zeitschrift*, 3(1), pp.144–156.
18. Rundkvist, M. (2011). *Mead-halls of the Eastern Geats: elite settlements and political geography AD 375–1000 in Östergötland, Sweden*. Kungl. Vitterhets historie och antikvitets akademien.

Further Reading

19. Karras, R.M. (1990). Concubinage and slavery in the Viking Age. *Scandinavian Studies*, 62(2), pp.141–162.
20. Brink, S. (2021). *Thraldom: A History of Slavery in the Viking Age*. Oxford University Press.
21. Kamm, J.P. (2007). Two Large Silver Hoards from Ocksarve on Gotland. Evidence for Viking Period Trade and Warfare in the Baltic Region. *Archaeologia Baltica*, (8).
22. Carlsson, D. (2008). 'Ridanæs': a Viking Age port of trade at Fröjel, Gotland. *The Viking World*, pp.131–4.
23. Carlsson, D. (2020). Gotland: silver island. In *Viking-Age Trade* (pp. 225–241). Routledge.
24. Kilger, C. (2020). Long distance trade, runes and silver: a Gotlandic perspective.
25. Kilger, C. (2015). Hoards and sinuous snakes: Significance and meaning of ring ornaments in Early Viking Age hoards from Gotland.
26. Hennius, A. (2018). Viking Age tar production and outland exploitation. *Antiquity*, 92(365), pp.1349–1361.
27. Jesch, J. (1991). *Women in the Viking Age*. Boydell & Brewer Ltd.
28. Raffield, B., Price, N. and Collard, M. (2017). Polygyny, concubinage, and the social lives of women in Viking-age Scandinavia. *Viking and Medieval Scandinavia*, 13, pp.165–209.
29. Spatacean, C. (2006). Women in the Viking age: death, life after death and burial customs. Master's Thesis.
30. Sigfússon, B. (1934). Names of Sea-Kings (Heiti Sækonunga). *Modern Philology*, 32(2), pp.125–142.
31. Maixner, B. (2020) Sæheimr: Just a Settlement by the Sea? Dating, Naming Motivation and Function of an Iron Age Maritime Place Name in Scandinavia. *Journal of Maritime Archaeology*, 15(1), pp.5–39.
32. Bill, J. (2006). The Skuldelev and Roskilde Ships from Excavation to the Building of Replicas: The Price of Perfection.
33. *De bellis Parisiacæ urbis*
34. Cooijmans, C. (2023). Hostile in tent: Reconsidering the roles of viking encampment across the Frankish realm. In: *Viking Camps*. Routledge.
35. Jennings, A. and Kruse, A. (2009). From Dál Riata to the Gall-Ghàidheil. *Viking and Medieval Scandinavia*, 5, pp.123–149.
36. Anderson, J. ed. (1873). *The Orkneyinga Saga*. Edmonston and Douglas.
37. Duncan, A.A.M. (1979). Scandinavian Kings in the British Isles 850-880.
38. Corráin, D.Ó. (1998). Vikings in Ireland and Scotland in the ninth century. *Peritia*, 12, pp.296–339.
39. Breeze, A. (1997). The 'Anglo-Saxon Chronicle' for 949 and Olaf Cuaran. *Notes and Queries*, 44(2), pp.160–162.
40. Parker Pearson, M., Brennan, M., Mulville, J. and Smtih, H. (2018). Cille Pheadair: a Norse farmstead and Pictish burial cairn in South Uist.
41. James, H.F., Lorimer, D.H. and Roberts, J. (2000), November. Excavations of a medieval cemetery at Skaill House, and a cist in the Bay of Skaill, Sandwick,

Orkney. In *Proceedings of the Society of Antiquaries of Scotland* (Vol. 129, pp.753–777).

42. Barrett, J.H. and Slater, A. (2009). New excavations at the Brough of Deerness: Power and Religion in Viking Age Scotland. *Journal of the North Atlantic*, 2(1), pp.81–94.

43. Caple, C. (2020). The Yarm Helmet. *Medieval Archaeology*, 64(1), pp.31–64.

44. Price, N., Hedenstierna-Jonson, C., Zachrisson, T., Kjellström, A., Storå, J., Krzewińska, M., Günther, T., Sobrado, V., Jakobsson, M. and Götherström, A. (2019). Viking warrior women? Reassessing Birka chamber grave Bj. 581. *Antiquity*, 93(367), pp.181–198.

45. Negus, T. and Rocks, M.A. (2023) The Birka Warrior of Grave BJ 581: How Archaeology Erases Female Narratives.

46. Brown, N.M. (2021). *The Real Valkyrie: The Hidden History of Viking Warrior Women*. St. Martin's Press.

47. Jesch, J. (2021). Women, war and words: A verbal archaeology of shield-maidens. *Viking*, 84(1), pp.127–142.

48. Hilberg, V., (1995). Hedeby in Wulfstan's days: a Danish emporium of the Viking Age between East and West. *Annales regni Francorum*, p.205.

49. Dobat, A.S. (2009). The State and the Strangers: The Role of External Forces in a Process of State Formation in Viking-Age South Scandinavia (c. AD 900–1050). *Viking and medieval Scandinavia*, 5, pp.65–104.

50. Bauer, Albert and Reinhold Rau (1971). Die Sachsengeschichte des Widukind von Korvei. In: *Quellen zur Geschichte der sächsischen Kaiserzeit. Freiherr-vom-Stein-Gedächtnisausgabe 8*.

51. Kennedy, M. (2011). evidence for unknown Viking King airdeconut found in Lancashire. *The Guardian*.

52. Thijs, P. and EV, M.J. (2014). How Cnut became Canute (and how Harthacnut became Airdeconut). *NOWELE: North-Western European Language Evolution*, 67(2), pp.237–243.

53. Hvass, S. (1983). Vorbasse: The development of a settlement through the first millenium AD. *Journal of Danish Archaeology*, 2(1), pp.127–136.

54. Wood, R. (2014). The pictures on the greater Jelling stone. *Danish Journal of Archaeology*, 3(1), pp.19–32.

55. Bolender, D.J., Steinberg, J.M. and Damiata, B.N. (2011). Farmstead relocation at the end of the Viking Age: results of the Skagafjörður archaeological settlement survey. *Archaeologia Islandica*, 9, pp.77–99.

56. Steinberg, J.M., Bolender, D.J. and Damiata, B.N. (2016). The Viking Age settlement pattern of Langholt, north Iceland: Results of the Skagafjörður archaeological settlement survey. *Journal of Field Archaeology*, 41(4), pp.389–412.

57. Benediktsson, J. (1966). Landnámabók. *Saga-book*, 17, pp.275–292.

58. Jónsson, E. and Jónsson, F. eds. (1896). *Hauksbók*. Thieles bogtr.

59. Bell, A. (2010). Þingvellir: archaeology of the Althing (Doctoral dissertation).

60. Nygaard, S. (2021). ein lǫg ok einn siðr: Law, Religion, and their Role in the Cultivation of Cultural Memory in Pre-Christian Icelandic Society. *Scandinavian-Canadian Studies*, 28, pp.144–177.

Further Reading

61. Williams, D.G.E. (1997). The Dating of the Norwegian leiðangr System: A Philological Approach. *NOWELE. North-Western European Language Evolution*, 30(1), pp.21–25.
62. *Laurentian Codex.*
63. *Hypatian Codex.*
64. (2012) *Ibn Fadlān and the land of darkness: Arab travellers in the far north.* Penguin UK.
65. Schjødt, J.P. (2007). Ibn Fadlan's Account of a Rus Funeral: To what degree does it reflect Nordic myths? In: *Reflections on Old Norse Myths* (pp. 133–148).
66. Gruszczyński, J., Jankowiak, M. and Shepard, J. eds. (2020). *Viking-age trade: Silver, slaves and Gotland.* Routledge.
67. Mägi, M. (2018). *In Austrvegr: The Role of the Eastern Baltic in Viking Age Communication across the Baltic Sea.* Brill.
68. Woolf, A. (1998). Erik Bloodaxe Revisited. *Northern History*, 34(1), pp.189–193.
69. Roesdahl, E. (1989). Prestige, display and monuments in Viking Age Scandinavia. *Actes des congrès de la Société d'Archéologie Médiévale*, 2(1), pp.17–25.
70. Jørgensen, L.B. and Eriksen, P. (1995). *Trabjerg: en vestjysk landsby fra vikingetiden.*
71. Livingston, M. (2011) *The Battle of Brunanburh: A Casebook.* (Liverpool Historical Casebooks)
72. Livingston, M. (2021) *Never Greater Slaughter: Brunanburh and the Birth of England.* Osprey Publishing.

Nemeses

1. Lund, N. (2002). *Harald Bluetooth, A Saint Very Nearly Made by Adam of Bremen* (Vol. 5, pp.303–15). Woodbridge: Boydell.
2. Wangerin, L. (2017). The governance of Ottonian Germany in historiographical perspective. *History Compass*, 15(1), p.e12367.
3. Chiarantini, L., Villa, I.M., Volpi, V., Bianchi, G., Benvenuti, M., Cicali, C., Donati, A., Manca, R. and Hodges, R. (2021). Economic rebound versus imperial monopoly: Metal provenance of Early Medieval coins (9th–11th centuries) from some Italian and French mints. *Journal of Archaeological Science: Reports,* 39, p.103139.
4. *Gesta Normannorum ducum.*
5. Breese, L.W. (1977). The persistence of Scandinavian connections in Normandy in the tenth and early eleventh centuries. *Viator*, 8, pp.47–62.
6. Worm, O. *Danicorum monumentorum libri sex: e spissis antiquitatum tenebris et in Dania ac Norvegia extantibus ruderibus eruti. Apud Ioachimum Moltkenium Bibliopolam ibidem primar.*
7. Gullbekk, S.H. (2016). Vestfold: a monetary perspective on the Viking Age. In: *Early Medieval Monetary History* (pp.365–382). Routledge.

8. Draganits, E., Doneus, M., Gansum, T., Gustavsen, L., Nau, E., Tonning, C., Trinks, I. and Neubauer, W. (2015). The late Nordic Iron Age and Viking Age royal burial site of Borre in Norway: ALS and GPR-based landscape reconstruction and harbour location at an uplifting coastal area. *Quaternary International*, 367, pp.96-110.
9. Ödman, A. (2014). The trelleborg constructors. Small Things, wide Horizons. Studies in Honour of Birgitta Hårdh. Oxford: *Archaeopress Archaeology*, pp.267–272.
10. Ten Harkel, L. (2015). Else Roesdahl, *et al.* (ed.). *Aggersborg. The Viking-age settlement and fortress.* Højbjerg: Jutland Archaeological Society, Moesgård Museum.
11. Runge, M. (2017). New archaeological investigations at Nonnebakken, a Viking Age fortress in Odense. In *The Fortified Viking Age*: the 36th interdisciplinary Viking age seminar, Odense (pp. 44–59).
12. Rosborn, S. (2021). *The Viking King's Golden Treasure: About the Curmsun Disc, the Discovery of a Lost Manuscript, Harald Bluetooth´s Grave and the Location of the Fortress of Jomsborg.* Rivengate AB.
13. Tys, D., Deckers, P. and Wouters, B. (2019). Circular, D-Shaped and Other Fortifications in 9th- and 10th-Century Flanders and Zeeland as Markers of the Territorialisation of Power(s). In: *Fortified Settlements in Early Medieval Europe* (pp. 175–191). Oxbow Books.
14. Büttner, H. (1956). *Zur Burgenbauordnung Heinrichs I.*
15. *Res Gestae.*
16. Schoenfeld, E. J. (1994) Anglo-Saxon burhs and Continental burgen: Early Medieval Fortifications in Constitutional Perspective. *The Haskins Society Journal* 6, pg. 49–66.
17. Balogh, L. (2007). A new source on the Hungarian raids against Byzantium in the Middle of the tenth century. *Chronica*, pp.16–25.
18. France, J. (2019). Bernard S. Bachrach and David S. Bachrach, Warfare in Medieval Europe, c. 400–c.1453. London and New York: Routledge, 2017.
19. Lind, J.H. (1984). The Russo-Byzantine Treaties and the Early Urban Structure of Rus'. *The Slavonic and East European Review*, pp.362–370.
20. *The Life of St. George of Amastris.*
21. Treadgold, W.T. (1983). Patriarch Photios of Constantinople: His Life, Scholarly Contributions, and Correspondence together with a Translation of Fifty-two of his Letters.
22. Fylypchuk, O. (2022). The Attack of the Rus' on Constantinople in the Light of the Chronicon Bruxellense. Studia Ceranea. *Journal of the Waldemar Ceran Research Centre for the History and Culture of the Mediterranean Area and South-East Europe*, (12), pp.417–435.
23. Vasiliev, A.A. (1951). The second Russian attack on Constantinople. *Dumbarton Oaks Papers*, 6, pp.161–225.
24. Jenkins, R.J.H. (1965). A 'Consolatio' of the Patriarch Nicholas Mysticus. *Byzantion*, 35(1), pp.159–166.

Further Reading

25. Polgár, S. (2005). A contribution to the history of the Khazar military organisation: The strengthening of the camp. *Acta Orientalia Academiae Scientiarum Hungaricae*, 58(2), pp.197–204.
26. Shpakovsky, V. and Nicolle, D. (2013). *Armies of the Volga Bulgars & Khanate of Kazan: 9th–16th centuries*. Bloomsbury Publishing.
27. Howard-Johnston, J. (2007). Byzantine sources for Khazar history. In: *The World of the Khazars* (pp. 163–193). Brill.
28. Constantine VII, *De Administrando Imperio*.
29. Stokes, A.D. (1960). Tmutarakan. *The Slavonic and East European Review*, 38(91), pp.499–514.
30. Solovyov, S.L. (2006). The Chora of Hermonassa. In *Ancient West & East* (pp. 121–142). Brill.
31. Зиливинская, Э.Д. and Васильев, Д.В. (2020). Миграции населения Хазарского каганата по материалам Нижнего Поволжья. *Stratum Plus Journal*, (5).
32. Марыксин, Д.В., Попов, П.В. and Крыгин, А.П. (2022). Работы на городище Кызылкала в 2021 году и предварительный анализ керамического материала. *Археология евразийских степей*, (3), pp.98–105.
33. *The Remaining Signs of Past Centuries*.
34. Ambrosiani, B. (2001). *Birka Studies 5: Eastern Connections. The Falcon Motif*. Stockholm.
35. Coco, F.S. (1921). *Historia Silense*. Rivadeneyra.
36. *Liber Chronicorum of Pelayo of Oviedo*.
37. *Chronicon Nairense*.
38. Christys, A. (2015). *Vikings in the South: Voyages to Iberia and the Mediterranean*. Bloomsbury Publishing.
39. Idhari, I. and Colin, G. (1948). *al-Bayan al-mughrib*. Vol. II, p.36.
40. *Castilian Anales Castellanos Segundos*.
41. *Anales Toledanos*.
42. *Chronicon Lusitanum*.
43. Scragg, D.G. ed. (1981). *The Battle of Maldon*. Manchester University Press.
44. Cavill, P. (2001). *Vikings: Fear and Faith*. Harper Collins.
45. Redknap, M. (2000). *The Vikings in Wales*. Cardiff: National Museums and Galleries of Wales.
46. Kovalev, R.K. (2002). Dirham mint output of Samanid Samarqand and its connection to the beginnings of trade with northern Europe (10th century) (Vol. 17, No. XVII-3/4, pp. 197–216). Éditions de l'EHESS.
47. Walker, J. (2021). Exploring the Significance of Islamic Dirhams in the Viking Age Silver Economy of the Danelaw. University of Sheffield.
48. Miechowicz, Ł. (2019). 'The Obol of the Dead' in medieval and modern Eastern Europe. *Wiadomości Numizmatyczne*.
49. Giv, A.L. (2016). The Effective Reasons for the Rise and fall of Abbasids State. *Mediterranean Journal of Social Sciences*, 7(3 S1), p.449.
50. Faith, R. (2012). The structure of the market for wool in early medieval Lincolnshire 1. *The Economic History Review*, 65(2), pp.674–700.

51. Crabtree, P.J. (2010). Agricultural innovation and socio-economic change in early medieval Europe: evidence from Britain and France. *World Archaeology*, 42(1), pp.122–136.
52. Jansson, S.B. (1966). *Swedish Vikings in England. The Evidence of the Rune Stones*. London: University College London.
53. Larsson, M.G. (2011). Early Contacts between Scandinavia and the Orient. *The Silk Road Journal*, 9, pp.122–142.
54. Minorsky, V.V. and Bosworth, C.E. (2015). *Hudud al-Alam, The Regions of the World, A Persian Geography 372 AH (982 AD)*. Gibb Memorial Trust.
55. Aliev, N. (2017). Influence of Shirvanshah State on Naval Affairs in Azerbaijan. *Journal of Defense Resources Management* (JoDRM), 8(2), pp.129–141.
56. Van Donzel, E.J. and Schmidt, A.B. (2009). The Political Landscape in Samarra, The Caucasus and Central Asia in the 8th and First Half of the 9th Century. In *Gog and Magog in Early Eastern Christian and Islamic Sources* (pp. 182–206). Brill.
57. Gambashidze, Givi G., And Askerkhan K. Abiev. (2020). Christian Burial Ground in the Village of Khunzakh (Based on the Materials of the Dagestan-Georgian Joint Archaeological Expedition). *History, Archeology and Ethnography of the Caucasus* 16, no. 2: 316-331.
58. Wheatcroft, S. ed. (2002). *Challenging Traditional Views of Russian History*. Springer.
59. Isitt, G.F. (2007). Vikings in the Persian Gulf. *Journal of the Royal Asiatic Society*, 17(4), pp.389–406.
60. Taylor, J.E. (2014), January. Vikings in the Gulf: fact or fancy? In *Proceedings of the Seminar for Arabian Studies* (pp.325–336). Archaeopress.
61. *Book of Roads and Kingdoms*.
62. Fedchenko, Oleg. (2018) Путешествие Ингвара из Гардарик в Серкланд (The Voyage of Ingvar From Gardaric to Serkland).
63. Mikkelsen, E. (2008). The Vikings and Islam. In *The Viking World* (pp. 567–573). Routledge.
64. Hedenstierna-Jonson, C. (2020). With Asia as neighbour: Archaeological evidence of contacts between Scandinavia and Central Asia in the Viking Age and the Tang Dynasty. *Bulletin of the Museum of Far Eastern Antiquities*, 81, pp.43–64.
65. Mikkelsen, E. (1998). Islam and Scandinavia during the Viking Age. *Byzantium and Islam in Scandinavia*, pp.15–16.
66. Larsson, M.G. (1986). Yngvarr's Expedition and the Georgian Chronicle. *Saga-Book*, 22, pp.98–108.
67. Nikolay, J. (2010). Little-known pages of the History of Georgian-Baltic relations in the 10th-18th centuries. *The Caucasus & Globalization*, 4(3-4), pp.147–154.
68. *The Georgian Chronicle*.
69. Tsetskhladze, G.R. (2015). Greeks, locals and others around the Black Sea and its hinterland: recent developments. *The Danubian Lands between the Black, Aegean and Adriatic Seas* (7th Century BC–10th Century AD), pp.11–42.

Further Reading

70. Hind, J.G. (1993). Archaeology of the Greeks and barbarian peoples around the Black Sea (1982-1992). *Archaeological Reports*, 39, pp.82–112.
71. Erdoğan, H. (2019). Ardanuç in the Middle Ages. Master's Thesis, Artvin Çoruh University.
72. Kjartansson, H.S. (2002). From the frying pan of oral tradition into the fire of saga writing: The precarious survival of historical fact in the saga of Yngvar the Far-Traveller.
73. Mueller-Vollmer, T. (2022). Yngvar the Far-Traveler. *Vikings: An Encyclopedia of Conflict, Invasions, and Raids*, p.284.
74. Fuglesang, SH (1998). Swedish runestones of the eleventh century: ornament and dating. In Runic Inscriptions as Sources of Interdisciplinary Research: *Proceedings of the Fourth International Symposium on Runes and Runic Inscriptions in 4th–9th cent.* August 1995 (pp. 197–218).
75. Krakow, A. (2021). The year of Olof Eriksson's death and the dating of the Ingvarståget. *The Ancient Friend*, 116 (2), pp.101–113.
76. Swift, C. (2000). Óenach Tailten, the Blackwater valley and the Uí Néill kings of Tara.
77. Cróinín, D.Ó. (2016). *Early Medieval Ireland 400-1200*. Taylor & Francis.
78. *Chronicon Scotorum*.
79. Fitzpatrick, D., Fitzpatrick, I. and Fitzpatrick, M. (2022). Mac Giolla Phádraig Dál gCais: an ancient clan rediscovered. *The Journal of the Fitzpatrick Clan Society*, 3, pp.1–45.
80. Gibson, D.B. (2020). Was There a Method to Their Madness? Warfare, Alliance Formation, and the Origins of the Irish Medieval State. Human Conflict from Neanderthals to the Samburu: Structure and Agency. In: *Webs of Violence*, pp.39–55.
81. Ward, F. (2007). *The Cenél Conaill and the Donegal Kingdoms*, AD 500–800.
82. Etchingham, C. (2020). The kings of Aileach and the Vikings, AD 800-1060. *Zeitschrift für celtische Philologie*, 67(1), pp.235–238.
83. Donoghue, C.N. (2015). The Irish Empire: *The Story of Niall of the Nine Hostages*. FriesenPress.
84. Bruford, A. (1992). Some implications of early Irish and Scottish names and epithets. *Études celtiques*, 29(1), pp.454–455.
85. *The Annals of Tigernach*.
86. Viron, O. (2016). The battle of Clontarf (1014) between memory and history. POLEN, Powers, Letters, Norms, pp.207-237.
87. Gøthche, M. and Strætkvern, K. (2017), The Roskilde 6 ship (Denmark). Reconstructing the longest warship find of the Viking Age. In *Ships and Maritime Landscapes: Proceedings of the Thirteenth International Symposium on Boat and Ship Archaeology, Amsterdam 2012* (p. 373). Barkhuis.
88. Buchanan, E.S. (1914). *The Book of Armagh*.
89. Marzocchi, S. (2017). Renovatio imperii Romanorum: quando Crescentius decollatus suspensus fuit. An analysis of the meaning of Otto III's first lead bulla. *Journal of Medieval History*, 43(2), pp.193–211.

90. Matthews, S. (2009). King Edgar and the Dee: the ceremony of 973 in popular history writing. *Northern History*, 46(1), pp.61–74.
91. Walsh, P. (1940). *The Annals of Loch Ce*.
92. Duffy, S. (2013). *Brian Boru and the Battle of Clontarf*. Gill & Macmillan Ltd.
93. Mulcahy, C. (2016). Seán Duffy (ed), *Medieval Dublin: proceedings of the Friends of Medieval Dublin*, 15 vols. Four Courts Press.
94. Wallace, B. (2003). L'Anse aux Meadows and Vínland: An Abandoned Experiment. In: *Contact, Continuity, and Collapse: The Norse Colonization of the North Atlantic*. Brepols Publishers. pp.207–238.
95. Batey, C. (2007). Birgitta Linderoth Wallace. Westward Vikings: The Saga of L'Anse aux Meadows. *Scandinavian-Canadian Studies*, 17, pp.117–119.
96. McGhee, R. (1984). Contact between Native North Americans and the Medieval Norse: A Review of the Evidence. *American Antiquity*, 49 (1), pp.4–26.
97. (1866). *Nuzhat al-mushtaq fi ikhtiraq al-afaq*. Ibrahim.
98. Phelpstead, C. (2003). *Historia Norwegie*.
99. Perkins, R. (1972). An edition of Floamanna saga with a study of its sources and analogues. Doctoral dissertation, University of Oxford.
100. Vebk, C.L. (1991). *The Church Topography of the Eastern Settlement and the Excavation of the Benedictine Convent at Narsarsuaq in the Uunartoq Fjord* (Vol. 14). Museum Tusculanum Press.
101. Rink, H. (1974). *Tales and traditions of the Eskimo*. London: C. Hurst.
102. Perkins, R. (1976). *The Furðustrandir of Eiríks saga rauða*.

Flux

1. Bolton, T. (2009). *The empire of Cnut the Great: conquest and the consolidation of power in Northern Europe in the early eleventh century*. Brill.
2. Skeie, T. (2021). *The Wolf Age: the Vikings, the Anglo-Saxons and the Battle for the North Sea Empire*. London: Pushkin Press.
3. Bartlett, W. B. (2016). *King Cnut and the Viking conquest of England 1016*. Stroud: Amberley.
4. Simek, R. (2006). *Dictionary of northern mythology*. Brewer.
5. Novotná, M. (2015). Hamr of the Old Norse Body. In The Sixteenth International Saga Conference Sagas and Space, p.223.
6. Lewis, S. and Sturluson, S. (2019). 'High in the howes of the kin who are gone'. Dancing with ghosts in The Waking of Angantyr.
7. North, R. (2009). Sighvatr Sturluson and the authorship of Víga-Glúms saga. *Analecta Septentrionalia: Beiträge Zur Nordgermanischen Kultur-Und Literaturgeschichte*, pp.256–80.
8. Miller, W.I. (1992). Emotions and the Sagas. From sagas to Society: Comparative approaches to early Iceland, pp.89–109.
9. Casteel, A. (2020). Cognizing as the Wind and Metaphors of Mind: A Reconsideration of Old Norse hugr and Huginn. Master's Thesis.
10. Turville-Petre, G. (1944). *The Road to Hel, a Study of the Conception of the Dead in Old Norse Literature*.

Further Reading

11. Картамышева, Е.П. (2021). Древнескандинавские индивидуальные и родовые покровители fylgja, hamingja, disir-пути трансформации мифологем. In *Dísablót* (pp.75-84)..
12. Sommer, B.S. (2007). The Norse concept of luck. *Scandinavian Studies*, 79(3), pp.275–294.
13. Stankovitsová, Z. (2015). Eru þetta mannafylgjur. A Re-Examination of fylgjur in Old Norse Literature. Doctoral dissertation.
14. Wade, J. (2016). Going berserk: Battle trance and ecstatic holy warriors in the European war magic tradition. *International Journal of Transpersonal Studies*, 35(1), p.5.
15. Schröder, F.R. (1958). *Grímnismál*.
16. Gowen, M. and Scally, G. (1996) A summary Report on Excavations at Exchange Street Upper/Parliament Street, Dublin. *Temple Bar Archaeological report number 4*, Temple Bar Properties.
17. Duffy, S. (2009). *Medieval Dublin IX: proceedings of the Friends of Medieval Dublin Symposium, 2007*. Dublin: Four Courts Press.
18. Zori, D. (2007) Nails, Rivets and Clench Bolts: A case for typological clarity. *Archaeologia Islandica*. 6. 32-47
19. YAT. (1991) Report on an Archaeological Evaluation at 26-34 Skeldergate, York. York Archaeological Trust Report.
20. Reeves, M. (2022). The waterfronts of Viking Dublin and York: a comparative study. MA, York: University of York.
21. Milne, G. and Goodburn, D. (1990). The early medieval port of London AD 700-1200. *Antiquity*, 64 (244), pp.629–636.
22. Wallace, P. F. (1992). The Archaeological Identity of the Hiberno-Norse Town. *Journal of the Royal Society of Antiquaries of Ireland*, 122, pp.35–66.
23. Vince, A. (2016). Lincoln in the Viking Age. In: *Vikings and the Danelaw*. Oxbow Books. p.157.
24. Hilberg, V. (2024). Hedeby & Denmark around the year 100. *Dorestad Congress IV*.
25. Edberg, R. (2013). Subterranean Maritime Archaeology in Sigtuna, Sweden: excavated evidence of Viking Age boat building and repair. *The International Journal of Nautical Archaeology*, 42 (1), pp.196–204.
26. Oehrl, S. (2017). Documenting and interpreting the picture stones of Gotland: Old problems and new approaches. *Current Swedish Archaeology*, 25(1), pp.87–122.
27. Moore, E. (2022). Landscapes of Early Medieval stone sculpture: How can digital humanities further our understanding of the placement of stone sculpture? In: *Early Medieval Britain: Continuity & Change*. 2022. University of Lancaster.
28. Malaterra, G. (1927). *De rebus gestis Rogerii Calabriae et Siciliae comitis et Roberti Guiscardi Ducis fratis eius* (Vol. 5). N. Zanichelli.
29. Stevens, C.E. (1933). Inventaire Archéologique De La Seine-Inférieure, Période Gallo-Romaine. By L. Deglatigny. Evreux: 4 rue de la Banque, imprimerie Hérissey, 1931. pp.241. *Antiquity*, 7(27), pp.379–381.

30. Degorog, R.P. (1963). On dating the change -s->-z- in Old French. *Word*, 19(3), pp.342–346.
31. Bachrach, B.S. and Fanning, S. eds. (2004). *The'Annals' of Flodoard of Reims, 919-966* (Vol. 9). University of Toronto Press.
32. Wladyslaw, D. (2004). Viking Rus: Studies on the Presence of Scandinavians in Eastern Europe.
33. Sobkowiak-Tabaka, I. (2015). 3 Bodzia: Site Location and History of Research. In *Bodzia* (pp.45–53). Brill.
34. d'Amato, R. (2011). The Golden Age of the Varangian Guard. *Medieval Warfare*, 1(2), pp.24–27.
35. Airinei, A. (2015). The Varangian guard and its contribution to the manifestation of the imperial power in Byzantium. *Revista Română de Studii Baltice și Nordice*, 7(2), pp.7–26.
36. Brock, R. (2013). *Hetaireia. The Encyclopedia of Ancient History*. https://www.graverini.net/pubs/
37. Werkenthin, S. and Papalexandrou, A. (2019). The Varangian Guard in the Byzantine Empire.
38. Åhfeldt, L.K. (2021). Rune Carvers in Military Campaigns. *Viking*, 84(1), pp.207–230.
39. Källström, M. (2016). Byzantium reflected in the runic inscriptions of Scandinavia. *Byzantium and the Viking World içinde*, pp.169–187.
40. Holloway, D. (2021). *The Last Viking: The True Story of King Harald Hardrada*. Osprey Publishing.
41. Fodstad, H. and Ljunggren, B. (1995). The saga of King Harald Hardrada and Viking chieftains with injured necks. *Journal of Medical Biography*, 3(2), pp.105–109.
42. Hendy, M.F. (1970). Michael IV and Harold Hardrada. *The Numismatic Chronicle* (1966-), pp.187–197.
43. Böhm, M. (2019). *Zoe Porphyrogenita and the Varangians*.
44. *Strategikon of Kekaumenos*.
45. *Alexiad*.
46. Mel'nikova, E.A. (2016). A New Runic Inscription from Hagia Sophia Cathedral in Istanbul. *Futhark: International Journal of Runic Studies*, 7, pp.101–110.
47. Thomov, T. (2014). Four Scandinavian ship graffiti from Hagia Sophia. *Byzantine and Modern Greek Studies*, 38(2), pp.168–184.
48. Blackburn, M. and Chown, J. (1984). A die-link between the Sigtuna coinage of Olof Skötkonung and some Long Cross imitations reading 'OCLOD'. *The Numismatic Chronicle* (1966-), pp.166–172.
49. Lindow, J. (2008). St Olaf and the skalds. In: *Sanctity in the North: Saints, Lives, and Cults in Medieval Scandinavia*, Ed. T.A. DuBois, pp.103–27.
50. Jackson, T.N. (2010). The cult of St Olaf and early Novgorod. In *Saints and their Lives on the Periphery: Veneration of Saints in Scandinavia and Eastern Europe* (c. 1000-1200) (pp. 147–167).
51. Keynes, S. (1998). *Encomium Emmae Reginae* (Vol. 4). Cambridge University Press.

Further Reading

52. Garmonsway, G.N. (1964). *Canute and his Empire*. HK Lewis.
53. Townend, M. (2001). Contextualizing the Knútsdrápur: skaldic praise-poetry at the court of Cnut. *Anglo-Saxon England*, 30, pp.145–179.
54. Speed, J. (1623). *The Histoire of Great Britaine Vnder the Conquests of the Romans, Saxons, Danes and Normans. Their Originals, Manners, Habits, Vuarres, Coines, and Seales: with the Successions, Liues, Acts, and Issues of the English Monarchs, from Iulius Cæsar, to Our Most Gracious Soueraigne King James*. Iohn Beale. 1980.
55. Bolton, T. (2007). Ælfgifu of Northampton: Cnut the Great's 'other woman'. Nottingham *Medieval Studies*, 51, pp.247–268.
56. Tveit, M. (2011). *Lawmaking and consolidation of power – Cnut's laws and the developing Norwegian kingdom*.
57. Hadley, D.M. (2000). Burial practices in the northern Danelaw, c. 650–1100. *Northern History*, 36(2), pp.199–216.
58. Hadley, D.M. (1996). Multiple estates and the origins of the manorial structure of the northern Danelaw. *Journal of Historical Geography*, 22, pp.3–15.
59. Stafford, P. (1981). The laws of Cnut and the history of Anglo-Saxon royal promises. *Anglo-Saxon England*, 10, pp.173–190.
60. Holman, K. (2001). Defining the Danelaw. In *Vikings and the Danelaw*: Select papers from the proceedings of the Thirteenth Viking Congress (pp. 1–11).
61. Matthews, S. (2009). King Edgar and the Dee: the ceremony of 973 in popular history writing. *Northern History*, 46(1), pp.61–74.
62. Thornton, D.E. (2001). Edgar and the eight kings, AD 973: textus et dramatis personae. *Early Medieval Europe*, 10(1), pp.49–79.
63. Cavill, P. (2001). *Vikings: Fear and faith*. Harper Collins.
64. Cownie, E. (1998). The Cult of St Edmund in the Eleventh and Twelfth Centuries: The Language and Communication of a Medieval Saint's Cult. *Neuphilologische Mitteilungen*, 99(2), pp.177–197.
65. Royal, S. (2020). The Martyrdom of St Edmund (d. 869) at the Hands of the Danes and its Legacy in Early Modern England. *Northern European Reformations: Transnational Perspectives*, pp.269–294.
66. Rosenwein, B.H. (2016). *Rhinoceros Bound: Cluny in the Tenth Century*. University of Pennsylvania Press.
67. Banton, N. (1982). Monastic reform and the unification of tenth-century England. *Studies in Church History*, 18, pp.71–85.
68. Meyer, M.A. (1977). Women and the tenth-century English monastic reform. *Revue bénédictine*, 87(1-2), pp.34–61.
69. Norton, E. (2013). *Elfrida: The First Crowned Queen of England*. Amberley Publishing.
70. Chaney, W.A. (1970). *The Cult of Kingship in Anglo-Saxon England: The Transition from Paganism to Christianity*. Univ of California Press.
71. Dumville, D.N. (1986). *The West Saxon Genealogical Regnal List: Manuscripts and Texts*.

72. Anlezark, D., 2002 (Sceaf), Japheth and the origins of the Anglo-Saxons. *Anglo-Saxon England*, 31, pp.13–46.
73. Ashby, S.P. (2015). What really caused the Viking Age? The social content of raiding and exploration. *Archaeological Dialogues*, 22(1), pp.89–106.

Faith

1. Laidoner, T. (2020). *Ancestor worship and the elite in late Iron Age Scandinavia: a grave matter*. Routledge.
2. Raudvere, C. (2008). Popular religion in the Viking Age. In: *The Viking World*, pp.235–243.
3. Wilson, D.M. (2008). The development of Viking art. In: *The Viking World* (pp. 347–362). Routledge.
4. Graham-Campbell, J. (2021). *Viking Art*. Thames & Hudson.
5. Owen, O. (2001). The strange beast that is the English Urnes style. In: *Vikings and the Danelaw*: select papers from the proceedings of the thirteenth Viking Congress (pp. 203–22).
6. Vikstrand, P. (2001). Gudarnas platser. *Forkristna sakrala ortnamn i Malar landskapen*, Uppsala,
7. Price, N. (2014). Nine paces from Hel: time and motion in Old Norse ritual performance. *World Archaeology*, 46(2), pp.178–191.
8. Molin, J.J. (2015). Ullr: A God on the Edge of Memory. Doctoral dissertation.
9. Hopkins, J.S. (2012). Goddesses Unknown I: Njǫrun and the Sister-Wife of Njǫrðr. *RMN Newsletter*, 5, pp.39–44.
10. Andersson, G. (2006). Among Trees, Bones and Stones – the Sacred Grove at Lunda, in A. Andren. Jennbert and C. Raudvere (eds) *Old Norse Religion in Long term Perspectives, Origins, Changes, and Interactions*, Vagar till Midgard 8, Lund, 195–9.
11. Carlie, A. (1998). Karingsjon. A Fertility Sacrificial Site from the Late Roman Iron Age in South West Sweden, *Current Swedish Archaeology* 6, 17–37.
12. Hagberg, U.E. (1967). *The Archaeology of Skedemosse 1. The Excavations and finds of an Oland fen, Sweden, Stockholm*. Almqvist & Wiksell. Stockholm, Sweden.
13. Hagberg, U.E. (1967). *The Archaeology of Skedemosse 2. The votive deposits in the Skedemosse fen and their relation to the Iron Age settlement on Oland, Sweden, Stockholm*.
14. Ilkjaer, J. (2000). *Illerup Adal. Et ark ologisk tryllespejl*, Moesgard.
15. Henriksson, G. (2003). The pagan Great Midwinter Sacrifice and the 'royal' mounds at Gamla Uppsala. Calendars, Symbols, and Orientations: Legacies of Astronomy in Culture. Uppsala. *Uppsala Astronomical Observatory Report*, (59).
16. Watt, M. (2004). The gold-figure foils ('Guldgubbar') from Uppåkra. Continuity for centuries. A ceremonial building and its context at Uppåkra, southern Sweden. (Uppåkrastudier 10) *Acta Archaeologica* Lundensia, Series in 8: 167-221.

Further Reading

17. Burstrom, M. (1990). Järnframställning och gravritual. En strukturalistisk tolkning av järnslagg i vikingatida gravar i Gästrikland. (Iron production and grave ritual. A structuralistic interpretation of iron-slag in Viking Age burials in the province of Gästrikland.) *Fornvannen* 85,261-71.
18. Von Schnurbein, S. (2000). The Function of Loki in Snorri Sturluson's 'Edda'. *History of Religions,* 40(2), pp.109–124.
19. Bonnetain, Y.S. (2006). Potentialities of Loki. *Old Norse Religion in Long-Term Perspectives,* pp.326-330.
20. Müller-Lisowski, K. (1952). Some Traditions about Cocks and Death. *Anthropos*, (H. 1-2), pp.287–288.
21. Di Sciacca, C. (2019). Crossing the bridge: insular eschatological imagery in the Eiríks Saga Viðfǫrla., pp.161–213.
22. Leake, J. (2018), January. Christianity and the Norse Otherworlds of Glæsisvellir and Ódáinsakr. 2018 MLA Annual Convention. MLA.
23. Santesson, L. (1989). En blekingsk blotinskrift. En nytolkning av inledningsradernap? Stentoftenstenen, *Fornvannen* 84, 221-9.
24. Niles, J.D., Christensen, T. and Osborn, M. (2007). *Beowulf and Lejre.* ACMRS, Arizona Center for Medieval and Renaissance Studies.
25. Simek, R. (2022). The Sanctuaries in Uppsala and Lejre and their Literary Antecedents. *Religionsvidenskabeligt Tidsskrift*, 74, pp.217–230.
26. Tang, L. (2015). Number Symbolism in Old Norse Literature: A Brief Study. Doctoral dissertation.
27. Simek, R. (1993). *Dictionary of Northern Mythology*, Cambridge.
28. Turkan, E.A. (2015). National-Cultural Vocabulary and Methods of its Translation (on the Example of Names of Sami Realities). In: Xiii Maslov's Readings (pp. 141-149).
29. Barraclough, E. R. (2017). Arctic frontiers: Rethinking Norse-Sámi relations in the old Norse Sagas. *Viator* 48. pp.27–51.
30. Hansen, L. I., and B. Olsen. (2014). *Hunters in Transition: An Outline of Early Sámi History.* Leiden.
31. Mundal, E. (1996). The perception of the Saamis and their religion in Old Norse sources, *Shamanism and Northern Ecology*, ed. J. Pentikäinen. pp. 97–116
32. Olsen, B. (2003). 'Belligerent Chieftains and Oppressed Hunters? Changing Conceptions of Interethnic Relationships in Northern Norway during the Iron Age and the Early Medieval Period', in *Contact, Continuity, and Collapse: The Norse Colonization of the North Atlantic*, ed. J. Barrett.
33. Williams, H. (2012). '*Dead in White Clothes': Modes of Christian Expression on Viking Age Rune Stones in Present-Day Sweden.*
34. Larsson, A. (2007). Kladd krigare: Skifte i skandinaviskt draktskick kring cir 1000. *OPIA, Occasional Papers in Archaeology.* 39. Uppsala.
35. Roslund, M. (2017). Bringing 'the periphery' into focus: Social interaction between Baltic Finns and the Svear in the Viking Age and Crusade period (c. 800 to 1200). In *Identity Formation and Diversity in the Early Medieval Baltic and Beyond* (pp. 168–204). Brill.

36. Schulte, M. (2015). Runology and historical sociolinguistics: On runic writing and its social history in the first millennium. *Journal of Historical Sociolinguistics*, 1(1), pp.87–110.
37. Cole, R. (2023). Runes and Rye: Administration in Denmark and the Emergence of the Younger Futhark, 500–800. *Comparative Studies in Society and History*, pp.1–25.
38. Robertson, J.S. (2012). How the Germanic Futhark came from the Roman alphabet. *Futhark: International Journal of Runic Studies*, 2, pp.7–26.
39. McKinnell, J., Simek, R. and Düwel, K. (2004). *Runes, Magic and Religion: a Sourcebook*. Fassbaender.
40. Harris, J. (2009). The Rök Stone's iatun and Mythology of Death. Analecta Septentrionalia: Beiträge zur nordgermanischen Kultur und Literaturgeschichte. *Ergänzungsbände zum Reallexikon der germanischen Altertumskunde*, 65, pp.467–501.
41. Myrvoll, K.J. (2022). Theodoric on the Rök stone. *Sagas and the Circum-Baltic Arena*, p.245.
42. Kyhlberg, O. (2010). The Great Masterpiece: The Rök Stone and its Maker. *Current Swedish Archaeology*, 18(1), pp.177–201.
43. Hermann, P. (2015). Memory, imagery, and visuality in Old Norse literature. *Journal of English and Germanic philology*, 114(3), pp.317–340.
44. Lindow, J. (2014). Memory and Old Norse Mythology. In *Minni and Muninn: Memory in Medieval Nordic Culture*, pp.41–57.
45. Daimon, R. (2020). How White is Heimdallr? *Viator*, 51(1), pp.121–136.
46. Staecker, J. (1999). Thor's Hammer – Symbol of Christianization and Political Delusion. *Lund archaeological review*, 5, pp.89–104.
47. Danilenko, N. (2020). What Is the World Like? Geographic Writing until the Tenth Century. In: *Picturing the Islamicate World* (pp. 14–48). Brill.
48. Hampton, V.D. (2011). Viking age arms and armour originating in the Frankish Kingdom. *The Hilltop Review*, 4(2), p.8.
49. Thomas, G. (2012). Carolingian culture in the North Sea world: rethinking the cultural dynamics of personal adornment in Viking-Age England. *European Journal of Archaeology*, 15(3), pp.486–518.
50. Martens, I. (2004). Indigenous and imported Viking Age weapons in Norway – a problem with European implications. *Journal of Nordic Archaeological Science*, 14, pp.125–137.
51. Garipzanov, I. H. (2014). Conversion and identity in the Viking Age. *Medieval Identities* volume 5. Turnhout: Brepols.
52. Antonsson, H. (2014). The conversion and Christianization of Scandinavia: A critical review of recent scholarly writings. In *Conversion and Identity in the Viking Age*, pp.49–73. Turnhout: Brepols.
53. Walker, J., (2010). In the Hall. *Signals of Belief in Early England: Anglo-Saxon Paganism Revisited*, Carver, M.O.H., Sanmark, A. and Semple, S., pp.83–102.
54. Christensen, T. (2008). Lejre and Roskilde. In: *The Viking World*, pp.121–5.
55. Christensen, T. (1991). Lejre beyond legend, the archaeological evidence. *Journal of Danish Archaeology*, 10(1), pp.163–185.

Further Reading

56. Carlie, A. (2008). Magnate estates along the road: Viking age settlements, communication and contacts in southwest Scania, Sweden. *Acta archaeologica*, 79(1), pp.110–144.
57. Nicklasson, P. (2002). Central places in a peripheral area or peripheral places in a central area – a discussion of centrality in Halland, western Sweden. *Central Places in the Migration and Merovingian Periods*, Almqvist & Wiksell, pp.111–23.
58. Larsson, L. (2007). The iron age ritual building at Uppåkra, southern Sweden. *Antiquity*, 81(311), pp.11–25.
59. Hårdh, B. (2010). *Viking Age Uppåkra. Från romartida skalpeller till senvikingatida urnesspännen*, pp.247–316.
60. Line, P. (2007). Chapter Five. Kings And King's Men. In *Kingship and State Formation in Sweden* 1130-1290 (pp. 175–205). Brill.
61. Karkov, C.E. (2022). Alternative Histories: Phantom Truths in Stone. Vera Lex Historiae: Constructing Truth in Medieval Historical Narrative Traditions, edited by Kelley, Michael and Taranu, Catalin. Binghamton, NY: Gracchi.
62. Taranu, C. (2023). The Figure in the Carpet: Narrative Structure and Theories of History in Old English Heroic Poetry. In: *Thinking about History through Old English Literature: Networks & Entanglements*. 2023. University of Leeds.
63. Taranu, C. (2016). The making of poetic history in Anglo-Saxon England and Carolingian Francia. PhD, University of Leeds.
64. Curzon-Siggers, S. (2017). Ancestor worship. *Meanjin*, 76(3), pp.70–76.
65. Gomo, G., Rød-Eriksen, L., Andreassen, H.P., Mattisson, J., Odden, M., Devineau, O. and Eide, N.E., (2020). Scavenger community structure along an environmental gradient from boreal forest to alpine tundra in Scandinavia. *Ecology and evolution*, 10(23), pp.12860–12869.
66. Lacey, M.E.R. (2015). 'When is a hroc not a hroc? When it is a crawe or a hrefn! A case study in recovering Old English folk-taxonomies. In *The Art, Literature and Material Culture of the Medieval World* (pp. 138–152).
67. Blum, C. R., Fitch, W. T. and Bugnyar, T. (2020). Rapid Learning and Long-Term Memory for Dangerous Humans in Ravens (Corvus corax). *Frontiers in Psychology*, 11.
68. Taylor, A.H. (2014). Corvid cognition. *Wiley Interdisciplinary Reviews: Cognitive Science*, 5(3), pp.361–372.
69. Lacey, M.E.R. (2014). Birds and bird-lore in the literature of Anglo-Saxon England (Doctoral dissertation, UCL (University College London)).
70. Rudkin, E.H. (1955). Folklore of Lincolnshire. *Folklore*, 66(4), pp.385–400.
71. Chiacchia, B. (2021). King Alfred's Successful Peace with Vikings: Making Legitimate Peace through Oath-Swearing. Unpublished essay. University of York.
72. Düwel, K. (1988). On the Sigurd Representations in Great Britain and Scandinavia. *Languages and cultures*: Studies in honour of Edgar C. Polomé, 36, p.133.
73. Kopár, L. (2012). *Gods and Settlers: the Iconography of Norse Mythology in Anglo-Scandinavian Sculpture* (p. 3). Turnhout: Brepols.

74. Lang, J.T. (1984). *Corpus of Anglo-Saxon Stone Sculpture*, Volume VI: Northern Yorkshire (Vol. 6).
75. Lang, J.T. (1976). The sculptors of the Nunburnholme cross. *Archaeological Journal*, 133(1), pp.75–94.
76. Peck, W. (1815). *A topographical account of the Isle of Axholme being the west division of the Wapentake of Manley in the county of Lincoln*. London: Epworth Mechanics' Institute.
77. Rawnsley, W. F. (1915). Highways and Byways in Lincolnshire. *The Geographical Journal*, 45 (6), p.522.
78. Bagge, S. (2004). *A Hero between Paganism and Christianity. Håkon the Good in memory and history*. Peter Lang.
79. IJssennagger, N.L. (2013). Between Frankish and Viking: Frisia and Frisians in the Viking Age. *Viking and Medieval Scandinavia*, 9, pp.69–98.
80. *Kitab al-Tarikh*.
81. Mikkelsen, E. (1998). *Islam and Scandinavia during the Viking Age. Byzantium and Islam in Scandinavia*, pp.15–16.
82. Fernstål, L. (2008). A Bit Arabic: Pseudo-Arabic Inscriptions on Viking Age Weights in Sweden and Expressions of Self-image. *Current Swedish Archaeology*, pp.61–71.
83. Knutson, S.A. and Ellis, C. (2021). Conversion to Islam in Early Medieval Europe: Historical and Archaeological Perspectives on Arab and Northern Eurasian Interactions. *Religions* 12: 544.
84. Faulkes, A. 91993). The sources of Skáldskaparmál: Snorri's intellectual background. *Snorri Sturluson*, 51, pp.59–76.
85. Nordvig, M. (2021). Volcanoes in Old Norse Mythology. *Volcanoes in Old Norse Mythology*, pp.1–100.
86. Blind, K. (1903). A Prehistoric Sun-Chariot in Denmark. *Westminster Review*, Jan. 1852-Jan. 1914, 160(5), pp.552–558.
87. Sparavigna, A.C. (2012). Ancient bronze disks, decorations and calendars.1203.2512.
88. Denninghaus, F.N. (2019). Arrangement of space inside Ölandic ringforts. A comparative study of the spatial division within the ringforts Eketorp, Sandby, and Ismantorp.
89. Andrén, A. (2005). Behind Heathendom: archaeological studies of Old Norse religion. *Scottish Archaeological Journal*, 27(2), pp.105–138.
90. i Riutort, M.R. (2019). The Myth of Sigurd of Norway as a Crusader. SVMMA. *Revista de Cultures Medievals*, (13), pp.56–73.
91. Thomson, R.M. and Winterbottom, M. (1998). *Gesta Regum Anglorum* (Vol. 2). Oxford University Press.
92. Ruiz, RA (2014). The Taifa of Denia and the 11th-century Mediterranean market. In *Studies on the Aftasí Kingdom*: [conferences], Badajoz, 2014 (pp.219–234).
93. Serreli, G. (2014). XXXIII *Jornades d'Estudis Històrics Locals: The millenary of the Taifa: Dénia-Balearic Islands* (1013-1115) Palma di Maiorca, 28-29 October 2014. RiMe. Rivista dell'Istituto di Storia dell'Europa Mediterranea, pp.205–212.

Further Reading

94. Hamblin, W. (2017). The Fatimid Navy during the early crusades: 1099–1124. In *Medieval Ships and Warfare* (pp. 215–221). Routledge.
95. Jensen, J.M. (2007). *Denmark and the Crusades, 1400-1650* (Vol. 30). Brill.
96. Christiansen, E. (1997). *The Northern Crusades* (Vol. 927). Penguin UK.
97. Doxey, G.B. (1996). Norwegian crusaders and the Balearic Islands. *Scandinavian Studies*, 68(2), pp.139–160.
98. S.J., Murphy G.R. (2013). *Tree of Salvation: Yggdrasil and the Cross in the North*. Oxford University Press.
99. Dreyer, J.L.E. (1907). The eclipse of 1030. *The Observatory*, 30, pp.354–355.
100. Henige, D. (1976). 'Day was of sudden turned into night': On the Use of Eclipses for Dating Oral History. *Comparative Studies in Society and History*, 18(4), pp.476–501.
101. Lubik, M., (2022). St. Olaf and Adam of Bremen's narrative pragmatics. In: *Adam of Bremen's Gesta Hammaburgensis Ecclesiae Pontificum: Origins, Reception and Significance*, Routledge, p.81.
102. Lönnrot, E. (1849). *Kalevala* (Vol. 14). Suomalaisen kirjallisuuden seuran kirjapainossa.
103. Rowe, E.A. (1991). Historical Invasions/Historiographical Interventions: Snorri Sturluson and the Battle of Stamford Bridge. *Mediaevalia*, 17, pp.149–176.

Fate

1. Le Rossignol, T.W. (2019). To what extent can we understand why the raid on Lindisfarne in 793 took place and what happened? Doctoral dissertation, University of the Highland and Islands.
2. Hadley, D.M. (1996). Conquest, colonization and the Church: ecclesiastical organization in the Danelaw. *Historical Research*, 69(169), pp.109–128.
3. Jackson, N., Petts, D., Wilkins, B., Jago, I., Kahlenberg, R., Swain, B. and Ungemach, J. (2021). *Lindisfarne: The Holy Island Archaeology Project*. https://digventures.com/
4. Hatherly, P. (2017). Serpent mythology and oxytocin; Psora unmasked. *Homeopathy*.
5. Rex, P. (2014). *The English Resistance: The Underground War against the Normans*. Amberley Publishing.
6. Battles, D., 2012. Reconquering England for the English in 'Havelok the Dane'. *The Chaucer Review*, 47(2), pp.187–205.
7. Matthews, S. (2003). William the Conqueror's Campaign in Cheshire in 1069–70: Ravaging and Resistance in the North-West. *Northern History*, 40(1), pp.53–70.
8. Strickland, M.J. (1994). *Against the Lord's anointed: aspects of warfare and baronial rebellion in England and Normandy 1075-1265*.
9. Ellis, C. (2022). Go West: Contextualizing Scandinavian Royal Naval Expeditions into the Insular World, 1013–1103. *Historical Research*, 95(270), pp.481–505.

10. *The Chronicle of Mann*.
11. McDonald, R.A. (2019). Heroes: The Manx Sea Kings Descended from Godred Crovan. Kings, Usurpers, and Concubines in the 'Chronicles of the Kings of Man and the Isles', pp.21–30.
12. Boüard, M.D. (1984). The Viking Age in the Isle of Man. Select papers from the 9th Viking Congress, Isle of Man, 4-14 July 1981, 1983. *Archéologie médiévale*, 14(1), pp.403–405.
13. Duncan, A.A. and Brown, A.L. (1959). Argyll and the Isles in the earlier Middle Ages. In *Proceedings of the Society of Antiquaries of Scotland* Vol. 90, pp.192–220.
14. Power, R. (1986). Magnus Barelegs' expeditions to the West. *The Scottish Historical Review*, 65(180), pp.107–132.
15. Caldwell, D.H., Hall, M.A. and Wilkinson, C.M. (2009). The Lewis Hoard of gaming pieces: a re-examination of their context, meanings, discovery and manufacture. *Medieval Archaeology*, 53(1), pp.155–203.
16. McDonald, R.A. and McLean, S.A. (1990). In Search of Somerled, King of Argyll and the Isles. *International Review of Scottish Studies*, 16.
17. McDonald, R.A. and McLean, S.A. (1992). Somerled of Argyll: a new look at old problems. *The Scottish Historical Review*, 71(191/192), pp.3–22.
18. McDonald, R.A. (2020). *The Sea Kings: The Late Norse Kingdoms of Man and the Isles c. 1066–1275*. Birlinn.
19. *Rotuli Litterarum Clausarum*.
20. Tait, C., and Duffy, S. (2009) The World of the Gallowglass: Kings, Warlords and Warriors in Ireland and Scotland, 1200-1600. *The Sixteenth-century Journal*, 40(3), pp.931–932.
21. Thomson, W.P. (2003). St Magnus: An exploration of his sainthood. *The Faces of Orkney: Stones, Skalds and Saints*, pp.46–64.
22. Smith, B. (1988). Shetland in Saga-Time. Rereading the Orkneyinga Saga. *Northern Studies*, 25, pp.21–41.
23. Mägi, M. (2018). Between Consolidating States: The Eastern Baltic Areas in the 11th and 12th Centuries. In: *Austrvegr: The Role of the Eastern Baltic in Viking Age Communication across the Baltic Sea* (pp. 348–420). Brill.
24. Bagge, S. (1993). Ideology and Propaganda in *Sverris saga*.
25. Hauksson, Þ. (2012). Implicit Ideology and the King's Image in Sverris saga. *Scripta Islandica*, 63, p.127.
26. Jakobsson, Á. (2015). King Sverrir of Norway and the Foundations of his power: Kingship ideology and narrative in Sverris saga. *Medium Ævum*, 84(1), pp.109–135.
27. *Heinrici Cronicon Lyvoniae*.
28. *Chronica Visbycensis*.
29. *Erikskrönikan*.
30. Mägi, M. (2019). *The Viking Eastern Baltic*. Amsterdam University Press.
31. Roslund, M. (2017). Bringing 'the periphery' into focus: Social interaction between Baltic Finns and the Svear in the Viking Age and Crusade period (c. 800 to 1200). In *Identity Formation and Diversity in the Early Medieval Baltic and Beyond* (pp.168–204). Brill.

Further Reading

32. Keller, C. (1989) The Eastern Settlement Reconsidered. Some analyses of Norse Medieval Greenland. University of Oslo, Unpublished PhD Thesis.
33. Forbes, J. (2010). *The American Discovery of Europe*. University of Illinois Press.
34. Saarse, L., Niinemets, E., Poska, A. and Veski, S. (2010). Is there a relationship between crop farming and the Alnus decline in the eastern Baltic region? *Vegetation History and Archaeobotany*, 19, pp.1728.
35. Šnē, A. (2008). The medieval peasantry: On the social and religious position of the rural natives in southern Livonia (13th–15th centuries). *Ajalooline Ajakiri*, 1(2), p.123.
36. Cotesta, V. (2021). The Islamic Vision of the World and Geography: Al-Khwarizmi, Ferdowsi, al-Muqaddasi, al-Idrisi. In *The Heavens and the Earth: Graeco-Roman, Ancient Chinese, and Mediaeval Islamic Images of the World*, pp.431–450. Brill.
37. Ducène, J.C. (2008). Poland and Central Europe in the Uns Al-Mushtag by Al-Idrisi. Rocznik Orientalistyczny (*Annual of Oriental Studies*), 2(61), pp.5–30.
38. Walther, S.H. (2022). Yngvar's expedition to Serkland: From historical event to cultural memory to fantastic literature in 15th-century Iceland. *Sagas and the Circum-Baltic Arena*, p.356.
39. Wanner, K.J. (2008). *Snorri Sturluson and the Edda: The Conversion of Cultural Capital in Medieval Scandinavia* (Vol. 4). University of Toronto Press.
40. Durrenberger, E.P. (1988). Stratification without a state: The collapse of the Icelandic Commonwealth. *Ethnos*, 53(3-4), pp.239–265.
41. Runolfsson Solvason, B.T. (1992). Ordered anarchy: Evolution of the decentralized legal order in the Icelandic commonwealth. *Journal des économistes et des études humaines*, 3(2-3), pp.333–352.
42. Vésteinsson, O. (2007). A divided society: Peasants and the aristocracy in medieval Iceland. *Viking and medieval Scandinavia*, 3, pp.117–139.
43. Andersson, T.M. (1994). The Politics of Snorri Sturluson. *The Journal of English and Germanic Philology*, 93(1), pp.55–78.
44. Jónsson, Þ. Ed. (1891). *Harðar saga ok Hólmverja* (Vol. 3). Sigurður Kristjánsson.
45. Poilvez, M. (2016). Vár lǫg: Outlaw Communities from Jómsvíkinga saga to Harðar saga. *Średniowiecze Polskie i powszechne*, (12), pp.90–107.
46. Smith, K.P. and Ólafsson, G. (2023). All that glitters is not gold: Multi-instrumental identification of Viking Age orpiment (As2S3) from Surtshellir cave, Iceland. *Journal of Archaeological Science: Reports*, 47, p.103724.
47. Smith, K.P., Ólafsson, G. and Pálsdóttir, A.H. (2021). Ritual responses to catastrophic volcanism in Viking Age Iceland: Reconsidering Surtshellir Cave through Bayesian analyses of AMS dates, tephrochronology, and texts. *Journal of Archaeological Science*, 126, p.105316.
48. van Houts, E. (2013). From Vikings to Normans. In: *The Normans in Europe* (pp.13–55). Manchester University Press.
49. Drell, J.H. (1999). Cultural syncretism and ethnic identity: The Norman 'conquest' of Southern Italy and Sicily. *Journal of Medieval History*, 25(3), pp.187–202.

50. Tabachnyk, D. (2013). Yaroslav the Wise as Statesman. *Law Ukr.*: Legal J., p.152.
51. Casey, R.P. (1949). Monastics and Seculars under Yaroslav the Wise. *Harvard Theological Review*, 42(3), pp.207–208.
52. Raba, J. (1967). The Fate of the Novgorodian Republic. *The Slavonic and East European Review*, 45(105), pp.307–323.
53. Fink, A. (2011). Under what conditions may social contracts arise? Evidence from the Hanseatic League. *Constitutional Political Economy*, 22, pp.173–190.
54. Salonen, K. and Jensen, K.V. (2023). *Scandinavia in the Middle Ages 900-1550: Between Two Oceans*. Taylor & Francis.
55. Liljegren, B. (2004). Rulers of Sweden. *Historiska media*.
56. Bøgh, A. (1997). On the Causes of the Kalmar Union. https://www.academia.edu/19195091
57. Haine, T.W. (2011). Greenland Norse knowledge of the North Atlantic environment. In: *Studies in the Medieval Atlantic* (pp. 101–119). New York: Palgrave Macmillan.
58. Vebk, C.L. (1991). *The Church Topography of the Eastern Settlement and the Excavation of the Benedictine Convent at Narsarsuaq in the Uunartoq Fjord* (Vol. 14). Museum Tusculanum Press.
59. Panagiotakopulu, E., Skidmore, P. and Buckland, P. (2007). Fossil insect evidence for the end of the Western Settlement in Norse Greenland. *Naturwissenschaften*, 94, pp.300–306.
60. Pringle, H. (1997). Death in Norse Greenland. *Science*, 275(5302), pp.924–926.
61. McGovern, T.H. (1980). Cows, harp seals, and churchbells: Adaptation and extinction in Norse Greenland. *Human Ecology*, 8, pp.245–275.
62. Star, B., Barrett, J.H., Gondek, A.T. and Boessenkool, S. (2018). Ancient DNA reveals the chronology of the walrus ivory trade from Norse Greenland. *Proceedings of the Royal Society B*, 285(1884), 20180978.
63. Arneborg, J., Nyegaard, G., Vésteinsson, O. and Hammond, A. (2009). Norse Greenland. *Selected Papers from the Hvalsey Conference* 2008.
64. Mead, William R. (2007). Scandinavian Renaissance Cartography. In: Woodward, David (ed.). *The History of Cartography, Volume Three, Part Two*. University of Chicago Press. pp. 1781–1805.

Index

Index to individuals, legendary figures and gods. Space precludes indexing more comprehensively.

Abd El Melik Ben Moghith 70-71
Abbo the Crooked 180
Adam of Bremen 143, 186, 188, 250, 270
Áed, King 114
Ælfgifu of Northampton 237, 337
Ælfred the Great 33, 35, 44, 91, 93, 101, 105-6, 109-12, 176, 183, 185, 202, 205, 208, 229, 241
Ælle, King 102
Ælle of Sussex 39
Æthelberht, King 39, 41
Æthelflæd of Mercia 112, 117, 183-4, 216
Æðelfrið, King 39, 41, 48, 52, 55
Æthelred the Ill-Counselled 44, 117, 208, 210, 222, 236-7, 239, 242, 291
Æthelstan, King 108, 180, 183, 185, 195
Æthelwold 111, 112, 117, 263
Æðelwulf, King 101
Aidan 61
Amarelo Mestáliz 201
Ambrosius Aurelianus 109
Anna Komnene, Princess 234
Anna Porphyrogenita 231
Anulo/Ale 81, 84
Alcuin of York 55, 77

Aldgisl, King 48
Alexander III, King 284
Alexander III, Pope 270
Alfonso III 147
Alfonso V 207
Alsviðr 264, 270
Amlaibh, King 181
Ansgar, Archbishop 95-6, 253
Ari Marson 171
Arnfithr Matr 269
Arnulf, King 111, 198-9
Arthur 26, 107-9
Arrow-Odd 297
Árvakr 264, 270
Åsa Eysteinsdottir 65
Ásfriðr 188
Askold 191
Asmund 233
Asser, Bishop 33, 105
Atli 24
Attila the Hun 202
Augustus, Emperor 172

Bacsecg 101
Bældæg 241

Bagrat IV, King 213-4
Baldr 167, 241, 269
Baldwin I, King 268
Basil II, Emperor 231, 233
Beaduheard, Shire-Reeve 56
Bede, The Venerable 39, 41, 96
Benedikt 269
Beohtric, King 56
Beow, King 37
Beowulf 22, 224, 27, 37-9, 125, 131, 252, 257-8, 297
Bjorn, King 95, 107, 130
Bjorn Breiðvíkingakappi 169
Bjorn Ironside 91, 100, 123, 148, 289
Blaecca, Prefect 96
Blot-Sweyn/Håkan the Red 293
Boniface, Saint 20
Bragi 120
Brendan, Saint 169
Brian Bóramha 214-6, 225-6
Brynhild 167
Bryhtnoth, Ealdorman 208
Burnt Njal 132

Canute, the Holy 278-, 285-6
Cassiodorus 26
Cædbæd, 'Battle-Crow' 39
Ce Acatl Topiltzin 170
Cennétig 215-6
Charlemagne 48, 51-6, 71, 74-84 passim, 91, 93-4, 97-9, 102, 145, 151, 198-9, 253, 263, 265
Charles he Bald 93, 112
Charles he Simple 128, 229-30
Claudius, Emperor 90
Claudius Clavus 297
Claudius Ptolemy 174
Cnut the Great 29, 80, 210-11, 218, 222-7, 236-241, 269, 275, 277, 292
Colm Cille 62, 180
Conrad II, Emperor 222
Constantine VII, Emperor 161

Constantin of Alba, King 185
Cormac Cas 215
Cuthbert, Saint 16, 61-2, 100, 119, 188, 275
Cwichelm 242

Dagr 264
Dalk 233-4
Dicuil 135, 138
Dir 191
Domnall mac Taidc 280
Drożko 75-6, 78, 87
Dudo 200

Eadgar, King 217, 238-9
Eadgils, King 37
Eadward the Elder, King 111-12, 117, 183-5, 216
Ealswitha 33
Ebo of Rheims 88
Ecgberht, King 97
Edmund, King 240-41,
Edmund Ironside 222, 277
Edgar the Ætheling 277
Edward the Confessor 62, 238
Edwin, King 39, 41, 48, 102
Eirikr of York/Erik Bloodaxe 93, 107-9, 119-20, 190, 200
Egbert, Count 80, 87, 198
Egil 42, 120
Egil Skallagrimmrson 120, 195
Emma of Normandy, Lady 237, 275
Eógan 215-6
Eoghann, King 114
Eohric, King 111-12
Eowils 112
Erik the Red 153, 156, 290, 297
Erik the Victorious 193, 200
Erlend Thorfinsson 284
Eystein, King 288

Fenrir 118, 133, 228, 264, 264, 272, 276
Fergus, Abbot 113

Index

Finn 40, 131
Freyr 20, 130, 140, 142-3, 150, 160, 165, 253, 272
Frīcg 20, 25
Frigg 25, 249
Fosite 20
Forseti 20

Ganger-Hrolf/Rollo 81, 93, 76, 229-31, 292
Garmr 272
Gauk Trandilsson 269
Genghis Khan 202, 293
Gerald of Wales 96, 226
Gildas 34-5, 41
Glum, Jarl 87
Gnupa, King 188
Godafrid 100
Godfrid, King 42, 45, 73-81, 84, 87-8, 98, 180, 187-8, 199, 201
Godred Crúbach 279-80, 282, 284
Godred the Black 282-3
Goffredo Malaterra 229
Gorm the Old 188-9, 193
Gormflaith 217
Gregory of Tours 37-8
Grimur Kamban 137, 289
Gudfrid 111
Gudleif 122, 169
Gundered 206
Gunnhild, Queen 65
Guthlac, Saint 259
Guthred, King 93, 119, 188, 199
Guthrum 101, 105, 109-10, 112, 119, 185, 197, 241, 262

al-Hakam, Emir 85
Haakon the Good 107-9, 189, 193, 262
Haakon IV, King 289
Håkon, King of Norway 284
Haesten 81, 91, 111, 123, 148-9, 151-2, 266-7
Halfdan 78

Halfdan the Generous 40
Halfdan, Great Army leader 101, 106, 110, 181
Halfdan/Ṣaltān 85, 93
Halfdan the Black 81, 107
Halfdan the Generous 40
Halfdan 'Whiteshanks' 81
Harald Bluetooth 57, 74, 76, 188-9, 193-4, 197-203, 223, 231
Harald Fairhair/Haraldr Lúfa 65, 93, 107-8, 120, 130-31, 134, 139, 143, 149, 181, 190, 249, 289, 291
Harald Harðráði 109, 165, 234, 238, 242, 266-6, 269, 271-2, 277-8, 285
Harald Hen 278
Harald Klak 81, 84-5, 88, 93, 96, 98-100
Harold Godwinson, King 271
Harold Hafi 233
Harold Harefoot, King 238
Harthaknut/Hardegon 188
Harthacnut, King 226, 238, 241
Healfdene 112
Heimdallr/Rig 86, 272
Helgi, King 186-7
Henry I, King 183, 267, 280
Henry of Huntingdon 102
Henry the Fowler 198, 202-3
Hereward the Wake 278
Herigar, Prefect 95-6
Hernando Cortez 170
Higbald, Bishop 77, 274
Hildr 277
Hisham, Emir 70
Hønir 272
Horik, King 56-7, 81, 87-9, 94, 98-100, 107, 188
Horik II, King 100, 107
Hrímfaxi 264
Huginn 260-261
Hygelac/Chlochilaicus 37-8, 49
Hywel Dda, King 185, 194

Ibn Fadlan 167, 177, 191, 232, 258
Ibn Habīb 263
Ibn Khaldun 148
Ibn Khurradādhbih 212, 254
Ida the Flamebearer 39
Ingeld, King 37
Íñigo Arista, Prince 85
Isa ibn Shuhayd, Chief Minister 145
Ivar 112
Ivar Bardarsson 296
Ivarr the Boneless 81, 101, 115, 181-2
Jakob, Anund 232, 236
John, King 226, 283, 299
John of Worcester 56, 240
Jǫrmungandr 227, 249, 264, 272, 276
Jon, Archbishop 274
Jon Grøenlander 298
Justinian, Emperor 27, 151, 153

Kjetill Flatnose 181, 190
Knútr, King 93, 119, 188, 199
Kollgrimr 296

Lambert, Count 69
Leo V, Emperor 87
Lif 269
Liparit IV, Duke 213-4
Lithrasir 269
Liudger 98
Lǫgmaðr 280
Loki 19-21, 25, 129, 131, 165, 224, 228-9, 248, 264, 276
Lothar, King 99-101
Lothair, King 200
Louis the Pious 85, 88, 94, 97, 99-100, 128, 190, 200, 263
Louis II, King 99
Lucan 141

Maccus 120, 239
Mael Sechnaill, Rí 97, 116, 181
Mael Sechnaill II, Ruiri 216-7

Magnus the Good 238, 285
Magnus Berfœttr 267, 280, 282
Magnús 284
Martin Knudsson 297
Michael the Syrian 26
Michael V, Emperor 234
Mimir 272
Mordred 26
Mstislav 232
Mstiszlav the Great 292
Muninn 260-261
Nīþhǫggr 272
Nerthus 174
Niall, Rí 96
Niall of the Nine Hostages 215
Nicholas Mysticus, Patriarch 204
Njǫrðr 246
Nór 130
Notker the Stammerer 77, 80
Nótt 264

Óðinn/Odin 13, 18-25, 28-9, 53-4, 57, 63, 86, 102, 120, 129, 131, 142-3, 154, 160, 165-7, 174, 224, 228, 241, 244, 249, 255, 260-261, 266, 270, 272
Odinkar 188
Odo, Count 93, 110-111
Oengendus/Angantyr 52, 73-4
Offa the Great 51-2, 56, 61
Ogmund 297
Ohthere 123, 125, 130, 131, 133
Olaf the Black 283
Olaf Guthfrithsson 182, 185, 194
Olaf Kyrre, King 163, 266, 279
Olaf Trygvasson, King 210, 236, 253, 263
Olafr Godredsson 280
Olafr Haraldsson, King 131, 206, 210, 236-8, 262, 269-70, 284, 292
Olav/Olaf Cuarán 182, 216
Oleg the Wise 93, 191, 202, 204
Olga 231

Index

Olof the Brash 186-7
Olof Tax-King 200, 211, 236
Onlafbal 275
Orm 116, 239
Örn 233
Osberht, King 102-3
Oswald, King 39, 41, 48, 50-51, 61-2, 102
Oswiu, King 39, 51-2, 102
Otta 96
Otto I, King
Otto II, Emperor 199
Otto III, Emperor 199, 217
Owain of Strathclyde, King 185, 194

Paulinus, Bishop 39
Paul Thorfinsson 284
Penda, King 39, 41, 48
Pepin of Aquitaine 99, 263
Perkūnas 20, 162
Perun 20, 162, 231
Philibert of Jumièges 72
Photios, Patriarch 204
Plutarch 141
Poppo 197
Porphyrios 153, 158
Procopius 19, 26, 30-31, 153
Publius Quinctilius Varus 172

Quetzalcoatl 170

Rædwald, King 39
Raghnall 283
Ragnall 119, 182, 185, 275
Ragnar 233-4
Ragnar Loðbrók Sigurdsson 102, 111, 240
Ragnar of Paris 56, 81, 91
Ragnhild Siggurdsdottir 107
Ralph de Guader 278
Ran 249
Rannveig 251
Redbad, King 48

Ref the Sly 196, 297
Reginfrid 79, 81, 84
Reginherus/Ragnar of Paris 56, 81, 91
Richard I of Normandy 200, 231, 237
Richard II of Normandy 292
Rhodri Mawr, King 116
Robert, Count 278
Robert Guiscard 229
Rodulf 101
Roger of Wendover 120, 240
Roger I, Count 229
Roger II, Count 267-8
Roger II, King 219
Rorik of Dorestad 93, 98-101, 190
Rurik 190-191

Saemund Oddson 297
Saxo Grammaticus 72, 187, 255, 285-6
Sclaomir 87
Scula 275
Sidonius Apollinaris 19
Sigefrid 111, 198
Sigfrid, King 81, 186-7
Sigfrøðr, King 93, 119, 188
Sigmundr 120
Sigtrygg, King 188
Sigtryggr 119, 182, 185
Sigurd the Crusader 267
Sigurd the Dragon-Slayer 259
Sigrid Björnsdóttir 297
Sindri/Eitri 142-3
Sineus 191
Sitriuc Silkbeard 217-8
Siward, Earl 238, 278
Skinfaxi 264
Snæfríð, Princess 134, 249
Snorri Sturluson 19-20, 25, 40, 81, 86, 92, 124, 133, 137, 140, 142, 150-151, 154, 164-7, 223, 242, 244-9, 252, 255, 264, 269, 289
Sól 264
Søren Norby 297

Steinunn 296
Stenkil, King 293
Stilicho 151
Sumarliði 282-3
Surtr 140, 143, 272
Sweyn Forkbeard 80, 201, 208, 210-11, 222, 236, 239, 240-241
Symeon of Durham 55, 62
Svein Estridsson, King 238, 277
Sverre Sigurdsson, King 285
Sviatopolk the Accursed 232
Sviatozslav 204-6, 231

Tacitus 20, 23, 172-3
Ṭāriq ibn Ziyād, Governor 143
Tiw 20, 25
Theodoric the Goth 252
Thiebault, Count 200
Thietmar of Merseburg 249
Thjodhild 153
Þórr/Thor 13, 19-20, 24-5, 36, 129, 142-3, 155, 160-162, 165, 241, 246, 248-9, 253-4, 256, 265, 272
Thoragalles 249
Thorir 249
Thorgils 249
Thorkell 249
Thorstein Olafsson 296-7
Thunor 20, 24-5
Thyrvé, Queen 198
Tóla 197
Torgrim Sölvesson 296
Tostig Godwinson, Earl 272
Truvor 191
Turgesius/Thorgest 90, 96
Týr 20, 25, 53, 57

Ubbe 81, 100
Ulf the Galician 120

Ulph 288
Ullr 133, 246
Ungortok, Chief 220
Urien of Rheged 109

Valdemar II, King 285-6
Vladimir the Great 231-3
Vidgaut 286
Víðarr 272
Visaeti 249
Vǫlundr/Völundr the Smith 143, 228, 229, 247-8, 259

Wahballah ibn Hazm, Chief Minister 145
Waltheof 238, 278
Weohstan 257
Widukind 53, 84
Widukind of Corvey 188, 202
Wiglaf 257-9, 297
Wilfrid, Bishop 150
William of Jumièges 72, 100
William of Malmesbury 108, 244
William Longsword, Count 230
William the Bastard 236, 238, 271, 273, 277-9
Willibrord, Saint 52
Winta 40
Wōden 20, 24-5, 28-9, 40, 53, 241, 241-2, 249
Wulfstan of Hedeby 63, 123, 125-7, 131, 187

Yaropolk 231
Yaropolk II 292
Yaroslav the Wise 191, 232, 234, 292
Yngvar the Far-Travelled 123, 166, 166-7, 197, 211-14, 232, 268, 289

Zoe, Empress 234